'Keep me warm
one night'

PUBLISHED BY

UNIVERSITY OF TORONTO PRESS

IN CO-OPERATION WITH THE

ROYAL ONTARIO MUSEUM

'Keep me warm one night'

Early handweaving in eastern Canada

HAROLD B. BURNHAM AND

DOROTHY K. BURNHAM

Toronto and Buffalo

Printed in Canada

ISBN 0-8020-1896-3

Microfiche ISBN 0-8020-0239-0

LC 72-83388

In memory of

CHARLES TRICK CURRELLY

1876–1957

First Director, Royal Ontario Museum of Archaeology

Professor Emeritus of Archaeology

Victoria University

Contents

Introduction

The first textile handwoven in Ontario to reach the Royal Ontario Museum was a blue and white overshot coverlet donated by Miss Florence McKinnon in 1941. This still holds a place of honour in the collections and is illustrated as no. 258. It was this gift that inspired the Ontario Textile Project which, since 1947, has been the major research venture of the Textile Department of the Museum: the pursuit of records and information regarding the textiles made and used in the province. Between these two dates a few more pieces came our way, but it was realized that far too little was known of what had been produced in earlier days. This was a serious lack in the provincial museum, and it was decided that a project should be undertaken before it was too late. This publication presents some of the results that have been learned to date. Other aspects of early weaving in Canada remain to be pursued in depth, but it is hoped that in due course they too will receive attention.

The original project was launched at a booth at the Canadian National Exhibition offered to the Museum by the University of Toronto when this great annual event re-opened following the Second World War. The project was the idea of Dorothy K. Burnham, then Keeper of Textiles, and she laid down its principles. The aim was to record material that was still in existence together with the history of individual pieces in the hope that the bits of information would fit together to form a homogeneous whole. The building up of a collection for the Museum was incidental. It was strongly felt that material still owned by the families for whom it was made should remain in their hands and it was this aspect of the project that proved to be one of its greatest strengths. As news spread, more and more doors opened, and we were able to see and record material that would otherwise have remained hidden.

The display at the booth at the Canadian National Exhibition showed the blue and white overshot coverlet mentioned and the few other pieces with an Ontario history that had come in during the following years. This display was supplemented by examples from the United States representing types that it was felt should be found in Canada. Over the booth was a sign reading 'If your family has been in Canada for more than two generations, maybe you can help us.' The response was overwhelming. The booth was constantly staffed, and many people filled in a questionnaire telling what they knew and giving the names of others who might help or have material. Despite this response, it was still not certain whether a full-scale effort should be launched: it might already be too late. With the close of the Exhibition, a two-week trip in a borrowed car was made across the southern part of the province sampling some of the 'leads,' as they came to be called. We were welcomed wherever we knocked on a door and each inquiry gave rise to another half dozen names. This multiplication of possibilities has remained one of the difficulties of the project, since it has proved physically impossible to follow up all the suggestions that have been offered over the years. In the initial trip, the distance covered was about eighteen hundred miles. This now seems little, but with the recent end of the wartime gasoline rationing, it was a long trip.

The results of this preliminary investigation proved more than promising so the decision was made to launch a genuine project. The textile industry in the province was approached and ten firms undertook to contribute a hundred dollars each for two years. In 1948, Mrs K.B. Brett became Curator of Textiles and in this capacity inherited the infant project. She spent the summer of that year visiting various parts of the province in an old converted ambulance lent by the Ontario Department of Education, borrowed material from people wherever she went, and brought it back to Toronto for photography and recording. When this was done, she went back on the road to return what she had borrowed and to find more. In the autumn of 1948, she put on a special exhibition showing what had been learned. About the same time, Miss Annie R. Fry was contacted and found to have a wealth of knowledge and material concerning her grandfather, Samuel Fry, who had been a part-time professional weaver near Vineland in the Niagara Peninsula. Miss Fry had treasured all that she could find concerning his work, and this now forms the Annie R. Fry Collection in the Royal Ontario Museum. Mrs Brett worked with Miss Fry during the summer of 1949, tracing down examples of Samuel Fry's work through the entries in his account book. In the autumn of that year, another special exhibition was put on displaying what had been located, as well as examples of the work of his brother-in-law, Moses Grobb, who had had a jacquard loom.

From 1950 on, expeditions to many parts of the province were made, often organized through the historical committees of the various branches of the Women's Institutes. They were of the greatest help in tracing down old coverlets and other handwoven pieces in various neighbourhoods and in extending hospitality to members of the Museum staff. Without the wholehearted support of the Women's Institutes far less would be known today, and all people interested in the history of Ontario owe them a debt of gratitude for the co-operation they extended so freely to the Museum.

Through the later 1950s and the early 1960s, the programme was pursued whenever time and opportunity permitted. In 1956, Mrs Brett prepared the pamphlet *Ontario Handwoven Textiles*, the first information on the subject to be published. It is only natural that all members of the staff of the Textile Department of the Museum, past and present, as well as others connected with the Museum who helped on a volunteer basis, have made a contribution to the programme, and all may take their share of pride in the Department's accomplishment. Special thanks are due to Mrs Nora Priverts; she has typed not only the text presented here, but also the mass of notes which now form the archival record on which it is based.

In 1964 Mrs Brett handed the project over to Harold B. Burnham, who had joined the staff in 1958. It was decided that its scope should be enlarged to cover textiles handwoven in Canada and a terminal date of 1900 was set. It was realized that this eliminated much of the western part of the country, but to set a later date would have given the project too wide a base for proper research. Even within the limits set, thoroughly detailed research has not been possible out-side Ontario. This can only be done by a person living in a province and pursuing the work at the grass roots level. Outside Ontario much has been accomplished, but much more remains to be done on the spot. It is to be hoped that before long people living in the other provinces will collect the data that should be preserved for the future.

In 1964, as part of the expanded project, it was decided to record material in other museums in Canada. Their co-operation has been invaluable. Examples from a number of these collections are illustrated, and to the Museums, as well as to the others who allowed their material to be studied, grateful thanks are extended. It was about this time that two events threw the project into high gear. The grant in 1965 of a contract to Mr Burnham by the History Branch of the National Museum of Man, Ottawa, made it possible to prepare a detailed catalogue of its collections, which added immeasurably to both knowledge and experience. In 1966, the award of a Senior Fellowship to Mr Burnham by the Canada Council made research possible on an even more extensive scale. A wide-ranging expedition was made through Quebec and the Atlantic provinces during that summer photographing and recording what was in various museum collections and much that was still in private hands. This expedition was followed the next year by research in Great Britain and Europe for traces of the traditions from which handweaving in North America had sprung. This trip provided an opportunity to gather new facts and to consolidate knowledge gathered on previous occasions.

It has been pointed out that the major premise of both the Ontario and Canadian research projects was not to build up a collection, but this has happened incidentally through the generosity of many individuals who desired to have their heirlooms preserved and to make their own contribution to preserving the heritage of this country. Others have helped obtain material by donations when other funds were not available. To all these people the Royal Ontario Museum owes a great debt and is proud to pay tribute to their generosity; many names will be found in the appropriate places where these gifts are illustrated. It must never be forgotten that much of the great wealth of the collections of the Royal Ontario Museum has been brought together by gifts large and small, and to all these donors the people of the province are indebted.

Other more recent factors have aided in building the truly representative collection of Ontario materials that the Museum now has, supplemented by examples from other parts of eastern Canada. With an increased and more generous budget since 1968, it has been possible to grasp the opportunity to fill the voids that were known to exist. During the past three years, every effort has been made to make the Ontario collection as representative as possible of what was produced and used in the province. The antique dealers have been more than co-operative, often beyond the call of business. They have been of great help and to them a special word of thanks is due.

Two other Museum departments have always been most helpful and co-operative: Canadiana and Photography. It has always been possible to rely on the former in case of need when items have become available. It has been part of the policy of the various heads of this Department – Mr W.B. Scott Symons, Miss June Biggar, and Mr D.B. Webster – to acquire Canadian items for the Textile Department when other sources have failed.

Almost without exception, the photographs used for the illustrations here are the work of the Museum's Photography Department, and in addition to these they have taken many others that form part of the archival record. They have made every effort to supply the best work possible, even with intractable material. Our thanks are expressed to all those connected with the Department, both past and present: Mr Leighton Warren, Head, Mr Brian O'Donovan, Mr Art Williams, Mr Alan McColl, Mr Lyn Gardiner, and Miss Margaret Cooke who consolidated all their efforts.

Outside the Royal Ontario Museum, a special word of thanks is owed to Mrs F.M. Mackley of Sydney, Cape Breton. In 1966 and again in 1970, she dropped everything in a busy life and shared her detailed knowledge of the island with us. She made sure that we saw all that was pertinent to our research, and met everyone who might be of help. A number of pieces are illustrated from the collections she has gathered for a Museum of Cape Breton which it is hoped will soon materialize. These are the only examples in the entire book that are not already in public collections in Canada.

In Prince Edward Island, the late George Leard of Souris had a wide knowledge of the history of the province and in him we found an ally in ferreting out the information we were after. He and his wife spent a Saturday taking us on a tour out to East Cape visiting every farmhouse where he thought there might be a coverlet or other handwoven material. It was a day never to be forgotten and filled many gaps in our knowledge of the Island's textile history.

Mrs W.R.D. McNeill of Fredericton is another person who has helped in every possible way and has drawn our attention to material from New Brunswick that we might not otherwise have seen. Miss M.P. Jenkins of Gagetown has filled many gaps in our knowledge of old weaving in the same province, all of which has been incorporated. Dr Ivan Crowell of Fredericton gave photographs of coverlets and weaving drafts that he had seen, and these also have been of great help. To all of these, and to all the other people in the Maritime Provinces who have taken an interest and have supplied information, we are most grateful.

The most constant support and encouragement has been received from Mr Fred J. Thorpe, Chief Historian, National Museum of Man, Ottawa. He not only arranged the contract granted in 1965, but has shown a constant interest in the project throughout. In addition he undertook to read the first part of the introductory chapter. If differences of opinion over this section should arise between the authors and other historians, it is no fault of his.

Mention has already been made of help and co-operation received from the smaller museums in Ontario. Similar help is acknowledged from museums outside the province, particularly Musée Acadien, Miscouche, The Confederation Art Gallery and Museum, Charlottetown, the Nova Scotia Museum, Halifax, the New Brunswick Museum, Saint John, the York-Sunbury Museum, Fredericton, and the various members of the staffs of these institutions who have been helpful. One pleasant recollection is a rewarding day spent at the former Village de Jacques de Chambly, the passing of which is sadly regretted.

In the United States several colleagues have co-operated with information and photographs: Mrs Florence M. Montgomery of the Henry Francis du Pont Winterthur Museum, Winterthur, Miss Rita J. Adrosko of the Smithsonian Institution, Washington, Shelburne Museum, Shelburne, and especially Miss Mildred Davidson, who has wide knowledge of the American field based on the excellent collection of coverlets at the Chicago Art Institute.

In Scotland in 1965 and 1967, many people helped in trying to locate examples of overshot weaving with an unquestioned Scottish provenance. That these did not turn up is no fault of theirs, but other facts of Scottish weaving did emerge. Those to whom special thanks are due are Mrs A. Halifax Crawford, Kilbarchan; Mr Maxwell Stuart and Mr Alexander Fenton of the National Museum of Antiquities, Edinburgh; Miss Marion Campbell of Kilberry at Auchindrain; Miss Greta Michie of the Museum of the Glens, Glen Esk, Angus; Mr George Davidson of the Highland Museum, Kingussie; and the staff of the West Highland Museum, Fort William.

Elsewhere in Great Britain, we were welcomed at many museums, but the traditions in England for which we were searching have long vanished. In Lancashire, the museums at Bolton and Blackburn deserve special mention. In Wales, some of the traditions live on, and reference will be found in the text to the help received from the Welsh Folk Museum at St Fagans near Cardiff.

On the continent, a number of colleagues have shown an interest in the project, and have been of great help. These include Dr Marta Hoffman, Oslo; Dr Agnes Geijer, Stockholm; Dr Brigitte Menzel, Berlin, and Museum für Volkskunde and Museum für Deutsche Volkskunde in that city; Frau Flury-Lemberg, Bern; Dr Rugh Grönwoldt, Stuttgart; and the staff of Musée des Arts et Traditions Populaires, Paris.

The publication of the results of almost a quarter century of research has been aided by a generous subsidy from the Canada Council, by a grant from Dominion Textile Limited, and by encouragement from the Royal Ontario Museum, and particularly from the Board of Trustees. For this support, both authors wish to express their most grateful thanks.

CREDITS

Photographs: Photographic Department,
Royal Ontario Museum
(unless otherwise specified)
Diagrams and drafts: The authors

ABBREVIATIONS

AIC	Art Institute of Chicago, Chicago, Illinois
BCPV	Black Creek Pioneer Village, Toronto, Ontario
DCB	Dictionary of Canadian Biography
CAGM	Confederation Art Gallery and Museum, Charlottetown, Prince Edward Island
CGC	Canadian Guild of Crafts, Montreal, Quebec
HFDM	Henry Francis du Pont Winterthur Museum, Winterthur, Delaware
MATP	Musée des Arts et Traditions Populaires, Paris

MEN	Musey Etnografii Narodov SSSR, Leningrad
MUM	Musée de l'Université de Moncton, Moncton, New Brunswick
NBM	New Brunswick Museum, Saint John, New Brunswick
NFM	Norsk Folkemuseum, Oslo
NGC	National Gallery of Canada, Ottawa, Ontario
NM	National Museet, Stockholm
NMM	National Museum of Man, National Museums of Canada, Ottawa, Ontario
NSM	Nova Scotia Museum, Halifax, Nova Scotia
RAPQ	Rapport de l'Archiviste de la Province du Québec
ROM	Royal Ontario Museum, Toronto, Ontario (see appendix)
SI	Smithsonian Institution, Washington, DC
UCV	Upper Canada Village, Morrisburg, Ontario

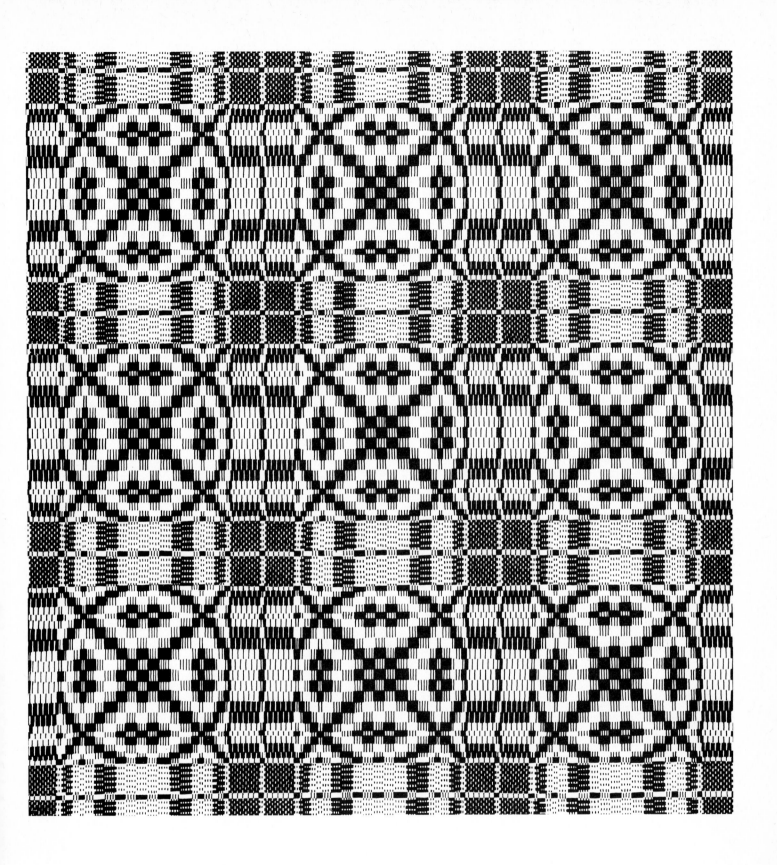

'Keep me warm one night,' the pattern from which this book
takes its name, is described on page 53

Figures

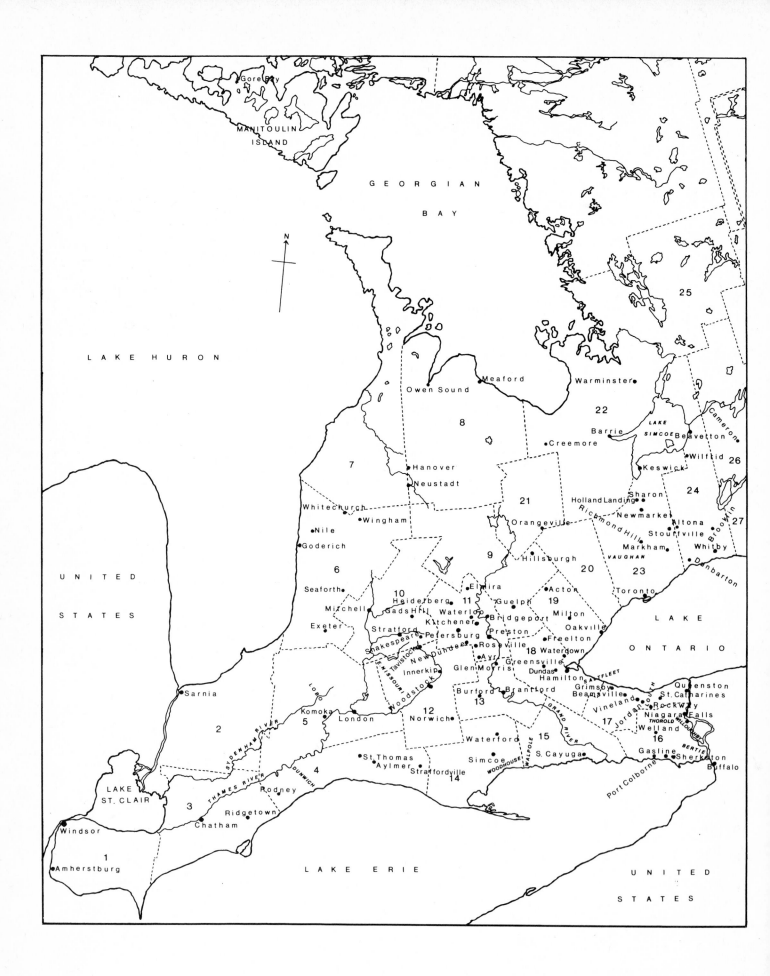

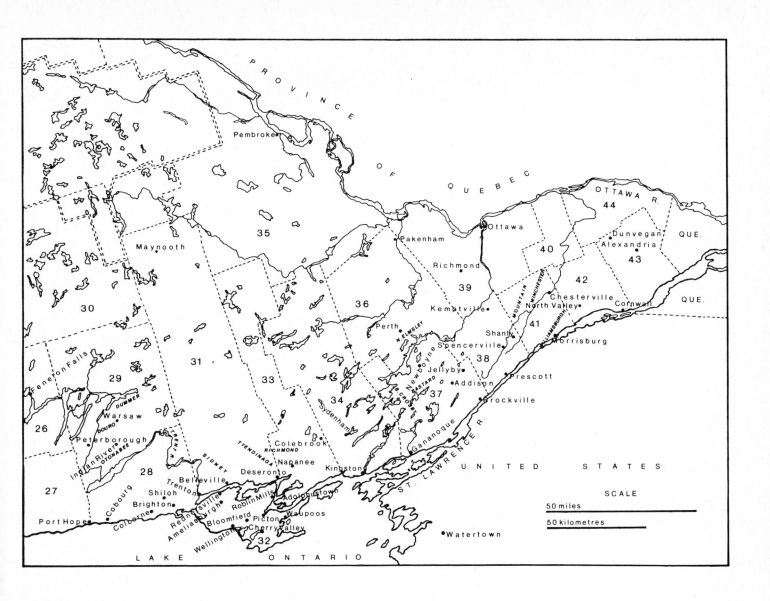

SOUTHERN ONTARIO COUNTIES

Brant 13	Grenville 38	Lincoln 17	Prince Edward 32
Bruce 7	Haldimand 15	Middlesex 5	Renfrew 35
Carleton 39	Haliburton 30	Muskoka 25	Russell 40
Dufferin 21	Halton 19	Norfolk 14	Simcoe 22
Dundas 41	Hastings 31	Northumberland 28	Stormont 42
Durham 27	Huron 6	Ontario 24	Victoria 26
Elgin 4	Kent 3	Oxford 12	Waterloo 11
Essex 1	Lambton 2	Peel 20	Welland 16
Frontenac 34	Lanark 36	Perth 10	Wellington 9
Glengarry 43	Leeds 37	Peterborough 29	Wentworth 18
Grey 8	Lennox and Addington 33	Prescott 44	York 23

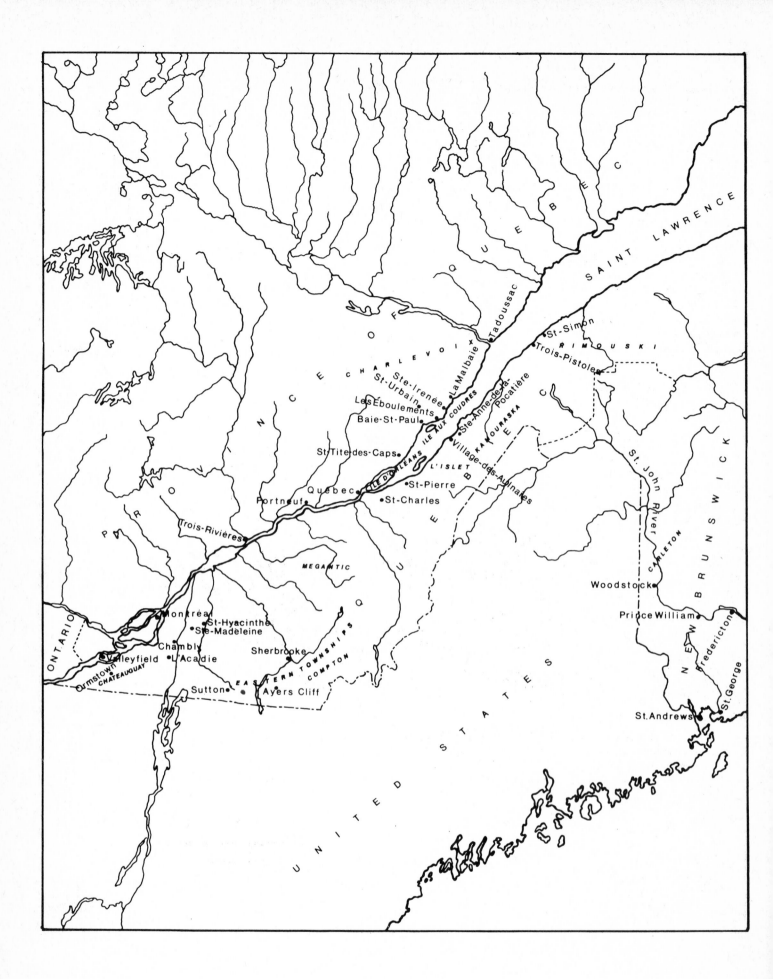

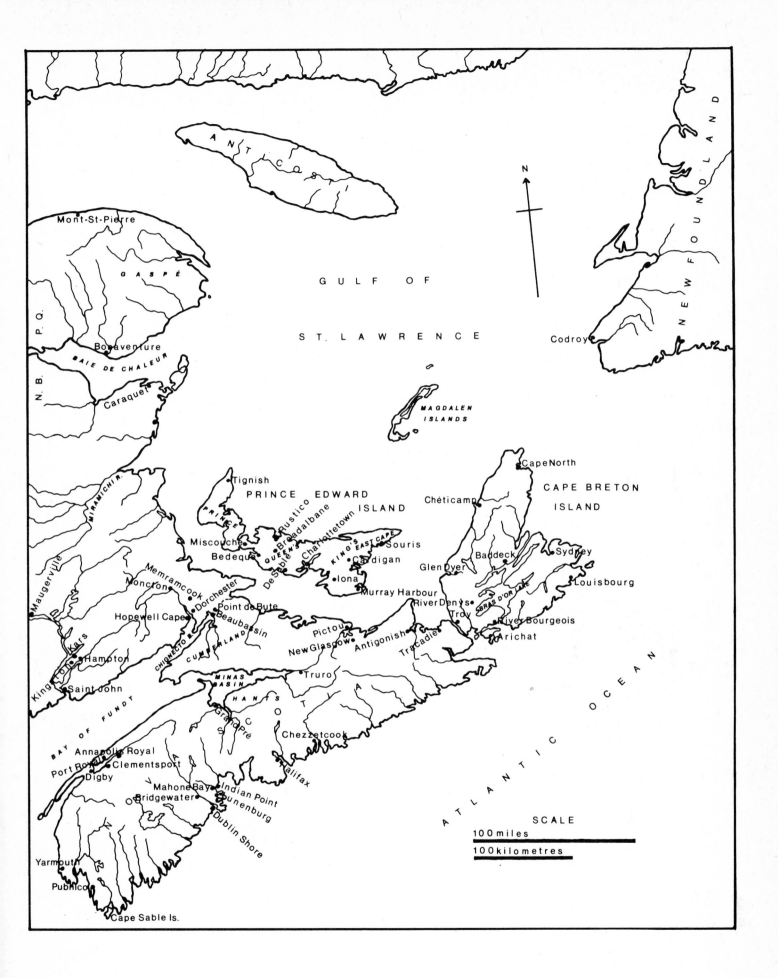

N

GULF OF

ST. LAWRENCE

NEWFOUNDLAND

Mont-St-Pierre

GASPÉ

P.Q.

N.B.

BAIE DE CHALEUR

Bonaventure

Caraquet

Codroy

MAGDALEN
ISLANDS

MIRAMICHI R.

Tignish

PRINCE EDWARD

ISLAND

CapeNorth

CAPE BRETON
ISLAND

Chéticamp

Rustico

PRINCE

Miscouche

Balbane

Charlottetown

Bedeque

QUEEN'S

EAST CAPE

Souris

De Sable

KING'S

Cardigan

Baddeck

Sydney

Memramcook

Iona

Glen Dyer

BRAS D'OR LAKE

Louisbourg

Moncton

Dorchester

Murray Harbour

River Denys

Hopewell Cape

Point de Bute

Troy

River Bourgeois

Maugerville

Beaubassin

Pictou

Antigonish

Arichat

Kars

CHIGNECTO B.

CUMBERLAND

New Glasgow

Tracadie

Hampton

Truro

King's Co.

MINAS
BASIN

HANTS

N O V A

S C O T I A

Saint John

Grand Pré

Chezzetcook

BAY OF FUNDY

Annapolis Royal

Port Royal

Clementsport

Digby

Mahone Bay

Indian Point

Halifax

Bridgewater

Lunenburg

Dublin Shore

Yarmouth

Publico

Cape Sable Is.

A T L A N T I C   O C E A N

SCALE

100 miles

100 kilometres

QUEBEC AND THE ATLANTIC PROVINCES

'Keep me warm
one night'

The background

The old traditions of handweaving in Canada, both domestic and professional, are limited to the eastern half of the country where the primary settlement took place before 1800. Except in isolated areas, many of the techniques used were little more than a memory a hundred years later, the terminal date of this study, although a few have survived or have been revived in somewhat altered form in modern craftwork. To understand the roots from which they sprang, one must know something of the phases and waves of immigration that have led to the complex national mosaic that now forms the country.

Although prior attempts had been made, the first successful settlement was that of De Monts and Champlain. Their party arrived in 1604 and spent the winter on Dochet's Island in the Ste-Croix River, the present boundary between New Brunswick and the state of Maine. Nearly wiped out by scurvy, the curse of many of the early settlements, enough of the party survived to move across the Bay of Fundy to the Annapolis Basin in Nova Scotia. Here *L'Habitation* was built on the western shore, which led to the founding of Port-Royal, near modern Annapolis Royal. Colonists from France came to this new outpost, mainly from Saintonge, Poitou, and Aunis, between 1632 and 1651, and developed the fertile lands of the Annapolis Valley. The area around the Minas Basin was first settled in 1675 with Grand Pré as the centre. From these places, outlying colonies developed as men went to find other alluvial farmlands at Peticodiac, Cobequid, Memramcook, and similar situations. These settlements constituted Acadia and the descendants of the quiet prosperous farmers are known as Acadians to this day.

By the terms of the Treaty of Utrecht in 1713, the present Atlantic provinces of Canada were partitioned between France and Britain. Ile Saint-Jean (Prince Edward Island) and Ile Royale (Cape Breton) went to France, and it was on the latter that the fortress of Louisbourg was to be built to guard French interests. Newfoundland and mainland Nova Scotia became British, but the western boundary of the latter was not clearly defined, and modern New Brunswick became an area claimed by both crowns. The result was that the peaceful Acadian farmers found themselves in the front line of fire in the continuing struggle between France and England for the control of North America. They refused to take an oath of allegiance that would have compelled them to bear arms against their mother country, but did undertake to maintain a strict neutrality in the struggle between the two major powers. For Governor Lawrence this was not enough, and in 1755 he ordered the expulsion of the Acadians from the rich diked farmlands they had claimed from the tidal flats. Of some fourteen thousand deported before peace was restored in 1763, half were sent to the American colonies, where they were far from welcome. Others fled to uninhabited areas particularly in those parts of the continent that were still French, or to the West Indies; some found refuge in France. Many, perhaps three thousand, died of privation, but after peace was restored in 1763 a considerable number found their way back to their homeland, and founded new settlements in various parts of the Maritime Provinces.

Acadians continue to make their contribution to Canada in the parts of Quebec where they settled after the expulsion, in New Brunswick, Prince Edward Island, Cape Breton, and Nova Scotia. They are found on both shores of the Baie de Chaleur, in the upper St John River valley, along the northern coast of New Brunswick, and in the Chignecto Isthmus separating that province from Nova Scotia. In Prince Edward Island, the main areas are Rustico and the western part of the island from Miscouche to Tignish. In Cape Breton, the older settlements in the southern part are around Arichat on Isle Madame, and River Bourgeois. Shortly after 1800, groups from Prince Edward Island settled on the western coast to found Chéticamp, and the villages that surround it. On mainland Nova Scotia, the main region of concentration is around the southern end from Cape Sable Island through the Pubnicos, and along the French Shore between Yarmouth and Digby. There are smaller communities in other parts of the province.

With the founding of Quebec in 1608 by Samuel de Champlain, the second and more important French colony in Canada was established. Settlement spread from Quebec down the St Lawrence River towards Tadoussac, primarily a trading post, then upriver to Montreal where Ville Marie was founded by Chomedey de Maisonneuve in 1642. Between these two points, the first fortification at Trois-Rivières was built in 1634. This was an additional protective post along the river highway.

The economy of Canada was oriented primarily to the rich Atlantic fisheries and secondarily to the fur trade, but small agricultural communities did grow up in the shelter of the fortified centres. Greater expansion was limited by the dangers of Iroquois raids, especially during the seventeenth century when the Five Nations adopted an aggressive policy aimed at preventing the French from trading with the more westerly tribes. They hoped to deflect the fur trade from Montreal to the English post at Albany with themselves as middlemen. With more peaceful times after 1700, the settlements expanded along both shores of the St Lawrence from well below Quebec to Montreal and up the Richelieu River. This trend was accelerated when peace became general with the cession of New France to Britain in 1763 by the Treaty of Paris.

During the period after 1608, the population was small, but grew slowly with continuing immigration from the various provinces of France. The welfare of the colonists and the hope of converting the Indians drew many religious to the new land, the wilds of America called the adventurous to the possibility of a life in the fur trade free from restrictions, and soldiers sent for the defence of the colony remained to settle and strengthen the scattered communities. Compared to the English colonies along the Atlantic coast from Maine to Georgia, the population of New France was never large. The census of 1666 ordered by the Intendant, Talon, lists 3418 souls. Just before 1685 an outbreak of influenza decimated the population, and some fourteen hundred of an estimated eleven thousand died during the epidemic. In 1760, the population of the colony was about seventy thousand, but with the change of sovereignty in 1763, a considerable number emigrated to France and to various French colonies.

Strong French traditions have survived in Quebec, but these have naturally been affected by outside influences that have been absorbed. During the French regime, New Englanders captured in raids on various communities were sometimes converted to Roman Catholicism, and perhaps made some contribution to their new environment. Some names in Quebec still bear witness to this period, such as Phaneuf (Fansworth), Stébenne (Stebbin), and Sayer (Sayward). After 1759, immigration from France ceased and was replaced by immigrants from the British Isles. Those who were Protestant formed a separate entity, but Scottish and Irish Roman Catholics were easily absorbed into the French community.

The first English settlements in what is now Canada were on the eastern coasts of Newfoundland, but these were fishing stations supposedly of a seasonal nature. The letters patent received by the Company of Adventurers to Newfoundland in 1637 forbade any settlement within six miles of the coast. These restrictions were firmly supported by the fishing interests in the west of England, but despite all efforts a permanent population did become established in the outports with St John's as the centre. The Newfoundland Act of 1699 somewhat eased the situation, but it was not until the nineteenth century that the restrictive laws were finally repealed. The corresponding French colony at Plaisance (Placentia) ceased to exist in 1713 when the whole community was moved to Louisbourg on Cape Breton.

What may be considered the first permanent English-speaking settlement in Canada under official auspices began with the founding of Halifax in 1749. This was primarily a military operation to counter the threat of the powerful French fortress of Louisbourg. Following the expulsion of the Acadians, fifteen hundred settlers moved in from New England in 1760 to take up the rich farm lands made vacant in the Annapolis Valley and around Grand Pré. After the fall of Quebec in 1759, other groups from New England settled in the St John valley of New Brunswick. These people from the American colonies who came prior to the Declaration of Independence are generally known as the 'Planters.'

The first heavy wave of English-speaking settlement resulted from the American Revolution when those who declared their loyalty to the Crown, or endeavoured to remain neutral in the struggle, were forced to flee their homes. Most of those able to travel by sea went to Nova Scotia and New Brunswick; others who had to travel overland found refuge in the Eastern Townships of Quebec or became the first settlers in Ontario along the shores of the upper St Lawrence River, Lake Ontario, the Niagara Peninsula, and Lake Erie. Those who came between 1776 and 1783 are the United Empire Loyalists and were followed by others who found the new republican regime not to their taste. With reports sent back of rich fertile lands to be had almost for the asking, a further stream of immigration flowed north from the new United States of America until the War of 1812–14. Like the Planters who had preceded them, many of the pioneers of this period were of English descent, but some were descendants of French Huguenots who had found refuge in New England. Others were the families of Scottish regiments that had been disbanded in the American Colonies following the Seven

Years' War or that had been involved in the battles of the Revolution.

People of other national origins left at the same time, both during and after the conflict. Some of Dutch descent came from New York State where their families had settled around New Amsterdam and in the Hudson Valley when it was a Dutch colony. Others had German ancestors such as the 'Queen Anne Protestants' who came mainly from the Palatinate and were victims of the European wars of the early eighteenth century. A number who had found homes in the Mohawk Valley and elsewhere travelled overland to the Niagara Peninsula. Of the Hessian mercenaries employed by the British government in their efforts to suppress the Revolution, some were discharged in Canada and took up land in Ontario. The Mennonites had been forced to leave Switzerland because of religious persecution in the seventeenth century. They moved first to Germany, and in the eighteenth century to Pennsylvania, where freedom of religious choice was a fundamental principle of the colony. Many of these people, often referred to as Pennsylvania Dutch, later came to Ontario, immigration being heaviest during the decades just before and after 1800.

As the country was opened up by pioneers from south of the border, it became more attractive for immigration from across the Atlantic, and new settlers arrived from the British Isles and later from continental Europe. People whose ways of life were changing as a result of the technological advances of the Industrial Revolution looked to North America as a land with a bright future, as an escape from overcrowding, or as a place where lost fortunes might be repaired.

Immigration from England and Wales was on a voluntary basis, though few came from the latter country. Those who did emigrate were often lured by handbooks published to advertise the advantages of various parts of Canada. These gave information, often unreliable, about life in the new land. A number who came from Britain were the younger sons of landed families who had to make their own way in the world; others were naval and military veterans who had completed their service and for whom there was no place in the new industrial economy. Periods of economic uncertainty and depression, particularly those that followed the Napoleonic Wars, gave an impetus to those who gambled on the possibility of a brighter future in the new world.

Additional factors affected Scotland: the growth of the population beyond the point where the primitive agricultural system could support the people, accompanied by poor harvests and changing markets. The old clan system had begun to break up in the seventeenth century, but was still a vital factor in the Highlands in raising support for Bonnie Prince Charlie in the '45. Its suppression by legislation after this tragic event, combined with the other factors, led to both voluntary and forced emigration. Tacksmen with their people sailed across the Atlantic to the Carolinas and Nova Scotia. In 1791, a report made to the Society for the Propagation of the Gospel stated that 'since the year 1772 no less than sixteen vessels full of emigrants have sailed from the western parts of the counties of Inverness and Ross alone, containing, it is supposed, 6400 souls.' One chief was probably among these, John Macdonald of Glenalladale. Roman Catholic and Jacobite, he had bought land in Prince Edward Island in 1772, and brought both tacksmen and sub-tenants to this new home from South Uist, Moidart, and Arisaig.

Higher rents could be obtained for land when the southern breeds of sheep were introduced into the Highlands: Lintons at Balnagowan in the 1760s, and the great Cheviot to Caithness and Ross in 1790. This led to the total collapse of the mutual responsibilities of the old clan system. The chief became the sole owner of the clan lands and could rent them to the highest bidder. The introduction of the more efficient English farming methods led to the Clearances and the mass displacement of the people who lived in the glens. They had to leave and find new homes. The sheep runs were new, but the principle of forced emigration was older. In 1739, Macdonald of Sleat and Macleod of Dunvegan sold some of their people as indentured servants in the Carolinas. Deliberate evictions commenced in the lands of Clanranald, Macdonell of Glengarry, in 1785, with families forcibly emigrated. Some of them joined those that had left earlier and had founded a new Glengarry in Ontario after the American Revolution. Here they were joined by later victims of their chief's needs for funds to gratify his extravagant tastes, or his successors' efforts to unburden themselves of the heavy debts they had inherited. By the 1860s, there were some twenty thousand of Clanranald's clansmen in Ontario, and none in the old Glengarry.

In the Isle of Skye in the twenty years following 1840, seventeen hundred and forty writs of removal were served affecting some forty thousand people. In some cases the crofters were loaded directly onto boats that took them across the Atlantic; in others they found their way south to the Lowlands to find employment that would enable them to pay their passage. Some lairds assisted former tenants to emigrate. The endeavours of the Earl of Selkirk in Prince Edward Island and the Red River Colony are perhaps best known, but as well, the Duke of Hamilton bought land in Megantic County, Quebec, and settled his tenants from the Isle of Arran there. Benevolent societies were formed to help those who moved south and who could not pay their own way. The settlement pattern of the Highlands was completely altered by the Clearances. As any observant person is aware in travelling through the glens today, and seeing the low mounds marking the remains of shielings and cornkilns, or the lines of the run-rig fields in the valley floors, this story was repeated again and again in the wide lands controlled by the hereditary Highland chiefs.

In Ireland, the overcrowding of a depressed tenantry was a serious problem and emigration the only possible solution. Societies were formed to assist those who were prepared to leave, and people sometimes came in organized groups under official auspices to settle in pre-arranged locations. Potatoes were the staple and often only food, and when the crops were struck by blight in 1845, famine was inevitable. Masses fled across the Atlantic to the United States and Canada. Many reached Quebec and Ontario, and in the latter province settlement was often on religious lines. In Peterborough County, two adjacent townships were settled by Irish: Douro was Roman Catholic while Dummer was Protestant.

During the Napoleonic Wars, Polish and Lithuanian mercenaries formed part of the French armies. Some of these men captured by the British as prisoners of war were taken to England. With the outbreak of the War of 1812–14 in North America, they were given the opportunity of fighting again in Canada on the British side. As they were mercenaries, national feelings were not involved, and a number accepted the offer. When the war was over, some of these men took up land and settled in Ontario.

The first German settlement in Canada was established in Nova Scotia in 1753 at Lunenburg, south of Halifax. This was an officially sanctioned venture, and the pioneers were Hanoverians, subjects of George II of England as Elector of Hanover. Later German immigration followed the Battle of Waterloo. The final defeat of Napoleon brought serious depression to Europe, and this was combined with the problems of increasing industrialization. Unemployment was high and many trained artisans could find no work. Germany was particularly hard hit, and a trickle of emigrants started across the Atlantic. Political unrest before the middle of the century and the introduction of compulsory military service, turned this trickle into a steady stream that lasted until the outbreak of the Great War in 1914. Most went to the United States, but a considerable number reached Canada, either directly or by finding their way north across the border. Once arrived, the majority of them settled in Ontario and tended to gravitate to areas such as Waterloo County already opened up by German-speaking pioneers.

Early handweaving in eastern Canada will be shown to stem from three cultures: French in Acadia and Quebec, Scottish in Ontario and the Maritime Provinces, and German-speaking in Ontario. These were accompanied by the traditions brought from the United States by the Loyalists and those who followed after them. The results can seldom be considered as a 'folk art,' since a peasant class in the European sense did not exist. The influences mentioned all date from before the middle of the nineteenth century. After this time, immigration increased and became more varied with many people coming from other cultural backgrounds. Some of these people have wisely treasured their national customs and traditions, but their arrival was too late to have an effect on older handweaving in Canada, which was already dying out by the time that they arrived.

The development of weaving, both domestic and professional, is dependent on settled agricultural communities that raise the fibres to be processed. This dependence is clearly illustrated in the case of Newfoundland. In the outports scattered along the rugged coastline, the people looked to the sea as their means of livelihood, the raising of crops and herds being a sideline. A limited number of sheep was sometimes kept for meat and fleece; the wool was used for knitting heavy sweaters, undergarments, and mitts to protect the fishermen from the elements. The basic needs for clothing and warmth could be obtained by trade. Supplies of this kind would be brought when the fishing fleets crossed the Atlantic from England and Europe to harvest the Grand Banks. Goods imported directly from England would also have filled these

needs. It was in the Codroy Valley in the southwest corner of the province that a basically agricultural community developed, and it is only from here that information about weaving has been obtained.

No examples of woven materials from this area have been seen, but some have been described from memory. Despite the nearness to Cape Breton where many overshot coverlets were woven, there was no recollection that these were ever made in the Codroy Valley. Blankets and clothing were the usual products. Some bed coverings were woven of strips of salvaged cloth. One informant with an Irish background remembered an aunt preparing resist-dyed, or ikat, yarn for the weft to be used for weaving material for a dress. The fine handspun skeins of wool were made the same length as the specific width she intended to weave; cotton was firmly tied at regular points to produce the pattern she knew and wanted. After being dyed red, the ties were removed, the skeins wound on bobbins, and used as weft on a cotton warp. As weaving progressed, a repeating pattern of small crescents appeared, arranged in half-drop repeat. Although the resist-dyeing of skeins of wool was widely used for the splashed patterns found in warp-faced carpeting (nos. 110–13), this is the only reported instance of the weft-ikat process being used in Canada.

The area known as Acadia covers parts of all the Maritime Provinces and Quebec and is quite distinct from any political boundaries. The agricultural communities that developed in the Acadian mainland grew up through the determination of the settlers and almost in spite of the colonial policies of the French government. The official attempts to encourage agriculture on Ile Saint-Jean (Prince Edward Island) in the eighteenth century were wholly inadequate. Some flax and even some hemp were raised in Acadia, and the census returns show that some sheep were kept, but these may well have been primarily for meat rather than for wool. Traditionally, Port Mouton on the Atlantic coast of Nova Scotia gained its name because a sheep that De Monts was carrying to the new colony fell overboard and was drowned there. One weaver is known: Mathieu Martin, seigneur of Cobequid (Truro, NS) is known to have been trained as one, and perhaps followed this trade, as well as dealing in furs and establishing his seigneury (DCB, II, 462).

The population in the Acadian communities grew slowly. The census of 1686 shows a total of 885 persons with 986 cattle, 608 swine, and 758 sheep. Even with this number, wool production would have been slim for the needs of the colony. With the sheep of the period, a three-pound fleece would have yielded only about half this weight of wool. A simple calculation based on the total population will show that this would mean only about twelve ounces per person per year. In actual fact, the main settlement was around Port-Royal, and it was here that the majority of animals were to be found, with a small number at Minas and almost none elsewhere. This meant that around Port-Royal, there was a limited supply of wool to be used for clothing, this supply being supplemented by flax and hemp.

Joseph Robineau de Villebon was Commandant in Acadia from 1690 to 1700, and in 1699 forwarded memoirs to France dealing with both Port-Royal and Minas. In connection with the former settlement, he wrote that 'Flax and hemp, also, grow extremely well, and some of the settlers use only the linen, made by themselves, for domestic purposes. The wool of the sheep they raise is very good and the clothing worn by the majority of the men and women is made of it.' Minas was still a comparatively small centre at this time, but Villebon reports that the women are always busy, 'and most of them keep their husbands and children in serviceable linen [hempen?] materials and stockings which they make skilfully from the hemp that they have grown and the wool produced by their sheep' (Webster, 128, 132). Nothing remains of the materials that were produced in these early settlements. The limited amount of wool would have stimulated the expenditure of time and patience needed to produce serviceable, long-wearing materials like the fine banded skirt materials known from the post-Expulsion period.

The 1752 census for Ile Saint-Jean shows a population of 2223, with only 1230 sheep. This figure would have meant an even smaller proportionate yield of wool. In the same return, one finds that 1817 bushels of grain were sown, mainly wheat, against one bushel of flax seed (Blanchard, 36–7). Following the Expulsion three years later, refugees from the mainland fled to Ile Saint-Jean, most arriving in a destitute condition. As there were no local supplies available, desperate pleas were sent by the governor of the island to Louisbourg for help and were met with shipments of such food and blue French cloth as could be spared. Despite this aid, many are believed to have been without clothing during the first winter and were forced to huddle indoors to escape the cold.

Such weaving as may have been done in the early period was done by women domestically and by men professionally, as suggested by Mathieu Martin's occupation, but it is not until some years after the Expulsion that actual examples are known. By this time it had become women's work. The basic loom in Acadia had only two shafts, and it was not until fairly well into the nineteenth century that four were adopted. The earliest known examples of Acadian weaving are two fragments, probably skirt materials, in the Confederation Centre at Charlottetown (no. 77). These were traditionally woven by Harriet Gallant at Rustico in 1796. They show a style known from other Acadian centres with multiple bands of coloured wools on a fine cotton warp that entailed a time-consuming amount of work. Plain linens and heavier woollen materials also seem to have been woven for clothing, but these have failed to survive. Blankets were made with the usual coloured bands decorating the ends, but perhaps the most characteristic examples of surviving Acadian weaving are the banded bed coverings woven of wool and cotton yarns, or woollen and cotton cloth strips salvaged from old materials. A number of these are illustrated. It is in them that the remnants of heavier clothing materials as well as blanketing can be recognized.

In Quebec, the occupation of primary official concern was the fisheries: for a Roman Catholic population in Europe, the cod from the North Atlantic fisheries was the staff of life. Once settlers arrived in Canada, the fur trade proved a greater attraction as a source of quicker and easier profit. Agriculture was less attractive, although some did turn to this way of life. André Vachon has expressed this attitude clearly (DCB, II, 166):

It has been said with a good deal of justice that the settlers of New France, craftsmen or soldiers rather than farmers, attracted moreover by the fur trade, had only a slight interest in farming. For many of them cultivating their land remained a marginal activity and simply constituted, in the final analysis, a necessary means of supplementing their income but one which they endured impatiently and got rid of at the first opportunity.

With this attitude, the climate could not be less conducive to the development of textile arts. The inventory and other records from Quebec are remarkably full and very informative. In studying them it becomes obvious that they tell the same story and prove that the needs of the colonists were met by materials brought from France. Compared to imports, the references to locally produced textiles are negligible (Séguin, 494–7). The colonists were, of course, dependent on the annual supply ships to bring what they required, and should these fail to arrive in any one year, shortages could result. A letter dated 4 September 1640 and written by Marie de l'Incarnation, expresses gratitude for gifts just received by the Ursuline Convent established in Quebec the year before, and says that 'all this has relieved us of the necessity of using our bed-valances to make garments for our girls, as we had resolved to do.' Granted, this necessity was due in great part to the newly established house's lack of funds, but twenty years later in a letter to her son dated 17 September 1660, she reports that the country 'can exist without France as far as food is concerned, but depends on it entirely for clothing, tools, wine, brandy, and an infinity of small commodities, and all these are brought to us through trade.'

The charter issued to the Compagnie des Cent Associés in 1627 included instructions to establish manufactures in Canada (Fauteux, 442), but these were ignored. Despite assurance that they would take action, the directors of the company preferred the people of the new colony to be obliged to obtain the goods they required from the mother country. This allowed the monopoly company, and others that followed, to control trade and increase profits by having a dependent population.

The instructions given to Jean Talon when he came as Intendant in 1665 contained similar clauses: 'Whether the inhabitants are too occupied in assuring their survival, and that of their families by the cultivation of the land, whether the administrators of the country have lacked zeal and initiative, it has been necessary up to now to export to New France the materials which the inhabitants need to clothe themselves, and the shoes for their feet' (Fauteux, 446). With the support of Colbert, Louis XIV's great minister who was able to enlist the interest of the king, Talon was to employ himself to better this state of affairs. Reports had been sent back to France that the land was suitable for raising both flax and hemp. In fact, both coarse and fine hemp cloth of local manufacture are listed in an inventory dated 1657 (Séguin, 497). Talon took this information to heart. He placed looms in selected houses, and was able to report to Colbert in 1669 that hemp had been harvested, and that thread and cloth had been made. Progress was much slower with woollen goods due to the small number of sheep, but a few pieces of *droguet* had been produced that would have been woven using a linen or hemp warp, and a wool weft. The first listing of locally produced fulled material of this type that has been found occurs in 1685 when tenants of Châteauguay sold to their seigneur thirty-three ells of fulled grey cloth (Séguin, 493). All wool goods are found just afterwards in 1688 when both *étoffe du pays* and *étoffe à capot* are mentioned (Séguin, 497). Talon in addition to encouraging the growing of hemp and flax realized that knowledge and skill in spinning was an integral part of the production of cloth. Marie de l'Incarnation in a letter to her son dated 27 August 1670 writes: 'The women and girls are urged as strongly as possible to learn to spin; we are encouraged to teach our seminarians, both French and Indian, and we are offered materials for this.'

Talon's term of office ended in 1672 and there was no successor until the appointment of Duscheneau in 1675. With the break in administration and the fact that the new Indendant took little interest in the economic development of the colony, all the projects commenced and strongly supported by Talon, often out of his own pocket, ground to a halt. When Brisay de Denonville became Governor-General in 1685, he also endeavoured to encourage the production of textiles. He pointed out the need of showing the women and girls how to spin, 'for they were almost unable to handle a spindle.' Colbert, who had supported Talon, was gone: Denonville asked for help from France, but his appeals met with little support.

It was not until the beginning of the eighteenth century when the bottom fell out of the market for beaver that the inhabitants showed any real interest in producing goods for their own needs. This was from necessity, not from choice: their purchasing power was gone. Antoine-Denis Raudot, with his father Intendant of New France from 1705 to 1710, estimated in one of his official reports that there was a twenty-year supply of coat beaver in the warehouses of France (DCB, II, 551). The depression caused by the failure of the main staple market hit hard, and fewer and fewer ships came from France with supplies or to carry back the fish and lumber that was available for export. During this period there was considerable illicit trade with New England. British materials were always less expensive than French, and as the price of the latter rose the former became more tempting, particularly to those in the Montreal area. In 1731 a search was ordered of all the houses in the city. Fines were imposed if any contraband goods were found and only fifty-three families escaped unscathed (Palardy, 363).

It was as a result of the shortage that the Sisters of the Congrégation de Notre Dame decided to install looms. Bégon reported in 1712 that he had been shown samples of cloth as good as any made in France, both black for priests and blue for the boarders at the convent. The best known result of

the depression was the weaving shop established by Mme Legardeur de Repentigny in a house she owned in rue Saint-Joseph in Montreal. Here she installed nine New Englanders whom she had ransomed from the Indians, and they proceeded to produce plain cloth, wool twill, and *droguet*. To supplement the ever present shortage of the usual fibres (linen, hemp, and wool), she experimented with others that were used by the Indians: bark (probably the inner bark of elm and basswood), nettle, and buffalo wool. In 1705, she sent samples of nettle cords to France explaining that if the cards she had ordered had not been lost at sea, the products would have been better. In 1707, the New Englanders grasped the opportunity to return to Boston, but the establishment was not abandoned until 1713 (Fauteux, 465–6). It is difficult to know just what was produced through Mme de Repentigny's endeavours, but Antoine-Denis Raudot pleaded with the Minister of Marine to permit, even to support, her efforts as the rough materials she produced were a boon to the poor (DCB, II, 552).

Throughout this period in Quebec, and well into the eighteenth century, weaving was a man's affair as it had been in much of Europe since the introduction of the horizontal loom about the eleventh century. Certainly there were professional weavers in Quebec at this period, but they were very few in number. They are mentioned both in the general census of 1666 ordered by Talon (RAPQ, 1935–6), and in that of 1681 (Séguin, 622). Whether all the eleven listed in the earlier census followed their craft is doubtful. Nine list other additional occupations, and weaving may have been the trade they followed before leaving France. Those in the later census appear to have been actual weavers. One was at Montreal and three others were on the South Shore. It was not until the second quarter of the eighteenth century that locally produced textiles came to be used to any great extent. As the demand grew, the craft became a means of professional livelihood. Boys were apprenticed to learn the trade, and such agreements made by Pierre Fontigny of Pointe-aux-Trembles are known from February and December 1745, and October 1751 (Séguin, 494).

With increased population and more peaceful times after the middle of the eighteenth century, the demand for locally woven materials continued to grow. Weaving gradually became part of the domestic occupations of rural households, and more and more a woman's occupation. These developments were hastened by a serious economic recession in Quebec in the second quarter of the nineteenth century (Ouellet, 257). Wheat had by then become the main cash crop of the farmers, but the demand for their produce failed probably because of the growth of the new settlements in Ontario. A longer growing season and rich soil made Ontario the granary of the country until it was supplanted in turn by western Canada.

With this loss of buying power, rural communities of Quebec were forced to become as self-sufficient as possible. Even though the materials available were becoming less and less expensive (through the growth of factory production in Britain), only the most prosperous farmers could consider buying cloth. The women of rural Quebec took over the tasks of processing fibres, spinning them, and weaving to keep their households supplied with clothing, bedding, and other domestic needs. This development has given rise to the unfounded belief in a long tradition of handweaving in Quebec. The craft continued to flourish in this province into the present century, long after it had died out in most of the rest of the country.

The shortage of textile tools as shown in the records of early Quebec tells the same story of the late development of textile production. Only two references have been found in the seventeenth century: a break (*broie*) for flax or hemp in the effects of Léonard Barbeau of Montreal in 1651, and a spindle (*fuseau*) owned by Jeanne Mance in 1673 (Séguin, 619, 621). The earliest reference to spinning wheels (*rouets*) is in 1708 when three old ones are reported at Saint-Lambert. In 1716 both large and small wheels were owned by Julien Choquet at Verennes (Séguin, 623). The earliest looms were for weaving tabby and are found in lists dated 1710 and 1717 (Séguin, 623). Up to 1759, the records indicate the existence of about a dozen others in the Montreal area (Séguin, 623). Fauteux, on the other hand, quotes a letter written by Bégon in 1712 which says that there were about twenty-five looms in Montreal at that time (475). Some of these would have belonged to the Congrégation de Notre Dame and to Mme de Repentigny's establishment, and would not have appeared in the inventories. Compared to the nineteenth century when weaving had become an essential part of domestic rural life in the province and the loom part of the standard equipment of almost every farmhouse, these figures are small.

As has been mentioned, successful attempts at growing hemp and flax in Quebec had been made in the seventeenth century, the cultivation of the former having been particularly sponsored by Talon. These efforts were repeated by some of the later administrators such as Bochart de Champigny (Indendant, 1686–1702), and Dupuy (Intendant, 1725–8). The endeavours to develop the cultivation of hemp were successful in the early part of the eighteenth century when the government was prepared to purchase the crop at a supported premium price that was almost triple that obtained by the farmers of Brittany. This product was not used for textile production, but exported to France where it was destined for rope and cordage. Once the government lowered the price to a more normal level, interest in hemp production flagged. Later attempts to encourage its cultivation under both the French and English regimes met with no success.

Flax is not as heavy to process as hemp, and its cultivation grew slowly and steadily until in the nineteenth century it became a staple crop both for seed and for fibre. Most of what was produced was used locally, and the fibres filled the domestic needs for textiles.

Sheep were more difficult to bring from France than flax or hemp seed, but efforts were made. Champlain mentions that there were sheep in the new colony in 1619 (Séguin, 565), but there were probably few. Fifty were included in the cargo of the *Saint-Jean Baptiste* when she sailed from La Rochelle for Quebec in 1671. The same ship carried other animals, a hundred men, a hundred and twenty *filles du roi*, cloth, blankets, and many essential items (DCB, II, 181). The census of 1681 shows that the best flocks belonged to the religious institutions (Séguin, 565). There were 625 sheep in the colony in 1683, 787 in 1685, and 900 in 1686 (Séguin, 566). This number meant an even smaller proportion than existed in Acadia at the same time, and an almost negligible amount of wool per capita per year. Obviously there would have been very little wool available in Quebec for textile production at this period.

As everywhere in Canada in the early days, sheep were not easy to raise. In the wooded countryside lurked wolves, wildcats, bears, and other predators, as well as dogs, that could wipe out a flock overnight. No matter how good the original stock, the animals degenerated due to inbreeding of the small flocks and the lack of knowledge of the rules of animal husbandry. These factors led to a decreased yield of fleece of inferior quality. Peter Kalm, the Swedish naturalist who was in Canada in 1749, confirms this. He mentions that each habitant ordinarily raised some sheep to supply wool for clothing, but that the better materials came from France. He states that the imported sheep degenerated, and their progeny more so, and gives the lack of proper feed during the winter months as an additional reason for the poor stock.

Wool production in Quebec remained low until the nineteenth century. In 1765, there were an average of 2.4 sheep per farm. This average rose to 4.4 in 1784, and 7.5 in 1831 (Ouellet, 86). In 1765, the farms in 81.2% of the seigneurial parishes had four sheep or less, and the remaining 18.8% had five to sixteen. In 1784, these figures show a marked change: 31.3% had four or less, 65.8% five to sixteen, and 2.9% more than the latter number. In 1844, almost 85% of the farms had five to sixteen sheep (Ouellet, 342).

Even with the growth of the flocks, other problems arose. The skinny, poorly nourished sheep produced less and less wool, and of an inferior quality. The habitant knew little about improving his flocks by the import of fresh stock and was even less able to afford to do so. In the long run, it became necessary for him to raise more and more sheep of low yield to supply the wool for his family's immediate use.

It was this wool, the homegrown flax, and later the inexpensive cotton yarns that could be obtained through barter, that clothed the families of rural Quebec and supplied almost all of their textile needs throughout the greater part of the nineteenth century and into the twentieth. The failure of the market for Quebec wheat after 1830 changed the emphasis on agriculture in the province. Each farm became more and more self-sufficient, and tended to produce everything that was required for the family's needs, with a small surplus that could be sold or bartered in local markets. The shortage of wool was sometimes acute, as is shown by Mme de Repentigny's experiments with buffalo wool. 'Two old blankets made of dog's hair and a four-poster bed' are listed in an inventory probably of the eighteenth century (Palardy, 364), and cow hair obtained from local tanneries was frequently used, and called 'poor man's wool.'

The basic loom in Quebec had two shafts. There were obviously a few four-shaft ones as early as the first part of the eighteenth century for weaving the twills that are mentioned. During the course of the nineteenth century, this latter type became steadily more common. All that was woven was for utilitarian use. Even with the sometimes scant supplies of materials, not always of the best quality, the use of colour in many of these everyday things shows the innate sense of design and artistry possessed by many of the women of Quebec. Catalogne with balanced and contrasting bands was made with a weft of strips of salvaged cloth for decorative bed covers and is possibly the best known material woven in the province. Although now usually considered a floor covering, there is no record of its use for this purpose before the latter part of the nineteenth century. Few, if any, old catalogne coverlets have survived, leaving the imaginative *boutonné* and *à la planche* ones from the lower St Lawrence as the most distinctive contributions that are to be found in the older textiles that have survived in Quebec.

In those parts of Canada where settlement was non-French, the picture of traditional handweaving presents fewer problems. The history is shorter and the settlers were able to establish a way of life peacefully without the upheavals that affected Acadia and Quebec. Until the end of the American Revolution in 1783, domestic manufacture of any kind in all the British colonies was always discouraged in the interests of maintaining a market for English products. It was considered part of the duty of a colony to obtain what it needed from the home country in exchange for raw materials and for the protection afforded by the British forces in times of trouble. Despite the restrictions, a weaving tradition did develop in New England and the colonies to the south, and this tradition was brought to Canada during and after the American Revolution. It explains the existence at an early date of certain weaves that are found in Nova Scotia, New Brunswick, and Ontario. These include twill diaper, double-cloth, 'summer and winter,' and many of the patterned weaves for linens. In the Maritime Provinces, it may have joined a tradition brought by the Planters who had come from New England some years earlier, but no material from this period is known to have survived. It seems unlikely that a German tradition was brought to Lunenburg in Nova Scotia when this settlement was founded in 1753. It would most certainly have met with official discouragement, and if it ever existed, it appears to have vanished without a trace. The woven materials known from that county differ in no way from what was produced in other parts of Nova Scotia.

The first settlement in Pictou County in Nova Scotia was by Rhode Islanders in 1767, but they were soon joined by the group that came on the *Hector* directly from Scotland in 1773. Among these people there was probably at least one weaver who brought the traditions of that country to the new world. The same would be true of John Macdonald of Glenalladale's settlement in Prince Edward Island. It would be surprising if there was not one man, perhaps more, among the sub-tenants who accompanied him who was a weaver by trade. In any case, there is little doubt that some among the group had an adequate knowledge of making cloth. From the start, it had been planned that this venture would be as self-sufficient as the clan had been before leaving Scotland.

In the early nineteenth century in Nova Scotia, a number of men are listed in official records as professional weavers. Many of these were new settlers who carried on the trade they had learned in their youth. As is known to have happened in Cape Breton, their daughters rather than their sons appear to have inherited their knowledge and to have become the custom weavers for the areas in which they lived. The same appears to have been true of the other Maritime Provinces, which would be one explanation why the more complex weaves died out in Nova Scotia and New Brunswick in the earlier part of the nineteenth century.

Although now part of Nova Scotia, Cape Breton was once a separate province. Its cultural development has a different background, and is quite independent of the mainland except for neighbouring Pictou County. The early English-speaking settlement was Loyalist, but this was of short duration. Most of those who came soon moved away in the face of the forbidding hills and deep shaded intervales to which they were unaccustomed. They were followed by Highland Scots forced to emigrate in the face of the Clearances, and shiploads of whom were landed at various ports along the coast. Parts of the island undoubtedly reminded them of the land they had left and they settled down to make new homes. Some preferred the sheltered coves along the shore, others the wider river valleys, but many established farms on the uplands of the hills where the hours of sunshine were longer and the snow perhaps less deep in winter.

Once settled, they carried on the Scottish traditions of weaving, and as time passed and flocks became established, this included not only clothing materials, sheets and blankets, but overshot coverlets and carpeting, examples of which will be described later. Flax was also an early crop, used for coarser linens for heavy use, and finer ones for the households. It was also used as a pattern weft for both coverlets and tablecloths in overshot weave, using a cotton warp when this yarn became available. There were men among the first settlers who were professional weavers, but the first call on the energies of all men was to raise or obtain food for their families by clearing the land for farming or by lumbering and fishing. The weavers' skills were not passed on to their sons, but to their daughters, and it is through them that the copies of the pattern drafts now in the Mackley Collection have descended. Weaving was added to spinning as part of the regular domestic duties in almost every home. Women generally taught their daughters to handle the shuttle and to produce clothing materials and blanketing from the yarn that they had spun.

The old traditions have survived longest in Cape Breton, and are not yet dead today. From the knowledge that still exists, the fact was verified that the weaving of patterned materials such as overshot remained an occupation for professional specialists. They wove the coverlets, overshot carpeting, and the patterned table linens on order on their own looms with the yarns supplied to them, or they would sometimes go to the customer and weave on the loom in the farmhouse. The last professional coverlet weaver died in 1971 in Cape Breton. Mrs John P. Munro was in her nineties and had woven overshot coverlets on order since her marriage shortly after 1900. She knew the answers to questions that had arisen in studying the old materials and was able to confirm rumours heard from others whose memory was not as long, and conclusions reached on a theoretical basis.

Mrs Munro, whose family had come from South Uist, had been taught to weave plain materials at home by her mother and grandmother when she was quite young. When she was in her teens, two overshot coverlets were wanted by her family, and Catherine MacIsaac, a professional weaver in a neighbouring community, was called in to make them on the loom in the farmhouse. She set up a sufficient warp for the pair and commenced weaving, carefully watched by the girl, who followed every action intently. Soon the first coverlet was completed, and Catherine MacIsaac went home to celebrate Christmas and Hogmanay, planning to come back after the first of the year to complete the order. When she returned, she found that the girl who had observed her so carefully had woven the second coverlet. The last professional coverlet weaver's career was started.

Mrs Munro remembered that the old type of cotton found in most coverlets had been imported as skeins of singles, that these were bought at the general stores, and that they were then plied by hand to give strength necessary for warp without sizing. Her loom was set up in a small shed behind the house. A strip of cloth was stretched between the two front cords that passed over the top pulleys. On this, the pattern draft was attached and a pin with a black head was placed in a pattern block of the draft to show that it had been completed, whether threading the loom or weaving the pattern.

Another professional weaver in Cape Breton had been left a widow with small children. Most of the food could be raised on the farm, but hard cash was needed for taxes and some other requirements. Yarn was brought to her from the surrounding community and woven to order. She wove some coverlets and wool plaids, but while her children were small her main production was blanketing. In the 1930s, she produced this in thirty-yard lengths at ten cents per yard, using handspun wool on a singles cotton warp that had to be sized with starch.

The handwoven materials that have survived in the Maritime Provinces are now dominated by the overshot coverlets, but wool carpeting, many patterned linens, blankets, sheets, and clothing materials were also produced in quantity. In the Nova Scotia Museum, Halifax, there is one quilt made of homespuns from Cumberland County. It dates from the early nineteenth century, and is entirely sewn with handspun woollen thread. The checked materials of which it is pieced are similar to those known from Ontario. Most of the homespun clothing materials and many of the blankets from the Maritime Provinces have disappeared into hooked mats where they are no longer recognizable. The making of these was a very popular pastime during the winter months. They are not too durable and the old ones would have been worked on a coarse linen ground like the rare example in the New Brunswick Museum, Saint John, dated 1865. Virtually all hooked mats that have survived are on jute sacking, a material that was not available before the 1870s and did not come into general use until later in the century.

One question that presents a problem for the Maritime Provinces, and especially Nova Scotia, is the source of the vast amounts of linen sailcloth that must have been required. Some was probably imported, but there is a good possibility that much was woven by hand from the flax that is known to have been extensively grown.

The development of weaving in Ontario was similar, but included settlements with cultural backgrounds, particularly German-speaking, that were neither Loyalist nor Scottish. In this province, each group made its own contribution, as will be shown later. From census returns, it is known that there were many professional weavers, and all but about one per cent were men. The small number of women listed are unmarried and of uncertain age, or widows with dependent children who were forced by circumstances to earn their livelihood. Almost the only other occupation that was open to them was 'laundress.' The majority of the men were immigrants from Scotland, Ulster, and Germany, and the supply was constantly replenished by new arrivals. In the 1871 census, some three thousand weavers are listed, and almost every township had its own weaver. All these men wove clothing materials, carpeting, blanketing, and linens using the yarns supplied by their customers. This is clearly shown in the account books of John Campbell of Komoka and Samuel Fry of Vineland. Some, but not all, would also have woven coverlets to a customer's order, each weaver usually having one or perhaps two types in which he specialized. The districts in Ontario where professional weavers are not listed are those settled by Irish Roman Catholics from the southern part of the country where weaving, unlike the rest of the British Isles, had become part of the domestic duties of the women.

William Thomson, a Scottish weaver suffering from consumption, visited the United States and Canada, and an account of his travels was published in 1842. He gives an account of one of the weavers in Ontario whom he came to know (143–5):

Here there is a numerous class of country weavers, who make a good living, working for farmers, and cultivating a piece of land for themselves. There was one of these, in the last-named township [Vaughan], that I used to visit, of whom I shall take particular notice, as he is a fair example of this class of tradesman. His name was John Kelly, an Irishman; he came out here five years ago, and all the knowledge he had of the business was learned in weaving dowlas [a coarse linen for shirtings, usually blue] at a factory near Belfast. He has a little farm house, with a *butt and a ben*, and a stair leading between the apartments to a roomy garrett, where he has his warping stakes. He has a cow and a calf; two swine; lots of cocks and hens; four children; with dogs and cats, and all the etceteras of a thriving household. His loom was in a corner of the apartment they lived in, and all around were bundles of woollen yarn. He wrought with the hand shuttle; his children filled the *pirns,* and he taught them to read while at work; now and then swearing 'By Jesus' he would murder them. He has four acres of cleared land; plenty of potatoes, oatmeal, Indian corn, &c. The wife said, such a thing as wanting provisions for themselves or for their children never came into her mind, for John had more work than he could do.

Due to the efforts of his grandaughter, Miss Annie R. Fry, Samuel Fry is the weaver in Ontario about whom most is known. The collection that Miss Fry saved and treasured is now in the Royal Ontario Museum, and a number of examples of his work will be found illustrated later. She not only preserved these, but also his pattern and account books, some letters, and the weaver's original handbill (fig. 1). She was able to supply much information about her grandfather when the Museum was first in touch with her in 1948. The collection forms the most valuable archive on any weaver who worked in Canada.

WEAVING.

SAM'L FREY, respectfully informs the Inhabitants of the Niagara district, that he is prepared to WEAVE all kinds of PLAIN and FANCY

COVERLETS,

DIAPERS, &c. at reduced prices, in a workman-like manner, and on reasonable terms, at the house of Jacob Frey, about half a mile west of Ball's Mill, on the 20 mile creek.
SAMUEL FREY.
CLINTON, October 4, 1836.

FIGURE 1

The Fry (Frey) family were Mennonites who had settled in Pennsylvania in the eighteenth century, one branch of which moved to Ontario following the American Revolution. Samuel Fry's father married the widow of Abraham Nash, a linen weaver in Pennsylvania, and settled in South Grimsby Township in Lincoln County. Samuel was born here in 1812 and three years later the family moved to a new and better farm a short distance south of Vineland on the border between Clinton and Louth Townships. A two-storey log house was built. This was moved to a new location a few years ago and now forms part of the Jordan Historical Museum of the Twenty. From an early age young Samuel showed an interest in the processing of the flax that grew on a special field on the farm and in the wool that came from the sheep kept. Even then, weaving apparently caught his fancy, an interest encouraged both by his father and by his mother.

When he was old enough and could be spared from the farm, he was sent back to Bucks County, Pennsylvania, to learn the craft probably from another member of the Nash family. Fry returned to Vineland with the book of patterns suitable for doublecloth and twill diaper that he had learned, as well as with a knowledge of weaving plain and twill materials. In 1836 he issued the handbill in which he 'respectfully informs the Inhabitants of the Niagara district, that he is prepared to WEAVE all kinds of PLAIN and FANCY COVERLETS, DIAPERS, &c. at reduced prices in a workman-like manner, and on reasonable terms.'

Fry had planned to devote his full time to weaving, but with the death of his father he was compelled to take over the management of the family farm. This was about 1843, which is when the first entries appear in his account book, and from then on he wove only during the off seasons, particularly in January and February. No account book was kept when he was weaving full time, as all the proceeds would have been turned over to his father. Fry had two looms, a four-shaft one for clothing materials and blankets and a multiple-shaft one for weaving doublecloth and twill diaper coverlets. After he died in 1881, his eldest daughter inherited one loom and continued to weave in Campden, a few miles west of the family farm. By this time, the only demand for handweaving was for rag carpeting. This she wove for her neighbours until a fire destroyed the house and what was left of Samuel Fry's equipment.

In the Annie R. Fry Collection, formed of material that Samuel Fry wove for his own family, there are examples of checked homespuns for clothing that have survived in woollen quilts, plain winter sheets, checked blankets, and superb bird's-eye ones. There are examples of plain linens and an outstanding twill diaper tablecloth, coverlets in the same technique, and an overshot one. In the Jordan Historical Museum of the Twenty is his wedding suit made of fulled dark blue cloth that he wove himself, while the winter shawl he made at the same time is in the Annie R. Fry Collection. From the time he took over the farm, he wove very few doublecloth coverlets, but some are known that he must have woven before. The main bulk of his coverlet production was in twill diaper, but there are a few overshot or 'floatwork' ones from late in his career. Most of the pieces calling for a multiple-shaft loom have four-block designs requiring sixteen shafts, but Fry's pattern book includes five-block ones requiring twenty shafts. Examples of these latter are known to have been woven for members of his own family and still belong to his descendants. All his known work shows a superb sense of colour and balance combined with faultless workmanship.

When Fry first kept records in his account book, the entries are in the pounds, shillings, and pence of York Currency, with a pound valued at $2.50. Later, the entries are in dollars and cents when the decimal currency became fully official. Between, there is a section when the entries are very confused and it is sometimes uncertain which method of accounting is used. The account book shows that most of the weaving was paid for in cash, but a few entries showing barter throw an interesting light on the life of the community. Most of these accounts are with his near neighbours, Abraham and Samuel Moyer.

An entry for February 8, 1848, shows a charge of £2/8/0 for two single (twill diaper) coverlets woven for Abraham Moyer. The following August, payment was made in the form of 1000 bricks.

Samuel Moyer's indebtedness covers a longer period. In 1849, Fry supplied him with three ploughpoints for 3/0 and wove a twill diaper coverlet for £1/4/0. In 1851, he charged 2/0 for a 'kettel boiling saus,' and received eighteen brooms worth £1/2/0, and the remaining 7/0 in cash. In 1856, he wove 17 yards of tow linen for £2/1/0, in 1857 25¾ yards of flannel for £3/1/9, and in 1858 16¾ yards of checked flannel for £2/5/4. In the autumn of the same year, he received part payment in the form of five bushels of wheat credited at £5/5/0. After weaving a bird's-eye coverlet that winter, £1/2/0, the balance of £3/5/1 was settled in cash.

The costs of some of the items in John Campbell's account book (now at the Ontario Science Centre, Toronto) supply additional information. All the yarns he used were supplied by his customers, and he wove lengths that ran from ten to fifty yards. The basic charge was 1/– York currency (12½ cents) per yard, which covered fulled cloth, bordered blankets (cf. no. 139) and checked ones, woollen twills, both plain and striped, and rag carpeting. Plain flannels and drugget (wool on a cotton warp) were cheaper at 10 cents per yard, but wool carpeting undoubtedly of the warp-faced type cost 1/6 or about 19 cents. Plaids, by which he meant checked woollens, were 1/– if in two colours, but 1/1 if in three, and 1/2 if in four.

The names of many of the professional weavers who worked in Ontario are known, but the great majority are no more than impersonal entries in the census returns, or the occasional notice in one of the business directories published in the second half of the nineteenth century. Biographical information on those about whom more is known will be found in the discussion of their work, but a glance at what is known about the Jordan-Vineland area of Lincoln County will show the services available in this very prosperous and self-sufficient rural area. In addition to Samuel Fry, there were other weavers. Wilhelm Armbrust had the first jacquard loom in Canada, and worked from 1834 to 1848 (nos. 425–30). Moses Grobb did similar work from 1853 until about 1872 (nos. 444–6) and is known to have woven simpler materials both during this period and before. Richard Banks' loom is now in the Jordan Historical Museum of the Twenty. It is a heavy one, firmly constructed of oak planks, with a pine warp beam, and a beater of fine grained hardwood. It is a simple two-shaft one limited to weaving plain materials for everyday use. Banks is known to have worked independently, but is also believed to have used this same loom when weaving at the woollen mills that used to stand by the upper falls at Ball's Mills, now Balls Falls Conservation Area. Frederick New worked in the village of Jordan. Little is known of his work, but on his death his daughter Kitty continued as a rag-carpet weaver into the present century.

Hester and Rosanna Young were sisters who wove in Picton in Prince Edward County as early as the 1840s (no. 301). Hester married John Abercrombie in 1852 and continued to weave, but probably on a less professional scale (no. 172). It was through their daughter, Miss Annie Abercrombie, that the Royal Ontario Museum was enriched by the gift of the collection of pattern drafts that her mother and aunt had used (nos. 65–71), and frequent reference will be found to these in dealing with coverlets. These drafts were probably gathered from several sources, but many were sent to the Young sisters by friends, or relations, named Sing who lived in Watertown, New York.

Most of the weaving done in Ontario, as in the rest of eastern Canada, was plain material for sheets, blankets, and clothing, produced in great quantity both professionally and domestically. Being plain and utilitarian, little remains; it is the patterned coverlets that were always special that have been treasured, although their frequent survival gives an unbalanced picture of what was actually made. Overshot coverlets occur throughout the province, but are found most commonly in areas of Scottish settlement as in the Maritime Provinces. 'Summer and winter' weave, and the appearance of twill diaper and doublecloth shortly after the first settlements seem to derive from the traditions brought during and after the American Revolution. Twill diaper occurs again later in the areas of German-speaking settlement, and is accompanied by other multiple-shaft weaves in this tradition. The weavers of the jacquard coverlets, with a few exceptions such as John Campbell, William Withers, Christopher Armstrong and a couple of others, were mainly German immigrants. Some appear to have brought the necessary knowledge with them, while others adapted their skilled training on shaft looms to this new medium.

From time to time, certain coverlets are reported to have been woven by itinerant weavers, including all types from overshot to jacquard-woven ones, as well as imported carpeting of the scotch ingrain or kidderminister types. That there were a few weavers in districts of rural Ontario who would move from farmhouse to farmhouse that had looms when other casual work was not available is more than likely, but they were a definite minority. It is not likely that these men wove coverlets; they would have worked up the yarns prepared on the farm into blanketing and clothing materials. The true professional weavers who wove coverlets as a specialty line had their own workshops and expected their customers to come to them. Almost all of those listed in the census returns are shown as married men with families and small plots of land on which to raise food. John Campbell's account book shows that his customers came from as far west as Goderich and Sarnia and from Woodstock to the east, a stretch of about a hundred miles. One thing is absolutely certain: no weaver of jacquard coverlets was ever itinerant. The sheer size, complexity, and weight of their equipment would have made this impossible. Pedlars are known to have carried samples of the work of Albert and Edward Graf in their packs, taking orders and probably taking back the customer's yarn. The finished coverlets were delivered on their next round. In the same way, some weavers may have been itinerant to the extent that they possibly travelled around the neighbouring countryside soliciting business, but they would have brought the customer's yarns back with them to their workshops to be woven.

In Quebec, it is known that almost all the handwoven materials were produced in the farmhouses of the province. In Ontario, in addition to the volume woven by professional weavers, there was also a great amount produced domestically in the rural areas, and the same is probably true of the Maritime Provinces. Michael Smith published *A Geographical View of the Province of Upper Canada and Promiscuous Remarks on the Government* in Hartford, Connecticut, in 1813. He reports that 'hats, shoes, boots and tin and crockery were manufactured in great quantity. Linen and woollen cloths are made in abundance. Whiskey, and apple and peach brandy are also made in considerable quantity' (Craig, 43). William Thomson was in Canada about 1840, and mentions that there were 13,400 domestic looms in Ontario at that time (145).

Firm figures for both Quebec and Ontario are found in *Census of the Canadas, 1851-2*. At the time the returns were made, the population of Lower Canada is given as 890,261, and of Upper Canada as 952,004. Relevant figures are tabulated in fig. 2. It will be noted in comparing the number of woollen mills in the two provinces and their production, that industrialization was already heavier in Ontario. Of

the hands employed in these operations, some would have been weavers, but others would have been employed in other necessary functions such as carders, spinners, dyers, and finishers. After deducting a percentage from the totals of the hands employed for these operations, there are still very few men in Quebec who would have been independent professional weavers, compared to the much greater number in Ontario.

In addition to the mill production of cloth, other figures are found in the agricultural returns, including both what was produced domestically and what was made by the professional weavers, almost all of whom lived in the rural areas. The amount of woollen cloth produced in the two provinces was about equal, with a different proportion between fulled and flannel. Although wool production per animal was slightly higher in Ontario, the figures are again comparable. The excess not used for the production shown in the agricultural returns would have gone to the mills. The most striking difference between the two provinces is shown in flax production and the weaving of linen yardage. It remained a major and important crop and product in Quebec, but of minor importance in Ontario where it was being replaced by imported goods.

FIGURE 2

Manufacturing and agricultural production figures

WEAVERS AND TEXTILE MILL RETURNS

	QUEBEC	ONTARIO
Weavers	166	1738
Woollen Mills	18	74
Hands employed	154	632
Cloth production	86,000 yards	1,022,500 yards
Carding and Fulling Mills	193	147
Wool processed	125,672 lbs	582,000 lbs
Cloth processed	81,072 yards	206,430 yards

AGRICULTURAL RETURNS

	QUEBEC	ONTARIO
Sheep	647,465	1,050,168
Wool produced	1,428,783 lbs	2,619,434 lbs
Fulled cloth	764,532 yards	531,560 yards
Flannel	856,445 yards	1,157,221 yards
Totals	1,620,977 yards	1,688,781 yards
Flax	1,189,018 lbs	59,680 lbs
Linen	929,249 yards	14,711 yards

Source: *Census of the Canadas, 1851-2*, II

Tools and equipment

Wool, linen, and cotton are the yarns found in the Canadian handwoven textiles covered in this book. Some substitutes were tried on occasions of shortage of the usual materials, and these will be mentioned in due course. Wool and flax could be raised and processed, but cotton yarn had to be imported from the United States, and probably Great Britain, until mills were established in Canada.

The sheep from which the wool was obtained were difficult to raise when settlement was sparse. Only small flocks were found in Quebec before the nineteenth century. In Ontario and the Maritime Provinces, the basic stock had to be brought across the Atlantic from Britain, where certain export restrictions were in force, or obtained from the United States. When they arrived, the sheep had to be protected from the various wild animals that roamed the wooded countryside. In the late eighteenth and early nineteenth centuries, the farmer who managed to obtain a small breeding stock and to protect them well until he had a flock of twenty or thirty, which was more difficult to guard, might wake up one morning and find half the animals dead (Ryerson, 241, 247). Steadily, as the frontiers of settlement pushed the predators back the flocks increased. Joseph Pickering was employed by Colonel Talbot on his Settlement in Elgin County in 1825–6 as 'foreman or overseer of his farm,' and published an account of his experiences when he returned to England shortly after. He mentions that each farmer had 'five or six to twenty or thirty, and in some instances fifty and sixty, but rarely more' sheep (Craig, 77). By the middle of the nineteenth century, wool and the production of woollen cloth had become a major item in the economy of Quebec and Ontario as the figures from the 1851–2 census show (fig. 2).

The sheep known to have been brought to Prince Edward Island were medium wool Southdowns and long wool Leicesters, with cross-bred animals of these two stocks. Some others are also mentioned, such as a Leicester ram and ewe crossed with long Scotch, and a Lincolnshire ram and some ewes (Harvey, 210–12). All these came from England. Southdowns and Leicesters were the usual sheep found in Ontario according to Charles Richard Weld, who was in Canada about the middle of the century (Craig, 203). He also reports that an attempt made near Peterborough, Ontario, about 1850 to introduce fine wool Merinos did not succeed despite all care. Pickering mentions that Colonel Talbot received a sample of the long staple Lincolnshire wool, and intended to bring some animals out, but it is not known whether his efforts met with success (Craig, 76).

Before wool is ready for spinning into yarn, several preliminary processes must be followed. The fleece must be washed or scoured to remove accumulated dirt and as much of the natural oils as possible. In Ontario, this appears mainly to have been done before shearing. The animals would be driven down to a suitable stream on a fine warm day in late spring or early summer, and, when the worst of the dirt had been removed, would be let loose in a clean pasture for the fleece to dry. They were then sheared, and each fleece would generally be roughly sorted into grades for different purposes. The wool was still matted in locks even after washing. These were teased apart by hand to break them up and separate them. The entangled dirt would fall out and the fleeces would be transformed into a loose fluffy pile ready to be combed or carded.

The combing of wool is the older of the two processes, its origins lost in the mists of antiquity. The use of cards, primarily for preparing short-staple wool, appears to be a western European invention of the fourteenth century which did not reach eastern Europe until later (Hoffmann, 284–8). As is usual with novel tools and processes, the first mention of cards is in ordinances against their use.

The results of the two processes are quite different. The aim in combing is to lay the individual fibres parallel, and it is most suitable for wools of fairly long staple. Combs are always used in pairs. Few have been found in Canada. All known examples appear to be no later than the early part of the nineteenth century. The pair illustrated comes from New Brunswick (no. 2), but others have been seen in the collections of the Wolfville Historical Society, Wolfville, Nova Scotia, and of the York Pioneer and Historical Society, Sharon, Ontario. A pair from Quebec was in the former Village de Jacques de Chambly. Combed yarn is now generally known as worsted. In the textiles described here, this yarn is usually of a fairly long staple, lustrous wool, lightly spun. Its presence normally implies a date prior to the middle of the nineteenth century and will be noted in describing some of the items in which it occurs.

Cards are also used in pairs when preparing wool for spinning, and most of those that have survived were made commercially in great quantity during the second half of the nineteenth century or in the present one (no. 3). A few older ones are basically handmade (nos. 4–5). In carded yarn, now generally known as woollen, the fibres are not parallel as in combed yarn, but arranged irregularly without order, and usually have a softer handle. Most of the wool yarns found in the materials described here are carded, but no special note is made of this in the descriptions.

Although a considerable amount of wool was carded by hand, carding is an operation that may be done equally well by machine, a development from a patent of 1748. Small carding machines may be worked by hand and larger ones by water power in a mill. In both cases the wool is placed on a circular drum covered with leather in which are inserted fine wires of the same type as those in hand cards (cf. nos. 3–5). The drum revolves against stationary cards and the wool is spread smoothly on the surface of the drum. The result is similar to that produced by hand cards. Hand-operated carding machines are known to have been used in Ontario during the latter part of the nineteenth century, and perhaps earlier. Carding mills were established on suitable streams in various parts of Canada shortly after 1800, and grew steadily in number (cf. fig. 2). Women faced with the task of preparing the wool for spinning usually took advantage of this labour-saving service whenever it was within reasonable range. A small charge of two or three pence per pound was made for processing the wool, or it might be done on a share basis, a certain proportion being retained by the mill in lieu of cash payment.

When wool was in short supply, various substitutes were tried. Mention has already been made of Mme de Repentigny's experiments with buffalo wool, and she also tried goat hair. R.M. Ballantyne in *Hudson Bay* mentions seeing the French settlers in the early 1840s on the banks of the Red River in Manitoba eking out their scanty supplies of wool with that from the buffalo in order to make yarn to be used to 'weave an excellent kind of cloth' (70). Cow hair was used in Quebec as a substitute on the North Shore of the St Lawrence (nos. 122, 133), and examples using this 'poor man's wool' from Gaspé are in the National Museum of Man, Ottawa.

Flax was the one textile crop that could be raised by settlers as soon as they had a plot cleared for the purpose. It was often raised in considerable quantity to help fill immediate needs. In 1775, eight years after the arrival of the Rhode Islanders, and a year after that of the Highlanders who came on the *Hector*, the returns for Pictou County in Nova Scotia show a crop of 34,000 lbs. for the year. It became of prime importance in Quebec as shown in the census returns for 1851–2, when the annual crop was almost a million pounds (fig. 2).

The flax seed was closely sown on the newly cleared land to produce tall unbranched stems. As the plants grew, the clear blue flowers added a bright note of colour to the landscape. The women of the household tended and weeded them, pulled the crop when ready, and spread the stems out to dry. If a fine quality linen was wanted, the crop was harvested as soon as the seeds had set, but if a coarser fibre was required, the crop was harvested after it was fully ripe, when it would yield a larger amount of stronger fibres. Once dry, the various processes began that would transform the brown straw into linen.

The first of these was rippling, or the removal of the seed-pods. It was done by drawing the heads of the plants through a flat coarse comb. If the flax was gathered when ripe, the pods spilled into a pile on the barn floor. They were gathered up, threshed, and winnowed. After a sufficient stock had been set aside for the next year's sowing, the remainder was a valuable by-product as feed or as a source of oil. Then, other processes commenced that would recover the fibres so that they could be spun. Some of the steps were physically heavy and normally undertaken by men, but in Quebec and Cape Breton the entire series of tasks became women's work.

The fibres from which linen is made are long fine ones arranged in groups known as bast bundles that are incorporated in the stem of the plant between the outer bark and the central woody core. These bundles must be separated from the cellular tissue surrounding them, which is done by the combined action of bacteria present on the straw and moisture. The process is known as retting, and may be carried out in one of two ways depending on climate. In dew retting, the straw is laid out on grass so that the action of the bacteria, combined with that of dew, sun, and air, breaks down the bark and the woody tissue and dissolves most of the gummy substance that surrounds the bast bundles.

Water retting, the more usual method, involves immersing the tied bundles of straw upright in still or slow-moving water such as a natural or a dammed pond. The action of the bacteria breaks down the structure of the stems and the ret is finished when the bark and woody core may be easily separated from the intervening bundles of fibres. The wet straw is dried and put aside to cure for at least a month, often longer, before further processing. If the climate is suitable, the straw may be sun-dried, but the Acadians of southern Nova Scotia spread it on covered racks over a small fire.

Once retted, the bark and woody sections of the stem, known as the shive, are removed to free the bast bundles. This involves two processes: breaking (no. 6) and swingling or scutching (nos. 8–9). These two latter terms are synonymous, the first derived from an English root, the other from a French one. Once the bast is separated from the shive, it is hackled (nos. 10–12), and the handfuls of long fine fibre are tied in hanks known as line linen. During swingling and hackling, the short fibres, called tow, are removed. After carding, they are spun separately to be used as weft in materials of lower grade than those woven of yarns made of line linen. The better quality of tow results from swingling and the lower grade from hackling.

All the other bast fibres used in Canada passed through the same processes as flax and the same tools would have been used. Mention has been made of hemp, and in the late seventeenth and early eighteenth centuries considerable amounts were grown. Outside Quebec, hemp cultivation was encouraged by the government during the early part of the nineteenth century when there was need for this fibre for cordage during the Napoleonic Wars. It may have been grown sporadically after this until its cultivation was banned by legislation. To meet a shortage during the Great War of 1914–18, some was planted in southwestern Ontario, but the crop was destroyed by government agents before it could be harvested. Some hemp was certainly woven in Quebec in the late seventeenth century, but no materials have survived except perhaps as the ground of a few rare contemporary embroideries.

Some indigenous bast fibres known to the Indians were tried as substitutes for flax, such as nettle and milkweed. In both cases, the fibres were from the bast bundles incorporated in the stems. Neither appears to have had any great popularity. There are reports of the use of milkweed bast from Gaspé, but no surviving examples are known. The silky seedpod fibres of this plant have sometimes raised hopes that they might be used for yarn, but they have no cohesive qualities and cannot be spun. It was probably a sample of this fibre that Marie de l'Incarnation sent home to France in her letter of 13 September 1640 to the Superior of the Ursulines of Tours, remarking that it 'is finer than silk or beaver.' She requested that it be seen by some skilled person in the hope that it might be put to use, but this experiment would have met with the same failure as did later attempts to exploit the material.

As cotton cannot be grown in Canada, supplies have always depended on imports. Very little was ever spun in this country, and the only definite reference known is an entry in the account book of William Nelles of Grimsby that covers the period from 1791 to 1828. In 1805, note is made of payment of 4/- to a girl for three days' work spinning cotton. Good handspun cotton is difficult to distinguish from early mill spinning, but that used in two tablecloths from Markham Township in Ontario probably falls into this class (nos. 176–7). They are rather coarse and heavy, but suitable for the use intended and totally unlike any of the other cotton yarns found in Canadian textiles.

Most of the cotton reaching Acadia, the Maritime Provinces, and Ontario came from mills established in the United States. The first of these was Slater's at Pawtucket in Rhode Island and was established in December 1790. Alexander Hamilton, Secretary of the Treasury, in *Report of Manufactures* that he presented to Congress a year later wrote: 'The Manufactory at Pawtucket has the merit of being the first in introducing into the United States the celebrated cotton mill which not only furnishes materials for the manufactory itself but for the supply of private families for household manufactures.' Slater's mill was followed by others often equipped with machinery that he had made. These appeared first in New England and then in the upper Mohawk Valley of New York State. Whether a mill met with eventual success or failure, a supply of cotton yarn was assured throughout North America.

The yarns from the mills south of the border rapidly reached Canada. Boats coming to the Maritimes from New England to trade brought supplies with them, and for many purposes the fine strong yarn rapidly replaced the use of the laboriously processed linen. Away from the Atlantic coast, it probably reached the inland settlements by way of the St Lawrence River, and later by way of Buffalo, New York, when it became a wholesale outlet for many imports into Ontario. The yarn coming from the mills in the United States arrived in the form of skeins of z singles of about 10's count that would have measured about 8400 yards to the pound (no. 58). In light blankets, winter sheets, and clothing materials it was used for warp as singles that had to be sized with starch before weaving. If not sized, it could be plied by hand, usually on a spinning wheel to give the necessary strength. The smooth controlled spinning, and the looser, sometimes uneven, ply are characteristic of the warp found in the ground of many early coverlets. Later, with increased industrialization, heavy mill-produced carpet warp makes its appearance in the last quarter of the nineteenth century. This is a strong z, 4s yarn designed as warp for rag carpeting, but also used as weft in the woollen warp-faced type and in the ground of some late overshot coverlets.

The first cotton mill in Canada was opened in Sherbrooke, Quebec, in 1845, and was successful for several years. The next opened at Thorold, Ontario, in 1847, and operated intermittently until destroyed by fire in 1864. A more successful mill was founded in Montreal in 1853, and lasted until 1870. In 1861, a mill was established in Saint John, New Brunswick, which remained in operation until after the Second World War. In the same year, another was opened in Dundas, Ontario, and by 1866 employed over 150 hands. These mills gradually filled the demands of the domestic market and replaced the need to import cotton yarns.

To spin is to draw out and twist fibres into threads or yarns.

The fibres must have certain cohesive qualities so that they will cling together. The inherent microscopic roughness that wools, bast fibres, and cotton naturally possess makes it possible for a mass of short fibres to be formed into long unbroken threads of even thickness with useful strength. The fibres may be twisted into yarn with the hands alone by rolling the ends of a few between the fingers and drawing the hands apart at the same time, but this is a slow, tedious process that gives an unsatisfactory product. The simplest device for spinning is a spindle, usually weighted towards one end to give it momentum, that is twirled with the fingers of one hand while the draw is controlled by the other. In spinning wool and flax it is usually allowed to drop to the floor as it twirls, drawing the fibres out and inserting a twist at the same time. The yarn is held near the upper end of the spindle by a half hitch, and when a length is spun, this is loosened, the yarn wound on, another half hitch taken, and the steps repeated. The finest quality yarn may be made using this simple device. It was used in Canada (Spencer, 17), but must have been of rare occurrence. Most of the handspun yarns were made with spinning wheels.

In using the spindle and some types of spinning wheels, the prepared flax and sometimes wool was arranged on a distaff that was held under the left arm with the end often tucked into a belt. Acadian ones are known. One from the western part of Prince Edward Island is in Toronto (ROM 966.157.14). It is a simple tapered shaft of wood, about 80cm long, square in section, with notches along the upper part to help hold the fibres in place. The more usual type has a small cage at the top over which the fibres could be tied, examples of which are in Moncton (MUM). The importance of spinning as a womanly occupation is shown by the fact that the female side of the family is known as the 'distaff' side, as opposed to the male 'spear' side. The legal use of the word 'spinster' for an unmarried woman shows the importance that this task once held.

A knowledge of spinning was essential during the early periods of settlement so that the family could be clothed and household necessities supplied. Walter Johnstone's letters from Prince Edward Island published in 1822 advise English families against emigrating as 'Their women frequently can spin neither flax nor wool, and many are both unable and unwilling to take the hoe' (Harvey, 143). Girls were taught to spin at an early age and were expected to produce a certain amount of yarn regularly. In Ontario, in families where there were no daughters, it sometimes became a boy's chore to learn to spin in order to help the mother supply enough yarns for the family needs. Several elderly men have confessed this somewhat shamefacedly. In addition to the spinning done by members of a household, there were also professional spinners who would work for their neighbours. In the Ontario census returns, women are listed as married, unmarried, or widows, but some of all of these are also listed as 'spinsters.' Girls as young as ten, married and unmarried women, and widows are found with this occupation. They would have been paid for spinning the prepared fibres of their neighbours, either in a farmhouse or at home.

The simplest type of mechanically driven spinning equipment is found in the great wheel (no. 13) and in one type from Acadia (no. 14). The first of these is also known as the wool or walking wheel, and as the muckle wheel in Scotland. In these two types, an iron spindle with attached pulley wheel is mounted horizontally some distance from a larger driving wheel. A belt connects the two, and by turning the larger one the spindle is made to rotate rapidly.

In using the great wheel, the spinner stood holding the prepared wool in her left hand. A few fibres from this would be attached to the already spun yarn on the spindle. She turned the driving wheel in a clockwise direction with her right hand, the spindle rotated, and the twist ran from the yarn on it through the tips of the fibres, and into the loose wool. As the spinner stepped back, she moved her left arm out away from the tip of the spindle and a long single strand of yarn was formed. When a length had been spun, the direction of the driving wheel was reversed just sufficiently to disengage the yarn from the tip, and was then turned clockwise again to roll the length of yarn onto the spindle. The actual movements were quite simple, but a considerable amount of practice was required to judge the exact amount of draw that was needed as the twist went into the fibres, and to produce a thread of uniform thickness and quality.

In *The Backwoods of Canada*, Catharine Parr Traill describes its use in Ontario (29). 'There is something very picturesque in the great spinning-wheels that are used in this country for spinning wool, and if attitude were to be studied among our Canadian lasses, there cannot be one more becoming, or calculated to show off the advantages of a fine figure, than spinning at the big wheel. The spinster does not sit, but walks to and fro, guiding the yarn with one hand while with the other she turns the wheel.'

The great wheel was not suitable for spinning flax, for which an even greater control is required, but was widely used throughout eastern Canada for spinning wool. In its simpler form, the spindle was rotated directly by the action of the belt on the driving wheel (no. 13), but after the middle of the nineteenth century a firm in New Hampshire manufactured a patented head that had double driving action (cf. no. 22), and this type was widely adopted. An axle with a small and a larger pulley was mounted between the driving wheel and the spindle. A belt from the driving wheel went round the small one, and a second shorter belt around the larger one and the pulley of the spindle. In this way, the spindle could be made to rotate even more rapidly. Great wheels were made locally, and any competent wheelwright could make the driving wheel. The base is a finished wood plank supported by either three or four legs. These are normally plain, but the uprights supporting the driving wheel and spindle usually have simple turning. In the 1860s, a patented form of great wheel was introduced in which the spindle was attached to a weighted arm that would swing to and fro so that the spinner could stand rather than walk back and forth. These are sometimes referred to as 'spinning jennies,' a catchy name taken over from James Hargreaves' invention in the 1760s for spinning cotton that was a major advance in the Industrial Revolution (Aspin and Chapman, 13–16).

Few of the great wheels are marked, but a man named Donaldson is known to have made them near Pakenham in Lanark County. Darius Card had a sawmill near Maynooth in the northern part of Hastings County on a lot he obtained in 1869. He made various articles, including wheels, probably great ones (Groves, 98). Others of this type are reported at Upper Canada Village with the name of the maker at Kemptville, Ontario, stencilled on the inside of the rim (Spencer, 18).

The Acadian wheel shown in no. 14 works on the same principle as the great wheel, but the spinner sat rather than stood. The draw was shorter, and the wheel could be used either for flax or wool. A hollow length of reed was placed on the spindle and on this the yarn was wound. In its older form, the driving wheel was turned by hand, and the addition of a treadle as shown in no. 14 is a later development. Many of these wheels are much plainer (ROM 970.202.28); this one with its simple decorative turning and well finished construction is the work of an expert woodworker.

In the two types of wheel with straight spindle just described, the movements of spinning required two actions. The drawing and twisting of the fibres occurred simultaneously, but the yarn had to be wound on the spindle in a separate operation. In Europe in the fifteenth century, an invention, probably German, was perfected that made it possible for drawing, twisting, and winding to continue without interruption. This was the flyer, a horseshoe-shaped wooden attachment that was mounted on the spindle over the bobbin on which the yarn was wound. The detailed illustration of no. 17 shows the various parts, and the flyer's action is described there. This attachment is used only on small wheels, and makes their use for spinning flax possible. For this reason, they are often referred to as 'flax wheels,' but they are equally suitable for spinning wool. The flyer mechanism comes in two forms; in both it is attached to the spindle while the bobbin is free. In one form, the latter is tensioned by a separate cord that passes over one end (nos. 15, 18, 19); in the other, the driving belt is double – one part rotates the spindle, while the other controls the bobbin (nos. 16, 17, 20, 21). The former is a French type sometimes called a 'Picardie' wheel; the latter is that used in the British Isles, Germany, and most of northern Europe.

The standard form of wheel with flyer is seen in the examples mentioned, but a variation known as the 'castle wheel' is thought to have been developed because it took up less space in a small room. It is sometimes said to be an Irish invention, but the type occurs widely in Germany, Byelorussia, and the Ukraine. A few have been seen in Ontario and one recorded in Quebec, but they are far from common. The example illustrated was made in a Byelorussian community in Kamsack, Saskatchewan (no. 23).

The 'Picardie' type mechanism is known from Acadia (no. 15). It is used in conjunction with a treadle, which leaves both hands free to control the yarn, but in the older form the driving wheel was turned by hand (Mackley Collection). Although the more usual type with the bobbin controlled by the driving belt was later used at Chéticamp, these wheels were imported from Quebec (ROM 966.157.44).

Both types of flyer are known from Quebec, the 'Picardie' being the older (nos. 18–19). The other is found on wheels made from the middle of the nineteenth century on, and these often have makers' marks. 'F.O.' for François Ouellet is stamped on no. 20, and 'Paradis' on no. 21. This stands for Aram Paradis, the mark on a wheel in Musée des Ancêtres, Mont-St-Pierre, Gaspé. Another earlier one is marked 'Amable Paradis' (ROM 969.274.2). The two families were related: one worked at Village-des-Aulnaies, Cté L'Islet, the other in adjacent Kamouraska. St-André in this county became the major centre of spinning wheel production in the province in the present century. Three other marks have been recorded in Quebec: 'Fr. Borduas, St-Charles,' 'J. L'Heureux, L'Acadie,' and 'F.L.,' possibly Portneuf (ROM 969.40.3).

In Nova Scotia, even more makers' names are known. Alexander McIntosh (no. 16), and later his son I.S., worked in Pictou, and William McDonald at New Glasgow. S. Mackay, J. McK., and R. Stewart (ROM 970.202.27) are other names from Pictou and Antigonish counties that have been seen. In Cape Breton, Hector Fraser worked at Baddeck Bay, and A. Mackenzie worked either on the island or on the neighbouring mainland. The most famous group of wheels outside these strongly Scottish areas were made by the Young (Jung) family in Lunenburg County. The name is normally branded on one side of the platform (no. 17). The few unmarked examples of this family's work are easily identified by their characteristic turning, highlighted by banding in colour. In Prince Edward Island an unidentified maker incised a number at one end of the platform, and a date at the other. Some idea of his production may be guessed by the fact that examples numbered in the 600s have been seen.

No wheels with flyers have been found in Ontario marked with local makers' names. They were often the only piece of household equipment brought across the Atlantic by emigrants, and many of the wheels used in this province reached the country in this way. The one belonging to the family of Samuel Pentland (cf. no. 42) was brought from Ireland. One found in the province is marked with the name 'Peter Nisbet, Coltnes,' a place in Lanarkshire (ROM 966.33.1). Another with double flyer and inset pan for water marked with the name 'James Duff' is also of Scottish origin (ROM 946.14).

The yarn coming from the spinning wheel is called 'singles,' as it consists of an individual strand. The twist inserted in it may be in either direction dependent on the equipment and how it is used. Several terminologies have been used at various times to describe the direction of the twist of a yarn, but the one in generally accepted use today describes the angle formed in relation to the slant of the central bar of the letter z, or of the letter s. If the angle resulting from the twist matches that of the first letter, it is described as z spun and the twist as z; if it matches the second, the terms are s spun and s twist. This is shown graphically in fig. 3 with z twist to the left, and s twist in the centre.

Singles yarn may be used as it comes from the wheel either as weft, or as warp if it is sufficiently smooth, strong, and even. To give greater body or strength, yarns are often plied by twisting two or more spun ends together. The twist imparted in plying is the opposite of that in the individual strands but for rare exceptions. The appearance of a 2-ply yarn is shown at the right of fig. 3, where two z-spun ends have been twisted s. This would be described as a z, 2s yarn.

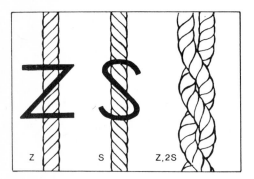

FIGURE 3

This formula tells that the twist of the individual ends is z, and that two of them have been plied s. This is the most usual plied yarn found in the textiles described here. In some sections, the spin of all yarns is noted in the descriptions; in others, particularly overshot coverlets where twist and ply are so consistent, note is only made when yarns depart from this norm. With plied yarns of other weights, for instance with 3 and 4 ends twisted together, the same type of formula is used.

Almost universally in spinning, the direction in which the driving wheel is turned is clockwise, which normally results in a z-twist yarn. This was formerly referred to as 'open band' twist, as opposed to 'closed band,' or s-twist. The reason for these terms is shown in fig. 4. If, as shown on the left, the belt (or band) of the great wheel simply encircles it and the pulley of the spindle, the latter rotates in the same clockwise direction as the driving wheel when it is turned in the usual way, and produces an open-band or z-twist yarn;

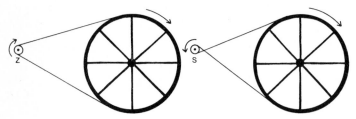

FIGURE 4

if, as shown on the right, the belt is arranged in a figure-of-eight so that it is crossed between the wheel and the spindle, the latter rotates in a counterclockwise direction resulting in a closed-band, or s-twist. In using a treadle wheel, an s-twist yarn is produced by turning the driving wheel counterclockwise. If the belt is doubled controlling both driving wheel and spindle, the two sections on the upper level are separate, or open, when spinning in the usual manner, and crossed below. If the wheel is turned in the opposite direction, the cross in the belt appears above, and the same terminology holds true.

The terms 'open-band' and 'closed-band' are of considerable age in the English woollen industry. The latter has long

been synonymous with warp spinning, and the former with the more lightly spun yarn destined for weft. It is possible that the extra drag given by crossing the belt on the great wheel made it easier to produce a more firmly spun strong yarn more suitable for warp. This practice was seldom followed in Canada where almost all yarn was z-spun for both warp and weft. In the blanket section, it will be noticed that some have singles warp spun s, combined with a weft spun z, in the traditional older way.

Yarns may be plied on a spinning wheel, but there were also tools specifically for this purpose. The great wheel was often used, and when this was done, the belt would be crossed as has been described. The spinner would still handle the wheel in the accustomed way, but without having to change the direction of the driving wheel. Plying with a treadle wheel was a different matter. It was immaterial to the action of the spinner's hands in which direction the wheel turned. To ply s, the wheel would simply be started counterclockwise rather than in the usual way.

The special tools for plying were the hurdy wheel (no. 22), and a type of dropped spindle known by the Gaelic name of *farsadh* (nos. 24–25). In the Scottish tradition, at least in Canada, it was felt that the plying of yarn put too great a strain on the treadle wheel and threw it out of balance. This would certainly be true in plying heavy yarns and special tools were needed for them. With the sturdier great wheel they would not have been needed.

The hurdy wheel turns up most frequently in Nova Scotia, but has also been recorded in Ontario. The one illustrated is the most usual type in the former province, and is normally supplied with a spindle head with double driving action of the type manufactured in New Hampshire and often found on great wheels. These tools were supplied with a clamp so that they could be attached to the edge of a table and were ideal for plying the heavy knitting wools required for fishermen's mitts, stockings, and sweaters.

The *farsadhs* illustrated come from Prince Edward Island and Cape Breton. In the type of treadle wheel used in Scotland, and the ones in this tradition made in Canada, there were usually one or two holes in the platform. These were either for a distaff or for a *farsadh*, usually missing when the wheel is found. If there is only one hole, it is not possible to know which accessory has been lost, but if there are two, both would have been present. A wheel seen at Auchindrain, near Inverary, in Argyll, still had its *farsadh* in place, and another has been seen in Ontario. In neither case was there a second hole for a distaff so it may safely be assumed that these wheels were made for spinning wool. A distaff is essential if spinning flax. The Scottish wheel already mentioned that was made by Peter Nisbet of Coltnes has both tools and would have been intended for spinning either wool or flax.

It is no longer certain how the *farsadh* was used. It could certainly have been twirled with the fingers and used as a dropped spindle, but one informant in Cape Breton had been told that it was rotated by hand and thrown across the room, the twist passing along the length of the ply as it twirled. If this was done, each stretch of yarn plied in one action would have been longer than would have resulted from twisting and dropping.

Prepared yarn, if it was to be used immediately, could be wound on spools or into balls. If it was to be kept for future use, it was wound into skeins where the fibre would not be under tension. For this, reels were used. The basic type is the hand reel, or niddy-noddy (nos. 30–1). When winding a skein with one of these, the upright was grasped in the left hand, the yarn guided over the tips of the cross bars with the other as it swung to and fro, or nidded and nodded. These tools are remarkably uniform in size, and made skeins of a standard length. They are found frequently in Nova Scotia, in both the Acadian and other parts of the province.

The more usual type of reel was a rotary device either vertical (nos. 32, 34) or horizontal (no. 33). The first occurs widely in the Maritime Provinces and Ontario; the second is also found on the Atlantic coast and was the standard type in Quebec. In both, the yarn was wound on cross-bars set at the end of arms that might be either four or six in number. Forty rounds of a reel was a standard known as a cut, when the circumference was ninety inches. As a cut was completed, a thread was passed around this part of the skein to mark the point. These actions were repeated with each additional cut until the skein was finished. A cut of forty rounds from a reel of the circumference specified was one hundred yards of yarn. The length of the finished skein could easily be determined by counting the number of cuts, and its grist or yarn number determined by its weight. Not all reels were exact in their measurements; a skein from no. 34 would be ninety-three inches and other measurements approximating the standard have also been seen. Another standard appears to have been eighty inches, and here a cut of forty-five rounds would have produced the same length of skein. This is true of almost all niddy-noddies, and also of the reel used by Peter Fretz, which has a circumference of a little over seventy-nine inches (ROM 970.257.26).

In the simpler reels, the number of rounds would have to be counted by the operator as the yarn was wound on, but in the more advanced type, a system of worm-gears and cogs kept count mechanically. One complete revolution of the final cog was equal to the number of rounds required for a cut. A small peg inserted in the side of the cog worked against a hardwood tongue, and caused it to click when a cut was completed. This type with a mechanical measuring device is usually termed a clock reel, and some have a clock-face counter placed on the front. This has a hand that may be moved to keep track of the number of cuts that have been made in the skein. There is one on that used by Peter Fretz mentioned above.

Skeins of wool, cotton, and linen could be dyed after reeling, but the first could also be dyed in the fleece before processing. Sometimes the finished lengths of drugget and flannel for clothing materials were dyed in the piece. The colour range was limited with blue dominant, followed by red, green, yellow, brown, and black. These hues were all obtained from natural sources, and are usually known as vegetable dyes. With the discovery in 1856 of aniline violet, a coal-tar derivative, these natural substances were steadily replaced and a wider palette from chemical products began to come into more general use from about 1870.

The characteristic blue was obtained from indigo, and the colour produced is rich, strong, and fast. It continued to be used into the present century in some parts of the country. The indigo plant does not grow in Canada. The prepared dyestuff was imported. It was the least expensive colouring agent that could be bought, which partly explains its popularity. It belongs to a class known as direct dyes that can be used without mordanting the fibres or yarn with a metallic salt, and was available at an early date; an entry in John Bonnyman's account book in the Museum at Tatamagouche, Nova Scotia, lists a sale as early as 1780. Indigo was used with wool, and less often with linen and cotton, which are more difficult to dye. The use of other colours was limited almost entirely to wool.

Reds were obtained from several sources. Camwood, one of several dyestuffs for this colour obtained from the wood of tropical trees, is the one mentioned most often in surviving lists and account books, but these dyestuffs are not as fast to washing and light as madder and cochineal. To what extent these red woods were used is uncertain as most of the surviving material that was dyed red has a characteristic brownish tone obtained from unpurified madder, a plant widely cultivated in Europe and imported into Canada. Cochineal, which comes from a small cactus-feeding insect indigenous to Mexico, occurs rarely. It gives a beautiful clear colour that was probably resisted because of its high cost.

Green could be obtained from verdigris, imported for the purpose, and a lovely soft shade obtained from wood ferns. The latter may be the source of this colour in New Brunswick. The more usual method was to top-dye with yellow after first dyeing with indigo. A good yellow could be obtained from quercitron, a substance in the bark of the black oak, a tree native to the United States. This could be bought, as could some other imported yellow dyestuffs, but in Canada local materials were available in the form of onion skins and goldenrod flowers. The difficulty with almost all local materials was the sheer volume required to extract sufficient dye. The busy housewife could and did save trouble and much valuable time by using bought supplies.

Brown could be obtained from a wide range of tree barks, but a considerable quantity of any of them was needed. Two stronger brown colouring agents were the hulls of black walnut and butternut. The latter seems to have been popular in New Brunswick, where the tree was quite common, for obtaining a soft brown. The former, which grew only in southern Ontario with its northern limit at Oakville, near Toronto, gives a strong direct dye.

In Prince Edward Island, and probably elsewhere in the Maritimes, foliose lichens known as crotal were widely used for warm browns. This common name comes from Scotland, where it is used for any lichen from which the colour could be obtained.

Wool was often treated with tannin to obtain darker colours, and iron mordants, known as saddening agents, were used for the same purpose. Tannin is contained in sumach and in oak galls, both of which could be gathered locally.

Iron has a corrosive effect on fibres, and with passage of time they gradually rot. Black was obtained from logwood, another import, when combined with saddening agents and often with indigo.

A purple shade is found rarely in a few pieces that pre-date the discovery of aniline violet. It is known from Prince Edward Island, Quebec, and Ontario. It is unidentified, but possibly comes from lichens of the species *Umbillicaria*. The best known of this group is rock tripe or *tripe de roche*. The colour would have been extracted by fermentation.

A tool often confused with the reel is the swift, but its use and purpose is the opposite. It is used to unwind the skeins and is not suitable for making them. When a skein is to be used, it is placed on a swift that is adjustable in size and wound off into a ball, or onto a spool or bobbin.

Some swifts are very primitive, consisting of the butt end of a tree trunk with roots attached that serve as legs. Two cross bars were set on a pivot on top so that they could revolve, and small pegs were inserted in the arms to hold the skein in position. Another simple type found in the Maritime Provinces and Quebec is illustrated (no. 35). It consists of an upright fixed in a heavy block. On this two sets of cross bars are placed, and the arms of both are drilled with series of holes. Through these holes, rods are placed so that they are slanted, and on them the skein rests, finding the point on the slanted rods that matches its circumference.

A more usual type is known as the umbrella swift (no. 36). It also has a central axle on which two small wheel-hubs are placed. Both revolve, but the lower one may also be raised or lowered and may be held in position by a peg through the axle. A set of ribs made of wooden slats is hinged on the upper hub angled down, and a matching set angled up on the lower one. Where pairs from the sets cross, they are held together with a pin. The ends of both sets of ribs are tied together with other slats that form a criss-cross cage to hold the skein. As the lower hub is raised, the circumference of the swift increases so that it may be adjusted to skeins of various sizes. A few old ones are fitted with a simple clamp for attachment, but many have a screw to hold them firmly to a support. Swifts of this type were widely used in the Maritime Provinces and Ontario, and probably in Quebec. They are found made in a wide variety of materials, from simple and everyday ones, to cabinet woods and ivory.

A more complex, but not necessarily more efficient type, is the barrel swift (no. 38). Two revolving cages shaped like small barrels are fitted on axles that project from an upright post. The lower one is stationary, but the upper may be moved to fit the size of the skein. This tool occurs in the Maritime Provinces and Ontario, but so far has not been seen from Quebec. Occasionally, double ones are found with two sets of cages, one on each side of the upright to hold two skeins when plying.

In preparing yarns for weaving on any scale, some device is needed to fill spools for the rack used in warping, and to fill bobbins that fit into the shuttles: special tools were made for this purpose (nos. 39–40). In many ways they resemble spinning wheels and are sometimes mistaken for them. The most usual type consists of a large driving wheel mounted on an axle with a single belt that rotates a spindle on which a spool or bobbin is placed. The driving wheel may be turned with a treadle or by hand. The spindle has a pulley fixed at one end and is normally held by upright supports. These may have a hole and groove or short lengths of leather with holes cut in them. Some winders have a box like no. 39 from Nova Scotia, where bobbins could be kept. Another winder of this type with smaller main wheel, but double drive, all set in a large box, comes from Quebec (ROM 966.211.2).

Although spools arranged on a rack was the usual way of setting up the threads when stretching a warp with a number of ends, a cage spool works equally well (no. 41). This is the only old one that has been found in Canada, and comes from south of Montreal. These were filled like spools on a special winder and stood upright on the floor when used.

The tools that have been described so far are those that are preliminary to weaving, but a loom is required to produce a textile. The loom has been defined as a tool on which a warp may be stretched and sheds opened mechanically for the passage of the weft. The one used by Samuel Pentland, a part-time professional weaver at Nile in Huron County, is shown in no. 42 together with his warping frame and spool rack. Other items from his equipment are shown in nos. 43, 47, 48, and 54. Still others are in the Royal Ontario Museum: a great wheel, a reel, a bobbin winder, a number of hand shuttles, and other incidentals. This loom has four shafts, and may be considered typical of the vast number of this capacity that were used throughout the Maritime Provinces and Ontario, and from the latter part of the nineteenth century on in Quebec and Acadia. They were for weaving tabby, a variety of twills and simple linen weaves, and overshot coverlets. The loom, as shown in the illustration, is set up with an overshot pattern, that of the first coverlet of this type in the Museum's collection (no. 258), which may be seen mounted in the screen behind.

The first step in preparing to weave is the stretching of a warp, the threads that are mounted on the loom and run lengthwise in the finished piece. This may be done either on a frame with projecting pegs of the type shown in no. 42, on a mill which is a large revolving cage with firm uprights and cross bars at the top and bottom in which the necessary pegs are set, or more simply on pegs set permanently in a wall in the weaver's workshop. Warps varied in length from enough for a simple coverlet up to a hundred yards, the capacity of Samuel Pentland's frame. From weavers' account books, it is known that twenty to forty yards was fairly normal. A warp may be stretched using any reasonable number of threads from one up, and in using up to four were often drawn directly from spools or balls. If from the latter, these would be wound around something with weight such as a small stone to prevent them from bouncing around, and placed in bowls or similar containers. If a greater number was being handled at one time, spools were usually mounted on a rack that could either stand (no. 42), or rest horizontally. The threads drawn from these could be handled manually or, more efficiently, by using a paddle (no. 29).

In either case, it was essential to keep the threads in correct and exact order for transfer to the loom. Two pegs will be seen on the upper bar of the warping frame in no. 42, and on these a cross is formed with the uneven-numbered threads going over the first peg and under the second, and the even-numbered ones following the opposite course, going under the first and over the second. When the warp is finished, this crossing of the threads is firmly tied, so that the threads cannot get out of order as long as the ties are in place. Usually a second cross is taken at the lower end of the warp, but this is formed by the groups of threads being handled, not by the individual ends. It too is firmly secured, and all these ties maintained until the warp is being put on the loom. To remove the warp from the frame or mill, it may be wound on a rod or, more usually, starting at the upper end with the single-thread cross, it is chained so that it resembles a stretch of very coarse crochet.

The use of a cross in warping to maintain the order of the threads is a very ancient method with a wide distribution. The one formed at the upper end of the warp by single threads is known as the porrey cross. That at the lower end formed by groups of threads is known as the portee cross, the portee being the round of threads carried together from the top of the mill or frame, down to the bottom, and back up again. The derivation of the term is the French *portée* (carried). The number of ends in a portee is usually the number required for all or an even fraction of a specific unit of width, such as an inch or half an inch.

Dressing the loom is winding the warp under tension onto the warp beam at the back of the loom. Rods are placed through the portee cross to maintain it, the ends of these tied together, and the ties holding the cross removed so that it may be spread. A sturdy rod, the cane roller, is placed through the loops at this end of the warp, and between it and the cross rods the raddle is placed. This is a comb-like tool made of wood with a removable cap, and acts as a spacer (no. 43). It has teeth set half an inch, or more rarely an inch, apart. A portee, or half a portee, is placed in each space in the raddle, and the cap replaced and pegged into position. It is then tied to the loom, and, using the cross sticks of the portee cross to spread the warp evenly, the warp is wound firmly onto the warp beam, and then the raddle taken off.

The rods holding the portee cross may then be removed, but are sometimes retained. Unless the portee cross is formed of only a small number of threads, and is used for entering the loom, additional rods are placed through the porrey cross and tied in place. The ends may be picked up individually from this cross for the threading or entering of the loom: the passing of the individual threads through the heddles on the shafts in the order wanted for the pattern chosen.

Old shafts consist of two stout horizontal bars of wood on which the heddles are arranged (no. 44). These are loops of cord, the earlier ones of handspun linen, the later of stout cotton. There are two basic types, one consisting of two interlocking loops known as clasped heddles, and the other with a separate eye in the centre. In the clasped type, the warp thread passes between two loops so that it is firmly held in place; with the other, it goes through the eye. In modern use each heddle is free on the shafts; in older types they are knotted with a single length of thread which joins them to-

gether and are evenly spaced along the length. These are referred to as knitted heddles and are the type that was in regular use. A frame for tying a set of knitted clasped heddles is in Musée Acadien at Bonaventure, Quebec.

Clasped heddles were used in many parts of eastern Canada, and were the typical older type in Acadia and Quebec. It was with this form that the *à la planche* technique (figs. 20–1) was possible; in turning the *planche* on its side, the threads over it could easily be raised but would have been blocked if eyed heddles had been used. Clasped heddles are difficult to thread and when a set was made the interlocking loops were tied over a rod to separate them. This rod remained in place until the first warp had been entered. When the weaving of the length was finished, the remaining ends of the warp were tied in bunches behind the shafts and in front of the reed, and the whole set taken off the loom and set aside. Several sets secured in this way are in the Jordan Historical Museum of the Twenty, left ready to be used again. When a new warp of the same type was to be woven, the shafts and reed were put back on the loom, the ends of the new warp were tied to those of the old one, and both were easily drawn through the heddles and reed. A weaver would own a set of shafts and a reed of a suitable spacing for each type of material he expected to produce.

The reed, named from the thin slips of cane or reed, often bamboo, of which old ones are made, is the tool that spaces the warp evenly across the width (nos. 45–6). It is like a fine comb, with the teeth firmly secured between two half-rounds of wood above and below. Reeds come in various sizes, with an exact number of teeth to a unit of measurement, the distance between the slips of cane being governed by a cord of the required diameter which is used to bind the half-rounds together. The most usual size of reed across eastern Canada appears to have had about ten dents, or spaces, per inch, or four per centimetre. Both finer and coarser reeds were certainly used for special purposes. Reeds were not easy to make and were often brought from the old country when a weaver emigrated. He could easily make a loom when he arrived, but reeds and shuttles were treasured possessions.

Once the ends of the warp are threaded through the shafts, they are passed through the spaces in the reed, an operation known as sleying. Usually they were entered two at a time, but for special purposes or effects this number could be varied. In the fine weft-faced Acadian skirt lengths (nos. 75–7), they were probably entered singly: in weaving doublecloth (fig. 39), four ends were usually put through one dent. After being sleyed, the ends of the warp are tied to a rod at the front of the loom which is attached to the cloth beam on which the material will be wound after it is woven.

The reed has a dual purpose. One is the even spacing of the warp as just described; the other is to beat the weft firmly into place to produce a sound piece of cloth. For this it is placed in the batten, or beater, which either hangs from the upper side beams of the loom, or which is sometimes pivoted at the base so that it is upright. In either case, its function is the same. After a shot of weft is put through the shed, or opening in the warp, the beater is brought smartly against the fell of the cloth, the reed held in the batten placing it firmly and evenly in position across the width.

To raise and lower the shafts so that a shed may be formed for the weft, treadles are required. The shafts may be tied directly to them or there may be intermediary levers known as lamms. These are pivoted at one side of the loom and the free end of each one connected to a shaft. If the shafts are tied directly to the treadles, a separate foot must be used to depress every one to be lowered. If there are lamms, one or more may be tied to a treadle, allowing one foot to control one or more shafts.

Using looms with more than four shafts, lamms are essential, and with multiple-shaft ones for complex weaving, two sets are used. These are tied so that each individual shaft may be raised or lowered independently of the others. Many four-shaft looms used the direct tie-up of the treadles, but for certain types of weaving, such as the overshot coverlets woven 'rose fashion,' the presence of lamms made the work easier. As will be pointed out, the pairs of treadles depressed in normal overshot weaving follow the pattern draft exactly. In weaving 'rose fashion' the order of the pairs of shafts depressed is reversed in order to change the basic pattern. If there are no lamms, this reversal would be difficult, but with their presence, no problem would arise. Once the tie-up had been altered as shown in fig. 33, the weaver would follow the treadling order indicated by the draft. The probable absence of lamms on many of the four-shaft looms used in Canada would be one reason why this method of patterning occurs so rarely.

For its passage through the shed, the weft is wound on bobbins that are inserted in shuttles. The old bobbins were usually short lengths of elderberry branches with the pith knocked out, but some may have been hollow reeds of the type used on some Acadian spinning wheels (cf. no. 14). The usual hand shuttle was boat-shaped with a short rod to hold the bobbin. This type had an eye in one side through which the yarn passed (nos. 50–5). This was often strengthened by inserting a short brad on either side of it, less often by an inset of bone (no. 51), a specially hard wood (no. 53), or some other wear-resistant material. Special longer shuttles of simpler type that would carry more weft were often, but not always, used in weaving rag carpeting. Two different forms are shown (nos. 48–9).

The hand shuttle is thrown by the weaver through the shed by a quick flick of the wrist and caught with the other hand. As the shuttle travels across, the hand with which it is thrown grasps the batten, and beats the weft into place as soon as the shuttle is caught on the other side. This means that the hands of the weaver perform two operations alternately: throwing and catching the shuttle and then handling the batten.

Many of the looms used by professional weavers in Ontario, and perhaps elsewhere in Canada, were equipped with a flying shuttle, an invention by John Kay in 1733. As an attachment to the looms used by the handweavers of this country, it was worked entirely by handpower. The fact that it is better known in its adaptation to the power loom does not mean that all materials produced with its aid are not handwoven, in spite of prejudices to this effect that have been expressed. Two of the fly shuttles used by Samuel Pentland on the handloom shown in no. 42 are illustrated (no. 54). Marks at the end of the race of the batten of the loom show that boxes to hold shuttles have been removed. John Campbell's jacquard loom now at the Ontario Science Centre, Toronto, still has the complete mechanism in place (fig. 40), as has a sixteen-shaft loom at the Halton County Museum, Milton.

The flying shuttle itself is heavier than the usual boat shuttle, and Kay widened the race, on the front of the lower bar of the batten, on which the shuttle travelled to support this extra weight. At each end, he built a box to catch the shuttle after it had travelled through the shed. A straight thin metal rod is fixed in each box at a height just greater than that of the shuttle. On each rod, a picker was set so that it could travel back and forth. Pickers were made of a stout piece of rawhide. Attached to each picker was a cord that travelled up through a ring and down to a wooden handle (at the centre of the batten) known as the picking stick. With the shuttle in the right-hand box, the picking stick was jerked to the left, which was sufficient to drive the shuttle out of the box, through the shed, and into the box at the other side. By jerking the picking stick to the right, the shuttle travelled in the opposite direction. The picking stick was always operated by the weaver with the same hand, leaving the other free to handle the beater (Hooper, 114–20). The resultant operation was faster and more efficient as the weaver did not have to change hands between throwing and beating. It had the added advantage that the weaver could cause the shuttle to travel a wider distance than was possible when the width he could weave was limited by the distance of his arms' reach as he threw the shuttle with one hand, and caught it with the other.

One other tool sometimes used in weaving is the temple (no. 47). The width of the cloth being woven must remain approximately the same as the width of the warp in the reed. If the cloth has a tendency to draw in and become narrower, the threads at the sides are subjected to excess wear by the reed, and break. To overcome any narrowing, the temple, which is adjustable, is fixed with the points at its ends in the selvages and the cloth stretched to the proper width.

To weave narrow bands for various purposes, a simple weaving device known as the rigid heddle was often employed. The examples shown come from Quebec, Nova Scotia, and Ontario (nos. 61–3). The first of these shows the rigid heddle in its simplest form, paddle-shaped with a broad blade in which long slits, closely set, alternate with small holes. The necessary length of warp is prepared and attached to a support. The rigid heddle is suspended from a hook or peg, the first end of the warp passes through a slit, the next through a hole, and so on. Once all are in place, the threads are tied together. To form sheds, they are alternately raised and lowered. Those that pass through the holes remain stationary and those in the slits move above or below them. A weft is passed through each shed and beaten into place with the fingers, or with a knife-like beater of the type shown with nos. 62 and 63. Unlike the simple rigid heddle from Quebec, those from Nova Scotia and Ontario are set in a box frame, and are usually called bandlooms. Except that they have simple warp beams to hold a considerable length, they operate in the same way.

In threading the loom, guides of some kind are needed, and these, as a rule, are also followed in treadling. They are known as weaving or pattern drafts. A selection of various types is shown (nos. 64–74). If a weaver planned to weave simple tabby or twill, no draft would be needed as the repeat of each threading and treadling unit is so short. If a patterned piece of cloth was to be set up on the loom, one of these scraps of paper with cryptic numbers became essential. They are found on strips from old account books and ledgers, on the backs of letters, on envelopes, and even on bits of wallpaper. Their mortality has been high, but all that can be found add more to the picture of handweaving in Canada.

The characteristic forms for patterns requiring four to six shafts are shown in nos. 64–71. Horizontal lines were usually drawn across the paper representing the shafts, and these were often divided by vertical lines to indicate the individual units or blocks that made up the pattern. Each block consists of a set number of threads, either even or uneven in number. The numeral '1' is placed on the shaft where threading is to begin and a higher numeral is placed on the shaft where the threading of that unit stops. If these two are 1 and 8, it specifies that the unit consists of eight threads entered alternately on the two shafts where the numerals occur. Where confusion might arise, the ends to be entered are numbered individually on the shafts (no. 69).

In the more complex draft for 'summer and winter' weave, a variant of this notation indicates that one end is threaded on the first shaft, one on the pattern shaft, one on the second shaft, one on the pattern shaft for four threads. This unit is repeated if the block is of greater size (no. 71). In a still more complex weave such as 'star and diamond,' the threading and treadling plans are constant, and only a tie-up is needed that shows the number of shafts used and how the treadles are to be tied (no. 72). Doublecloth and twill diaper patterns were often drawn out for the customer to see (no. 73). The threading plans for the loom might be written on the same page, but were often recorded in a separate book that could be kept private (no. 74).

Many of the old drafts for the simpler weaves are riddled with pinholes. A strip of cloth was fastened between the cords that ran over the pulleys and the draft attached to this strip. As each unit of the pattern was threaded, a pin with a coloured head was pushed in. When the next unit was complete, the pin was moved along. The same practice was followed in treadling, and the pin moved along as each block was woven. In this way, the weaver could leave the loom at any time and return knowing at exactly what point he had stopped.

Almost all names of patterns that are given in this book have been found on the relatively small number of drafts that have been collected or recorded in Canada. 'Keep Me Warm One Night,' a draft from Cape Breton has supplied the title (no. 64).

1 / Ontario. Sydenham district, Frontenac County. 1825-50
ROM 968.269.1. Gift of Mrs Edgar J. Stone
Wool basket. L. 50cm; diam. 32cm

Made of willow withes in the shape of a rugby ball, this type of basket is well known in Scotland, and another smaller example has been seen in Cape Breton (Mackley Collection). Although sheep were sheared in Canada, a certain amount of wool was caught on the bushes of the rough pastures, which was of value particularly when the flocks were small. With a basket like this under one arm, one would wander aimlessly through the fields 'wool gathering,' picking up the small flocks of wool. This is the source of the expression that has survived to the present day. Baskets of this type were also used when teasing wool.

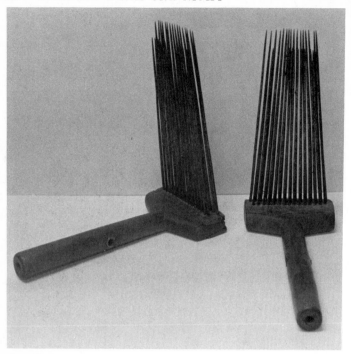

2 / New Brunswick. Beginning of the 19th century
NBM 22.844. Gift of Mr C.R. Peters
Wool combs (pair). L. 34cm; l. teeth 29cm

These wool combs are the typical form used in England in the eighteenth century and earlier. The rows of tapered steel teeth are inserted in a strip of horn inserted in a hardwood base from which a strong handle projects. In this pair, the wood appears to be maple, supporting a local provenance. Combs may be used in the hands, but the more usual practice is to set the handle of a comb in a support attached to a beam or post where it can be locked into position by placing a peg through a small hole in the centre of the handle. The teased fibres are placed on the stationary comb and gradually transferred to the other. By repeating the operation, all short fibres are removed and the others laid parallel to one another. The result is a smooth even length known as a roving that is ready for spinning. The combs were kept warm in a pot of oil over a small flame. The warmth and the presence of the oil helps the operation. (Photograph: Burnham)

3 / Saskatchewan. Used in Kamsack. About 1900
ROM 967.130.3. Gift of Mrs Marta Remekoff
Wool cards (pair). W. 23cm

4 / Ontario. Early 19th century
ROM 967.124. Gift of Mr andMrs Harold B. Burnham
Wool cards (pair). W. 26cm
5 / Quebec. 19th century
ROM 966.157.29. Gift of Mrs Edgar J. Stone
Wool cards (pair). W. 21cm

The first pair (3) is typical of the great mass of commercially produced cards that were widely used after the middle of the nineteenth century. Stamped on it is 'The Only Genuine Old Whitemore Patent Improved No. 8 Wool J.S. Watman & Co. Leicester,' showing they were made in England. The two older pair are basically handmade, and represent the type that would have been available at an earlier period. Every card consists of a rectangle of wood with a projecting handle attached to the back. On the face of each is a layer of leather in which close-set, fine steel wires are inserted. Each of these is bent so that the point is angled towards the handle. In carding, a handful of fibre is placed on one of the cards which is steadied on the knee; the other card is drawn across it so that the fibres are spread out in a smooth layer. Then, by reversing the direction of the upper card, the fibre is removed in the form of a loose roll known as a sliver that is ready for spinning.

6 / Nova Scotia. Lunenburg County. Early 19th century
ROM 966.157.46. Gift of Mrs. Edgar J. Stone
Flax break. H. 77cm; l. central blade 110cm

Breaking is the first process in freeing the retted flax straw of the woody waste known as shive. This process may be performed by beating the shive with a mallet, but the more usual method is to use a break, two layers of hardwood blades hinged together at one end. The lower one is stationary on a stand and the upper movable. The blades are set so that the upper ones fit into the spaces of the lower one. A handful of flax straw is placed on the lower layer, and the upper one brought sharply down, cracking the bark and woody core but only loosening the resilient fibres of the bast bundles. Much of the shive falls away and the broken bits still adhering are removed in swingling, the next process to which the straw is subjected.

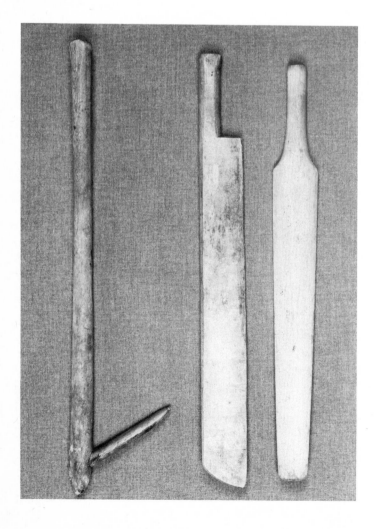

7 / Ontario. Meaford, Grey County. 19th century
ROM 955.121. Gift of Mr F.S. Knight
Retting hook. L. 62cm

This hardwood hook was used in moving the sodden bundles of flax straw while in the retting pond, and to remove them when this process was complete.

8 / Nova Scotia. Pictou County. 19th century
ROM 966.157.17. Gift of Mrs Edgar J. Stone
Scutching knife for swingling flax. L. 60cm
9 / Nova Scotia. Lunenburg County. 19th century
ROM 966.157.16. Gift of Mrs Edgar J. Stone
Scutching blade for swingling flax. L. 57cm

In swingling or scutching, the handfuls of flax straw received from the break are placed over the edge of an upright board, held by the left hand, and tapped and stroked with the right using hardwood tools of these types. The knife form is the usual type and is also known from Quebec and Ontario. The tapping loosened the bits of shive still adhering, which with the shorter fibres were removed by the stroking. The short fibres removed in swingling were the top grade of tow. Hand-operated swingling mills were also employed in which the action of blades mounted on a wheel cleaned the fibres which rested against wooden uprights. One of these is in the gallery of the church at Clementsport in Nova Scotia and another is at Black Creek Pioneer Village in Toronto.

10 / Quebec. Cté L'Islet. 19th century
ROM 966.157.30. Gift of Mrs Edgar J. Stone
Double hackle and cover. L. 68cm; w. 23cm

11 / Nova Scotia. Annapolis Valley. Early 19th century
ROM 966.157.31. Gift of Mrs Edgar J. Stone
Hackle with cover, initialled 'E.W.' L. 56cm; w. 19cm
12 / Ontario. 19th century, 1st half
ROM 955.26. Gift of Mrs Edgar J. Stone
Double hackle with covers. L. 57cm; w. 9.5cm

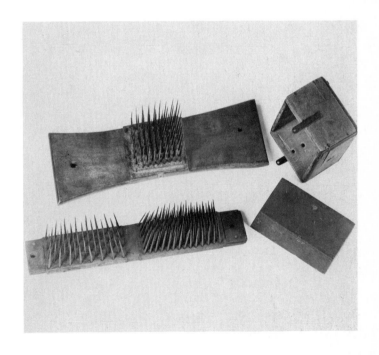

Hackling clears the flax of whatever shive remains after
swingling and separates the fibres in the bast bundles to give
the fine fibre characteristic of linen. It is usually processed
on a coarse hackle first and then on a finer one. For the finest
quality linen, a third hackle with smaller, more closely set
teeth is used. Handfuls of swingled straw are grasped at one
end and drawn repeatedly through the teeth of the hackle
until it is thoroughly clean and the bast bundles have been
separated into individual fibres. As well as being the final
cleaning, hackling removes the remaining short fibres, which
form the second grade of tow.

The hackle from Quebec has tapered hand-forged teeth
inserted through the oak base and protected by a pine cover.
In the examples from Nova Scotia and Ontario the teeth
are also in a hardwood base. There are holes at the ends of
these so that they could be pegged down to a firm stand.

13 / Quebec. Eastern Townships. 1830-50
ROM 966.211.1. Gift of Miss Emily Le Baron
Great wheel. Diameter of driving wheel 122cm

This is a typical example of the great wheels used throughout eastern Canada. It shows the earlier type of head with the spindle driven directly by the large wheel. The name 'Sabra Anthony' carved in beautiful flowing script on the platform is that of the owner. A wide variety of tensioning devices is found on these wheels, and this is one of the more complex. Catharine Parr Traill in *The Backwoods of Canada* (100) describes one of these large pieces of equipment: 'A large spinning-wheel, as big as a cart-wheel, occupied the centre of the room.'

14 / Nova Scotia. Tracadie, Antigonish County. 19th century
ROM 970.202.29. Gift of Mrs. Edgar J. Stone
Spinning wheel. Diameter of driving wheel 66cm

This shows a more highly finished example of the simple Acadian wheel with direct drive than is usually found. There is no device to control tension, which could only be adjusted by tightening or loosening the driving belt. The length of hollow reed on which the spun yarn was wound is still on the spindle. This could be removed with the yarn on it for storage, or used as a spool when warping. These reeds always seem to be too long to fit directly into a shuttle.

15 / Nova Scotia. Chezzetcook. 19th century
ROM 966.157.33. Gift of Mrs Edgar J. Stone
Spinning wheel. Diameter of driving wheel 64cm

A simple Acadian wheel equipped with a 'Picardie' type flyer. It has been somewhat altered, but shows the traditional form. An earlier type in which the driving wheel is turned by hand is in the Mackley Collection in Sydney.

16 / Nova Scotia. Pictou County. Dated 1819
ROM 966.157.34. Gift of Mrs Edgar J. Stone
Spinning wheel. Diameter of driving wheel 50cm

This is an excellent example of the standard type of treadle wheel with flyer that was used for both wool and flax spinning in the Maritime Provinces and Ontario. It is of a Scottish type and is marked 'ALEXR MCINTOSH 1819' at one end. Alexander McIntosh lived in Pictou County, and signed and dated all the wheels he made. The earliest date reported is 1809. A later group are signed 'McIntosh,' by which time his son was probably working with him. After the father died, the son continued making wheels of the same type with his own name, 'I.S. MCINTOSH,' into the 1870s.

17 / Nova Scotia. Lunenburg County. Mid-19th century
ROM 969.278. Gift of Mrs Edgar J. Stone
Spinning wheel. Diameter of driving wheel 50cm

A famous family of chair and spinning-wheel makers were the Youngs (Jung) of Lunenburg County. Their wheels are very distinctive in style, and usually have the name branded on the side of the platform. The turning is highlighted by bands of colour, red and black as here, but others were sometimes used. Wool was spun on these wheels holding the prepared fibres in the hands, but for flax a distaff was needed. This is the upright to the left of the wheel. Many distaffs throughout Canada were made by taking the upper tip of a spruce or fir tree, stripping it clean, and tying the tips of the branches together to form a cage over which the prepared flax could be loosely tied. The spinner simply drew from this supply while the spinning was in progress.

Flax is a much more inflexible fibre than wool and is frequently spun into finer yarns. With the fibres held on the distaff, both hands were free to manipulate them as it was fed into the spindle.

The detail at the bottom of the page shows the Young name clearly in bold letters. It also shows the working parts comprising the flyer head. The pulley cord is always double on this type of wheel. Both parts go around the driving wheel; one of these goes around the pulley at the back of the metal spindle held in position between the two upright posts, and the other around one end of the bobbin resting on the spindle. The spindle is a straight shaft of wrought iron which widens into a tube in front. This tube may be seen jutting through the leather support on the front upright. Just behind the support is a small hole through which the spun yarn passes to emerge through the front of the tube. The horseshoe-shaped flyer is attached rigidly on the spindle and is the part of the mechanism that imparts the twist to the yarn. Between the front end of the flyer and the back pulley, a wooden bobbin is held loosely on the spindle, and lies between the arms of the flyer. As mentioned, it is driven by half of the pulley cord.

The spun yarn can be wound up on the bobbin at the same time as the flyer is revolving and imparting a twist to the yarn. This twist runs down and out through the tube in the front end of the spindle into the loose fibres that the spinner is holding in the left hand. As it runs into these, the spinner draws the fibres out with the right hand. She can exert gentle pressure on the fibres, not allowing them to roll onto the bobbin until she feels that sufficient twist and draw have been given to produce the weight and type of yarn she wants. The metal hooks on the arms of the flyer are used to place the yarn evenly on the bobbin.

The whole flyer head is mounted so that it may be moved to decrease or increase tension on the driving belt. The handle jutting to the left of the stand turns a wooden screw on which the head is mounted. By turning it, the tension is adjusted so that the relative speeds of bobbin wind and spin are controlled.

(*in colour* PLATE I)

18 / Quebec. Late 18th – early 19th centuries
ROM 970.258.1. Gift of Mrs Edgar J. Stone
Spinning wheel. Diameter of driving wheel 50cm

This is an early type of spinning wheel from French Canada, one of the few that have survived intact. A contemporary one is in Centre de Marie de l'Incarnation in the Ursuline Convent in Quebec (Palardy, 348). Most of those now seen have been converted into spool or bobbin winders. The shape of the stand is characteristic of this early type, as are the remains of bright yellow paint. Wheels in Quebec were made to be gaily painted red, yellow, blue, or green to provide a bright spot of colour in the home. It is a tragedy that those coming on the market are promptly scalped of all original colour by the dealers through whose hands they pass.

The flyer head is of the 'Picardie' type, with no mechanical means of altering the driving belt tension. The wooden pan supported on a post fitting one of the platform holes is for water. Flax is spun wet; the spinner needs a handy supply of water in which her fingers may be constantly moistened. Here the dish occurs hewn from a block of wood. It is not as old as the wheel; the original probably split and was replaced. More sophisticated wheels often have a small rectangular platform opening for a water dish.

Another platform hole was for a distaff also used when flax was being spun. Like that described in 17, this distaff would have been made from the top of a spruce or fir. If wool were being spun, both the water dish and distaff could be removed.

19 / Ontario. Early 19th century
ROM 948.26. Gift of Mr Lawrence de la Franier
Spinning wheel. Diameter of driving wheel 77cm

This is a fairly large wheel with 'Picardie' type flyer, a single untensioned driving cord, and a tensioning cord for the bobbin at the front. It comes from the area of eighteenth-century French settlement in Southwestern Ontario along the Detroit River and is of a type known in Quebec. It was painted a soft red, much of which remains. The uprights supporting the wheel have been turned in one piece and then split down the centre to make the two posts.

20 / Quebec. Village-des-Aulnaies, Cté L'Islet. 1840-60
ROM 967.207.1. Gift of Mrs Gerard Brett
Spinning wheel. Diameter of driving wheel 57cm

The older wheels in Quebec had the 'Picardie' type flyer, but
were supplanted by ones with the more usual type of head.
This is an excellent example from this transitional period
marked 'F.O.,' for François Ouellet, a member of a well-
known family of wheel makers at Village-des-Aulnaies. It was
originally painted yellow with red wheel trimmed with dark
blue finials, but unfortunately has been stripped. Tension
may be adjusted by moving an arm that controls the position
of the flyer head. If this is raised, tension is increased as the
head moves slightly away from the driving wheel.

The treadle is attached to the axle of the driving wheel by
the pimstock, usually a thin slat of wood with a hole at the
top that fits onto the hook at the back of the axle. This may
be seen more clearly in no. 14. At the lower end of the pimstock are holes. A stout cord passed through these is tied to
the end of the treadle, loosely enough to allow a certain
amount of play.

21 / Quebec. Kamouraska County. 1875-1900
ROM 967.207.2. Gift of Mrs Gerard Brett
Spinning wheel. Diameter of driving wheel 74cm

This is the usual type of wheel considered characteristic of
Quebec. The large driving wheel is typical of those made in
the province from about 1875 well into the present century.
It has been painted a gay yellow and has the usual Quebec
tensioning device described in no. 20. It is stamped 'PARADIS'
for Aram Paradis, a prolific wheel maker in Kamouraska
County.

22 / Nova Scotia. Perhaps Pictou County. 1860-80
ROM 966.157.43. Gift of Mrs. Edgar J. Stone
Hurdy wheel for plying. Diameter of driving wheel 45cm

Wheels of this type were produced that could be clamped to the edge of a table and were excellent for plying the heavier yarns for knitting. They were often equipped with a skein holder for the yarn. In this one, the wheel is painted red with black semi-circles where the sections of the rim are joined. The spindle-head was bought readymade. It is shown with open driving belt as found, but the wheel would have been turned counterclockwise by the left hand to give an s-twist. The yarn would be controlled by the right.

23 / Saskatchewan. Kamsack. About 1904
ROM 967.130.1. Gift of Mrs Marta Remekoff
Spinning wheel. Diameter of driving wheel 53cm

Wheels with the standard type of flyer mounted above the driving wheel are usually called 'castle' wheels and occur rarely in Canada. This is typical of those used in Byelorussia from where the settlers at Kamsack came. It is painted red, blue, and black with a white flyer. Similar examples from Byelorussia are in Musey Etnografii Narodov SSSR, Leningrad, where undecorated wheels of the same type from the Ukraine are also shown.

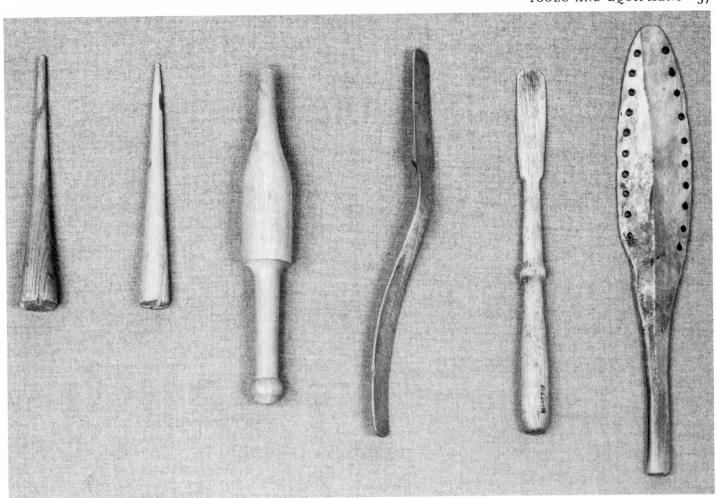

24–9 left to right

24 / Prince Edward Island. 19th century
ROM 966.151.32. Gift of Mrs Edgar J. Stone
Farsadh (yarn twister for plying). L. 22cm
25 / Nova Scotia. Cape Breton. 19th century
ROM 970.202.23. Gift of Mrs Edgar J. Stone
Farsadh (yarn twister for plying). L. 21cm

These small devices were used for plying yarn, and are also known from Scotland. They were probably twirled like a dropped spindle, but to date no one has been encountered who actually used one. The conical form is characteristic, with cross grooves in the base to position the yarn, and often a small bump at the top to help hold the half hitch by which the yarn was attached.

26 / Quebec. Eastern Townships. 19th century
ROM 966.211.13. Gift of Miss Emily Le Baron
Wheelboy (or spinning finger). L. 28cm
27 / Ontario. Napanee area, Lennox and Addington
Counties. 1825-50
ROM 970.257.25. Gift of Mrs Archie Lamont
Wheelboy (or spinning finger). L. 34cm
28 / Prince Edward Island. 19th century
ROM 966.157.15. Gift of Mrs Edgar J. Stone
Wheelboy (or spinning finger). L. 32cm

The great wheel was often turned by hand, but small devices such as these were sometimes used to give the spinner a longer reach and presumably to save her from getting her knuckles rapped. They usually had a cord at the end which went round the wrist: the tool could be dropped from the hand without losing it. The one from Quebec is a sturdy example of maple. That from the Napanee area was part of the equipment of Peter Fretz, a weaver, whose bobbin winder is shown as no. 40. As the winder has no handle, the beautifully worked and shaped maple wheelboy may have been used with it. The Prince Edward Island example is of oak, and at first glance resembles a spirtle for making porridge.

29 / Quebec. Eastern Townships. 19th century
ROM 966.157.18. Gift of Mrs Edgar J. Stone
Warping paddle. L. 39cm

When stretching a warp with a number of ends simultaneously, a paddle is often used to keep them in correct order and to facilitate the manipulation of them. This one could handle up to twenty threads, one through each of the holes in it.

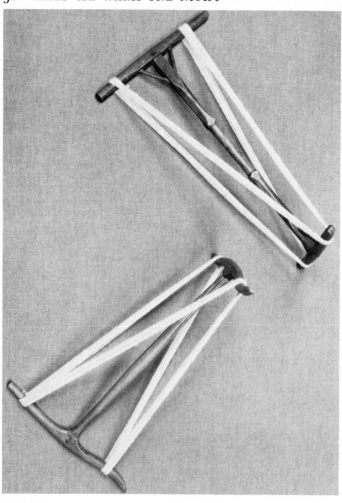

30 / Nova Scotia. Cape Breton. Mid-19th century
ROM 966.157.45. Gift of Mrs. Edgar J. Stone
Niddy-noddy (or hand reel) for skeining yarn. L. 50cm

When wool has been spun, it is usually taken from the bobbin and skeined. One of the oldest and simplest devices for skeining is this strangely shaped tool: a straight shank with one cross bar at one end and another at the other at right angles to the first. If one sees such a tool used, the derivation of the name becomes obvious: as the yarn is guided over the ends of the arms, it first nods one way and then the other. They are often beautifully made, and were widely used throughout the Maritime Provinces.

31 / Nova Scotia. Yarmouth-Digby Counties. 19th century
ROM 966.157.26. Gift of Mrs Edgar J. Stone
Niddy-noddy (or hand reel) for skeining wool. L. 46cm

This beautifully made example comes from the French Shore, an Acadian area of Nova Scotia. Three ends of the cross bars are curved to hold the skein in place, but one is straight so that the finished skein may be slipped off. Niddy-noddies vary slightly in size, but all make a skein approximately 79″ in circumference (about 198cm). The aim was probably 80″, and forty-five rounds would mean a hundred yards of yarn.

32 / Ontario. Kitchener, Waterloo County. Dated 1868
ROM 967.129.6. Gift of Mrs Edgar J. Stone
Clock reel. H. of stand 88cm; circumference of head 229cm (90″)

The clock reel may not be as picturesque as the niddy-noddy for skeining wool, but it is considerably more efficient. This was a commercial production, as is shown by the name 'HAILER BURCKLE 1868 BERLIN C.W. WARRANTED' printed on the base. ('C.W.' stands for Canada West; the name of Berlin was changed to Kitchener during the Great War of 1914–18. Even in 1868 it was becoming a considerable manufacturing centre.) The turning of the reel activates worm-gears that move a cog. After forty revolutions of the reel, a peg on the cog presses against the piece of lighter wood seen against the central post, causing it to click. This click indicates that forty rounds of 90″ have been wound: in other words, a skein of one hundred yards. Other reels have different circumferences and numbers of revolutions to indicate the length that has been wound. One reel from Ontario has a small clock counter on the face with a hand that could be moved along with each click to keep count (ROM 970.257.26).

33 / Nova Scotia. Lunenburg County. Early 19th century
ROM 966.157.39. Gift of Mrs Edgar J. Stone
Reel. H. of stand 39cm; circumference of head
147cm (58″)

This horizontal form of reel was widely used in Nova Scotia,
and was the usual type in Quebec in various simpler forms.
The incised carving of pairs of hearts is very much in the
German tradition of the original Hanoverian settlers of this
county in Nova Scotia.

34 / Nova Scotia. Annapolis Valley. 1800-50
ROM 970.248. Gift of Mrs Edgar J. Stone
Clock reel. H. of stand 92cm; circumference of head
236cm (93″)

The worm-gear and two cogs may be seen in the illustration,
as well as the wooden tongue that makes the click. Just above
the small handle on one of the arms that was used for turning the reel, a nodule may be seen that differs from those on
the other arms. This is a sliding support that can be pushed
up; the arm is hinged beneath it making it easy to remove
the skein after it is wound. Some clock reels have a rounded
end on one of the arms so that the skein will slip off.

35 / Nova Scotia. Digby County. 19th century
ROM 970.202.24. Gift of Mrs Edgar J. Stone
Swift. H. 96cm

Swifts are used for unwinding skeins of yarn, the opposite of
reels, which are for making them. A pair of hands to hold
the skein may be useful if only a small amount is to be converted into balls, but on a larger scale a tool becomes necessary especially if spools or bobbins are to be filled. The simple
swift shown here has been painted indian red and set in a
sturdy block of wood. The axle is hickory cut to hold the
lower cross bars in position.

36 / New Brunswick. Probably Carleton County. 19th
century
ROM 966.157.28. Gift of Mrs Edgar J. Stone
Umbrella swift. H. 75cm
37 / Nova Scotia. Lunenburg County. 19th century
ROM 969.243.7. Gift of Mrs Murray Oickle
Skein of handspun linen yarn. Circumference ca. 160cm
(64″)

The name of this type of swift comes from the fact that the
lower hub on the axle may be raised or lowered to adjust the
size of the cage on which the skein is held: it goes up and
down like an umbrella. If the hub is raised, the circumference
increases as the ribs are forced out, and it may be lowered
to lessen this circumference, or to collapse the cage completely for easier storage. Many of these tools have a cup at
the top in which an uncompleted ball of yarn may rest. This
example is set in a block, but most umbrella swifts have a
clamp arrangement so that they may be fastened to the edge
of a table. The skein shown as no. 37 is of handspun natural
linen.

38 / Ontario. 19th century
ROM 971.393.1. Gift of Mr and Mrs John E. Langdon
Barrel swift. H. of stand 125cm

This type of swift has gained its name from the revolving cages shaped like small barrels that hold the skeins. The lower one is stationary, but the upper one is adjustable. The cages are wide enough to hold two skeins side by side, which arrangement may have been used when plying. A few examples have two sets of cages, one on either side of the upright.

39 / Nova Scotia. Annapolis Valley. 1825-50
ROM 970.202.25. Gift of Mrs Edgar J. Stone
Bobbin winder. H. of stand 42cm; diameter of driving wheel
52cm

Winding, unwinding, and winding again are processes always
present with spinning and weaving. Yarns were stored as
skeins, but for weaving had to be wound on spools for making the warp, or on bobbins to fit in the shuttle. Either spools
or bobbins may be filled with a tool of this type by placing
them on the spindle, turning the driving wheel, and drawing
the yarn from a skein mounted on a swift. The spindle was
held in a hole at the back and in a slot in front for easy removal. Bobbins, usually a short length of elderberry branch
with the pith knocked out, could be dropped in the box
holding the spindle. The turned ridges on the uprights and
the legs have been painted red.

40 / Ontario. Napanee area, Lennox and Addington
Counties. About 1825
ROM 970.257.18. Gift of Mrs Archie Lamont
Bobbin winder. H. of stand 37cm; diameter of driving wheel
72cm

This bobbin winder belonged to Peter Fretz, a weaver who
also owned the set of shuttles (no. 55) and the wheelboy or
spinning finger (no. 27). As this bobbin winder has neither
treadle nor handle, the wheelboy may well have been used to
turn the driving wheel. The spindle is held in holes in strips of
leather attached to the sides of the supporting box. Although
Peter Fretz is known to have woven (no. 321), it was probably on a semi-professional basis as a sideline to farming
during the off season. This was done by many men in the
province.

41 / Quebec. South of Montreal. Mid-19th century
ROM 966.88.1. Gift of Mr and Mrs. Harold B. Burnham
Cage spool for warping. H. 61 cm; diameter 40cm

This is the only old cage spool that has been found in Canada. It would be mounted sideways on a special winder and could be filled quite rapidly with yarn destined for warp. When a group of these was ready, they would be set up side by side and the yarn would run off smoothly over the curved points. Each thread would pass through an eye or ring in a beam or bracket above, and then to the warper, either to be handled manually, or more probably with the aid of a paddle (no. 29). Cage spools have been widely used, and are known from representations of silk processing on stone bas reliefs of the Latter Han Dynasty (AD 25–221) in China.

42 / Ontario. Nile, Huron County. About 1845
ROM 947.62.1, .7, .21. Gift of Mr and Mrs Harold B. Burnham
Loom, warping frame, and spool rack

Samuel Pentland came to Ontario from Northern Ireland. He settled first at Amherst Island in 1825, and moved to the Huron Tract about 1845 while this area was being opened up by the Canada Company. He settled on a farm at Nile, north of Goderich, and wove professionally for his neighbours. The loom is the four-shaft type typical of the many used both domestically and professionally. It was suitable for weaving woollens and linens for clothing and household use, and for overshot coverlets. The heavy frame seems to be salvaged ships' timbers that were washed ashore on Lake Huron. The reeds used with the loom, and the shuttles, would have been the only equipment brought by Samuel Pentland when he emigrated and when he moved from Amherst Island.

The shafts are tied directly to the four treadles and are suspended over pulleys by cords tied to horizontal bars, called horses, that connect the shafts in pairs. This is a counterbalanced shedding mechanism. When a shaft is depressed, the others automatically rise, but it is only when two are depressed that the others rise an equal distance giving a clean shed. This was the usual type used in Canada. A few more advanced looms equipped with a countermarch system in which each shaft could be raised or lowered independently were used by full-time professional weavers.

Samuel Pentland's loom was originally equipped with a flying shuttle. The extensions at both ends of the shuttle race of the batten may be clearly seen. These held the boxes which were removed when the loom was converted to a two-shaft one for rag-carpet weaving.

On the warping frame at the left, a warp of over a hundred yards could be stretched drawing the threads from the spools on the rack.

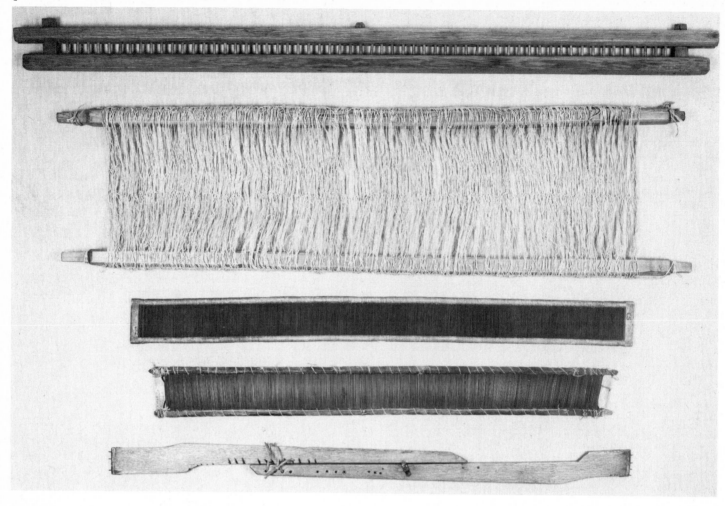

43 / Ontario. Huron County. About 1845
ROM 947.62.13. Gift of Mr and Mrs Harold B. Burnham
Raddle. L. 152cm; h. 11cm

This raddle of typical form was used by Samuel Pentland, whose loom has just been discussed (no. 42). It is made of oak with a removable cap held by pegs, and each space is half an inch wide.

44 / Ontario. Seaforth, Huron County. Mid-19th century
ROM 948.250.1. Gift of Mr Lawrence de la Franier
Shaft with knitted heddles. L. shaft 140cm, heddles 38cm, eyes 3cm

This is one of a pair of shafts with heddles of handspun linen cord. The joining ties may be seen along the upper shaft.

45 / Ontario. Pelham Township, Welland County. Mid-19th century
ROM 969.94. Gift of Mrs Jozina Goldring
Reed. L. 110cm; h. 9cm; approximately 7 dents per cm

46 / Quebec. Eastern Townships. Mid-19th century
ROM 966.211.19. Gift of Miss Emily Le Baron
Reed. L. 103cm; h. 10cm; approximately 7 dents per cm

These two reeds with bamboo teeth are typical of those used throughout eastern Canada before metal ones were available. The one from Quebec has been strengthened by a wrapping of dressed leather, and the cord holding this shows clearly. Both are finer than were generally used and would have been suitable for linen, which explains their survival. The coarser ones were subjected to much more use.

47 / Ontario. Huron County. Mid-19th century
ROM 947.62.25. Gift of Mr and Mrs Harold B. Burnham
Temple. L. arms, 84 and 79cm

This tool made of oak was used to keep the width constant while weaving. The points at the ends of the arms were inserted in the selvages of the cloth at the fell to stretch it so that it was equal to the width of the warp in the reed.

48 / Ontario. Huron County. Late 19th century
ROM 947.62.11. Gift of Mr and Mrs Harold B. Burnham
Carpet shuttle. L. 56cm
49 / Ontario. Haldimand County. Late 19th century
ROM 964.32.1. Gift of Mr and Mrs Harold B. Burnham
Carpet shuttle. L. 45cm

These shuttles were used for weaving rag carpeting. The first
came with Samuel Pentland's weaving equipment (no. 42),
and the other, more carefully made, was found with a carpet
weaver's loom of the late nineteenth century.

50 / Quebec. Eastern Townships. 19th century
ROM 967.45. Gift of Miss June Biggar
Hand shuttle. L. 31cm
51 / Quebec. Eastern Townships. 19th century
ROM 966.157.1. Gift of Mrs Edgar J. Stone
Hand shuttle. L. 24cm
52 / Quebec. Cté L'Islet. 19th century
ROM 966.157.6. Gift of Mrs Edgar J. Stone
Hand shuttle. L. 30cm
53 / Prince Edward Island. 19th century
ROM 966.157.5. Gift of Mrs Edgar J. Stone
Hand shuttle. L. 31cm

These show hand shuttles of the standard boat type. In all,
the bobbin would have been held on a short length of cane
as in no. 51. The initials on no. 50 are those of the owner.
The eyes through which the weft passed are in the side,
strengthened in no. 51 by an inset of bone, and by one of
ebony in no. 53.

54 / Ontario. Huron County. Mid-19th century
ROM 947.62.2, .6. Gift of Mr and Mrs Harold B. Burnham
Pair of fly shuttles. L's. 38cm

These show the fly shuttles available to the handweavers of
Ontario, and were used by Samuel Pentland on the loom
shown in no. 42. The bobbins are tapered and set on a metal
pin that can be raised or lowered. The yarn is drawn off the
end, through a wire loop, and out of an eye in the side.

55 / Ontario. Napanee area, Lennox and Addington
Counties. 1825-50
ROM 970.257.19–24. Gift of Mrs Archie Lamont
Set of hand shuttles. L's. 27–34cm

This set was used by Peter Fretz, and his initials are incised
on two of them. He probably wove the overshot coverlet
no. 321. Other examples of his work are in the Museum's
collections (970.257.1–.3, .7, .8, .11, .12).

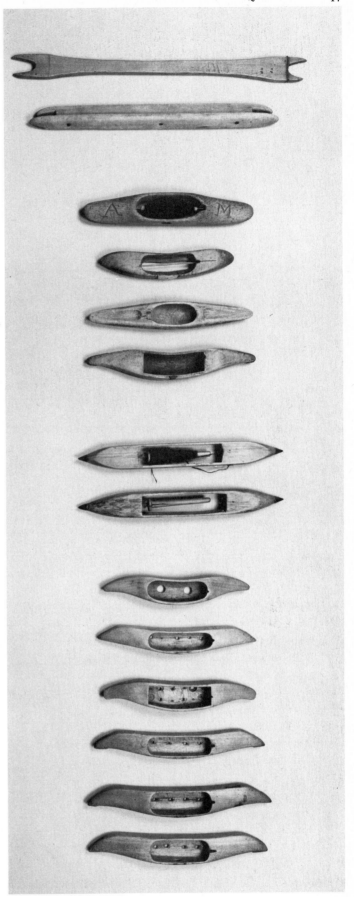

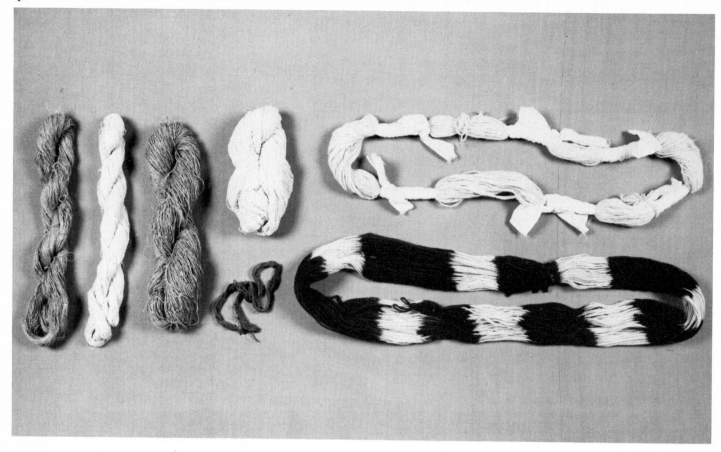

56 / Ontario. Elgin County. Mid-19th century
ROM 951.173.10, .9. Gift of the Misses F. and E. Pearce
Skeins of handspun linen: natural, z singles, and bleached,
z, 2s. Circumference 179cm (70")
57 / Nova Scotia. Bridgewater, Lunenburg County. Late
19th century
ROM 968.4.4. Gift of Mrs Murray Oickle
Skein of handspun linen, natural, z, 2s. Circumference
179cm (70")

These are typical of the linen yarn produced domestically.
The bleached one might have been used as sewing thread.

58 / Collected in Prince Edward Island. 19th century
ROM 970.202.22. Gift of Mr and Mrs Harold B. Burnham
Skein of natural white mill-spun cotton, z singles. Circ.
137cm (54")

59 / Ontario. Mid-19th century
ROM L965.11.60. The Annie R. Fry Collection
Skein of cotton, z singles, dyed red. Circ. 122cm (48")

The natural skein of about 10's count is typical of the thousands that were imported from the United States, and used
in this form, or after being plied by hand. The small skein
was probably for embroidery, but large skeins of this colour,
and of blue, were also used for weaving.

60 / Nova Scotia. Cape Breton. 1968
ROM 969.31.1, .2. Gift of Mrs F.M. Mackley
Skeins of resist-dyed or ikat yarn, woollen. Circ. 158cm
(62")

These show two stages in preparing yarn for the splashed
patterns found in warp-faced carpeting (nos. 110–13). The
upper has been tied ready for dying; the lower after this
with the ties removed from the reserved areas.

61 / Quebec. 19th century
ROM 970.87.34. Gift of Mr and Mrs John E. Langdon
Rigid heddle. H. 69cm; w. 21cm

This paddle-shaped tool is for weaving narrow bands and
tapes for all sorts of domestic purposes. It would be suspended over a peg or hook. The warp threads passed alternately through the twenty-five slits and corresponding holes.
By raising and lowering the threads, sheds were formed.
The threads through the holes remained stationary; those in
the slits moved above and below them; the weft was passed
through and beaten into place.

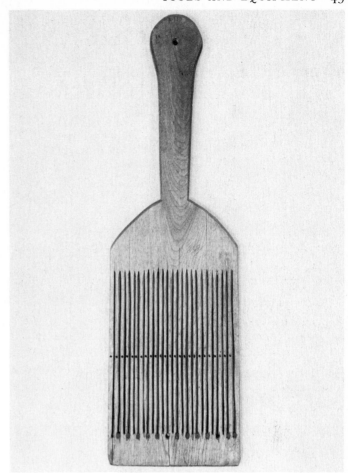

62 / Ontario. Niagara Peninsula. Mid-19th century
ROM 947.74.1. Gift of Mr J.S. Beatty
Bandloom with rigid heddle. H. 64cm; w. 30cm; l. 70cm

When the rigid heddle is mounted in a frame, the device becomes a bandloom. Both this and no. 63 have simple warp beams at the back on which a considerable length may be wound and let off as required. The weft was beaten into place either with the fingers or with a knife beater like the ones shown here and in no. 63. The tapes and narrow bands woven with these tools were used for garters, men's suspenders, laces and ties for clothing, suspension loops for towels, and a host of other purposes.

63 / Nova Scotia. Lunenburg County. 19th century
ROM 966.157.20. Gift of Mrs Edgar J. Stone
Band loom with rigid heddle. H. 32cm; w. 19cm; l. 50cm

This bandloom has a smaller capacity than no. 62, but was
used in the same manner. This particular one was specifically
used for weaving wicks for oil lamps. A small knife beater is

shown beside it. A similar bandloom is in the Desbrisay
Museum at Bridgewater, Nova Scotia.

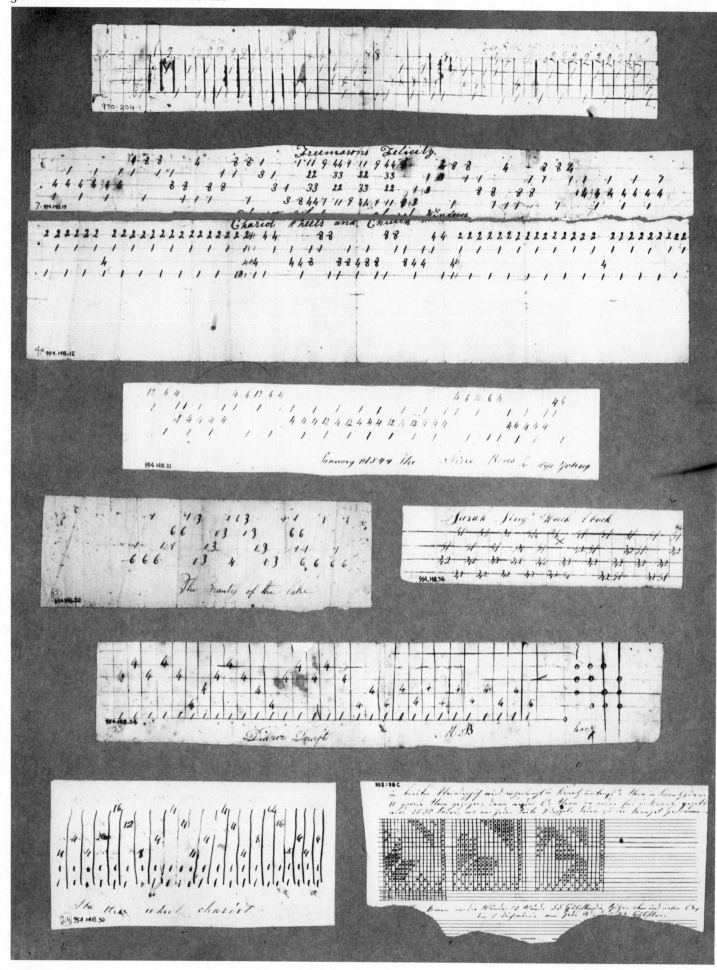

64 / Nova Scotia. Cape Breton. 19th century
ROM 970.204.1. Gift of Mrs. F.M. Mackley
Four-shaft overshot pattern draft: 'Keep Me Warm One
Night'

This draft from Cape Breton is the source of the title of this

book and is one of the loveliest pattern names that has been
found in Canada. The design is similar to another with a
wide distribution and a constant name: 'Chariot Wheels
and Church Windows' (nos. 66, 347). This draft has a larger
nine-part table.

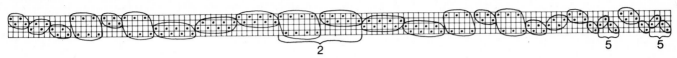

65–8 / Ontario. Prince Edward County. Mid-19th century
ROM 954.148.15, .12, .21, .20. Gift of Miss Annie
Abercrombie
Four-shaft overshot pattern drafts

These are representative of the overshot drafts in the Abercrombie Collection, which has proved a mine of information on pattern names and on the old methods of drafting for various techniques. The drafts were used by Hester and Rosanna Young, two sisters who lived in Prince Edward County and who were weaving as early as the 1840s. They are typical of those used throughout eastern Canada, and show transverse lines to indicate the shafts and numbers to indicate the placing of the threads. Coverlets in these patterns are illustrated: 'Freemason's Felicity' (no. 324), 'Chariot Wheels and Church Windows' (no. 347), 'Nine Roses' (no. 280), and 'Beauty of the Lake' (no. 240).

69 / Ontario. Prince Edward County. Mid-19th century
ROM 954.148.36. Gift of Miss Annie Abercrombie
M's & O's pattern draft: 'Sarah Sing Huck A Buck'

This is called a huckaback, but is actually a simple M's & O's pattern. Sarah Sing was a friend or relation of Hester and Rosanna Young.

70 / Ontario. Prince Edward County. Mid-19th century
ROM 954.148.34. Gift of Miss Annie Abercrombie
Diaper draft

This shows five transverse lines for the five shafts needed, and

the vertical ones delimiting the individual pattern blocks. 'Diaper' or 'spot' weave is the old name for the one christened 'Bronson' in the present century.

71 / Ontario. Prince Edward County. Mid-19th century
ROM 954.148.30. Gift of Miss Annie Abercrombie
'Summer and winter' pattern draft:
'The Three Wheel Chariot'

No coverlet in 'summer and winter' weave has been seen in this pattern, but it is similar in type to the overshot shown in no. 255. Here a slight variation of the usual notation may be seen. The notation shows one thread on each of the two front shafts as required for this weave, the balance on a pattern shaft where the total number in each block is indicated.

72 / Ontario. Preston, Waterloo County. Mid-19th century
ROM 955.138, c. Gift of the Toronto Spinners and Weavers
Star and diamond tie-ups

This shows three tie-ups for star and diamond coverlets to be woven on seventeen shafts. They were found on a loose sheet in Wilhelm Magnus Werlich's pattern book (ROM 955.138). Once the principle of this construction is known, only a tie-up is required by an experienced weaver. The outer two are more typical while the central one would have produced an eight-petalled flowerhead rather than the usual star. The legend in German script is translated in the section dealing with coverlets of this type.

73 / Ontario. Near Vineland, Lincoln County. About 1836
ROM L965.11.63. The Annie R. Fry Collection
Page from Samuel Fry's pattern book

This pattern suitable for either twill diaper or for doublecloth
is no. 31 in Samuel Fry's pattern book. It has been drawn
out across the two pages of the open book and the number
shown at the side. It is a four-block pattern with reversing
motifs to give a longer repeat, and would have required sixteen shafts in either technique. The early doublecloth coverlet in no. 414 shows the same design woven. The drawing
is typical of Samuel Fry's careful work. There are thirty-
seven patterns drawn out in the book, two three-block and
seven five-block ones. All the rest are four-block. These would
have been shown to Fry's customers for them to make a
choice. In addition to the pattern book, a number of other
drafts and patterns are on separate sheets of paper. Some are
of this type, one is for 'star and diamond,' several are for
mulitple-shaft twills suitable for linen, and two are for
overshot weave.

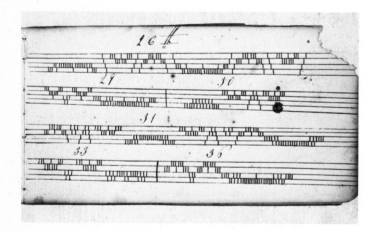

74 / Ontario. Vineland area, Lincoln County. About 1836
ROM L965.11.64. The Annie R. Fry Collection
Page from Samuel Fry's cording book

This page from the cording book shows the drafts for six of
Samuel Fry's designs that are drawn out in the pattern book.
That on the third line is the one required for the design
shown in no. 73. These are all given in shortened form. Each
space between the lines represents four shafts, and each short
line in these spaces indicates that four threads would be entered in twill on the specified group of shafts. On a separate
page in the cording book are full tie-ups for twill diaper and
doublecloth.

This and the pattern book would have been brought back
to Vineland by Samuel Fry after completing his apprenticeship in Bucks County, Pennsylvania.

The basic weaves, tabby, twill, and simple patterns

The three basic weaves on which all textile constructions are founded are tabby, twill, and satin. With the exception of the damask coverlets derived from satin that are the work of one weaver (nos. 484–9), Canadian handwoven materials are based on tabby and twill. The weaves of the jacquard-woven coverlets that are described in a later section are all derived from tabby, and for these a special patterning mechanism, the jacquard machine, was mounted on the loom to produce the complex realistic patterns. All the other textiles made in this country were woven on shaft-looms of varying complexity and with these a threading or entering plan was required to show the order of placing the warp ends in the heddles of the shafts to produce the weave wanted.

Diagrams are shown in this book so that a reader may gain a better knowledge of the different constructions that occur. In this chapter, a series provides a foundation on which knowledge may be built and in later sections dealing with specific pattern weaves further explanatory diagrams will be found. All are of the same form. A large-scale drawing shows the weave expanded so that the interlacing of warp and weft may be clearly seen. In line above this, the entering draft shows the shafts of the loom in schematic form, and the placing of the warp threads in the heddles on them indicated by a mark. To the right of this is the tie-up of the shafts of the loom to the treadles; in all cases they are shown as if the looms were equipped with lamms so that one or more shafts may be controlled by the same treadle. Below the tie-up, and in line with it and the diagram of the weave, the order in which the treadles are worked is indicated.

In addition to these full diagrams, entering drafts are shown wherever applicable with the descriptions of the individual pieces. As most of the old drafts are written to be read from right to left, the same convention is followed here. Except in the simple weaves, one single pattern unit is shown. If the piece has a border, one repeat of the unit, or occasionally more, is shown to the extreme left. Four-shaft overshot weave uses a standard tie-up that is shown in the relative diagrams; in other cases, the tie-up is shown to the left of the pattern draft, or between this and the border if one is present. With the drafts, the treadling order is not shown as it almost always follows the same order as the threading: the standard way of weaving called 'as drawn in.' If this has not been done, a note is made as to how the treadling differs from normal.

The diagram for plain tabby in fig. 5 shows two shafts indicated by the two rows of horizontal squares. Each square represents a heddle, and reading from the right the first end is passed through a heddle on the front shaft of the loom, the next through one on the back, and so on alternately across the width. The tie-up to the right shows that the first shaft is connected to the right treadle as indicated by the small cross, and the second shaft to the left treadle. Below this is the treadling order showing how the two of them are depressed in turn. When the left treadle is stepped on, it takes down all the warp threads that are entered on the back shaft which is attached to it. When the weft is passed through the resulting shed or opening in the warp, it will show at each point where it passes over a warp end, as can be seen in the top line of the schematic weave. When the other treadle is depressed, the other shaft is taken down with all the threads that it controls and the next shot of weft passes over all the alternate warp ends. The use of the two treadles in turn combined with passing the weft back and forth through the sheds produces a piece of plain tabby. This is the most ancient, basic, and common weave found in textiles and is the foundation of many patterned fabrics.

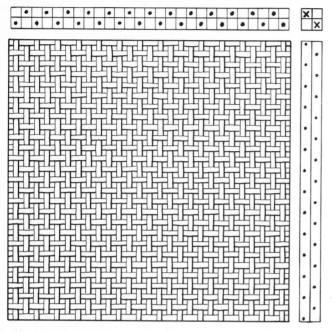

FIGURE 5

Tabby may be decorated with coloured stripes in the warp, or bands in the weft, or by combination of both to produce a wide variety of checks (no. 86). A subtler form of colour change is shown in fig. 6. The elusive pattern results from the use of an uneven number of contrasting threads entered alternately. As this unit is repeated, two threads of the same colour come together regularly. In the diagram, groups of nine are shown. The threading, tie-up, and treadling order

are the same as in fig. 5, but by using the two colours in the same order in the weft as well as in the warp, an indefinite check results known as 'log cabin' colour and weave effect. This was used in the fine weaving of shawls (nos. 101–3), and also occurs most effectively in one blanket (no. 151) which is slightly warp-faced. If the same principle of patterning is used with weft threads that are alternately heavy and light as well as in contrasting colours, the whole effect is accentuated. This is found in some carpeting (nos. 117, 120).

In 'log cabin' colour and weave effect, the construction is usually balanced with similar spacing of warp and weft threads. Fig. 7 shows another type of tabby patterning that sometimes occurs in carpeting (nos. 108–9). In this type the warp is closely set, almost covering a much heavier weft, producing a transverse rib. A section of the warp is threaded alternately in two colours combined with plain stripes and ladder-like patterns appear that are known as 'picket fence' colour and weave effect.

The second and more important basic weave is twill, for which three or more shafts are needed. The warp ends always pass under one or more, and over two or more weft threads, and in each passage of the latter the point of binding steps over one warp end resulting in a characteristic diagonal line. Only one three-shaft twill is shown (no. 78). The great majority are based on four, but some of the more complex patterned pieces described under multiple-shaft and twill diaper coverlets require up to twenty-four.

Fig. 8 shows a four-shaft twill in its simplest form. As seen in the draft above, units of four threads are entered in order on the four shafts from right to left and from front to back. The shafts are tied up singly to the treadles and the order of using these follows the draft exactly. In the resulting weave, each pick of weft passes over one warp and under three. With every passage, it steps over one thread to the left producing the diagonal line across the material that is characteristic of twill. The one shown here is known as a 3/1 twill

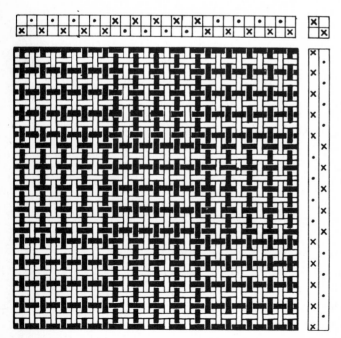

FIGURE 6

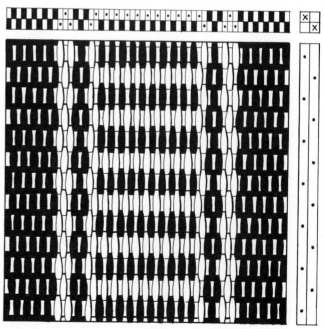

FIGURE 7

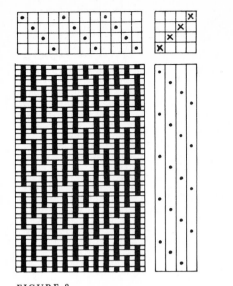

FIGURE 8

FIGURE 9

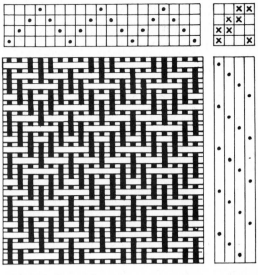

FIGURE 10

as each warp passes over three wefts, and under one. The reverse of the fabric would show the exact opposite with the weft predominating.

A 2/2 twill, shown in fig. 9, is the most usual of all weaves of this type. It is the common one for blankets and a number of other materials. The draft and treadling are identical to that in fig. 8; only the tie-up is changed. Here, two shafts are tied to each treadle with the result that the warp threads are taken down in pairs, and the weft travels over two and under two regularly.

A variation of 2/2 twill is shown in fig. 10. The tie-up and treadling remain unaltered but the order of threading reverses regularly on the shafts. This will result in a series of chevrons running across the width of the cloth. It is known as herringbone weave (no. 138). Here the repeat of the threading unit is seven ends, but this may be extended to produce larger chevrons, and a considerably stronger herringbone effect, as shown in fig. 11, which is based on a fourteen-thread repeat.

At first sight, the twill shown in fig. 12 is very similar to the one just described, but it will be seen that instead of threading running in sequence, there is a break of one thread at every point where the direction of the threading changes.

The result is a very ancient twill variation, and it has been discovered that it is the only possible way to produce the characteristic chevrons of herringbone patterning on the warp-weighted loom (Hoffmann 187–93). This very simple loom, perhaps the first type that evolved, is of prehistoric origin which survived in Lapland until the present day (ROM 960.130.1). It gradually died out, but was used in Iceland, Scandinavia, the Orkneys, Shetlands, and Faroes into historic times. It is fascinating to find the characteristic broken herringbone patterning continuing in side borders of blankets woven in Scotland, and in the tradition brought from there to Canada (nos. 139–40; ROM 968.30.3), even though they were woven on horizontal looms.

If a firm weave is wanted, this construction has a distinct advantage over the normal herringbones shown in figs. 10 and 11. If these are examined, it will be seen that there are three-thread floats at each point where the direction of the threading reverses. In fig. 12, no float is over more than two threads and a distinct break appears at the points of the chevrons. Broken herringbones occur in many variations, and some will be found in the drafts for both blankets and linens. If they are woven with contrasting colours in warp and weft, a more interesting pattern effect is gained: the arms

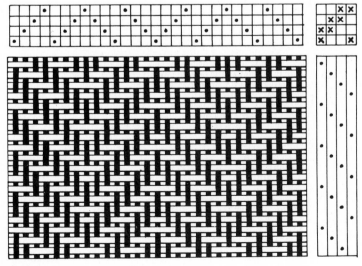

FIGURE 11

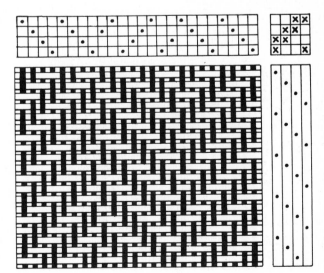

FIGURE 12

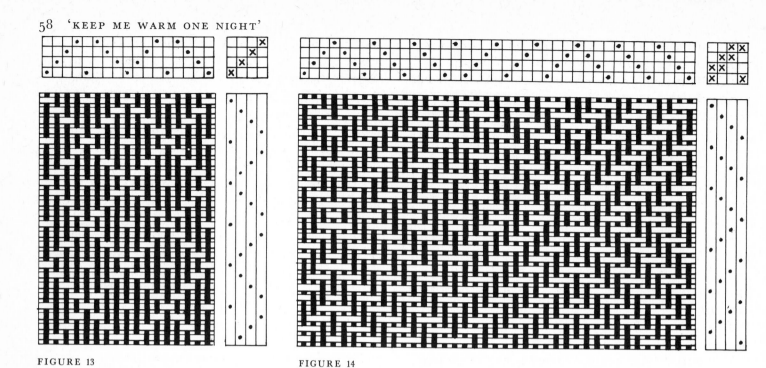

FIGURE 13   FIGURE 14

of each chevron are in contrast to one another, a dark one meeting a light one at the points of the angles.

By reversing the treadling regularly so that it follows the threading order of the chevron or herringbone twills, a whole new series of variations is opened up, and two basic ones are shown in figs. 13 and 14. These have an allover lozenge lattice which in its simplest form is centred by a small spot (fig. 13). If the straight threading order is repeated before reversing, each central spot is surrounded by concentric lozenges within the lattice (fig. 14). Both these variations have traditional names, the first being known as bird's-eye, and the larger as goose-eye. There are different ways of producing both these patterns and a number will be seen in the linens and blankets described later (nos. 171–4; 145–50).

The bird's-eye weave shown is derived from the simple 3/1 twill shown in fig. 8 with a slight extension in the threading, and may equally well be woven in a 2/2 twill. Similarly, the threading shown for the goose-eye weave is an extension of the herringbone in fig. 11.

The weaves of many patterned fabrics are derived from twill, a group with simple motifs often being referred to as 'linen weaves.' It is in this material that these weaves are best known, but they are equally adaptable to wool, cotton, and other yarns (no. 152). All have a long tradition of use behind them and belong to the European heritage in North America.

The best known is huckaback (fig. 15), which is familiar as the ground of many hand towels. The name is now usually shortened to 'huck,' a term that made its first appearance in a catalogue of The Great Exhibition of 1851 in London. Its derivation from a simple herringbone threading becomes obvious by comparing the draft with that in fig. 10. By duplicating the entering of two threads at every point where the herringbone reverses, a new threading plan results. With an altered tie-up, but still following the threading plan for treadling, an entirely different weave appears with small allover motifs in offset rows formed by warp floats on the face and weft floats on the reverse (no. 175).

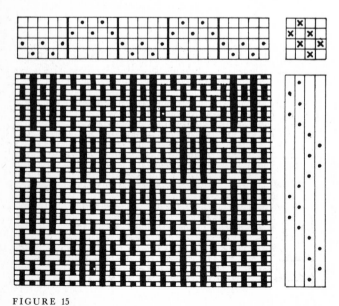

FIGURE 15

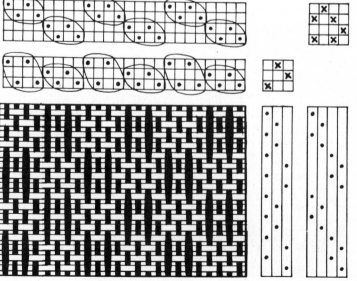

FIGURE 16

The standard huck weave just described is based on five-thread units, but a simpler one may be woven on four (fig. 16). This threading produces a similar effect, but the motifs are slightly closer together. There are three possible ways of writing the draft, an excellent demonstration of how the same result may be achieved with different threadings. Two drafts are shown with the diagram and the third is to the right with the description of no. 176. By comparing this one with that for the five-end huck shown in fig. 15, the connection is obvious. In the upper draft in fig. 16, a twill sequence of threading is maintained, but every pair of threads is doubled. With a special tie-up, having two treadles each controlling the same pair of shafts as was sometimes done for convenience, and weaving 'as drawn in,' the warp floats appear on the face and the weft floats on the reverse in the same manner as in the standard huck. The other draft given with the diagram is on three shafts, and is the simplest version of the weave known as diaper or spot.

In pattern weaving, motifs are built up of small units used either singly or in combination with others. Each of these is usually called a block if the design is geometric rather than realistic, and a pattern is described as being made of so many blocks. In the drafts given in this book where the patterning principle of combining units is involved, each individual block has been circled so that it may be clearly seen. This has been done with the drafts accompanying this diagram (fig. 16) where only two blocks form the pattern and in fig. 17, which shows a four-block pattern. Occasionally two units form one block, as in M's & O's weave, but this is unusual, and in the drafts for this weave each unit is encircled individually.

Diaper or spot weave is the old and traditional name for one that has been christened with the genteelism 'Bronson' in the revival of handweaving as a hobby in the present century. It was named after J. and R. Bronson, who published drafts for it which they called diaper in *The Domestic Manufacturer's Assistant* in 1817. The same term is found on the old draft from Prince Edward County (no. 70), and others. The connection of diaper weave with twill may be understood by studying the draft with the diagram (fig. 17), and may also be seen by looking at the old draft (no. 70). Although this weave occurs in its simplest form with three shafts (fig. 16), it is seldom used with less than five. One of these is used for the ground, and every second warp thread is entered on it. The other threads are entered on the remaining shafts in pairs in twill sequence showing the derivation. For shots of ground across the width, the four pattern shafts shown in the diagram are depressed and alternate with a pattern shot using the first shaft and one of the pattern shafts together. Although closely related to huck, where the warp forms a pattern on the face, diaper weave is usually woven with the weft floats appearing on the right side and with the warp ones on the reverse. This weave is highly suitable for simple table linens, two examples of which are illustrated (nos. 178–9). Both show an extension of the patterning principle of the diagram with pairs of units repeated to produce larger motifs.

The last of the linen weaves is now called M's & O's; a name of uncertain origin. During the eighteenth and nineteenth centuries, huckaback was used for both constructions, and it is only in the present century that a distinct division has been made. The old draft shown in no. 69 shows the basic form of the weave, and it is called 'Huck A Buck'; similar instances occur in other old drafts. The confusion may well arise from the fact that both constructions are very suitable for towelling, and were widely used for this purpose.

The basic construction of a two-block design is shown in fig. 18, and the pattern is formed by weft floats that are on both the face and the reverse. Each block consists of two units, often repeated, the blocks alternating to produce an allover pattern. Although other bases are practicable, the M's & O's draft shown here is derived from twill, as in the other linen weaves. In this case, it is two simple broken twills, one threaded 1, 2, 4, 3 and the other 1, 4, 2, 3. By duplicating every pair of threads, using the usual tie-up for a 2/2 twill, and weaving 'as drawn in,' the pattern results.

With a four-shaft loom, three pairs of two shafts are available (1, 2 and 3, 4; 1, 4 and 2, 3; 1, 3 and 2, 4). The

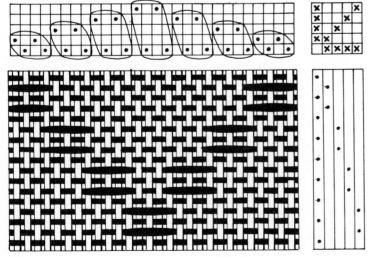

FIGURE 17

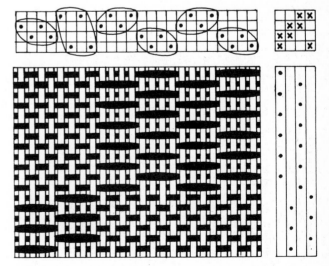

FIGURE 18

patterning principle of the two-block M's & o's weave uses two pairs of shafts working against each other. All old drafts that have been seen use the first two combinations, the method that has been followed here. Many modern books employ the first and third pairs, a threading plan that produces the same result with an altered tie-up. All three pairs may be used to produce a three-block pattern (fig. 19). This differs from the usual type as the two units forming a block are not side by side, but separated. In this weave, the tabby areas are not true and faults occur automatically in the ground. These would also result from old drafts that have been seen. In the towel illustrated (no. 187), the only piece that has been seen, they are present but are completely inconspicuous and detract in no way from the weaving. Another way of producing a three-block M's & o's pattern is to place the two units side by side as is shown in the two-block examples (Frey, 93).

The most common pattern weave'for a four-shaft loom is overshot, which is dealt with in detail in the section on coverlets using this technique (figs. 32–4), but it also occurs in carpeting and linens. Several old drafts are illustrated (nos. 64–8) and all will be found transposed to modern notation for easier understanding. Drafts are given with the descriptions of the examples of overshot weave illustrated. All are based on the same layout. The 'table' motif is usually a dominant one in these pieces and has been chosen as the starting point. The two blocks of which it is built up are always placed on the same pair of shafts (1 and 2, and 2 and 3) unless the motif is drafted 'on opposites,' when it is shown on shafts 1 and 2, and on 3 and 4 to obtain the proper separation of units. As has been mentioned in describing fig. 16, each block used to build up motifs has been circled so that every one may be distinguished clearly.

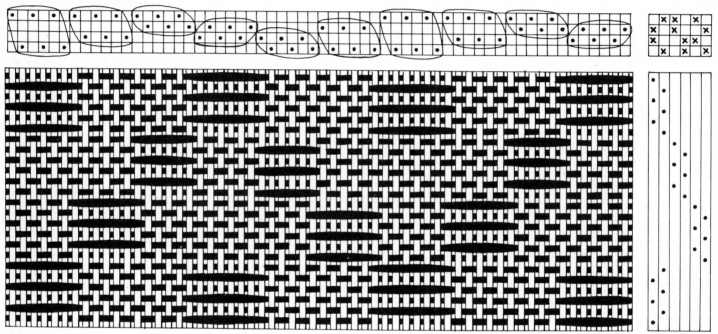

FIGURE 19

PLATE I

134, 102, 87, 17, 145, 107

Costume

It is very difficult to generalize on the development of costume in pioneer Canada; conditions varied as different parts of the country were opened for settlement. In all areas textile fibres were inevitably in short supply at first. For some years, the settlers were dependent on what they brought with them. Some came well supplied, and their stock lasted until the country could supply their needs. Others from ignorance or of necessity arrived with little more than the clothes on their backs. It was flax, the pedlar's pack, and dressed deerskins on which they had to depend. Flax was grown as soon as a field was cleared for the purpose. The pedlar's pack supplied the little luxuries, but these were expensive and few could afford any great amount. Deerskins were a ready source of clothing in all parts of the country, and in the Maritime Provinces and parts of eastern Quebec there were herds of caribou. Both deer and caribou were killed for food and the skins carefully dressed and kept until needed. People, of necessity, reverted to a pre-textile period. As the fabrics they had brought with them wore out, some turned to leather to fill their needs.

It was natural for the men of Quebec to adopt Indian dress when following the fur trade and to become accustomed to wearing clothing of dressed skins. The habitants of Quebec also used them to clothe themselves from head to foot. Shirts, an old pair of breeches, and other leather garments appear in the seventeenth-century Quebec inventories (Séguin, 487). Garments of this type were practical and windproof, but seldom smart. There is one exception shown in a watercolour of about 1830 by J. Crawford Young in the McCord Museum, Montreal. This shows a group of four habitants, one of them wearing an elegant painted caribou-skin coat of the type made by the Naskapi-Montagnais Indians of Labrador.

Buckskin was sometimes all that was available and was much better for rough work in the bush than cloth that would have snagged and torn on thorns and branches. Peter Horning came to Barton Township, now part of Hamilton, Ontario, from Pennsylvania in 1788. He had nothing to wear but buckskins until Jacob Burkholder, a trained weaver from the same state, settled on the next concession in 1794. Horning by this time must have managed to raise a small flock of sheep that provided the wool for the first order to Burkholder for material for a homespun suit (Powell, #3, 69; #5, 51). From the few references that have been found, women were less often dependent on leather. A member of the Harris family of London, Ontario, remembered a girl hired as a nursemaid in 1798 who had been left without a garment when she ruined her only dress of deerskin through careless washing. Light is thrown on the shortage of materials by the fact that her clothing when she arrived at the Harris's was a woollen slip made out of her mother's second petticoat (Ryerson, II, 240). The account book of William Nelles of Grimsby that runs from 1791 to 1828 has many entries for moccasins, spelled in various wonderful ways, showing the widespread use of this kind of footwear. The usual price was 6d York currency for a pair obtained from Indians.

Once sheep were established, wool was added to linen as material for clothing. The first scanty supplies were eked out by using the wool as weft on a linen warp to produce drug-get (Fr. *droguet*, Gael. *drogadh*). The derogatory name 'linsey-woolsey' had long been used for this material as it was not 'all wool and a yard wide.' As cotton yarn became available through imports, it rapidly replaced the handspun linen as warp, and it is druggets of this type that have survived and occur in some of the pieces described here, particularly undergarments. With increasing supplies of wool, flannel and fulled cloth came into general use. The term used for the former in some early nineteenth-century records in Ontario is russetting and is described as both plain and checked.

From the few pieces of everyday clothing that have survived, no more than an incomplete picture can be put together. In the Acadian areas, the women wore full pleated skirts (nos. 75–7), probably with white linen blouses. They have parallels in the regional costume of France. Similar skirts were probably worn in Quebec, but none are known to have survived. Nothing is known of men's clothes in Acadia, but the three-piece, double-breasted suit of the mid-nineteenth century (no. 97), and a somewhat later hooded coat (no. 98) come from Quebec. Both may be considered characteristic of what was worn by men in the rural parts of the province. The hooded coat, or capote, is a typically Canadian garment often made of blanket cloth.

Few handwoven garments have been seen in the Maritime Provinces. Almost all have vanished into hooked rugs. One unglamorous and scratchy set of woollen underwear for a man remains almost unworn in the Albert County Museum, Hopewell Cape, New Brunswick. In Prince Edward Island, a man's waistcoat of about 1840 is banded with the unusual red-violet colour that may have come from lichens. In Cape Breton, the use of handwoven materials lasted into the present century, but few garments are still in existence. In the Mackley Collection in Sydney, there is a drugget petticoat from Cape North, a sample of hodden grey trousering, two lengths of mill-finished indigo blue flannel, and a piece of beautiful black coating material. This last was woven a yard wide and fulled by hand to twenty-seven inches.

Fulling was first done by hand, a practice that continued in some parts of the country, but as local mills were established they took over this heavy work. In the Scottish tradition, it was women's work, and when a length was ready a group would gather at the house of the weaver for a 'milling frolic.' One would act as leader, and sing a waulking song, usually in Gaelic, as the wet length of cloth was passed from hand to hand, thumped, and whacked as it passed around a long board. It was known how many songs were needed to shrink a piece of cloth the required amount, but to take it from a yard to twenty-seven inches was a full day's work. As more and more wool became available in the early part of the present century, men and boys were allowed to join in the task, and in some areas there would be a frolic almost every evening. Little is known about Irish communities, but in those from the southern part of the country, it was probably the work of two men who came round specially for the occasion and who would have worked the cloth with their feet against a board.

In Ontario there were professional fullers, but their services were not inexpensive. They received about three times as much a yard as did the weaver. A receipt in the Jordan Historical Museum of the Twenty is dated 1812 and records payment of £2/10/9 for fulling 14½ yards of cloth. Samuel Fry's account book lists payments on a similar scale to a Mr Madison.

Fulling mills were established in Ontario in the early part of the nineteenth century, possibly a little earlier in Quebec. The same is probably true of the Maritime Provinces, and Lippincotts at West River in Pictou in 1825 was probably not the first. The comparative figures from the census of 1851–2 given in fig. 2 show that there was a much greater production of fulled cloth in Quebec than in Ontario. Much was probably for outdoor wear in a more inclement winter climate and was probably like the material used for the hooded coat shown in no. 98. This material would be much warmer than the suitings known from Ontario (nos. 95–6) and is of the type known as double fulled (*foulé double*).

Most of the examples of handwoven clothing illustrated are from Ontario, where, scarce as they are, more seem to have survived. Linens of all qualities were produced. Ryerson mentions women making strong linen for shirts and checks for their own dresses about 1800 (II, 241); (nos. 90, 166). Much of this first linen was coarse, but as time passed and more effort could be expended, others of superb quality were woven. Little of the everyday quality has survived, except as fragments or as perfectly plain towels. The finer materials were used for undergarments for trousseaus (nos. 80–1) and for men's shirts for special occasions (no. 83). The neckerchief shown in no. 82 also fits into this class. These examples show the quality that was possible to meet a special demand, either on the farms, or by local professional weavers.

The most characteristic clothing materials of Ontario, woollen flannels (no. 86), were produced in quantity and used for dresses, children's clothes, men's work shirts, and underwear. The one dress shown (no. 88), and the plain drugget dress (no. 87), are the earliest in date that have been seen, but many examples of earlier materials found their way into the pieced homespun quilts. It is from these that a knowledge of the range and types may be learned. Flannels, frequently checked, were commonly worn throughout Ontario, and the one early quilt that has survived in the Maritime Provinces, now in the Nova Scotia Museum, Halifax, shows that similar materials were worn there. One shirt for a lumberman on the Otonabee River is in the Peterborough Centennial Museum and, like other late ones at King's Village Pioneer Settlement in New Brunswick, was sewn by machine. Old photographs survive of husbands and wives obviously wearing homespun clothes. The men's coats and jackets have no pretence of style; the women's clothes may not have been fashionable, but they did mirror the current trends.

Shawls were worn instead of overcoats by both men and women. The women's shawls were square, folded diagonally, and draped over the shoulders. They are known from Quebec (nos. 99–100; ROM 970.90.15), Ontario (nos. 101–2), and New Brunswick (NBM). Men's shawls have only been seen from Ontario, but were probably worn in the Maritime Provinces. They were not as wide as those of the women, but much longer, sometimes three or four yards, and resembled the Scottish shepherds' plaids in form. They were the usual wear in rainy and winter weather, and wrapped around the upper part of the body they gave protection whether riding or stepping out along a country road.

A shawl was expected to last a lifetime. The yarns were spun with special care and carefully woven so that it might be worn with pride. It is in shawls that some of the best handweaving is found.

75 / New Brunswick. Memramcook Valley. Early 19th century
NBM. Gift of Mme Emile Paturel
Skirt length, weft-faced tabby, with *à la planche*. L. 232cm; w. 80cm

Banded in fine black, light brown, and medium blue wool and natural white cotton on natural white cotton (all z singles). Above, this Acadian skirt length is shown gathered and hanging sideways as it would have been made up. The detail below shows the bands, which are more elaborate than in other examples known. Two types alternate, one centred by black and white yarn twisted together to give a marled effect in the centre, the other with short floats along the edges to give a dotted effect. These were produced on the two-shaft loom by using the *à la planche* technique, better known in coverlets from the North Shore of the St Lawrence (cf. fig. 20). This is the only documented example from outside the lower St Lawrence region in which this effective technique has been used.

The piece made up as a light bedcovering now in Musée Acadien at Miscouche was probably woven as skirting (no. 197). Pieces from skirt lengths are known from the Chéticamp area of Cape Breton (ROM 968.308.5; 970.202.9, .10) and have survived in the same way. When this style went out of use towards the end of the nineteenth century, the prudent housewives removed the lengths from the waistbands and used the warm materials for bed coverings.

76 / Nova Scotia. Chezzetcook. Early 19th century
Grand Pré National Park. Lent by the Nova Scotia Museum.
8031
Woman's skirt, weft-faced tabby.
Circumference 262cm; w. 90cm

Black and natural white wool entirely covering fine natural
white cotton warp (all z singles). The black ground is regularly broken by white bands, and two white pin stripes are
centred on each black one. This is the only old Acadian skirt
known to have survived in its original form. The length of
closely woven material has been joined by one seam, then
one edge has been pleated into a linen waistband. The use
of cotton warp shows that it is unlikely to be quite as old as
no. 77, but the sewing had been done with a woollen thread
and the waistband with a bleached linen one (s singles),
both of which are early features. The rest of the figure is
dressed in reproduction clothing, but the skirt is a very rare
and interesting piece. (Photograph: Burnham)

77 / Prince Edward Island. Chapel Creek, Rustico. End of
the 18th century
CAGM. Collection of Robert Harris
Skirt length (fragment), weft-faced tabby. L. 43cm; w. 30cm

Banded in medium and deep indigo blue and red wool, and
half-bleached linen entirely covering the half-bleached linen
warp (all z singles). This was tradionally woven about 1795
by Harriet Gallant, daughter of Grandpère Gallant, the
first Acadian settler at Chapel Creek. There seems no reason
to doubt the story as Robert Harris, the artist, obtained it
from her nephew Hubert Gallant, in 1901. At that time he
was 80, and could have received it directly from the weaver.
The use of linen indicates an early date, and the quality of
the wool and the fineness of the weave (7 ends and 20 picks
per cm) both support this. As is the case with almost all
everyday costume in Canada, little notice was taken of it by
chroniclers. The only firm evidence that we have about
Acadian clothing is the type of skirt worn by the women
made of fine materials such as this. They were woven with
bands entirely covering the warp, a tremendous amount of
work. When finished, the length was turned on its side and
pleated at the waist. The bands hung vertically, the width
being just sufficient for an ankle-length skirt.

78 / Ontario. Shakespeare, Perth County. Late 19th century
ROM 970.36.4. Gift of Mrs K. Oakes
Sample, 2/1 twill, corset material (coutil).
L. 75cm; w. 48cm

Half-bleached linen (z singles) with strong herringbone lines
showing on the face. This is a very strong and unstretching
weave that was made in linen especially for corsets. A 2/1
twill is what was originally meant by the term 'jean' and is a
very strong hard-wearing material when set and woven
properly. This piece is said to have been made by May and
Johnnie Bell, a brother and sister who were professional
weavers. If a local weaver could produce an article on a
competitive basis he had a market. Presumably the Bells had
a demand for linen corset material, which was stronger than
the commercially produced cotton equivalent. The country
women of the area would be well held in if their stays were
made of Bell's coutil.

79 / Ontario. North Elmsley Township, Lanark County.
1833-63
ROM 949.36.3. Gift of Miss Bessie Farmer
Width of petticoat material, tabby. L. 31cm; w. 83cm

Natural white cotton (z singles) fairly loosely set, banded at
intervals with quite heavy cotton. This was made by Duncan
McNab, who came from Scotland in 1818 and worked as a
professional weaver in Beckwith Township until 1833 when
he moved to North Elmsley Township. Here he supplied the
area with all sorts of plain cotton materials to be used for
sheets, tablecloths etc. until his death in 1863. This is another
example of a weaver filling a local demand. The material
was made for petticoats. The upper part was plain and the
bottom stiffened with the heavier cotton to help hold out
the full skirts, which even unstylish women wore.

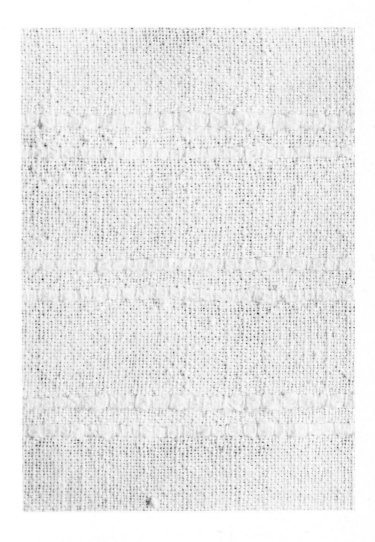

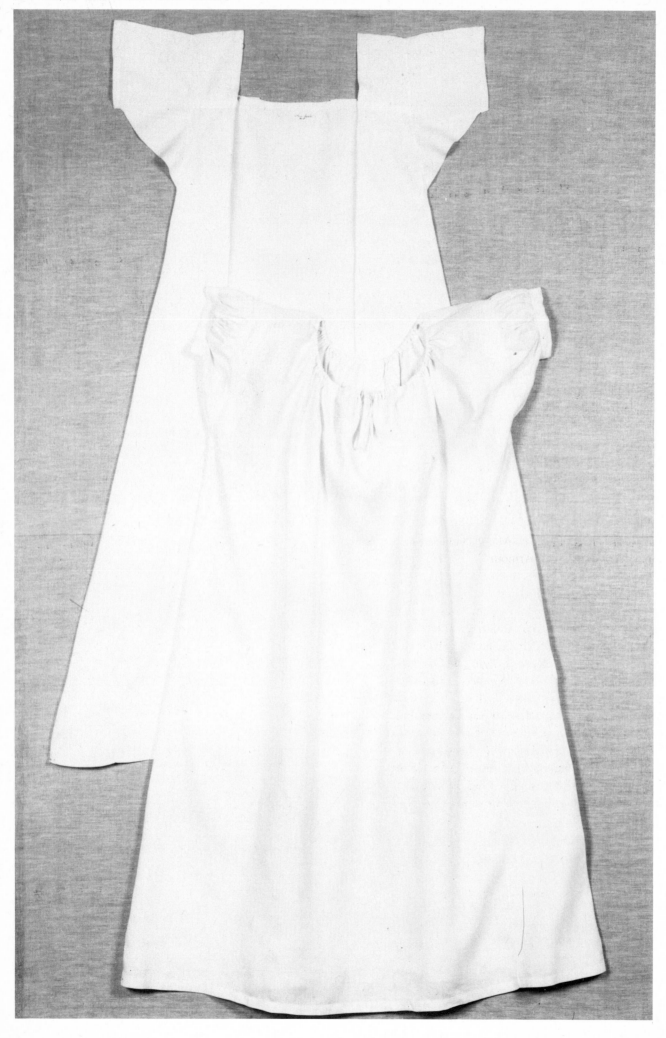

80 / Ontario. Dundas, Wentworth County.
Probably about 1840
ROM 944.45.7. Gift of Miss Marion F. Lesslie
Chemise, tabby. L. 118cm

Bleached linen of excellent quality (z singles, about 30 ends
per cm). At the front of the neck is 'Anna Lesslie No. 5' in
black ink. Much personal and household linen was marked
in this way. Laundry was done infrequently at this period,
and those who could afford it had good supplies of linen.
These were used in numerical order, and the names on the
garments made it easier to sort them out after a large seasonal
washing. This chemise is a beautiful example of the simple
basic undergarment worn by women beneath the corsets
and the petticoats of the period. The sewing is exquisite and
the weaving excellent. The material is typical of the finest
linen produced in Canada, sometimes for a family's own use,
and sometimes for sale. About 1820, an Irish community in
Beauce sent linen to Quebec that was reported to be of as
fine quality as what was imported (Ouellet, 262).

81 / Ontario. Prince Edward County. Mid-19 century
ROM 939.21.45. Gift of Miss H.M. Armour
Chemise, tabby. L. 115cm

Bleached linen of excellent quality (z singles). This is even a
little finer than no. 67, with 32 warp threads per cm. The
production of linen such as this was never large in the early
days of Ontario but a limited amount was grown and processed on farms. In this case probably linen was needed for a
daughter's trousseau and a special effort made to produce a
proper quality for her underwear. The sewing was undoubtedly done at home, probably by the girl herself, and is beautiful with tiny backstitch used around the inserts which have
been set in to allow for a fashionable mid-nineteenth century
bosom. The chemise comes from the same Barker family as
the shirt no. 83 and the blanket no. 137. They were Loyalists
who settled near Picton.

82 / Ontario. Port Hope, Durham County.
Early 19th century
ROM 969.277.4. Gift of Mrs Doris Wardenier
Kerchief, tabby. L. 75cm; w. 73cm

Linen (z singles) in bleached white, medium indigo blue, and golden brown. This and no. 166 are the only two pieces of linen known from Ontario with a colour other than blue. Few items of this kind have survived, making it impossible to form a true picture of what was made. This is probably a man's neckerchief, but it could equally well have served for a woman to trim a plain neckline on informal occasions. In one corner 'I' has been embroidered, probably the numeral 1. From the Choate family.

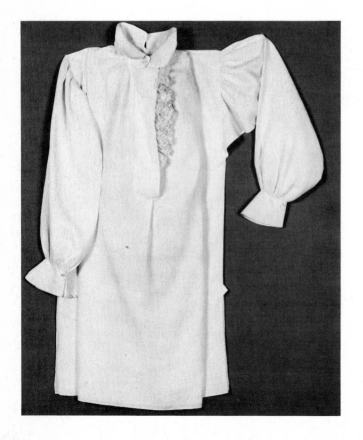

83 / Ontario. Prince Edward County. About 1825
ROM 948.180. Gift of Miss Maisie Tyrell
Man's shirt, tabby. L. 89cm

Linen (z singles) of almost as fine a quality as the woman's chemise no. 81, also from the Barker family of Picton. This is beautifully sewn, with fine back stitch outlining the front placket and the tiny shoulder gussets. The side seams are the selvage edges top-sewn together with almost invisible stitches. The front frill is of imported muslin edged with lace, but otherwise the shirt is a superb example of the excellent weaving and sewing sometimes lavished on a special garment. This must surely have been the wedding shirt of David Barker, whose name is on it.

84 / Ontario. Dunwich Township, Elgin County.
About 1860
ROM 952.214. Gift of the Misses F. and E. Pearce
Man's shirt, tabby. L. 94cm

Bleached linen (z singles). The flax was grown and processed on the farm of the donors' grandparents, and their
grandmother, Ann Moorhouse Pearce, wove the linen and
made the shirt. The linen is heavier than in no. 83 and is
probably much more typical of the quality normally produced.

85 / Ontario. Vineland area, Lincoln County. About 1843
ROM 966.192.1. Gift of Mr Norman Macdonald
Pair of man's trousers, tabby. L. 101cm

Natural white cotton warp with fine stripes in blue and
pinkish-red, woven with bleached linen (all z singles). These
trousers were worn by David Housser when he was married
in 1843. The material was either woven at home or by one
of the local professional weavers, possibly Samuel Fry who
was a near neighbour. The cutting and making up is expert,
but may well have been done at home. The brass buttons are
a stylish touch that would have been bought. A very smart
garment has been locally made from locally woven cloth.
A pair of white linen trousers of similar date is in the Jordan
Museum of the Twenty.

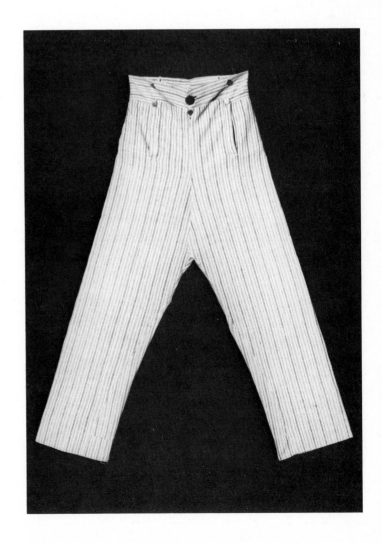

86 / Ontario. Essex County. Made about 1865
ROM 947.53.
Pieced quilt of homespuns, tabby and twill. L. 219cm; w. 178cm

This has been made from a range of checked woollen materials (all yarns z singles) that are older than the making of the quilt. The hand-woven garments worn in Canada for many decades, and by the large mass of the population, are now virtually gone. The examples illustrated in this section show the majority of the surviving pieces. Being ordinary garments, they were not treasured, and in a non-affluent economy material was used again and again.

Worn garments were cut down for smaller members of the family. In the Maritime Provinces, the ultimate end of these homespuns was the strips for hooked rugs; in Ontario, it was the warm pieced quilt. Here, all sorts of materials have survived and may be examined. From such sources, we may discover what was used for everyday clothes: women's dressses, men's jackets, trousers, and work shirts. These materials are the flannel that is listed in the census returns as part of the agricultural produce of rural Ontario in the middle of the nineteenth century.

This illustration shows a detail about 80 × 60cm of a quilt made of homespuns. The colours of the wool are basically red (probably madder) and a greenish-brown, with natural grey and white, and a little blue. A few cotton threads are used for emphasis. The quilt is backed with other pieces of homespun and filled with a woollen bat. It is typical of the woollen quilts that have survived, and that only vary in range of colour.

This was the first example of its kind to turn up in the Museum's research project, near its start in 1947. It was still being used as bedding: the owner could not do without it, although she did wish to see it preserved. The Museum was short of funds, so the old Ontario system of barter was revived. The owner ended up with a new blanket and the Museum with this important quilt.

Plain materials were also made for clothing but are infinitely rarer than the checks and stripes. These homespuns were woven domestically in quantity, but were also a staple production of the local professionals, who would take a woman's spun and dyed yarn and weave it for about a shilling a yard. One old lady to whom we spoke in Beamsville remembered how much she hated having to go to school in a handwoven dress of similar material about 1885–90 as everyone else in the class had clothes made of material from the store. It all depended on the part of Canada in which you lived. Another informant in Cape Breton, considerably younger, told us that when he was young there was no question of wearing anything but handwoven indigo blue material – everybody did. All the boys had homemade pants and the lucky ones jackets.

87 / Ontario. Probably Dunbarton, Ontario County. 1855-60
ROM 959.272. Gift of Mr Arthur Hunt
Woman's dress, tabby

Fine brown wool on a duller brown cotton warp (both fine z singles). This was woven by one of the fully trained professionals scattered throughout the province. Material with wool on a cotton, or earlier a linen, warp, is drugget, most of which was considerably coarser than this. The wool weft is beautifully spun with a hard twist that gives the material a very firm texture. It would have stood up to many years of wear. A point which cannot be emphasized too strongly is that these everyday dresses were never worn over a crinoline frame. Several petticoats would have been used to give the proper support but crinolines, even though in all the fashion books of the time, were only used by the very fashionable or for formal wear.

(*in colour* PLATE I)

88 / Ontario. Willoughby Township, Welland County.
1865-70
ROM 967.7. Gift of Mrs W.E.P. De Roche
Woman's dress, tabby

Checked in black, green and pink (now faded) wool (all z
singles). This simple dress was worn by the donor's grandmother and by some happy chance survived. It seems to be
the earliest remaining dress made of the checked flannels
that were the basic clothing material before being supplanted
by machine-woven goods. There are a few other examples
of homespun clothing of later date in various collections in
Ontario (Peterborough Centennial Museum, Peterborough,
Sombra Museum, Sombra, and the Glengarry Museum,
Dunvegan). The cut of this dress is typical of the simple
dresses of the late 1860s worn in rural Ontario and is given
in the ROM *Modesty to Mod* catalogue (Pattern no. 30).

89 / Ontario. Perth, Lanark County. About 1870
ROM 969.10.1. Gift of Mrs J.H. Stewart
Woman's petticoat, 2/2 twill. L. 99cm

Warp of fine cotton (z singles) in black with narrow stripes
in white; weft of fine wool (z singles) banded in red and
black. The skirt has been cut from five pieces which are
straight in front and with slanting fullness to the back. Although these handspun garments were certainly not the dress
of fashion, they usually reflect in modified form the style of
the period in which they were made. This would have been
an eminently suitable garment for the cold Canadian winter
before central heating became general.

90 / Ontario. Sharon, York County. About 1830
ROM 950.63.2. Gift of Mrs T.S. Jardine and
Miss Helena Daly
Apron, tabby. L. 96cm

Linen (fine z singles), bleached white with tiny check in
indigo blue. This is made from a straight length of linen,
hemmed at either end with a draw-string run through the
top. It was worn and woven by the donors' grandmother,
Elizabeth P. Doane.

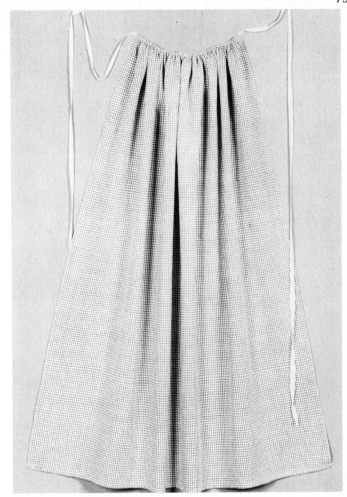

91 / Ontario. Perth, Lanark County. 1875-90
ROM 969.10.2. Gift of Mrs J.H. Stewart
Woman's drawers, 2/2 twill. L. 85cm

Natural white cotton warp woven with bright red wool (both
z singles). It is interesting that even with the woollen yarn
handspun and the weaving done by hand the making up
has been done by sewing machine. The cut of these drawers
with the two legs completely separate except at the waist
band was usual right up to the twentieth century. The length
of the leg would reach to about mid-calf; garments such as
this are the female version of the proverbial red flannel underwear.

92 / Ontario. Perth, Lanark County. 1863
ROM 969.161. Gift of Mrs J.H. Gibson
Woman's dress, gauze

The warp is very fine natural white cotton with tiny stripes in black (both z singles), and at intervals some of the white threads have been spot-dyed (ikat), producing small indefinite motifs scattered in more or less regular rows. The weft is a very fine combed grey wool (z singles) with narrow blue wool bands alternating with a line of white silk. The weave is gauze, which means that spaced pairs of warp ends twist backwards and forwards holding the fine wefts firmly between them. A detail is shown in the picture below.

It is a most unlikely material to have been handwoven in Ontario in the 1860s, but it was the wedding dress of Helen Forsythe Bell, grandmother of the donor, and was woven by the bride's father. It is known that he was a weaver who came to Canada from Scotland. Gauze weaving was an important trade in southwest Scotland and with this skill he must have come from this area. Drawing on all his early experience he wove his daughter a dress length suitable for a bride and produced this beautiful and delicate material. The dress is from the period when skirts were widest and, being for a formal occasion, was probably supported by a crinoline as well as the usual number of petticoats. The frills are all edged with violet silk, which was by far the most fashionable trimming of the period; the aniline dye to produce this colour had been discovered just a few years before.

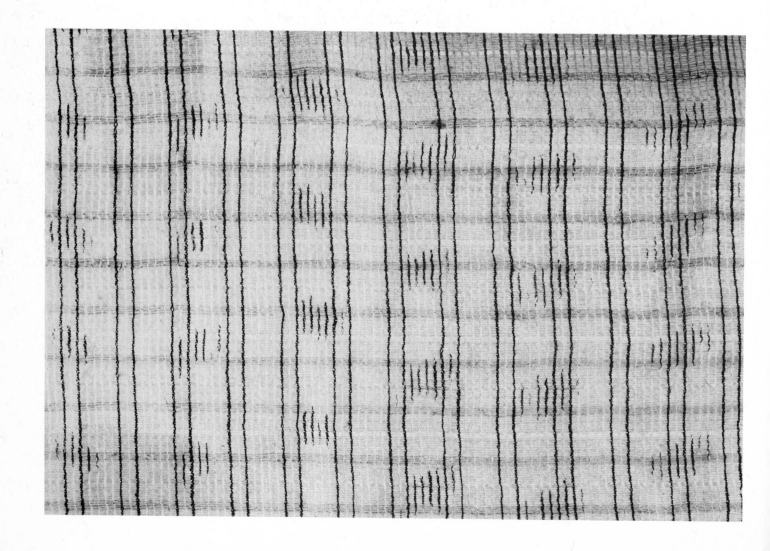

93 / Quebec. Mid-19th century
ROM 958.96.11. Gift of Miss Joan Arnoldi
Woman's petticoat, tabby. L. 88cm

Fine natural white cotton warp woven with wool (both z singles) in light brown with graduated bands around the hem in red and indigo blue separated by natural white. The bottom is decorated with scallops in coarse feather-stitch. It has been made up from two matching pieces sewn together at the sides, and the whole put on to a coarse white cotton yoke which gathers into the waist on a drawstring. The yoke, which is sewn by machine, seems to be a late addition, and the main part of the garment considerably earlier. It is difficult to date such pieces accurately, as both the plain drugget and these simple garments were made and worn over a long period. In Scottish areas, the bands around the bottom were called the 'listes.' An elderly lady of Irish extraction from the Codroy valley in Newfoundland was quite scathing about the Scottish girls in her area. When she was young, they could hardly wait to get down the church steps after Mass before tucking up their sober Sunday skirts. Ostensibly this was for the walk home, but she knew it was to show off the gay 'listes' on their shorter petticoats and, incidentally, a neatly turned ankle.

94 / Ontario. Welland County. Late 19th century
ROM 964.56. Gift of Mrs K. Sorensen
Woman's petticoat, tabby. L. 79cm, plus knitted scallops

Natural white cotton warp woven with fine red wool (both z singles). The spinning of the wool is tight and the weave very firm, giving a harsh handle which would be durable, but not pleasant to wear. It has been made from two widths of material, seamed at the sides, with a drawstring at the top, and is trimmed around the hem with knitted lace of red wool. This is a late example, but characteristic of the use of drugget for all sorts of garments in the nineteenth century. Blue was by far the most common colour for the coverlets and blankets, but red certainly predominates for undergarments.

95 / Ontario. Vineland area, Lincoln County. 1837
Jordan Historical Museum of the Twenty, Jordan, Ontario
Man's suit, fulled tabby

All black wool of excellent quality (z singles) woven plain
and then shrunk so that it is fulled to the consistency of a fine
English broadcloth. The material is the work of Samuel Fry
and was made up, probably by his mother, into this three-
piece suit of great sobriety for his wedding. It is well known
from written records and accounts that local weavers in
Canada made woollen material to be fulled and used for
men's clothing, but without a definite history such as accompanied this piece, it is difficult to tell which broadcloths were
local and which imported. The custom of weaving such
material locally carried on past the middle of the century
and the services of fulling mills for finishing became steadily
more available.

96 / Ontario. 1840-50
ROM 947.94. Gift of Mr Sidney Holmes
Man's coat, fulled tabby
Fine medium brown wool (z singles) woven plain and fulled.

This is a considerably smarter garment than Samuel Fry's
wedding suit; it was worn in this country, but little else is
known about it. With close examination of the material
it seems likely that it was woven here rather than imported.
There was a considerable production of handwoven fulled
cloth in Ontario, probably much of it mill finished (cf. fig.
2). In the agricultural returns of 1851 many of the farms
listing flannels as a part of their production also list some
fulled cloth.

97 / Quebec. Ile-d'Orléans. Probably mid-19th century
NMM A452-4
Man's suit, fulled and napped twill

The illustration shows the jacket of a three-piece suit of grey napped woollen twill (*étoffe du pays*). The material is fairly coarse, locally spun and woven, and entirely sewn by hand. It is a rare and excellent example of the clothing of rural Quebec

98 / Quebec. Made in Quebec City, and worn on the Ile-d'Orléans. Late 19th century

NMM A451

Man's hooded coat, fulled and napped twill

Natural grey wool (*étoffe du pays*). In the province of Quebec, thousands of yards of heavy woollen materials were woven by the country people for their own garments, but virtually nothing has survived. This coat is late, has a tailor's label 'Beaulieu & Godbout Québec,' is sewn by machine, but is made of the typical cloth of the countryside. Judging from prints and sketches of French Canada, these grey hooded coats and the capotes made from Hudson Bay blankets were the two most usual outdoor winter garments for men throughout the nineteenth century. It is shown here with a *ceinture flêchée*, the plaited sash so typical of Quebec.

99 / Quebec. St-Charles, Cté Bellechasse. About 1810
ROM 961.112.1. Gift of Miss Ninette Lachance
Woman's shawl, 2/2 twill. L. and w. 175cm, plus fringes

Dark indigo blue and natural white wool (exceedingly fine z singles, combed, and of very long staple). The body of the shawl is in a tiny white check on a blue ground, with borders in blue striped and banded in white. It has been made from two widths seamed together and very well matched. The fringe has small groups of threads twisted together; each group was originally held by a tiny knot at the end. This is a truly remarkable production, with superb wool, exquisite spinning, and expert weaving. It was made by the donor's great-great-grandmother Gaumont about 1810, and is the earliest surviving piece of domestic weaving recorded from Quebec. As a shawl, in addition to being useful and decorative, was expected to last a lifetime, everything from the selection of the wool to the final knotting of the fringe was done with the greatest care. Some of the best weaving done in Canada is found among the surviving shawls.

100 / Quebec. Ste-Madeleine, Cté St-Hyacinthe. 1860-80
ROM 970.90.33. Gift of Mrs. John David Eaton. Ex coll. CGC
Woman's shawl, overshot. L. and w. 154cm, plus fringes

All wool, brown warp with black main and pattern wefts
(all z singles), and with two shots of a different heavier
pattern weft at the centre of each unit. These are a yellow
and an orange end plied together. Both the black and brown
wools may be the natural colour of the sheep. The overshot
technique was not traditional in French Quebec, but a cultural borrowing from Scottish settlers. It made its first appearance around the middle of the nineteenth century, and
steadily came into more and more general use. The pattern
here is a simple diaper similar to the draft of no. 188. The
warp has been too closely set to take full advantage of the
technique, an early characteristic, but the pattern is only
slightly elongated. Although the black pattern weft barely
shows against the brown ground, it adds a richness and a
warm texture. The flashes of colour produced by the red
and yellow pattern weft show up as an allover spot pattern
against the dark ground resulting in a subtle and handsome
effect.

101 / Ontario. Winchester Township, Dundas County.
Mid-19th century
ROM 967.69. Gift of Mr Herbert Ide
Woman's shawl, tabby. L. and w. 175cm, plus fringes

All wool, black and natural white (both z singles) woven in
a 'log cabin' colour and weave effect (fig. 6). To produce
the check, the ends are entered one black, one white for 35
threads, and the next check is done in the same order, but
as the sections are always of an uneven number of threads,
two blacks come together at intervals making the order of
colour on the shafts change and when treadled in the same
sequence this indefinite check results. It seems to have been a
particularly popular pattern for shawls; this is a stunning
example of its use with excellent spinning and expert weaving.

102 / Ontario. Perth, Lanark County. 1850-75
ROM 969.10.4. Gift of Mrs J.H. Stewart
Woman's shawl, tabby. L. and w. 176cm, plus fringes

All wool (s singles, double) in red and green in a simple 'log cabin' check similar to fig. 6. The weaving of this shawl is expert, but the spinning is even more remarkable. It is entirely s-spun, very firm and fine and even. The singles yarn used double in both warp and weft gives quite a different handle. As with all women's handwoven shawls this is square: it is made of two widths neatly joined and with the borders matching well.

(*in colour* PLATE I)

103 / Ontario. Holland Landing, York County. First half of the 19th century
ROM 967.276. Gift of Mr and Mrs Harold B. Burnham
Man's shawl, tabby. L. 357cm, plus fringes; w. 136cm

All wool (fine z singles), in natural white and two shades of brownish-green. The body of the shawl is in a 'log cabin' colour and weave effect and is bordered with narrow solid bands of the two colours. Shawls were frequently worn by men during the early and middle parts of the nineteenth century instead of overcoats. They must have been a practical and comfortable garment whether walking or riding, and vivid accounts are given of men bundled up in their great shawls with a top hat perched above. The photograph shows how the great length can be swathed around the shoulders with a final wrapping firmly around the waist and the fringes hanging down. Like the women's shawls, the men's were expected to last a lifetime; the best wool available was spun by the best spinner in the family, and the weaving was always done with the greatest possible care. The draping quality of these old shawls is something that seems to have been lost with the end of handspinning.

104 / Ontario. Vineland area, Lincoln County. About 1836
ROM L965.11.31. The Annie R. Fry Collection
Man's shawl, 2/2 twill. L. 413cm, plus fringes; w. 96cm

All wool (very fine z singles) in dark green and natural white. The warp has been threaded two green, two white, and the weft has been used in narrow bands of four green and four white. When this repeating order is combined with the straight 2/2 twill a most interesting little colour and weave effect results with interlocking toothed bands in the weft. Plain bands and a simple warp fringe have been used at either end. This is not as wide as the previous shawl but is even longer and finer in quality and would have swathed a man most amply and draped beautifully. It was woven by Samuel Fry for his own use and traditionally was made about the same time as the broadcloth for his wedding suit (no. 95).

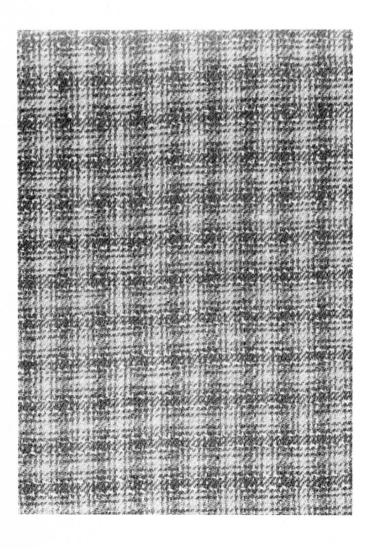

105 / Ontario. Probably Goderich, Huron County. About 1865
ROM 948.11. Gift of Mrs H.J. Cody
Man's shawl, 2/2 twill. L. 350cm, plus fringes; w. 141cm

All wool (fine z singles) with warp of natural beige-grey striped with natural darker grey which has had a little green-dyed fleece carded with it. The darker stripe is broken by two spaced threads which are 3-ply: two natural white singles and a dark grey-green. The weft forms a balanced check with similar but slightly darker yarns. This shawl belonged to the donor's grandfather, the Rev. William S. Blackstock, and is believed to have been woven for him between 1863 and 1868, when he had a church in Goderich. It is another example of the superb spinning and weaving that is found in both men's and women's shawls.

Carpets, blankets, linens

The handwoven textiles produced in eastern Canada, both domestically and professionally until the end of the nineteenth century, were all made in rural areas and with few exceptions were consumed entirely in the countryside. This was equally true of clothing materials, of the textiles required for household needs, and of the coverlets that added a note of warm colour to many an established settler's home. The people in the hamlets and villages were close enough to the farms to follow the same way of life, but the inhabitants of the towns and budding cities developed more sophisticated tastes and preferred imported goods. The fact that many city dwellers today still treasure coverlets and other handwoven pieces that they have inherited is due to the fact that many of the older families in Canada have a farming background somewhere in their past.

In the figures for the earlier census returns, there are categories for flannel, fulled cloth, and linen (fig. 2). All materials in which wool formed a part would be included in the first two, and all varieties of linens from bed ticks through sheeting and the fine materials for clothing to the simply patterned ones for towels and tablecloths would have been in the third category. Homespuns, plain and checked, druggets, plain and banded, and wool carpeting would have been listed under flannel, as well as special items of limited production such as coverlets. Blanketing might have been included with them as well, or under fulled cloth. Some blankets were certainly lightly milled to give them more body; the lighter ones used as winter sheets were not. It is no longer certain in which of the categories they would have been listed; it is possible that the decision often devolved on the individual enumerator.

The only floor coverings available to settlers at first were the skins of animals obtained through hunting and it was not until there was a surplus of wool available that anyone could dream of anything more decorative. Once this point was reached, the most popular carpeting in Ontario and the Maritime Provinces was the warp-faced type with gaily coloured stripes. It was similar to the Venetian carpeting manufactured in England, which is described as 'a common make of carpet, usually striped, in which the warp alone shows.' It might be mentioned that this carpeting has no connection with Venice; the term is a purely arbitrary trade name to enhance its sales appeal and to make it seem slightly exotic and more desirable.

The warp-faced carpeting was woven as yardage and strips were sewn together to cover the floors of parlours and sometimes other rooms. With greater prosperity as the nineteenth century passed the midway mark, and as more wool could be spared, it was used throughout some houses. The earliest reference that has been found is in a letter written in 1828 to relations in England by Mary O'Brien from Richmond Hill, Ontario, shortly after her arrival in Canada (Miller, 17). She was staying with her brother who had come out a few years before and had established a small flock of sheep. Just before Mary O'Brien arrived her sister-in-law had 'laboriously spun wool for a carpet. This is to be sent home shortly and will cost thirty shillings more than a bought carpet would have done, and she will be less housewifely in future.' This cost is more than a little puzzling, but probably the price that would have been obtained for the wool is included in the estimate. No examples of handwoven carpeting of as early a date appear to have survived; virtually all that are known show the presence of chemical dyes that precludes a date earlier than the 1860s. Floor coverings have always been subjected to hard usage, and wearing out was the inevitable fate of almost all that was woven.

Most of this carpeting was gaily patterned with bright stripes (nos. 106–13). A weft of cotton yarn or salvaged cotton cloth strips was usual. Due to the combination of the two fibres, the name drugget was sometimes used to describe it, a transfer of term that was more usual in the Maritime Provinces than elsewhere. From the many fragments and the fewer room-sized pieces that have survived, there is no question about the popularity of this floor covering.

Although strips of cloth were sometimes used as weft in wool carpeting, another type was woven on a cotton warp with the cotton rag predominating. There is a very strong misconception current that this type was widely used as floor covering from the early days of settlement, but cotton textiles had to be imported and were naturally scarce and expensive. They were not relegated to the rag bag until they had served a long and useful life. A sufficient hoard would not have been built until around the middle of the nineteenth century. In any case, the first call on the better parts of the materials would have been for patchwork quilts. There are a few entries in the account book of John Campbell of Komoka in the 1860s for weaving rag carpeting, but they are far outweighed by the orders for wool carpeting.

Little rag carpeting is known from the Maritime Provinces, where hooked mats were greatly preferred. In Ontario it was quite widely used by the less prosperous. This was particularly true in the latter part of the nineteenth century as the necessary skills for spinning wool steadily died out.

In Quebec, where the term catalogne is now used, the same holds true despite the wide use in the present century of this type of carpeting as a rustic floor covering. Material of this type woven with woollen rags had long been used in both Quebec and Acadia as bed coverings. A French dictionary of 1852 fails to mention the term catalogne, but another published in 1878 defines it as a bedcovering of wool. In 1894, in a dictionary published on this side of the Atlantic, it is described as 'a type of household carpet, made by families of all sorts of small leftovers, and which is especially used in the countryside' (Séguin, 390). As pointed out in the descriptions of the two catalogne lengths (nos. 121–2), both would be more suitable as bed coverings than as carpeting.

Carpeting in overshot weave was made, but it is a construction unsuited to heavy wear. Although only fragments have survived, there is evidence of its use both from examples and from drafts. On the basis of the few pieces that have been recorded, it seems probable that many had a coloured ground that would have soiled less easily than white.

A few more complex examples of carpet weaving are known. The one in twill diaper is the only example that has been seen, even though the construction would be ideal for the purpose woven of heavy wools (no. 126). A few jac-quard-woven pieces have been recorded that are obviously for such a purpose, but by the time they were made competition from the local carpet industry was already keen (nos. 127, 479).

No handwoven materials that were made to be used as curtains are known except for some lengths in overshot weave of the late nineteenth century from Nova Scotia. Undoubtedly more fashionable houses in towns and cities had curtains of imported materials that could be drawn for privacy and comfort, but in the countryside this was not necessary and they were not used. The privacy of farmhouses was ensured by their isolation and, until the advent of electricity, every scrap of daylight was valued and treasured. Most old farmhouses were equipped with shutters that would close out the glare and heat of summer, as well as darken the bedrooms when the days were long. A study of interior woodwork surrounding many old windows clearly shows that the fine mouldings and detail were never meant to be hidden. Even in winter, curtains were not needed to cut off draughts in the evening; in the country, people went to bed early and rose before the sun. In kitchens, the bright glare was sometimes lessened by blinds, but it was preferable to keep the windows open; wood-fired stoves rendered these fittings less serviceable than decorative.

In addition to the large amounts of carpeting that were woven particularly during the latter half of the nineteenth century and that have now vanished, an even greater quantity of blanketing was produced. Like the linen used for sheets, most of this was quite plain, and decidedly unphotogenic. Occasionally an initialled or dated blanket is found; a tabby one is shown to represent this vast group (no. 137). Many of the earlier blankets appear to have been woven in this way: twill ones became more usual at a later period. The reason was to conserve wool supplies; a greater amount of the same weight of yarn is needed for twill than for tabby to produce a well woven piece of the same width and length. In twill the warp must be more closely set and the weft packs down more firmly. All of these early handwoven blankets were of two widths joined by a centre seam. A few from the latter part of the nineteenth century were woven double-width using a flying shuttle.

If a blanket was decorated, the most usual method was the simple coloured bands across the ends. In the Scottish areas, a different tradition was followed – coloured stripes ran down each side. Both gay and simple checks were popular for blankets to add a note of colour and are found in a wide variety often used for patterned twills such as bird's-eye or goose-eye. With really colourful blankets, it is now difficult to know which were for household use and which for horses, but some of the heavier ones were undoubtedly for the latter purpose.

The lighter pieces were winter sheets to be used in cold weather instead of linen ones. Many of these were plain and were often woven on a fine cotton warp. In some areas, particularly around Waterloo County, they were always of wool brightened by being checked like many of the homespun clothing materials. A quilt with the set made from a winter sheet shows the type clearly (no. 134).

Most of the linen raised, processed, and woven in eastern Canada was for the immediate use of the families concerned, and varied from the coarsest grades to those suitable for clothing. It was woven in many parts of the country from an early period, but this production steadily died out almost everywhere except in Quebec where it was continued into the present century. When there was a surplus of the finer grades, as happened in this province, it found a ready outlet in the urban markets for shirts and underclothing, and for sheeting.

Until well into the ninetenth century, linen was the preferred material for sheets, and these come in a wide range of qualities woven in two widths with a centre seam. A few initialled sheets and pillowcases have been recorded that are dated in the 1820s and 1830s, but by far the greater part is perfectly plain with simple neat hems at both ends.

The simple weaves for patterned linens have already been discussed, and the purposes for which they were used will be seen in the illustrations. So little of this material has survived that it is difficult to know how much was produced, and most of the examples recorded in Canada are shown. A great deal must have worn out in daily use, and much of what was left probably went into bandages during the Great War of 1914–18.

The twill diaper construction is discussed in the section on coverlets using this technique (fig. 38), but it is also known from linens woven in Ontario. A few examples have been seen in Nova Scotia, but it appears more likely that they were brought from Scotland than woven in Canada. In Ontario, it was probably brought by German weavers who emigrated or who reached here as part of the Mennonite tradition from Pennsylvania, where the weave was popular (ROM 956.147.3; 959.274.1). Its use for household linens has a long history in Europe, both on the continent and in Great Britain. Examples in Toronto come from England (ROM 945.24.7; 970.115.1), Scotland (ROM 968.259.2; 968.271), France (ROM 920.34.1), The Netherlands (ROM 963.9.57, .58), and Switzerland (ROM 969.187.2, .3), either in this technique or the related damask diaper. The same patterns were used for both and were equally suitable for doublecloth.

Designs composed of up to six blocks are found in the pattern book that Wilhelm Magnus Werlich brought from Germany about 1850, in a number of pattern books, both printed and manuscript ones, in Germanisches National-Museum, Nürnberg, and in one in Historisches Museum, Bern. This last is dated 1855 and represents almost the end of a long tradition. All of these show tie-ups for both twill and damask diaper. One with dates from 1775 to 1782, but possibly going back to about 1760, belonged to William Jones of Holt, Denbighshire, Wales, a parish just inside the Welsh border with Cheshire. It was formerly in St Chad's Church there, but is now in the National Library of Wales with a copy at the Welsh Folk Museum at St Fagans near Cardiff. The patterns which also use up to six blocks are often considered to be for doublecloth, the Welsh *carthenni*, but all the tie-ups accompanying them are for straight and broken twill diapers, indicating that William Jones was more than probably a linen weaver.

Multiple-shaft point twill linens have not been found in Canada. They are known from the Mennonite areas of Pennsylvania, and there are drafts for them on loose sheets with Samuel Fry's pattern book. Some examples may yet be found, but like damask diaper ones, they call for fine yarn, which may well have been reserved for weaving the better quality linens for clothing materials.

106 / Ontario. Jellyby, Leeds County. About 1870-5
ROM 965.214. Gift of Mrs Ethel Stewart
Length of carpet, warp-faced tabby. L. 115cm; w. 90cm

Multicoloured wool warp (s, 2z) with brown cotton weft
(z, 4s). This type of carpeting with wool warp almost hiding
the weft was the usual handwoven floor covering in the
Maritime Provinces and Ontario. Wefts vary; in this piece
a dark cotton yarn has been used producing a fairly fine
material. As it is firmly woven it would have been durable
once fastened to the floor and properly padded with straw,
reeds, corn husks, seaweed, or newspapers. Commercial dyes
were available by the time it was woven; the stripes are
strong in a considerable range of colours: purple, yellow,
dark and light orange, and with a wide central stripe in
shades of brown centred with black; on one side a wide stripe
shades from pink to dark red, and on the other a similar one
from pale green to blue. As in most of these carpets, the repeat
is carefully arranged so that the widths can be sewn together
unobtrusively to make a room-sized piece without obvious
joins. The wool, which is spun and plied in the opposite direction to normal, was prepared by Mrs James Langry, grandmother of the donor, and taken to a professional weaver at
Jellyby. It must often have been a puzzle for the weaver to
take the set amounts of yarn supplied to him by the housewife in different strong colours and to produce an attractive
combination, using what was given to him without running
short of any essential colour while warping. This piece was
used in a house at Carleton Place.

107 / Ontario. Spencerville, Grenville County. About 1870
ROM 968. 202.15. Gift of Mr and Mrs Harold B. Burnham
Carpet (part), warp-faced tabby. L. 163cm; w. 170cm

Wool warp (z, 2s) almost covering brown cotton weft (z,
4s). Striped in shades of grey and tan with three narrow
stripes of bright red enclosing two striking sections threaded
alternately one yellow, one black. This is another example
of the popular carpeting, with top quality spinning and dyeing done at home, woven by one of the many professional
weavers who operated in almost all localities in Ontario.

(*in colour* PLATE I)

108 / Ontario. Near Cameron, Victoria County. About 1878
ROM 948.225. Gift of Mrs Ralph W. Dowson
Length of carpet, warp-faced tabby. L. 125cm; w. 75cm

Fairly coarse multicoloured wool (z, 2s) covering heavy
dark cotton rags. The wool was spun and dyed, and the
weaving done by the donor's mother. It is an excellent example of a domestic production that has produced an attractive and durable material. The stripes use red-brown for the
main colour, with narrower ones in red, green, blue, black,
and white, but the interest centres on the narrow 'picket
fence' effect (cf. fig. 7) in yellow and black. It is simple and
effective.

109 / Nova Scotia. Lunenburg County. 1870-80
ROM 970.90.25. Gift of Mrs John David Eaton
Width of carpet, warp-faced tabby. L. 80cm; w. 60cm

Multicoloured wool warp (z, 2s) covering white cotton
rags. The warp is in red, orange, and yellow, using natural
wools in white, brownish-grey, and black for the main stripes.

Only about half the wool would have required dyeing and
yet the effect is very colourful, with a different variation of
'picket fence' patterning. Black sheep were treasured because
their fleece could be used without dyeing.

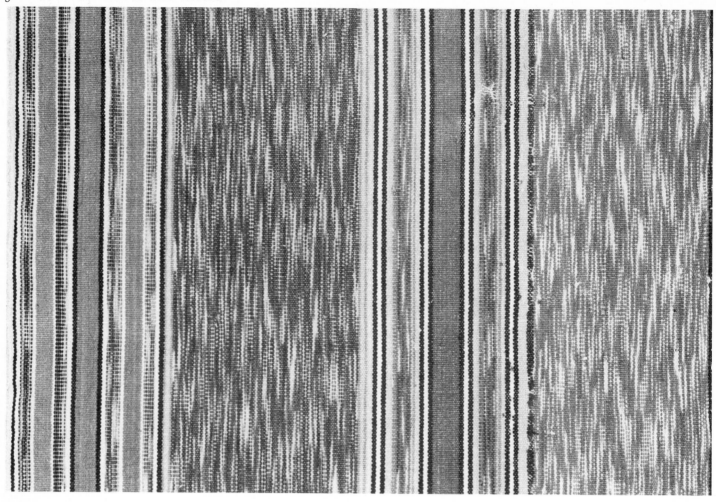

110 / Ontario. Ridgetown, Kent County. About 1875
ROM 949.228. Gift of Mrs H.E. Fries
Width of carpet, warp-faced tabby with ikat stripes. L. 66cm;
w. 86cm

Multicoloured wool warp (z, 2s) almost covering the weft
of natural white cotton (z, 4s). The warp is very gay with
narrow stripes in black, white, yellow, mauve, purple, red,
and blue, and with two wide stripes, one combining green
and yellow, and the other red and white. These were produced by a technique known as ikat. The skeins of yarn were
wrapped tightly at intervals with cotton rags or cords to
protect that part of the wool from the dye. The skein was

then immersed in the dye bath, and when removed and the
ties taken off, sections which were protected remained the
original colour (no. 60). When wool treated in this way was
used for the warp of a carpet, the result was an attractive
broken splashed effect. The yellow and green stripe was produced in two stages; first the wool was dyed yellow, then
wrapped to protect parts of it and dyed with green. Shading
occurred due to leakage at the edges of the ties, producing
variations from light to dark. This carpeting covered the
floors of the home of the donor's grandmother, whose daughter, Miss Elizabeth Green, prepared the yarns. A room-sized
piece of the same carpeting is also in the Royal Ontario
Museum (ROM 951.18).

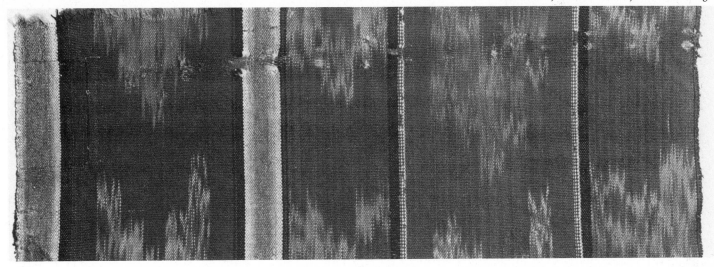

111 / New Brunswick. Pointe du Bute, Westmorland County.
Late 19th century
Keillor House, Dorchester, NB
Carpet, warp-faced tabby with ikat stripes. Room size.
Weaving width 90cm

Coloured wool warp (z, 2s) almost covering dark grey cotton weft (z, 4s). Wide bold stripes of brown, green, and dark red spaced by guards in black, white, and natural shades of grey wool. The splashed ikat motifs are more complex than in no. 110. All the skeins have been dyed at least twice. The red and brown ones have alternating colours of motifs requiring two separate wrappings. In warping, the threads were arranged so that the reserved parts produced effective arrow-like forms regularly spaced down the length. It was woven by Miss Carrie Read, a professional weaver at Pointe de Bute.

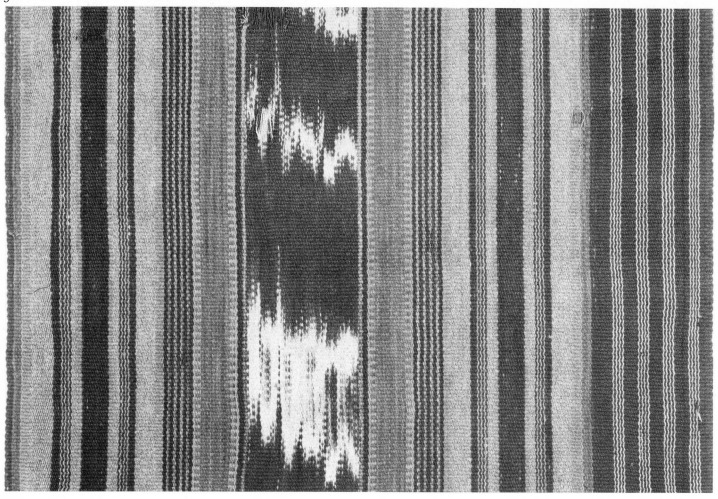

112 / Ontario. North Elmsley Township, Lanark County. 1876-95
ROM 949.36.9. Gift of Miss Bessie Farmer
Length of carpet, warp-faced tabby with ikat stripe.
L. 147cm; w. 96cm

Multicoloured wool warp (z, 3s) entirely covering the weft of grey cotton (z, 4s). The stripes are in grey, dark green, blue, yellow, purple, and red with two wide stripes which would alternate boldly when the widths of carpeting were sewn together. One stripe is brown with groups of pinstripes in pink, and the other red with a strong ikat pattern reserved in white. This length was woven by Elizabeth McNab between 1876 and 1895. She was the granddaughter of Duncan McNab, the weaver of nos. 79 and 173. The wool warp appears to be machine spun, but the dyeing with commercial dyes was undoubtedly done at home.

113 / Ontario. Near Gananoque, Leeds County. About 1890
ROM 964.15. Gift of Mrs Ward Alfred Davenport
Length of carpet, warp-faced tabby with ikat stripe.
L. 112cm; w. 64cm

Brightly coloured wool warp (z, 2s) hiding the weft of beige
cotton (z, 2s, double). The reserved areas of the wide, ikat
stripe were not tied firmly, and with one dyeing in bright red
a splashed pattern has been produced strongly shaded in
pinks. On both sides are guards in natural brownish-black
wool and wide stripes in shades of yellow. At the outer edges,
there are narrow ones in the same colours with the addition
of mauve. The wool was prepared by Mrs William J. Nuttal,
the donor's grandmother, at South Lake.

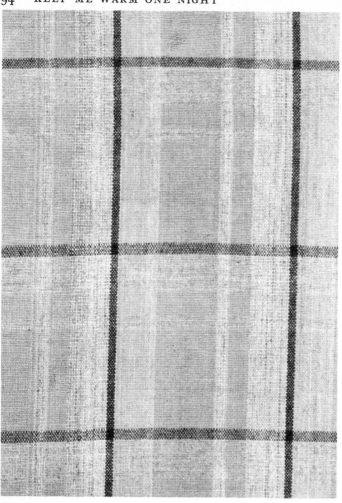

114 / Prince Edward Island. East Cape, King's County.
1840-60
CAGM. Gift of Mr and Mrs Willard Ching
Carpet, tabby. Three lengths; weaving width 88cm

All wool (z, 2s) checked in brown, red, and green with over-check in black. This type of carpeting with a balanced tabby weave in all wool is an old type that has only been seen in Prince Edward Island. The wool appears to be combed rather than carded and the brown dye is probably crotal, both facts pointing to a fairly early date. Its discovery was one of those magic moments that come very occasionally to the researcher. We had spent the most wonderful day with the late George Leard and his wife, going from house to house on the East Cape visiting everybody that he thought might have material to show us, or information that would help fill in the picture. Finally, in the early evening, we arrived at the Willard Chings and they took us to an abandoned house well back from the road on a farm they had bought. Some years before, the house had been vacated because of termites and the furnishings left in place for fear of contaminating other surroundings. It was one of those glorious evenings that seem clearest on the East Cape, but dusk was setting in and the little house was full of ghosts. In the fading afterglow, it was possible to distinguish the first old handwoven carpeting that we had ever seen still on the floor for which it was made.

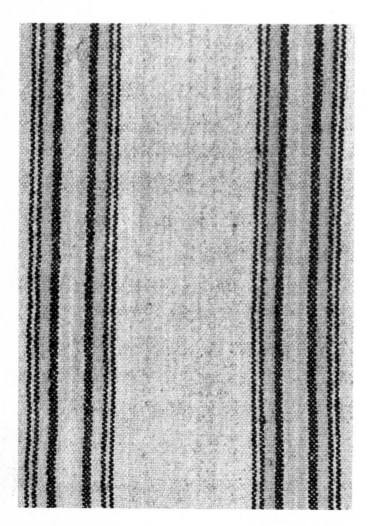

115 / Prince Edward Island. East Cape, King's County.
Mid-19th century
ROM 967.291.4. Gift of Miss June Biggar
Carpet fragment, tabby. L. 42cm; w. 64cm

All wool (z, 2s), soft brownish-yellow with warp almost covering the weft and with groups of stripes in light red, pale green, and black. The dye used for the brownish-yellow is said to have been maple crotal. This came from a house near Souris.

116 / Prince Edward Island. Probably Prince County.
1865-75
ROM 968.308.11. Gift of Mr and Mrs Harold B. Burnham
Four pieces of carpet, twill. Weaving width 91cm

All wool (z singles); the warp has wide beige stripes and
narrower ones of purple, blue, and yellow. In the weft, the
purple, blue, and yellow are banded in the same proportions,
while the beige is replaced by black, giving a 'salt and pepper'
effect. The weave has been threaded and treadled as a plain
twill, but the tie-up has been altered, as shown in the draft.
The result is a weave that has shots of tabby alternating with
shots of twill, producing a fabric that is firm and reversible.
Among old Canadian fabrics surprisingly few broken twills
have been found. This piece survived as upholstery, but was
probably woven as carpeting. The old man from whom it
was bought remembered that his grandparents' bed was
hung with curtains not unlike this in colour and weight.

 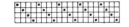

117 / Nova Scotia. Cape North, Cape Breton. Late 19th
century
Mackley Collection, Sydney, NS
Carpet fragment, warp-faced tabby. L. 22cm; w. 27cm

Wool warp (z singles) alternately red and black except when
the colour changes where two red threads are used side by
side. The weft is alternately black wool (z singles) and fine
light blue cotton (z singles), also used alternately except
when two picks of black in succession make a colour change.
This is a simple but effective colour and weave effect explained by fig. 6, but in this piece the result is emphasized by
the use of weft threads of contrasting weight producing a
strong rib.

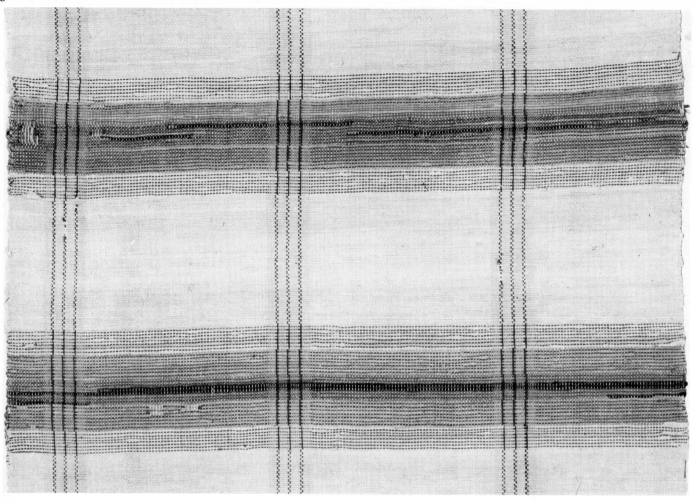

118 / Ontario. Warminster, Simcoe County. Early 20th century
ROM 947.80.2. Gift of Mr and Mrs Harold B. Burnham
Length of rag carpet, tabby. L. 337cm; w. 87cm

Cotton warp alternately pale green and pink, with light brown stripes at intervals (all z, 4s) broken by double ends of olive wool. In the brown stripes the warp is set twice as close as in the ground. The weft is basically grey and pink cotton cloth strips, with bands of brown cotton yarn used alternately with beige cloth strips to produce a colour and weave effect.

At the start of the Museum's textile research project in 1947, one of the first calls made was on the old professional weaver, Addie Mick, who wove this piece. We were nervous, as we were new at this kind of thing and did not know how we would be received. We were welcomed at the gate with the words, 'I was just praying that God would send me a visitor today.' At that time she was 85; she stood tall and slim with her grey hair pulled back in a little neat bun, her white shirt and pink apron spotless, and her legs seemingly quite ageless in faded blue jeans. That visit was memorable – in the course of four or five hours all sorts of information on the life of a professional weaver came between periods of reading the Bible to her. She had two looms, both with only two shafts. Her mother, who had come from Ireland as a young woman, had been a weaver, and she herself had woven all her life. In her time the only thing for which there had been a demand in the area where she lived was rag carpeting, and she had spent nearly seventy years weaving it. Eventually she brought out her treasured box of samples, and as she showed them it was evident that even this very limited medium was not able to curtail or hinder her artistic expression. With a weaver like Addie Mick, more things can be done with a rag carpet than the average weaver would dream possible.

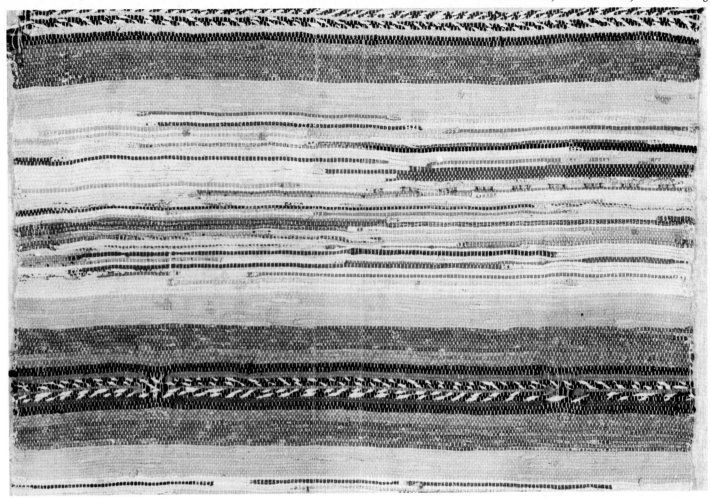

119 / Ontario. Indian River, Otonabee Township, Peterborough County. Late 19th century
ROM 954.95.4. Gift of Mrs Wilbert W. Graham
Width of rag carpet, tabby. L. 150cm; w. 86cm

Natural white cotton warp (z, 4s) with weft of varying coloured cotton cloth strips, both plain and printed, used hit and miss to form the ground. Blue bands at regular intervals are centred by twisted strips in black and white that make an arrow pattern between black and pink guards. Thousands and thousands of yards of rag carpeting have been woven in Canada from the latter part of the nineteenth century to the present day. People prepared their own rags and took them to a weaver. This was the last profitable production with which the local professional craftsmen could compete against the increasing industrialization. Informant after informant has told the same tale and surviving handlooms confirm it. Coverlet looms of more or less complexity were converted to two-shaft ones used solely for weaving rag carpets.

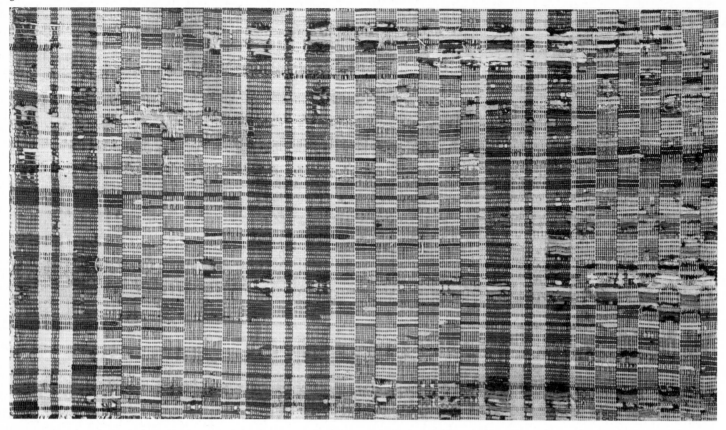

120 / Ontario. Oxford County. 1880-90
ROM 949.155.2. Gift of Mr John Wood
Width of rag carpet, tabby. L. 50cm; w. 92cm

Brown and white cotton warp (z, 4s) threaded alternately
light and dark, then dark and light with solid stripes at intervals. Woven with green cotton used alternately with rags of
different colours. By putting two shots of rag in succession

the colour emphasis in the warp changed. This is a colour
and weave effect similar to no. 117. As in most carpeting the
placing of the stripes is cleverly arranged so that lengths can
be sewn together unobtrusively to make a room-sized piece.

121 / Quebec. Ile-aux-Coudres, Cté Charlevoix.
About 1900
ROM 970.90.24. Gift of Mrs John David Eaton
Length of rag carpet, tabby (catalogne). L. 453cm; w. 87cm

Natural linen warp (z singles), with wide bands of cloth
strips in light colours alternating with stronger ones, mainly
blue. These are separated by narrow triple bands in red, light
green, and burnt orange jute. The colours are muted and
harmonious. It is not too old, but is in the best tradition of
Quebec catalogne weaving. The handspun linen warp adds
immeasurably to the quality of the piece. It is almost too fine
for a floor, and was possibly planned as a bed covering, the
earlier use for such weaving in Quebec. If cut in half and
seamed together it would be the right size for this purpose.

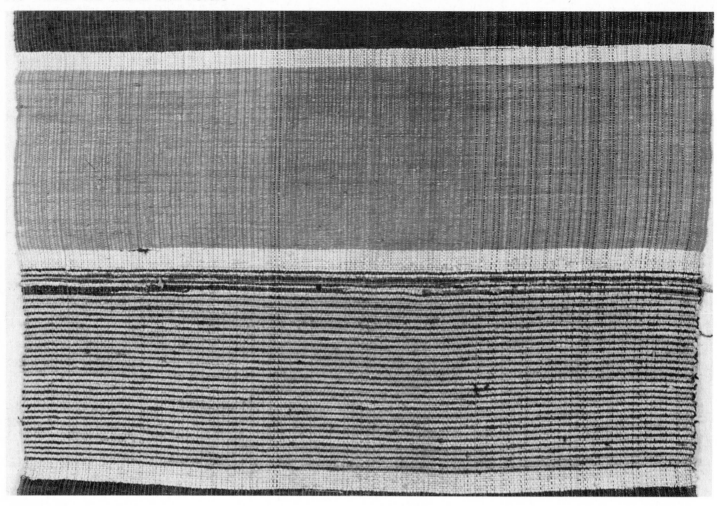

122 / Quebec. Pis-Sec, Baie-St-Paul, Cté Charlevoix.
About 1925
ROM 970.90.26. Gift of Mrs John David Eaton
Length of carpet, tabby. L. 350cm; w. 87cm

Warp of cotton (fine z, 2s) in three wide stripes, the central
one in two shades of green, and the outer in three shades of
brown. The colours in each stripe have been mixed in warping, and were dented irregularly. The weft is in three repeating wide bands, separated by guards of white cotton strips.

They are dark brown cowhair obtained at a local tannery
and spun by hand, green jute, and two shots of dark wool
used alternately with two of light cloth strips. From simple
materials an effective piece has been made.

123 / Nova Scotia. Indian Point, Lunenburg County.
About 1850
ROM 966.158.32. Gift of Mr and Mrs Harold B. Burnham
Width of carpet, overshot. L. 95cm; w. 76cm

Brown wool on yellow-brown cotton (all z, 2s). The over-shot weave, best known from coverlets, was used extensively for carpeting, but very little survives. While doing fieldwork in the Maritime Provinces in the summer of 1966, driving through Lunenburg, we spotted a battered piece of overshot weave on the front doorstep of a house. A quick stop was made and the owner of the house was a little startled when enquiries were made about her doormat. After an explana-tion was given, she said that she had another piece put away. She had obtained a full room-sized carpet at a country auc-tion many years before and knew that it had been woven at Indian Point. Her small mat and this piece were all that remained. The pattern is a variation of 'Monmouth' (no. 258), the most common of all overshot patterns.

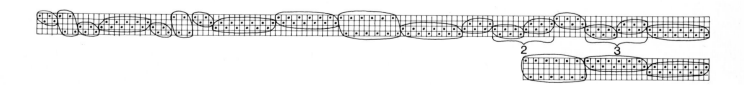

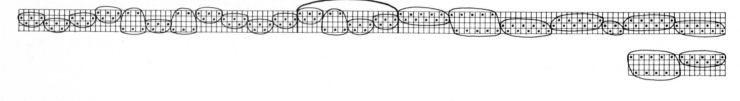

124 / Ontario. Probably Grey County. 1885-90
ROM 968.326. Gift of Mrs John Harrison
Width of carpet, overshot. L. 211cm; w. 70cm

Indigo blue wool (z, 2s) on natural white cotton (warp and main weft z, 3s). Although this is believed to have been woven as a coverlet, it was taken about 1900 by the family of the donor's mother to Saskatchewan, where it was used as a carpet. The heavier cottons of the ground made it very suitable for the purpose. The pattern is a further variation of 'Monmouth' (cf. no. 268), but the four blocks marked at the right of the draft have been omitted on the left giving a curious lopsided effect.

While travelling in Nova Scotia, we were told of bedrooms that had been furnished with overshot coverlets and carpeting in matched patterns, but sometimes in different colours.

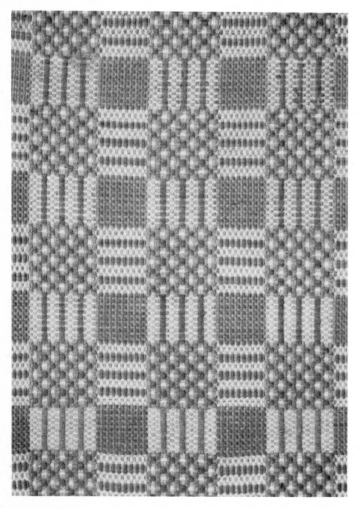

125 / New Brunswick. About 1850-75
King's Village Pioneer Settlement, Prince William, NB
M68.73.1
Carpet, overshot. L. 235cm; w. 210cm

Wool, golden-brown and light chartreuse green, on cotton that has faded but was probably red (all z, 2s). Overshot weave with a coloured ground is rare, and its use here supports the statement that this rather heavy piece was a carpet, rather than a coverlet. This allover pattern of squares has almost the appearance of tiles and would have looked well in a fairly small room.

Overshot drafts apparently for such a purpose are known: one from Ontario is labelled 'English Carpeting'; another marked 'Carpet' is from Cape Breton (Mackley Collection), where several fragments have been seen. Both were patterns that would have been suitable as floor coverings.

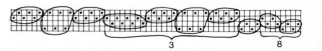

126 / Ontario. Innerkip, East Zorra Township, Oxford County. Late 19th century
ROM 953.159. Gift of Mr D.L. Isbister
Carpet length, twill diaper. L. 212cm, plus added fringes; w. 99cm

All wool (coarse, z, 2s), with beige warp banded in orange-red and blue. This length is even heavier than the horse blankets in this weave, and has a cotton fringe sewn to both ends. The weave is described in the section on multiple-shaft weaving (cf. fig. 38) and requires four shafts for each block of the pattern. As this has four blocks, it could only have been woven on a sixteen-shaft loom. This is a capacity that many of the professional weavers in the Waterloo County area owned; this is certainly the work of one of them. It is the only piece of this type that has been seen, but carpets have only survived by extraordinary chance. Many more of all types were produced than remaining samples suggest. The draft is shown in profile form.

127 / Ontario. Late 19th century
ROM 968.117.2. Gift of Mr and Mrs Harold B. Burnham
Carpet, jacquard. L. 212cm; w. 175cm

Doublecloth, all wool, red and yellow warp (z singles) with
red and black weft (z, 2s), (decoupure 2). This is one of
the few jacquard-woven pieces that has turned up that seems
definitely to have been woven as a floor covering. Other examples of the same design have been seen woven in red wool
and white cotton, a fashionable colour scheme for strip carpeting in the latter part of the nineteenth century. This carpet
shows a late survival of the 'Bird of Paradise' motif combined
with patriotic maple leaves and the Canadian beaver. This
may not be the work of an individual weaver, but may have
been produced by one of the Ontario carpet companies,
which were coming into full operation as the nineteenth century drew to a close. It is similar in type and quality to the
imported scotch ingrain and kidderminster carpeting.

128 / Quebec. St-Pierre, Cté Montmagny. Late 19th century
ROM 970.90.43. Gift of Mrs John David Eaton
Blanket, 2/2 twill. L. 227cm; w. 185cm

All wool (z singles) in natural banded at both ends with
pink. This twill blanket is typical: handwoven in two widths
that are seamed down the centre. It is the normal type in
both French and English traditions. The initials 'A.L.' in
cross stitch in pink wool are those of Amédée Letourneau,
several of whose linens are shown in nos. 153–9.

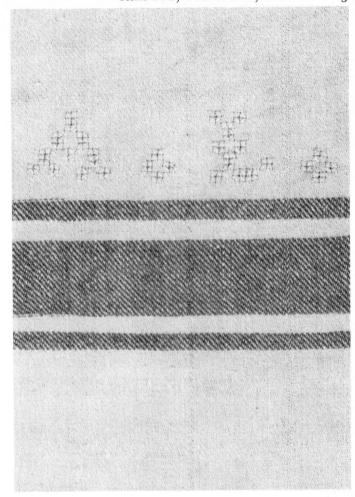

129 / Quebec. Eastern Townships. Second half of the 19th
century
ROM 966.211.23. Gift of Miss Emily Le Baron
Blanket, 2/2 twill. L. 200cm; w. 151cm

All wool (z singles): unevenly dyed grey-purple on natural,
with evenly spaced pairs of narrow stripes in grey-purple.
This unusual colour is not an aniline violet and is of vegetable origin.

130 / Quebec. Village-des-Aulnaies, Cté L'Islet.
Mid-19th century
ROM 970.90.42. Gift of Mrs John David Eaton
Blanket, tabby. L. 264cm; w. 153cm

Natural wool (z singles) with narrow pink and a wide mixed brown and pink band at both ends. The warp is fine, used double, and the weft is also used in pairs. The texture is unusual and pleasant with the fine hard warp of combed wool somewhat covered by the softer weft. This type with doubled warp and weft is probably the forerunner of the well-known 'basket-weave' Murray Bay blankets of the present century. It would be natural for this cottage industry to have been based on a familiar type of Quebec blanketing.

131 / Quebec. St-Tite-des-Caps, Cté Charlevoix.
About 1935
ROM 969.54. Gift of Dr Naomi Jackson Groves and Mrs Gerard Brett
Blanket, tabby. L. 209cm; w. 181cm

Fine cotton warp (z, 2s) in grey and orange separated by narrow white stripes, banded to form a large check with white overcheck in wools of similar colours (fine z singles). This gay and attractive blanket is a late survival of a traditional Quebec type. The orange wool has been dyed in two lots and the colour changes from quite bright to almost terracotta.

132 / Quebec. Second half of the 19th century
ROM 970.90.14. Gift of Mrs John David Eaton. Ex coll. CGC
Blanket, 2/2 twill. L. 212cm; w. 146cm

Natural wool (z singles) banded with medium indigo blue
between terracotta guards. This is a simple utilitarian blanket. It is not too well woven, but the weaver's innate sense of
design has produced an object of considerable artistic worth.
The proportion of the stripes is excellent and the small touch
of treadling most of the narrow bands in the opposite direction to the body of the blanket is imaginative.

133 / Quebec. St-Urbain, Cté Charlevoix. About 1900
ROM 970.90.16. Gift of Mrs John David Eaton. Ex coll. CGC
Blanket, tabby. L. 194cm; w. 180cm

Brown cow hair (fairly fine z singles) striped with pink wool
(fine z singles), woven with weft of lighter brown cow hair
producing a harsh texture. Cow hair was obtained from local
tanneries. Known as 'poor man's wool,' it was used in the
parts of Quebec where sheep's wool was in short supply.

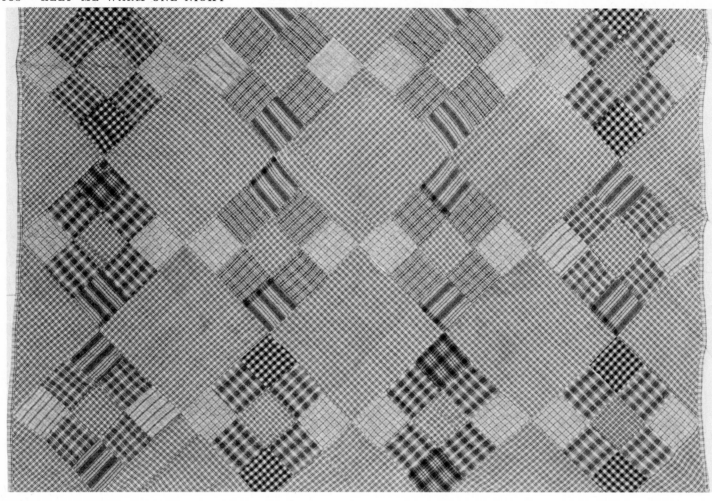

134 / Ontario. Made near Acton, Halton County. 1875-85
ROM 967.316. Gift of Mrs Keith Comfort
Quilt of homespun tabby. L. 195cm; w. 150cm

'Nine-patch' pieces of various checked homespuns set with
squares of black and red check. It is backed with two lengths
of banded homespun in grey with red and blue on a cotton
warp. As many of the patches use red as a basic colour, this
is an unusually bright and attractive example of the quilts
made of handwoven pieces which at one time were common
in the rural homes of Ontario. It has the additional interest
that the small check used for the set comes from a length
which was woven as a winter sheet. Materials woven at home,
lighter than normal blankets, often striped or checked in
quite bright colours, were used in the winter months instead
of linen sheets. Elderly informants give mixed reports of
their warm comfort and the itch which accompanied their
use. (*in colour* PLATE I)

135 / Ontario. Louth Township, Lincoln County.
Mid-19th century
ROM 948.166.2. Gift of Mrs Curtis Haynes
Winter sheet, tabby (fragment). L. 36cm; w. 69cm

Natural wool (z singles) on natural white cotton (z singles).
The fine narrow, red and green stripes which run across the
top and down the side, making a check at the corner, are of
two coloured threads used alternately with two natural ones.
The weight is suitable for a winter sheet, but this might also
have been used as a light blanket in summer.

136 / Ontario. North Grimsby Township, Lincoln County.
1820-40
ROM 964.204. Gift of Miss Elizabeth J. Smith
Winter sheet, 2/2 lozenge twill (fragment). L. 55cm;
w. 94cm

All wool (z singles): checked in rust-red and medium indigo
blue in a goose-eye pattern. The quality of the wool is remarkable: with the pattern units centred on the stripes, the
decorative effect and the handle are exceptionally fine. The
intention appears to have been as the draft is shown but
many of the units have got slightly off centre in the threading.

 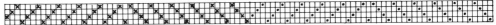

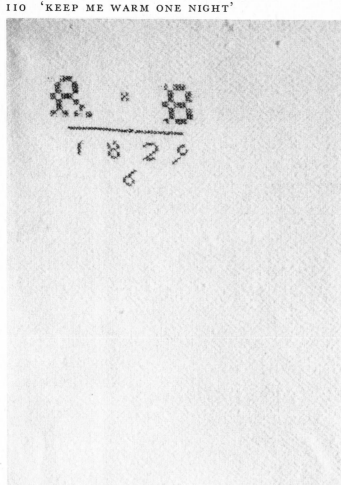

137 / Ontario. Prince Edward County, dated 1829
ROM 968.320. Gift of Miss H.M. Armour
Blanket, tabby. L. 208cm; w. 176cm

Fine natural wool (z singles) of excellent quality, with initials 'R.B.,' the date '1829,' and the number '6' embroidered in cross stitch in dark grey silk beside the centre seam. The initials stand for Rebecca Barker, an ancestress of the donor, and the number means that this was the sixth blanket for her trousseau. Other blankets of hers are at Upper Canada Village. Judging from the dates and numbers on them, it appears that not more than one blanket a year was woven, and each one put aside in preparation for her marriage in 1843. This would have been all the wool that could be spared from the everyday demands of the family.

138 / Ontario. Waterdown, Wentworth County.
About 1855
ROM 967.305.2. Gift of Mr and Mrs Hugh Flatt
Blanket, 2/2 herringbone twill. L. 218cm; w. 182cm

Natural wool (fine z singles) on natural white cotton (z singles). At each juncture, where the line of the herringbone turns, there is quite an obvious line. This is one of the small subtleties that can make an effective weave out of something basically simple. The warp has been taken through the reed in pairs except at these points, where three ends are in one dent, making a slight ridge with a tiny space on either side. The denting is marked on the accompanying draft. Each repeat of the pattern occupies one inch, showing that a reed with 14 dents to the inch was used.

139 / Ontario. Deseronto, Tyendinaga Township,
Hastings County. About 1857
ROM 969.246.1. Gift of Miss Grace Worts
Blanket, 2/2 twill. L. 188cm; w. 190cm

All wool (warp, s singles; weft, z singles), natural with
herringbone side borders in dark indigo blue. The two twists
of yarn give a good handle, coupled with excellent spinning
and firm weaving. Of special interest are the side borders
and the absence of bands across the ends. This is a feature
usual in Scotland, where many blankets were woven to be
used on box beds, and side borders would be quite noticeable.
Another interesting point is that the herringbone threading
breaks at every point as in fig. 12. This is normal in traditional Scottish blankets. It is an ancient form of patterning
stemming from the use of the vertical warp-weighted loom
in northern Europe (cf. Hoffmann). The draft is shown with
the border threaded from the right and an indefinite number
of natural threads for the centre of the blanket.

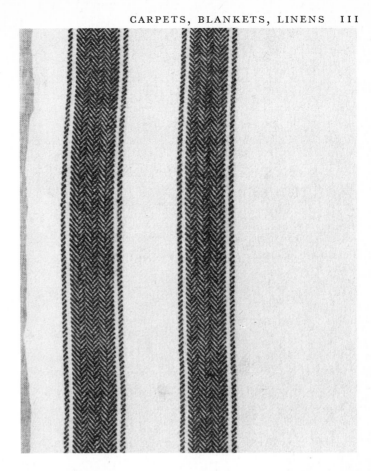

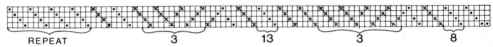

REPEAT   3   13   3   8

140 / Ontario. Glen Morris, Brant County.
Mid-19th century
ROM 969.66.3. Gift of Mrs Edgar J. Stone
Blanket, 2/2 twill. L. 194cm; w. 183cm

All wool (s singles), natural with check and side borders in
very dark indigo blue. As in the previous example the borders
are in the Scottish tradition with a broken herringbone. The
rest of the blanket is straight twill. A fine point of designing
shows up: checks always look better if they are slightly higher
than wide. The large squares are woven this way, and in the
draft it can be seen that the narrow vertical stripes consist
of eleven threads, a rather strange number. They have been
crossed by a matching band of twelve picks, the one-thread
difference being just enough to make the check a pleasant,
slightly elongated form. The draft shows the complete
threading of half the blanket starting on the right at the
centre seam.

6   44   4   22

141 / Ontario. Vineland, Clinton Township, Lincoln County. Mid-19th century
ROM L965.11.12. The Annie R. Fry Collection
Blanket, 2/2 twill. L. 215cm; w. 192cm

All wool (z singles), natural checked with indigo blue. The check is on quite a fine scale with a repeat of 44 natural, 22 blue, 22 natural, 22 blue in the warp and, as the weave is balanced, to make the checks slightly longer than wide, it has been woven 48 natural, 24 blue, 24 natural, and 24 blue in the weft. Both the quality of the yarn and the evenness of the weaving are superb. This is one of several similar blankets woven by Samuel Fry for the use of his own family.

142 / Ontario. Prince Edward County. Early 19th century
ROM 970.196.1. Gift of Mrs. Edgar J. Stone
Blanket, 2/2 twill. L. 206cm, plus knotted fringe; w. 198cm

Natural white cotton (z, 3s) and indigo blue wool (heavy s singles) forming a bold check. This type of blanket combining wool and heavy, very white cotton of beautiful quality, is an early type. Such blankets are now quite rare. They were made when wool was still in very short supply. As it became more plentiful, they were replaced by all wool ones. These blankets were probably the work of trained weavers who came to Canada at the time of the American Revolution, rather than a domestic production.

143 / Ontario. Hallowell Township, Prince Edward County.
1840-60
ROM 968.202.3. Gift of Mrs. Edgar J. Stone
Blanket, 2/2 twill. L. 219cm, plus knotted fringe; w. 190cm

All wool (s singles), natural checked with dark green, pale
pink, rust-red, and medium indigo blue. As there are errors
in the threading and the centre seam does not match, this is
probably a domestic production. It is a well-proportioned
pattern, showing that care and thought were taken to make
even such a utilitarian thing into a pleasure to possess.

144 / Ontario. Picton, Prince Edward County. 1825-50
ROM 969.220.5. Gift of Mrs Edgar J. Stone
Blanket, 2/2 twill. L. 203cm; w. 178cm

Wool (z, 2s) which has probably been dyed black, but is
now olive-brown, striped and banded with red, and with an
overcheck of natural white cotton. Here the cotton has
probably been used for artistic reasons to give the strong
contrast needed with the colours, rather than to eke out an
inadequate wool supply.

145 / Ontario. Vineland, Clinton Township, Lincoln County. 1840-60
ROM L965.11.16. The Annie R. Fry Collection
Blanket, 2/2 lozenge twill. L. 208cm, plus knotted fringe; w. 198cm

All wool (z, 2s) checked in dark indigo blue and red, with overcheck in pale blue, and woven in a small bird's-eye pattern. The striping is carefully arranged so that the change of colour always coincides with the centre of the doubled threads that are at the point of each pattern unit. The blanket was woven by Samuel Fry of Vineland for his own use, and his initials 'S F' have been embroidered at the centre seam towards one end. It is well woven and beautifully designed. Another bird's-eye blanket woven by him is in the ROM (L965.11.17). It is different in colour, but similar in weight and appearance. Interestingly enough it is woven on a different bird's-eye threading similar to no. 146.

(*in colour* PLATE I)

146 / Ontario. Waterloo County. Collected at Elmira.
1840-60
ROM 967.220.4. Gift of Mrs. Edgar J. Stone
Blanket, 2/2 lozenge twill. L. 197cm, plus fringe; w. 173cm

All wool (z, 2s) checked in dark indigo blue and bright red
with overcheck in pale blue. This has a small bird's-eye pattern similar in appearance to no. 145. It is also expertly
woven and the work of an excellent craftsman, but is not
quite as carefully planned. The stripes have no relation to the
threading. This is a very small point, but the total effect is
not as good as in the Fry blanket where the change of colour
always coincides neatly with the doubled threads.

 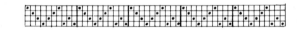

147 / Ontario. Probably Waterloo County. 1850-75
ROM 963.189. Gift of Mrs Edgar J. Stone
Blanket, 2/2 lozenge twill. L. 201cm; w. 173cm

All wool, checked in natural and indigo blue in a bird's-eye
pattern. All the yarn is singles with the warp spun s and the
weft z, in accordance with old traditions. For general spinning with the great wheel, the band that drove the spindle
was put on in a simple circular manner; if the wheel was
turned clockwise, as was usual, a z twist resulted. For plying,
or for spinning singles to be used as warp, a figure 8 turn
was put in the driving belt between the wheel and the
spindle, the wheel was moved in the same clockwise manner, but the cross in the belt turned the spindle in the opposite
direction, resulting in s-twist yarn (fig. 4).

148 / Ontario. Sydenham area, Frontenac County. Mid-19th century
ROM 968.269.2. Gift of Mrs. Edgar J. Stone

Blanket, 2/2 lozenge twill. L. 218cm, plus fringe; w. 200cm

All wool (z, 2s) checked in brownish-green and pink-red with overcheck in grey, in a goose-eye pattern. The pattern and the spacing of the stripes are unrelated so that the goose-eyes are not centred on the checks. This was probably a horse blanket.

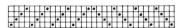

149 / Ontario. Victoria County. Mid-19th century
ROM 970.197. Gift of Mrs Edgar J. Stone
Blanket, 2/2 lozenge twill. L. 211cm; w. 185cm

All wool (z singles), natural checked with indigo blue in a
goose-eye pattern. This is undoubtedly the work of a professional weaver: the blanket is of superb quality and the design shows a complete mastery of technique. The threading
of the goose-eye has been carefully arranged so that a large
unit fits in each of the larger blocks in the check and a small
unit is centred on each of the narrower ones. It is simple but
very effective.

 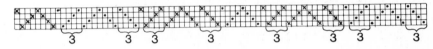

150 / Ontario. Gasline, Humberstone Township, Welland
County. Late 19th century
ROM 969.235. Gift of Mrs Edgar J. Stone
Horse blanket, 2/2 lozenge twill. L. 201cm; w. 177cm

All wool (z, 2s) checked in strong red and dull grey-green
with an overcheck in beige. This was woven either by Albert
Graf or by his father, Edward. They were professional
weavers with a wide loom for jacquard coverlets, but also
at least one other wide loom on which they wove linens and
blankets. Towards the end of the nineteenth century when
the market for coverlets was waning, they did a good business
in decorative horse blankets, such as this one, sometimes
woven to order in the colours of racing stables. Unlike all
the other blankets illustrated in this section, this is without
centre seam. The loom would have been entirely hand-
operated with a simple flying shuttle, making it possible for
one weaver to manage the wide width, and changing shuttles
by hand when the colour altered.

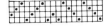

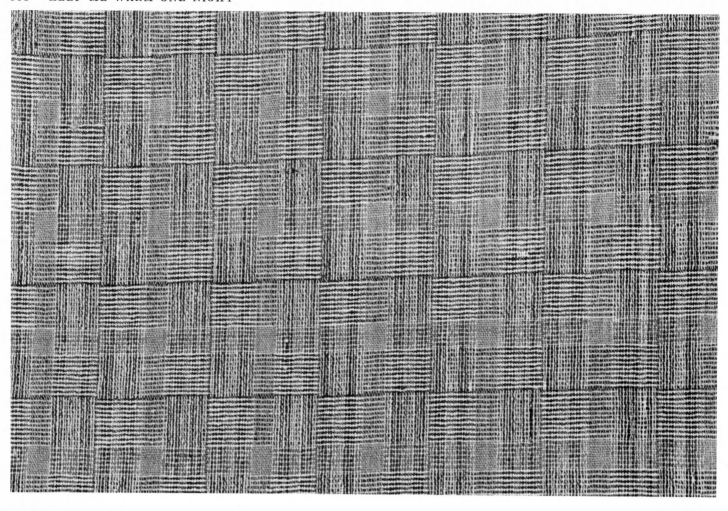

151 / Ontario. Northumberland County. About 1820
ROM 947.68. Gift of the Misses Philp
Blanket, tabby. L. 225cm; w. 208cm

All wool (z singles) in black (now dark green) and yellow
alternating to make a 'log cabin' colour and weave effect
check, with overcheck in orange-red. This is believed to have
been woven at Shiloh, north of Colborne, where the donors'
family first settled and from where they moved about 1825.

The weave is a plain tabby. The pattern of indefinite checks
results from the order in which the two colours have been
threaded: dark and light alternately to form one of the
checks, and then two dark threads together to change the
order to light and dark in the next check. The colours are
used in the same way in the weft (cf. fig. 6). Patterning like
this was used for shawls, but was exacting to weave and very
rarely used for blankets.

152 / Ontario. Probably Lincoln County. Mid-19th century
ROM 963.171. Gift of Mrs. Edgar J. Stone
Blanket, huckaback weave. L. 165cm; w. 150cm

All wool (z singles) in strong pink striped with dark indigo
blue, with the same colours in reverse proportions in the weft.
The way the colours have been used gives a beautiful, almost
shot effect. The construction is usual for linens: it is strange
to find it in a blanket, but it produces an excellent texture for
the purpose (cf. fig. 16).

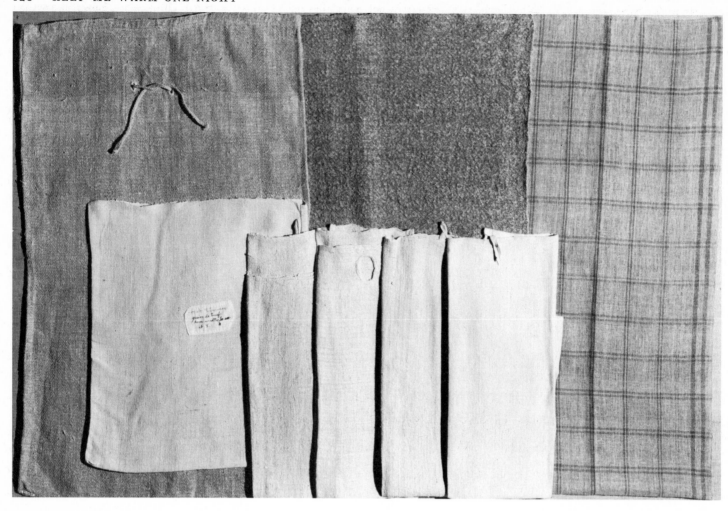

153–60 / LINENS: Quebec. Mid-19th to 20th centuries
ROM 970.90.35, .46–.49, .53, .54, .58. Gift of
Mrs John David Eaton

This is a selection of household linens from rural Quebec
woven with z singles yarn. All but no. 160 come from one
house at St-Pierre, Cté Montmagny, and date from the second half of the nineteenth century. They give an excellent picture of the quality and range of the simple linens woven on
the farms of the province. All the processes were carried out
at home. The volume each year was not large, and the linens
were durable. Quebec families were usually large, and any
surplus was put aside for the dowers of daughters.

153 / On the left is a large sack used to store or ship grain. It
is of unbleached linen, quite heavy in a firm 2/2 twill, and
with cords of plaited linen that could be wrapped and tied
around the neck. Modern jute sacking became available in
the latter nineteenth century. Before that, and for some time
afterwards, all sorts of sacks were made at home of linen.
(970.90.58. L. 95cm; w. 58cm)

154 / In front of the large sack this smaller bag for clover seed
('*graine de treuf*') of finer linen tabby has a handwritten
label asking for its return. When seed was sold, it was taken

away in a bag of this type that was to be returned to the
owner. (970.90.54. L. 50cm; w. 45cm)

155–8 / In the centre front, there are four towels of different
type and qualities of linen and in different stages of bleaching through use. Towels were usually tabby, as the basic
looms of the province were only equipped with two shafts.
Later, when four-shaft ones became more general, 2/2 twill
was also used in the province. (970.90.46. L. 85cm, w. 64cm;
970.90.48. L. 100cm, w. 58cm; 970.90.49. L. 94cm, w.
62cm; 970.90.47. L. 87cm, w. 34cm)

159 / The towel in the centre back is the dark grey colour of
the linen as it came from the loom. It has a very rough texture
and has been woven with linen tow weft. This is the part of
the fibre that is combed out in hackling the flax and consists
of short fibres, often with a considerable amount of the woody
stem still adhering. It was not used for fine purposes, but
made an excellent weft for coarse fabrics. (970.90.53.
L. 42cm; w. 63cm)

160 / The piece on the right is from Trois-Pistoles, Cté
Rimouski, and was made about 1930. It is a length of
towelling in natural grey linen with double check in blue
cotton and is a late example of a traditional type. (970.90.35.
L. 182cm; w. 47cm)

161 / Quebec. Possibly Eastern Townships. 1850-70
ROM 968.115. Gift of Mr and Mrs Harold B. Burnham
Tablecloth, tabby. L. 197cm.; w. 161cm

Checked in indigo blue wool (z singles), and natural white
cotton (z singles). Cloths of this type are very much in the
French tradition of Quebec. Similar ones of bleached linen
and indigo blue wool were formerly in the Musée de l'Institut
des Arts Appliqués in Montreal. These were probably earlier
in date. Some without specific provenance were patterned
in the *à la planche* technique (cf. fig. 20). This produced a
simple pattern of floats of indigo blue wool in a checkerboard
pattern.

162 / Ontario. Waterloo County. Dated 1840
Doon Pioneer Village, Kitchener, Ontario
Show towel, linen tabby, embroidered. L. 124cm, plus fringe;
w. 33cm

Plain linen (z singles) of good quality embroidered with red
cotton (z, 2s), and dark indigo blue linen (z, 2s). This was
made by Elisabeth Bauman, whose name appears at the top.
In the early days of Ontario, much plain linen of varying
quality was woven. It was used for all the normal utilitarian
items such as sheets and pillowcases, towels, tablecloths, and
napkins. Although a number have survived, they appear very
unimpressive in a photograph, and the most elaborate use
to which these materials were put has been chosen to illustrate this whole group of household linens. Among the Mennonites of Waterloo County, every family had a show towel,
embroidered with care as part of the dower linen and eventually hung over the utilitarian towel in the kitchen to hide it.
People soon learned to reach in and dry their hands on the
towel underneath.

These show towels were embroidered, usually in cross
stitch, in much the same way as a sampler, using a traditional
range of motifs originally brought from Europe by these
German-speaking settlers. The eight-pointed stars, the
Distelfink seated on a branch, the stylized carnations, the
peacocks, and the tulip tree are all parts of this repertory,
and will be seen later in the jacquard coverlets. A motif that
occurs on many show towels is the branched heart surrounded by the letters 'o E H B D D E' standing for 'O edel
Herz bedenk dein End' (O noble heart, consider thine end),
a constant reminder of human mortality. Show towels were
normally finished with an elaborate fringe, either with complex knotting or darned net.

163 / Ontario. Waterloo County. Dated 1832
Doon Pioneer Village, Kitchener, Ontario
Show towel, linen tabby, embroidered. L. 137cm, plus fringe;
w. 42cm

Plain linen (z singles), embroidered with red and blue
cotton (z singles) in cross stitch. This was made by Ania
Shoemaker in 1832. It was after this date that show towels
became more elaborate, as may be seen in no. 162. This
example shows a smaller range of the traditional motifs, but
one that dominates is the branched heart with the letters of
the same devotional precept.

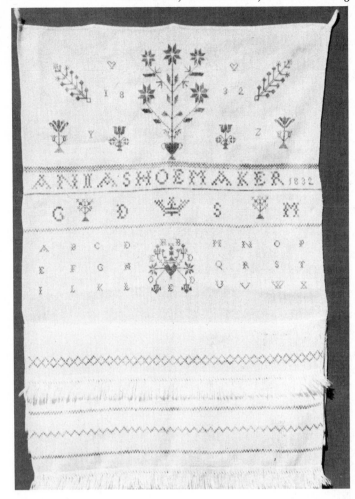

164 / Ontario. Waterloo County. Dated 1799
Doon Pioneer Village, Kitchener, Ontario
Towel, linen tabby, embroidered. L. 104cm, plus fringe;
w. 36cm

Plain linen (z singles) embroidered in cross stitch with
coloured silks: red (faded), and brown (probably faded
black). The motto within the frame between two stylized
lilies reads 'In dem Leben war ich dein in dem Tod vergesnet
mein' (In life I was yours, in death remember me), beneath
which are the initials 'E B,' probably those of the maker. With
this motto, it is uncertain whether this is a show towel, although the form is the same. It may perhaps be a commemorative one for some special purpose, or part of a funerary
cloth. It is the earliest piece of dated linen found in Canada.

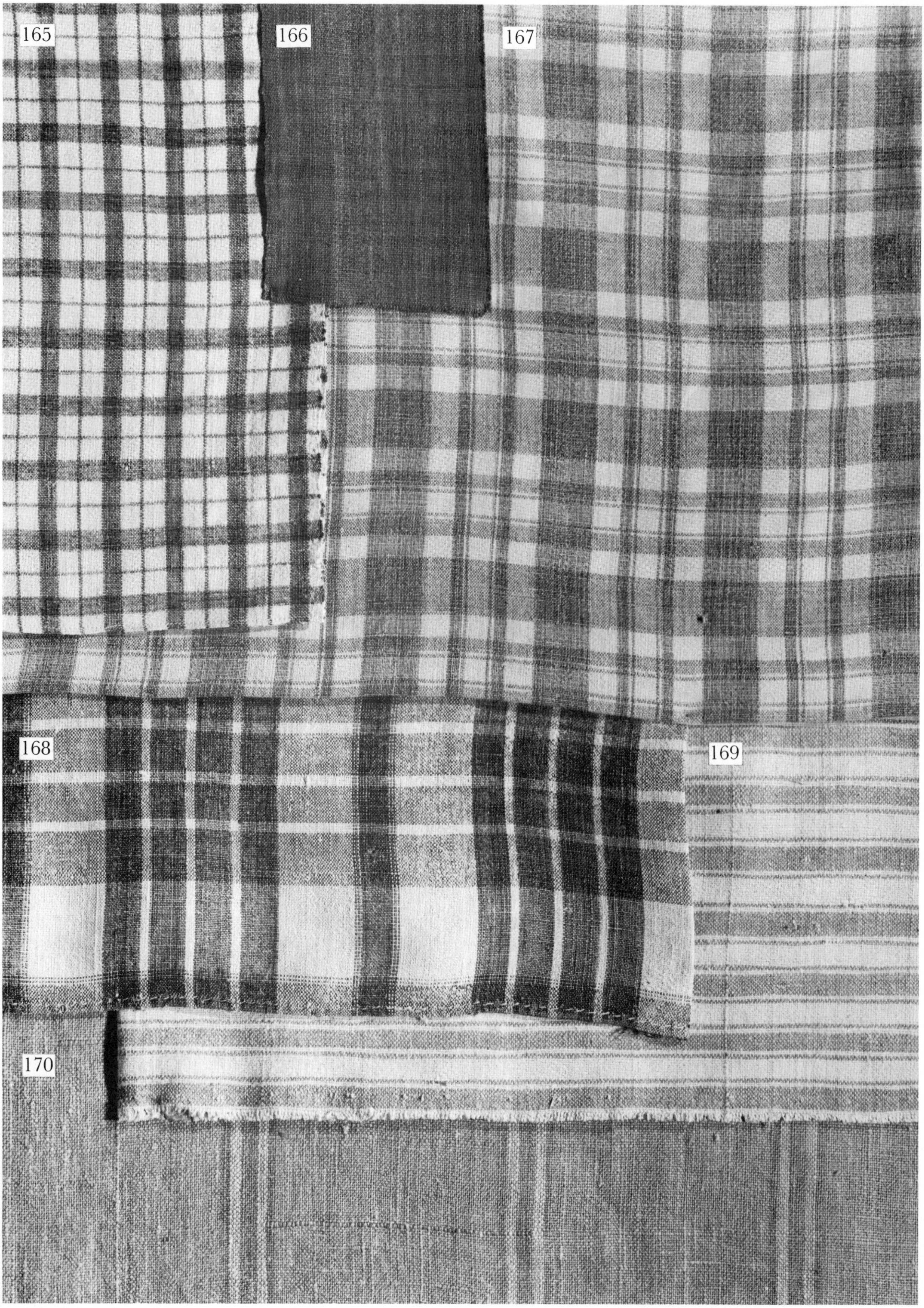
165
166
167
168
169
170

165 / Ontario. Kitchener, Waterloo County.
Mid-19th century
ROM 957.179.2. Gift of Mrs Phoebe M. Kolb
Fragment, tabby. L. 29cm; w. 30cm

Checked in bleached and indigo blue linen (z singles), with stripes spaced about 2.5cm (1″) apart. Linen does not take dye easily, and the colour is never as strong as with wool. This fragment is probably from a tablecloth, although such materials were also used for sheets and pillowcases.

166 / Ontario. Niagara Peninsula, probably Lincoln County.
1825-50
ROM 951.126.1. Gift of Mr and Mrs Harold B. Burnham
Fragment, tabby. L. 17cm; w. 9cm

Linen (z singles), with tiny check of six medium indigo blue and six golden-brown. This piece might have been for household purposes, but was more likely for clothing. It may have started life as a dress and then served as an apron, or a child's pinafore. Its survival is probably due to its being used in a quilt face, the usual end of many clothing materials. Except for the kerchief (no. 82), this is the only example of Ontario linen with yarn dyed other than blue that has been recorded.

167 / Ontario. Near Sherkston, Welland County. 1830-50
ROM 950.236.2. Gift of Mrs Verna Hall
Width, tabby. L. 48cm; w. 80cm

Checked in bleached and indigo blue linen (z singles). The spacing of the blue stripes is well planned with each repeat measuring about 7cm (2¾″). Judging from the shape of the piece and the traces of sewing around the edges, this is probably from a pillowcase. Checked blue and white linen for this purpose is known in Europe from pictorial records as far back as the Middle Ages. It is no surprise for it to turn up in the German-speaking areas of Ontario. The same donor gave the coverlets (nos. 231–2) from the Reeb family, who were Mennonites from Alsace-Lorraine.

168 / Ontario. Near Sherkston, Welland County. 1830-50
ROM 950.236.1. Gift of Mrs Verna Hall
Fragment, tabby. L. 16cm; w. 53cm

Checked in bleached and indigo blue linen (z singles) with bold stripes in a repeat of 15cm (6″). This fragment has a beautiful quality, and would be suitable for a tablecloth, but like the previous one from the same donor may also have been part of a pillowcase.

169 / Ontario. Norwich, Oxford County. 1823-33
ROM 950.55.4. Gift of Miss Alma Clutton
Fragment, ticking, tabby. L. 18cm; w. 89cm

Banded in blue and natural white cotton on bleached linen (all z singles). This piece was woven by Susanna Sutton to be used as ticking. It is firm and suitable for the purpose. Thousands and thousands of yards of such materials were woven at home for everyday use. Little has survived; such ordinary fabrics were not treasured, but when worn out were discarded and replaced by store-bought goods.

170 / Ontario. Simcoe County, found near Creemore.
1840-60
ROM 966.33.4. Gift of Mr and Mrs Harold B. Burnham
Bed tick, tabby. L. 159cm; w. 150cm

Half-bleached linen striped with bleached and pale blue linen every 11cm (4½″), and woven with fine natural tow linen (all z singles). This tick was used to cover a straw mattress; traces of the filling remained when it was found. It is a firmly woven and very durable material suitable for the purpose.

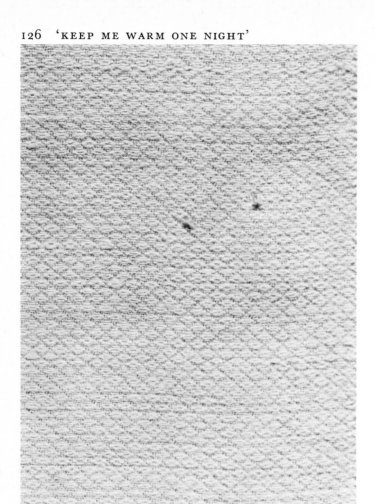

171 / Ontario. Dunwich Township, Elgin County.
About 1850
ROM 951.165.7. Gift of Mrs I. Moss
Towel, 3/1 lozenge twill. L. 44cm; w. 86cm

Bleached linen (z singles, with fine weft double), in a bird's-eye pattern. It has a lovely texture that would have been ideal for towelling, but would have been equally suitable for table linen. It was woven by Ann Moorhouse Pearce, threaded and treadled as shown in the draft. An old name for small allover repeating patterns is *diaper*. These materials are usually very absorbent, and were used for baby's wear; the name of the weave was taken over and used for the garment.

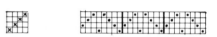

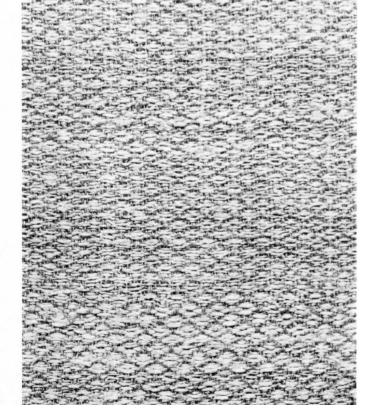

172 / Ontario. Prince Edward County. 1860-80
ROM 954.148.5. Gift of Miss Annie Abercrombie
Towel, 2/2 lozenge twill. L. 58cm; w. 93cm

Unbleached linen with fine firm warp and softer weft (both z singles). The small bird's-eye pattern has a less usual draft, but is treadled in the normal way like no. 171. It was woven by Mrs John Abercrombie, the donor's mother. Linen was woven in an unbleached state and locally made ones were usually bleached through use. With repeated washing, linen gradually changed from this dark grey to white. Housekeepers of the past well knew that if they laid their linen on the lawn on a sunny day, it would steadily whiten as it dried even though they knew nothing of the chemistry of the free ozone in the air acting as a bleaching agent.

173 / Ontario. North Elmsley Township, Lanark County. 1833-60
ROM 949.80.3. Gift of Miss Bessie Farmer
Towel, 2/2 lozenge twill. L. 59cm; w. 57cm

Natural white cotton (z singles) in a broken twill of traditional Scottish type in the draft (cf. fig. 12), and with unbroken chevron treadling, producing a broken goose-eye pattern. This towel was woven by Duncan McNab, the professional weaver who also wove no. 79. He supplied his neighbourhood with a wide variety of useful household materials.

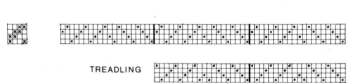

TREADLING

174 / Ontario. Near Chippewa, Willoughby Township, Welland County. 1850-60
ROM 959.57.3. Gift of Mrs W.E.P. De Roche
Towel, 2/2 lozenge twill. L. 79cm; w. 44cm

Bleached linen (z singles) of excellent quality. The piece has been made into a towel, but it is likely that it was originally part of a tablecloth. The twill lines of the threading repeat, resulting in a series of concentric diamonds, is known as a *goose eye* (fig. 14). Here, a mixture of larger and smaller units has been used giving an elusive pattern. The treadling follows the same order as the threading, but as the weft is considerably closer than the warp, each unit is increased in length with 32 picks rather than 20, and 10 rather than 8.

175 / Ontario. Norwich, Oxford County. 1823-33
ROM 950.55.3. Gift of Miss Alma Clutton
Width, huckaback. L. 130cm. w. 60cm

Very fine bleached linen (z singles), woven by Susanna
Sutton. This has a beautiful quality of the type made for finer
tablecloths and towels. The little pattern is the standard
huckaback and is treadled as drawn in (fig. 15). This weave,
with small floats of weft on the face and of warp on the
equally good reverse, was so suitable that the term *huck* became almost synonymous with linen towelling in the later
nineteenth century. The weave is an extension of a simple
herringbone twill threading, as may be seen by comparing
the draft and fig. 10.

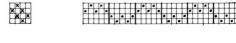

176 / Ontario. Markham Township, York County. 1840-60
ROM 964.191.2. Gift of Mr and Mrs Harold B. Burnham
Tablecloth, huckaback. L. 138cm; w. 140cm

Heavy bleached linen on natural white cotton of similar
weight (both z singles). This is a sturdy everyday tablecloth
made up from a full width and a half one. There are remnants of sewing around the edge suggesting that at one time
it may have been trimmed with a fringe as in no. 177. The
threading is a shorter form of huckaback than no. 175, with
only four threads in each unit (fig. 16). It can be threaded on
three shafts as shown at the right and in this form it looks
very like no. 175. It may equally well be threaded as shown
in the centre, and here another connection becomes obvious.
In this form, it becomes a two-block spot weave that should
be compared with fig. 17. It is unlikely that it was woven on
three shafts, so the four-shaft draft to the left is probably the
one that was used.

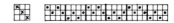

177 / Ontario. Markham Township, York County. 1840-60
ROM 964.191.3. Gift of Mr and Mrs Harold B. Burnham
Tablecloth, 'huck block' weave. L. 180cm, plus fringes;
w. 150cm, plus added fringes

Heavy bleached linen on natural white cotton of similar
weight (both z singles). This was made on the same farm as

no. 176 and uses similar yarns. It also consists of a full width
and a half. Additional pieces have been woven and joined
to the sides to supply fringes. The weave combines huckaback
and straight twill. Woven 'as drawn in,' the curious bars
that link the two elements occurred automatically, as the
huck part was treadled twill and the twill part was treadled
huck.

178 / Ontario. Near Milton, Halton County. 1830-50
ROM 969.111.2. Gift of Mr and Mrs Harold B. Burnham
Tablecloth, diaper weave. L. 220cm; w. 121cm

Fine natural cotton (z singles). This has been made from
two lengths of finely woven and pleasantly textured cotton,
but coarsely sewn by machine. The construction, an extension of huckaback, is threaded on five shafts (fig. 17). The
draft should be compared with the middle threading of no.
176. This weave always uses the first shaft for every other

thread and one additional shaft for each block of pattern.
Here, it has been partly treadled 'as drawn in,' but other
treadlings have also been used. It is possible that the material
was woven for another purpose, possibly towels, as it is considerably earlier than the machine sewing suggests.

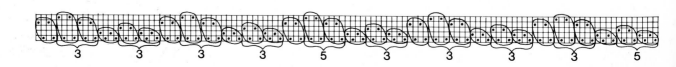

179 / Ontario. Vineland, Lincoln County. Dated 1865
ROM 953.151. Gift of Mrs D.C. Wills
Tablecloth, diaper weave. L. 146cm; w. 99cm

Fine bleached linen (z singles). This is made from a single
width that was probably woven by Samuel Fry. In one corner
is marked in fine red cross stitch: 'E + M' (Elizabeth
Moyer) and the date 1865. This tablecloth shows the design possibilities of extended huck or spot weave to much
fuller advantage than the previous piece. The pattern of

'table' and 'stars' resembles some in the overshot section. The
construction is equally good on both sides, making it highly
suitable for table linens, of which few have survived in
Ontario.

As in many weaves, the thread order of each pattern unit
is constant. Here it is four threads, alternately on the first
shaft, and on one of the pattern shafts. In writing the draft,
it is not necessary to show it in full: a profile with one block
for each pattern unit is all that is required. The profile form
is shown below the expanded draft.

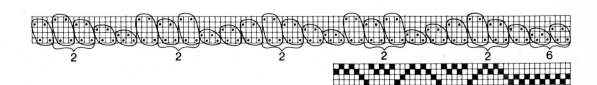

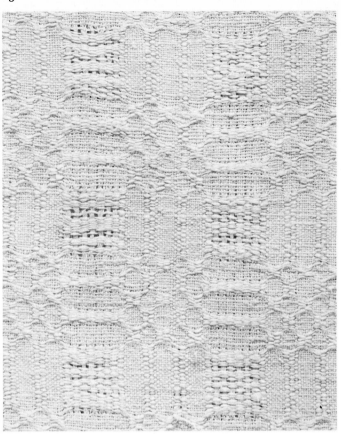

180 / Ontario. Prince Edward County. 1840-60
ROM 950.107.1. Gift of Miss Annie Abercrombie
Tablecloth, 'M's & O's.' L. 186cm; w. 155cm

Bleached linen (z singles) of medium weight; made from two lengths. Unlike huckaback and spot weave, the floats that form the pattern are always weft. The result is fully reversible. Fig. 18 shows how the treadling produces the pattern. The drafts are shown here using shafts 1 and 2 working against 3 and 4 to produce one pattern block, and the second is formed by 2 and 3 against their opposite, 1 and 4. This is how the weave is written in all the old drafts that have been examined. Many modern books use 1 and 3 working against 2 and 4 for the second block with identical results. A true tabby cannot be woven using a normal threading of this type.

181 / Ontario. Bloomfield, Prince Edward County. About 1860
ROM 950.104.2. Gift of Miss F. Barker
Fragment, 'M's & O's.' L. 23cm; w. 38cm

Bleached linen (z singles) of excellent quality. The draft is similar to the previous one, but the units are turned so that there is an overlap of one thread where the two pattern blocks meet. This is quite unnoticeable. The treadling differs as the large 'table' is woven in straight twill. From the Noxon family, and possibly woven by George Sanderson.

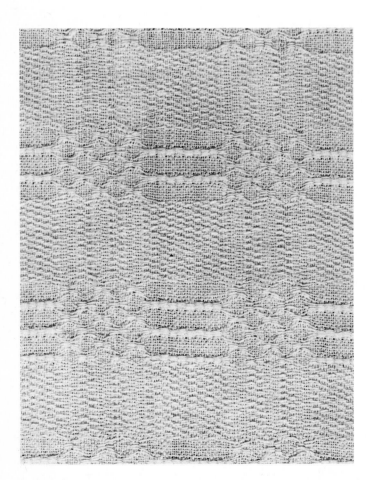

182 / Nova Scotia. Mahone Bay, Lunenburg County.
1840-60
ROM 966.158.28. Gift of Mrs Edgar J. Stone
Tablecloth, 'M's & o's.' L. 154cm; w. 164cm

Bleached linen on natural white cotton (both z singles).
Made from two widths seamed together. This makes a good
firm fabric and the linen weft supplies a sheen, although the
handle is not as good as in the all-linen examples. The threading is the standard 'M's & o's' with treadling as in the previous
tablecloth.

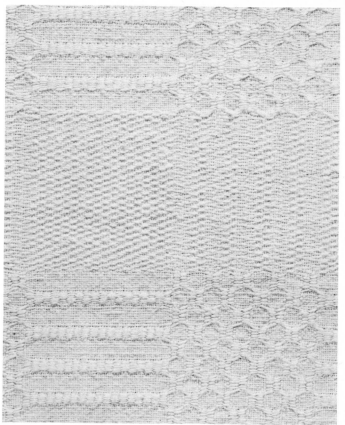

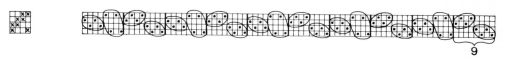

9

183 / Nova Scotia. 1840-60
NSM 57.21.1
Towel, 'M's & o's.' L. 66cm; w. 40cm

Bleached linen on natural white cotton (both z singles).
Another example of 'M's & o's' combined with twill treadling.
Here it is used for towelling. The material would be most
suitable for the purpose because the floats of linen create
good absorbency. Both the draft and treadling are the same
as for no. 182.

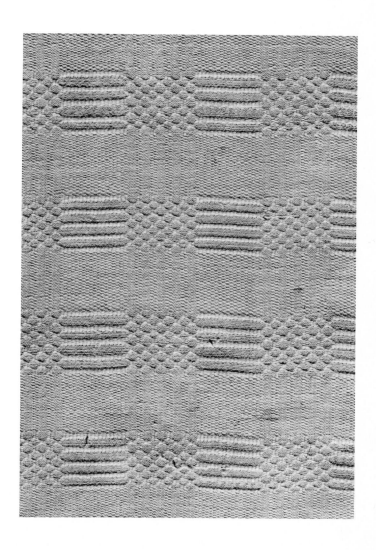

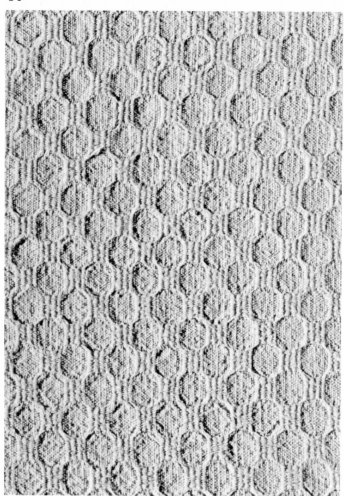

184 / Nova Scotia. Lunenburg County. 1850-75
NSM 68.31.17
Tablecloth, 'M's & O's.' L. 135cm; w. 130cm

Bleached linen on natural white cotton (both z singles).
This is the simplest 'M's & O's' pattern: the two small units are
repeated to form an allover checkerboard. There is a small
irregularity that gives a slightly different texture. Units of
the pattern have been turned as shown in the draft. This
deviation does not affect the patterned areas, but in the
ground doubled threads occur at regular intervals. It is hard
to tell whether subtleties of this kind are intentional, or just
a happy accident.

185 / Nova Scotia. Mahone Bay, Lunenburg County.
1840-60
NSM 59.20.3
Tablecloth, 'M's & O's.' L. 186cm; w. 160cm

Bleached linen (z singles), of two widths seamed together.
This is an interesting variation achieving a totally different
effect than usual. The threading is an elaboration of the
usual design with treadling cut in the large blocks and extended in the smaller ones.

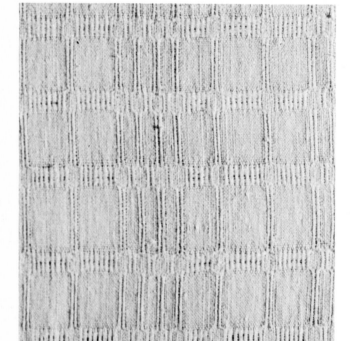

186 / Ontario. Port Hope, Durham County. 1825-40
ROM 969.277.1. Gift of Mrs. Doris Wardenier
Towel, 'M's & O's.' L. 78cm; w. 53cm

Bleached linen (z singles), woven the width of the towel,
and marked with the initials 'M S' in blue cotton. The pattern is a variation worked out on a very fine scale. A small
'table' is formed by one block and then there are two short
links joining it to another small 'table' on the other block,
making a charming little allover design. From the Choate
family.

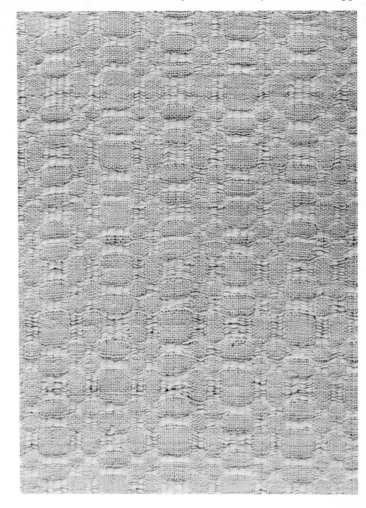

187 / Nova Scotia. Probably Pictou County. 1825-50
ROM 968.118.1. Gift of Miss Edith Taylor
Towel, 'M's & O's,' three-block variation. L. 85cm, plus
fringes; w. 66cm

Half-bleached linen (z singles), woven the width of the
towel. Near the upper edge the initials 'S. C' (Sarah Chase)
are worked in brown silk in cross stitch. The borders are
normal 'M's & O's,' but the body of the pattern is a clever
extension of the technique (fig. 19). The six pairs of shafts
available are used to form an allover lattice of eight-end
floats. The tie-up shows the six combinations. To produce a
pattern block, a treadle controlling two shafts is worked
alternately with the one controlling the opposite two. No
similar example has been seen in Canada, but among the
drafts in the Mackley Collection from Cape Breton there are
two for this design and technique. One is labelled 'Young
Man's Fancy.'

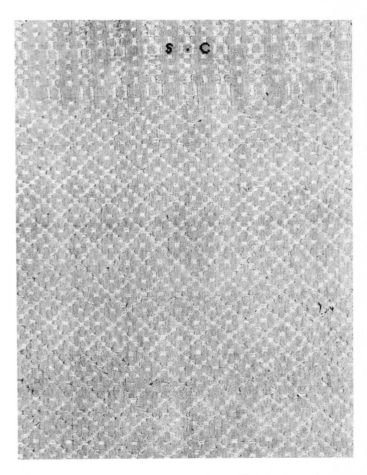

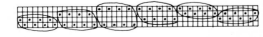

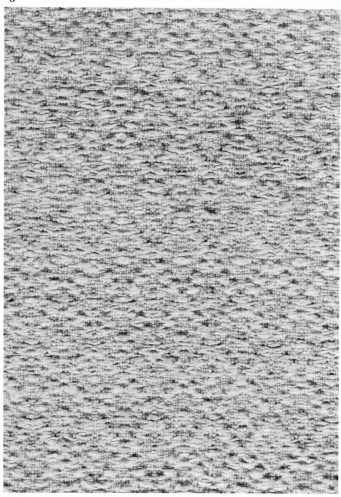

188 / Nova Scotia. Pictou County. 1850-60
ROM 966.158.22. Gift of Mrs Edgar J. Stone
Tablecloth, overshot. L. 159cm; w. 147cm

Bleached linen on natural white cotton (all z singles). The overshot technique is explained in the coverlet section (fig. 32). By some it is considered unsuitable for linens, and is called 'poor man's damask' in derision, but all depends on the scale of the pattern and the firmness of the weave. This piece with its simple lozenge formed of three-thread blocks produces a balanced pattern and a firm fabric eminently suited to its purpose. Among the old weaving drafts known from the Maritime Provinces are many small overshot patterns undoubtedly used for linen weaving.

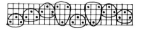

189 / Nova Scotia. Lunenburg County. 1850-75
ROM 966.158.27. Gift of Mr and Mrs Harold B. Burnham
Towel, overshot. L. 55cm, plus fringe; w. 50cm

Bleached linen on natural white cotton (all z singles). The pattern is a common one in coverlets woven 'rose fashion' (nos. 315, 354), and is more suitable for them than for towels as the eight-end floats are too long with a linen weft.

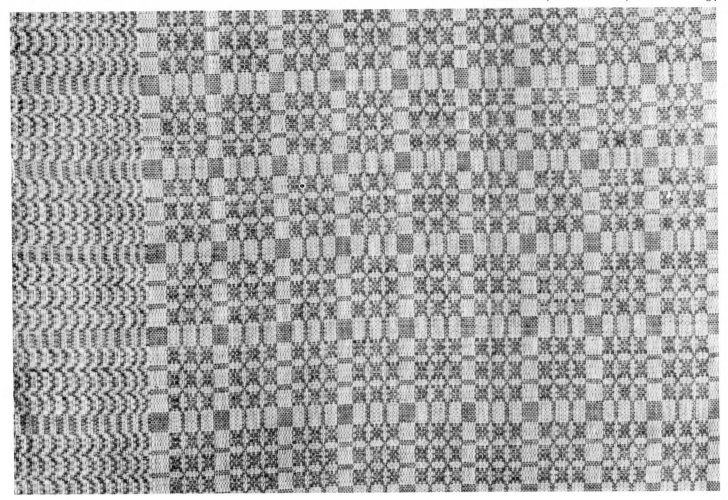

190 / Nova Scotia. Pictou County. 1850-75
NSM 61.23.56
Tablecloth, overshot. L. 159cm; w. 155cm

Unbleached linen on natural white cotton (all z singles).
This small pattern on a closely set cotton warp has a repeat
of only 6.5cm (2½″) making it most suitable for a tablecloth. A similar piece in Toronto (ROM 966.158.23), now

fully bleached, was undoubtedly also woven with unbleached
linen; the bleaching has come through use. Among the Cape
Breton drafts (Mackley Collection), a slightly larger version
of the pattern is called 'Ladies Delight.'

191 / Nova Scotia. Cape Breton. 1850-70
Mackley Collection, Sydney, NS
Tablecloth (part), overshot. L. 138cm; w. 74cm

Bleached linen on natural white cotton (all z singles). This material, of very good quality, is similar to the previous example in design, but with an extra repeat of the 'table.' This has not been used in the treadling, resulting in a curious lobed form in the main motif.

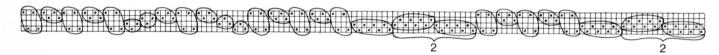

2   2

192 / Prince Edward Island. Bedeque, Prince County. 1825-50
CAGM 65.2.1
Tablecloth, overshot. L. 106cm, plus added fringes; w. 100cm, plus added fringes

Bleached linen of superb quality (z singles) with the pattern weft used double. The linen is so fine and the piece so firmly woven that the whole repeat of one hundred and four threads occupies less than 6cm (2¼"). On this scale, the familiar overshot technique is almost unrecognizable and serves as a substitute for damask that would satisfy even the most fastidious.

This is the work of a professional weaver. The names of two who worked in the Island are known: James Leard was described as a weaver when he married in Charlottetown in 1799, and James Thompson, who was active between 1830 and 1854, wove a tablecloth early in his career for the annual dinner given at Government House for the Legislative Council and the Legislative Assembly.

193 / Ontario. Preston, Waterloo County. Late 19th century
ROM 968.142. Gift of Mrs Robert Nix
Length of towelling, twill diaper. L. 109cm; w. 42cm

Unbleached linen (fine z singles) on natural white cotton
(z singles). This was woven by August Ploethner, a professional weaver in Preston. He is best known for his jacquard
coverlets (nos. 471–2), but he also wove a wide range of less
spectacular things to sell in the small shop he had near the
Kitchener market. This towelling was given to the Museum
by his granddaughter and is still in loom state. It is a two-
block twill diaper (cf. fig. 38) requiring eight shafts. Unlike
the coverlets in this weave that are illustrated, the twill is
broken, giving a good texture for towels.

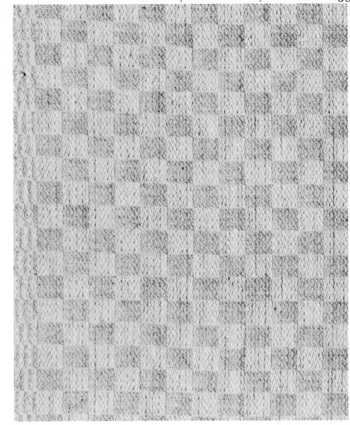

 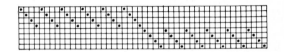

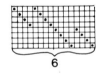
6

194 / Ontario. Vineland, Clinton Township, Lincoln
County. 1840-60
ROM L965.11.5. The Annie R. Fry Collection
Tablecloth, twill diaper. L. 189cm; w. 176cm

Bleached linen of excellent quality (z singles). Samuel Fry,
whose name is mentioned frequently in different sections of
this book, wove one of these tablecloths for each of his children. The flax was raised in a field reserved for this crop and
all processing was done at home on the farm south of Vineland. The field was only large enough to produce a sufficient
amount for the family's use. The pattern is no. 12 in Fry's
pattern book and is also known in coverlets made by him
(no. 386). It is a very rare piece and an outstanding example
of expert work.

 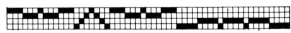

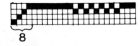
8

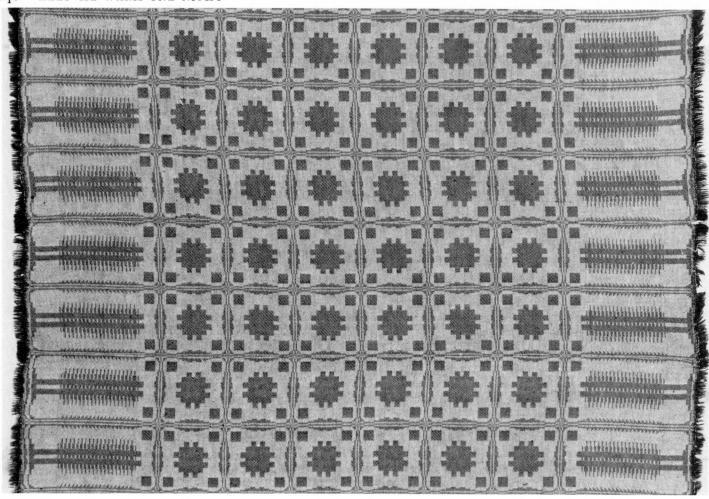

195 / Ontario. Waterloo County. Late 19th century
ROM 967.175.2. Gift of Mrs Elton Witmer
Tablecloth, twill diaper. L. 136cm, plus fringe; w. 121cm,
plus fringes

Fine cotton (z singles), indigo blue on natural white. This
is a late example of a purely traditional type that could have
been woven by any one of a number of professional weavers
in Waterloo County. As the demand for handweaving de-
clined, some of these weavers turned to using cotton rather
than the more expensive linen and wool. Another white
tablecloth from the area is in linen on cotton with a pattern
similar to that of no. 194 (ROM 955.50).

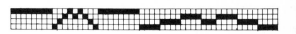

An introduction to coverlets

Whether called coverlets, kivers, coverlids, *couvrelits, couvre-pieds, couvertures*, draft rugs, storm blankets, bed mats, or *Depigs*, the coverlet has a unique place in Canadian social history. Throughout the course of development of western culture, the bed has had a place of special importance. It was the centre of the home where the members of the family were born and where in due course they expected to die. The bed and its furnishings were a matter of special note and pride in the gathering of a dower and in the division of an estate. Priscilla Nelles followed her husband from their home in the Mohawk Valley in 1776 after the outbreak of the American Revolution. She lived first in Grimsby and later on the banks of the Grand River. Her will, dated 1814, contained three specific bequests of bedding (Powell, #6, 63):

'I also give and bequeath unto Priscilla Nelles, daughter of Warner Nelles, my feather-bed and bedding –

'I also give and bequeath unto Catherine Nelles, wife of Henry I. Nelles and daughter of Abraham Young, my Bed Curtains which I brought with me and my large woolen [*sic*] wheel –

'I also give and bequeath to my daughter-in-law Elner, wife of Abraham Young, my Great Coat, my Red Cloak, and three coverlets – '

Household effects were limited in the early days of this country, but bedcoverings were brought by settlers when they came and supplemented as soon as possible once they were settled in their new homes. Supplies were far too limited to allow for anything that was solely ornamental, but even with life as hard as it undoubtedly was for many people, time and trouble were taken to produce bed coverings that were not only warm and serviceable but also beautiful. Many kinds of woven coverlets were used in different parts of eastern Canada, but all show that the pioneers wanted and worked for colour and pattern to brighten their plain way of life. In the small living space of the first one-roomed log cabin, the bed was inevitably a prominent feature, and a warm and attractive cover added greatly to the cheeriness of the confined space. The coverlets were not merely for show; many that have survived are very worn, particularly across the upper edge where they have been repeatedly pulled over the shoulders as some tired pioneer snuggled down between the woollen sheets into what was probably the only truly warm and comfortable spot in a chilly and spartan existence.

It is hard nowadays to grasp just how short supplies were on the pioneer level in Canada. Every tiny scrap of material was used and reused. Spinning and weaving were useful and essential accomplishments for the settler's wife, but were of little use until there were fibres to spin and weave. Flax for linen was grown as soon as land was cleared. It was used for the ground of coverlets in the very early days, but those with linen ground are now as rare as the proverbial hen's teeth. Reports and rumours of such coverlets reaching the Museum have been frequent over the past twenty-odd years, but on investigation all except a very few have turned out to have cotton grounds that have gone hard and discoloured with age. With the opening up of the country for settlement, cotton yarn arrived as an article of trade, the first source being the spinning mills established in Massachusetts, such as the one started by Slater in 1790. In coverlets and blankets, it almost immediately replaced as warp the home-grown flax that involved so much labour. It was difficult to establish sheep in the new land when the basic flock had usually to be brought across the Atlantic in sailing ships, and when wolves and other predators were numerous in the heavily forested countryside. Slowly the land was cleared and civilization pushed the predators back, but even as late as the 1850s wolves were still being hunted in the Niagara Peninsula.

The pioneers were prepared to work hard for what they could acquire in no other way, but they were not so stupid as to look for unnecessary work: if an article or service could be obtained by barter or purchase, they took advantage of it. In examining old coverlets, it must be realized that one is dealing with all sorts of combinations of home production and bought service. At an early stage imported cotton replaced the homegrown flax, but until well into the nineteenth century it arrived in the form of skeins of singles yarn that could be bought from pedlars or at the local general store. Any plying that was required was done at home using a spinning wheel or a dropped spindle. This is one undoubted explanation why the warp is plied and the main weft is not in almost all the earlier overshot coverlets. Unless a weaver had the necessary training and skill to dress a singles warp, the cotton had to be plied to provide the strength necessary to stand the strain of weaving. Plying the main weft would have been a wasted and unnecessary effort as no additional strength was needed. In general, it is safe to say that the older overshot coverlets have a 2-ply warp, and a singles main weft. This is one of the features that gives them their quality.

Wool was often processed entirely at home, but some help for the busy housewife was provided when the first carding mills opened. Writing about 1840, William Thomson reported that there were about thirty of these in Lower Canada, all with fulling mills, most of which did some spinning at 3d sterling a pound, and about seventeen or eighteen in Upper Canada (139). The scoured wool could then be taken to the mill, and a laborious part of the yarn preparation avoided. Either in the fleece before carding or spinning, or as yarn, the wool could be dyed. Native vegetable dyestuffs from plants, barks, and lichens were used to a limited extent, but it takes time and effort to obtain clear and fast colours from most of these sources. Whenever good strong imported dyestuffs were available the busy pioneer did not hesitate to buy them and to enjoy the fine clear colours obtained with less work. Numerous early account books tell of the availability of imported dyes from the earliest days and the coverlets that have survived show little trace of native dyes in comparison with the many for which indigo, and to a lesser extent madder, camwood, and the more expensive cochineal were used. Among the later coverlets, it is obvious that the chemical dyes were not scorned. In some areas where there was a mill with a trained dyer, his services would be called upon by the domestic weavers either to dye their handspun yarn or to supply them with yarn already spun and dyed. In southwest Cape Breton in the area around Macdonald's mill at Glendyer, established in 1848, many coverlets turn up with an unusually gay range of colours that originated there.

Two types of loom were used for weaving coverlets in Canada: those with shafts controlling the sheds for the passage of the weft and those with a jacquard mechanism mounted on top of the loom controlling all movement of the warp threads. The former were used wherever weaving was done either domestically or professionally, but the latter were always professional tools of scattered use, employed only in limited areas of Ontario. The coverlets woven on shaft looms are considered in this section: they fall into three general groups. The first includes the coverlets for which basically only two shafts were required, with the addition of a few closely related ones requiring a slightly more complex loom. The second group, the four-shaft overshot, is without question the best known and the most widespread; it is supplemented by a small group, technically similar, requiring eight or ten shafts. The third group consists of coverlets in various more complex constructions that require more than four shafts: 'summer and winter' weave, twill diapers and geometric doublecloths, the 'star and diamond,' and the lozenge twills. Although many of the surviving examples are professional work, the first two groups include the coverlets that might have been woven domestically. In contrast, those of the third group are, without doubt, professional work.

PLATE II

215, 203, 223

Two-shaft coverlets

Most of the two-shaft coverlets that have survived are woven with lengths cut into thin strips which may be either of woollen or of cotton cloth. These are often combined with yarns, either in the ground or for decorative purposes. This re-use of older fabrics has a wide distribution for materials for a variety of purposes. It is known from many parts of Europe and from the Far East. As bed coverings in Canada, it has several names: *catalogne* in Quebec, *laize du pays* at least in parts of Acadia, and probably *cloutie* in the Scottish settlements of Prince Edward Island and Cape Breton.

The Acadian term *laize du pays* or country length needs no further explanation. The Scots term is connected with the Gaelic *clud*, a rag, and *cludadh*, patching or mending, and is remembered in the proverb 'Ne'er shed a clout, 'til May be out.' The derivation of the term *catalogne* as presently used in Quebec presents a more difficult problem. Robert-Lionel Séguin has gathered the evidence and presented it fully and well (Séguin, 389–96). From the information available, one may conclude that the modern term seems to be derived from the older word *castelonge*, but the meaning of this is confused. That the *couvertures de castelonge* of the seventeenth century mentioned in the Jesuit *Relations* were not the same as the catalogne covers of the nineteenth century is undoubted: the former were blankets, perhaps originally from Catalonia, imported from France, of white wool, possibly fine, whereas the more modern descendants were made of strips of salvaged cloth, originally woollen, but later cotton. The only suggestion that might be added to Séguin's excellent contribution to the problem is that the *couvertures de castelonge* would have ceased to be imported after 1760 in favour of English blankets, and that, with the rise of domestic weaving for household needs, the name was transferred to the new covers made from the strips of the old worn-out blankets that could no longer be obtained.

Regardless of name, all were originally bed coverings. It was not until well on in the nineteenth century that catalogne came to be used as a floor covering in the rural parts of Quebec (Séguin, 390). Its use in France for the same purpose, and in comparatively recent times, is proved by examples from La Charente (MATP, nos. 39.24.1–.6) where they were known as *tapis de lirette* (*tissu lacéré tissé*). As mentioned previously, the occurrence of rag carpeting in Ontario was similar: it did not come into use until a sufficient volume of rags could be spared for such decorative purposes.

Of the thousands of pieces of catalogne that must have been woven in the whole of eastern Canada, only a fraction that can be dated prior to 1900 have survived. Undoubtedly many were of the type known as 'hit and miss,' where rags were used in whatever order they came to hand without any intention of producing a piece of work with regularly ordered bands that would have satisfied the weaver's urge for artistic expression.

Except for one piece from the Magdalen Islands, which has carefully arranged bands (no. 198), no example of catalogne from Quebec woven with woollen rags has so far turned up; at least none are known to exist in any of the public collections in Canada. It is probable that few pieces of simple catalogne made in that province before 1900 have survived.

Unlike the ornamented *à la planche* and boutonné coverlets from the lower St Lawrence that will be discussed later, these unpatterned coverings were purely utilitarian. When their useful life was over, they were relegated to the barn, or discarded.

In the Acadian areas of the Maritime Provinces, the possibilities of differently proportioned bands using the materials and colours available were exploited, whether using yarns or cloth strips. Where wool was plentiful from local sheep, the cloth strips were used only for emphasis. Blankets from River Bourgeois in Cape Breton show a confident mastery using a wide range of colours and effects (nos. 207–9). Others of this type with different banding are known from Memramcook and Beaubassin in New Brunswick.

It is in the coverlets from Chéticamp that one finds the use of woollen rags. Here, combined with yarns and cotton strips, the weaving shows yet another style of banding. In reviewing the limited evidence available, it would seem that different stylistic traditions may have grown up in the various scattered Acadian communities. Banded catalogne coverlets have certainly been used in Quebec since the late nineteenth century, but woven of cotton rags. It is possible that traditional regional differences may have developed there as well.

The Scots term for coverlets of this type is *cloutie*, and even fewer of these have survived from the nineteenth century in areas settled by Scots that may serve as a basis for conclusions, although some 'hit and miss' ones have been recorded in Canada that are quite like older examples seen in Scotland from Dumfries in the south to Kilmuir in Easter Ross in the north. This latter area was once the centre of a thriving linen industry that succumbed to the increasing use of cotton as the nineteenth century progressed. The one from there that was seen was basically white, woven 'hit and miss' on a linen warp. The owner remembered that the better ones that were still around in her childhood were patterned with blue bands on white.

The Scottish-Canadian examples shown here illustrate elaborations of the simple type. No. 228 from Prince Edward Island is rare in using rags in the warp, as well as in the weft, to produce a red check on a white ground. Two from Cape Breton show other variations (nos. 229–30); the former with a simple brocaded pattern in red, the other with white rags raised in loops to form lozenges. This has an indubitable history of having been woven by a Scottish-Canadian family, making it unique in this tradition. The method of patterning, generally known as boutonné, will be discussed later when dealing with coverlets from the lower St Lawrence, where it is best known.

One type of two-shaft coverlet from eastern Canada requires special mention: the all white one usually woven of cotton strips and yarns, although a few examples have no rags. These coverlets are traditionally *couvertures de mariage*, or bridal coverlets, one of which was an integral part of any dowry in Acadian areas, and at least in some Scottish ones. This special part of the trousseau might be made by the bride herself or by an older relation either for her or for the groom. The examples shown here are all Acadian and come from Tignish (no. 196), Chéticamp (nos. 200–1), and River

Bourgeois (no. 206). Others have been seen at Caraquet. Examples with a Scottish history from Prince Edward Island and from Cape Breton are known. They have also been reported from the Codroy Valley in the southwest corner of Newfoundland. It was from this isolated agricultural community that the information came that it might take as long as eight years to gather and treasure a sufficient store of white cotton rags to weave one of these bridal coverlets. Although not near an Acadian community, the cultural ties between this part of Newfoundland and neighbouring Cape Breton were very strong. It is probable that the appearance of these special white coverlets in a Scottish milieu was a cultural borrowing from the neighbouring Acadians. It must be remembered that many of the Scots coming to Prince Edward Island and Cape Breton were Gaelic-speaking Highlanders who knew no English. Granted they knew no French either, but many were Roman Catholics and religion brought them into much closer contact with the Acadians than with other settlers in the same area. Intermarriage did occur and it would be seen that a bride from either culture would have her *couverture de mariage*. This would have introduced the custom into purely Scottish areas.

Two means of patterning two-shaft coverlets were used in Quebec in addition to simple banding: *à la planche* and *boutonnue*, or boutonné, on the North Shore of the St Lawrence, and boutonné across the river on the South Shore. The surviving documented examples of *à la planche* patterning come from Ile-aux-Coudres, which lies off Baie-St-Paul in Charlevoix County. The motifs are usually in decorative chessboard bands across the width of the material, but were occasionally used for more adventurous patterning to produce brocaded geometric forms (no. 212). In both types, the two shafts of the looms were threaded to produce the ground; then the *planche*, a thin board two to three inches wide, was inserted through the warp ends behind the shafts regularly over and under a set number of threads across the width. From the Canadian examples seen, it appears likely that the number of ends in each unit was governed by the number of ends in one portee. If the warp was made using four balls of yarn, the number of ends in a portee was eight; if five were used, the result would be ten. This number would be what was required for half an inch of width with the warp set either sixteen or twenty ends per inch respectively. The portee cross would be used in winding the warp on the beam of the loom. It would be a simple matter to insert the *planche* before removing the cross sticks. Once in place, the board was pushed to the back of the loom, until wanted for patterning. It was then pulled forward and turned on edge, forming a special shed with groups of threads over the board raised and those underneath lowered, ready for a shot of pattern weft to be thrown. After another shot of ground had been inserted, the board was turned on edge again, and another shot of pattern weft put in. These steps were repeated as desired, usually until the motif was squared. In the simpler types of *à la planche* patterning only one board was used (fig. 20, nos. 210–11), but if the opposite block was wanted, the first board was pushed back and a second one inserted quite easily in front of it, passing over the threads that lay

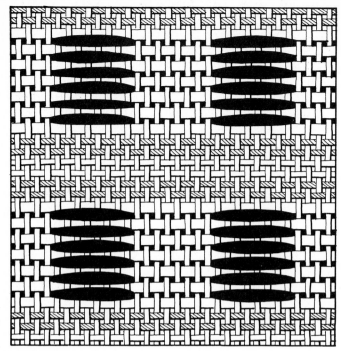

FIGURE 20

FIGURE 21

over the first board and under those that were beneath it. After the second board was used for patterning, it had to be removed before the first one could be used again (fig. 21). A brief glance at *à la planche* coverlets will show that most of those using the two blocks use first one, then the second, and return to the first for the characteristic chessboard bands. Away from the North Shore of the St Lawrence, only one documented example of *à la planche* patterning has been seen. This is an Acadian skirt length from the Memramcook Valley now in the New Brunswick Museum, Saint John (no. 75), suggesting that the technique may once have had a wider distribution in Canada. This is a point that should be borne in mind in considering the examples from Quebec that have no firm provenance.

In Europe, *à la planche* appears to be an old tradition. The head veil worn by Magdalena Meyer in the portrait by Holbein (Kunstmuseum, Basle) shows a simple banding in yellow on a sheer white ground that may well have been produced in this way. Although in its simplest form of use the *planche* was probably based on the portee, it could also be inserted arbitrarily in the warp in any order desired. A fair linen, *Abendmahlstuch*, in Bern (Historisches Museum, no. 4705) has bands across the ends that were undoubtedly patterned in this way. The ground is a fancy eight-shaft point twill and the wefts float over and under either four or seven ends depending on the threading plan of the twill. The technique has survived in peasant weaving. In numerous pieces from the Balkans in the Royal Ontario Museum, simple coloured bands as decoration for towelling and similar materials were probably produced using a single pattern board. A woollen bedcover from Transylvania (ROM 969.144.1) shows its use combined with boutonné. The possible origin of its survival in Quebec as part of the French tradition is supported by a group of nineteenth-century Breton aprons from Pont l'Abbé, Finisterre (MATP nos. 87.6.6.27–31). These examples, which may well be evidence of a once wide distri-

bution in France, have weft-faced patterns in coloured wools on a linen or hemp ground. An old type of Scottish coverlet used two-block patterns on a contrasting ground, and may be seen in an example from Strathspey (fig. 30). It is a type still being woven at Bridgend in Islay. A draft for a similar coverlet is found in Alexander Cameron's 'Draft and Cording Book' now in the National Museum of Antiquities, Edinburgh. This book dates from the late eighteenth century, and shows the pattern arranged on four shafts. Despite this, there seems little reason to doubt that the origins of these types lie in two shafts and two pattern boards. The same is true of the familiar 'monk's belt' patterns from Scandinavia. These are now invariably woven on four shafts; but may well be derived from an earlier use of the *à la planche* technique. In more advanced form, the use of a pattern board of this type has survived in this part of the world as the *skälblad* to produce pattern sheds for more complex constructions (Cyrus, 121, 144).

In Canada, the *couvrelit boutonnue* or *paresseuse boutonnue* (idly twisted knots) is found on the St Lawrence River below the city of Quebec, in Charlevoix County on the North Shore, in Kamouraska and Rimouski across the river. The alternate name *boutonné* is the one better known outside the local area, a fact that accounts for its use here. The technique employed in patterning these coverlets is a purely manual one and is used with either a yarn or a catalogne ground. The absence of loom control gives scope to individual endeavour in designing and presents a challenge that was successfully met by the domestic weavers in the rural areas where the technique was known. Their innate sense of colour and design made their creations a major contribution to the distinctive arts of Quebec.

The usual ground for boutonné is tabby or plain cloth, although a simple twill is found in a few late examples. The patterns are worked in contrasting wools, sometimes supplemented by cloth strips. Occasionally linen or cotton was

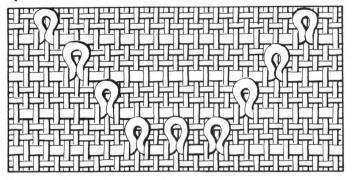

FIGURE 22

FIGURE 23

most effectively used for patterning all-white coverlets (nos. 223–5). In many of the more colourful examples from the North Shore, a catalogne ground is found, but where yarn has been used this is always of a finer grist than that used for patterning.

The motifs in the coverlets are formed by secondary wefts that are inserted after one or more shots of ground and pulled up in loops wherever they are required by the pattern, either with the fingers or aided by a small hook. When raised, these wefts may be placed on a gauge to ensure that all are the same size, but an experienced weaver might judge the height entirely by eye. The wefts may travel across the width from selvage to selvage (fig. 22) or be brocaded only in the areas required by the pattern. In the former case, there may or

may not be a shot of main weft in the same shed, but its presence adds slightly to the strength of the finished piece. The brocading wefts are always placed in the same shed as a shot of ground: they may be short strands slightly greater than the length required, the ends of which are held firmly in the shed (fig. 23; no. 226), or continuous lengths of yarn that turn on the face in moving from line to line of a motif (no. 215). In the latter case, they may be handled in a variety of ways (fig. 24).

Boutonné is an ancient and widespread technique known from about 2000 BC when it was used to pattern linen in eleventh-dynasty Egypt (Riefstahl [fig. 19], 17), and examples are common from the Coptic Period, both as plain weft-pile fabrics and as patterns in coloured wools on a linen

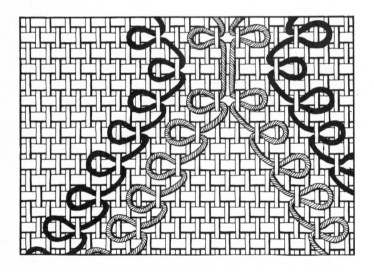

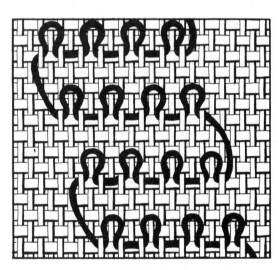

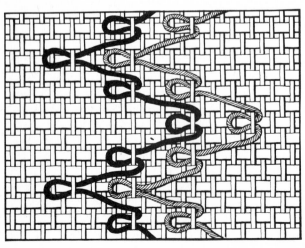

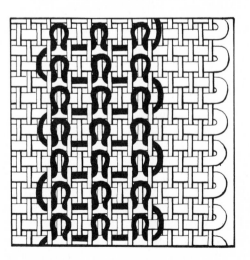

FIGURE 24

ground. Using gold thread, or sometimes silver, the technique added extra richness as *bouclé d'or* to many of the most sumptuous velvets woven in Italy and Spain in the fifteenth and sixteenth centuries. In these it might be used in different heights to produce rich motifs or scattered in the pile to add emphasis to the contours of the design. It has survived in south European folk art, and is known from various areas and countries: La Alpujarra in Spain (ROM 970.88.22, .23, .30), Italy (Studio, fig. 189), Transylvania (ROM 970.227.7), and Crete (ROM 959.148.62). It has been reported from Lithuania (Balcikonis, pl. 205), and is known from Finland (Henriksson, 237). It occurs in Mexico where it may well be a pre-Columbian technique (Start, 67, pl. 21). In England, in the nineteenth century, it formed the basis of a cottage industry centred on Bolton in Lancashire, and 'Bolton quilts' were produced in considerable numbers for the domestic market and for export. The Irish term *caddow* that was sometimes applied to them appears to have no other basis than romanticism for selling purposes.

The Bolton coverlets were always of white cotton and throughout their period of production employed a fairly consistent range of motifs that became more rigid as the nineteenth century progressed. Earlier examples had a centre seam, such as one dated 1773 now at Winterthur (HFDM 62.123), but throughout the nineteenth century they were woven double width on wide looms. An example of this type with loops in two heights is dated 1804 and was found in Ontario (ROM 969.2). One dated December 31, 1888 is in the Museum at Bolton (T 62.63). It has the name of Ann Eliza P. Morris woven in as well; she was a grocer's wife at nearby Doffcocker. Undated examples assigned to this centre may be identified by cryptic letters and numbers worked in one corner that may have signified either the weaver or the pattern. Examples of 'Bolton quilts' are well known in Canada, and have been found with various romantic histories attached. They have come from Acadian communities in New Brunswick (MUM), from Nova Scotia (Uniacke House), Quebec (formerly CGC), and Ontario (fig. 25; ROM 948.99). The extensive production for export inspired imitation in the United States. The motifs in one coverlet made in the Rutgers factory in Paterson, New Jersey, in 1822 for Colonel Henry Rutgers (Schwartz, 330–2) shows the strong stylistic influence of Bolton despite the dominant eagle in the centre. The Deborah Hayes coverlet at the Shelburne Museum in Vermont (no. 10–149), woven for her in 1838, also shows a borrowing in simpler form of motifs and layout inspired by the imported examples.

The origins of the use of the boutonné technique at Bolton remain undetermined. The cottage industry that produced them was probably well established by the latter part of the eighteenth century, and may have developed from a local practice that pre-dated industrialization. Equally, the background of its use on the lower St Lawrence remains unknown. In Egypt, knowledge of the technique survived the Coptic Period and with the advance of Islam across north Africa into Spain was probably introduced into this part of Europe. It may have spread farther and reached France, but proof

of this has yet to be determined. No example has been found in any of the museums of that country, nor could any knowledge of its former existence be determined. Claims have been made that the technique was known in Brittany (Carless, 8), but no evidence of any kind has been put forward in support. One coverlet ascribed by the donor to this part of France, where it may possibly have been collected, has all the earmarks of the Bolton products and was unquestionably woven there (ROM 943.24.16).

At the time that the oldest extant coverlets were woven in Quebec on the North Shore, this method of patterning was fully understood and the examples that have survived show a masterful command of the technique (no. 215). Some of the motifs are indigenous and original; others, such as the eight-pointed star and the stylized tree forms, belong to the general design repertory. No satisfactory origin of this knowledge can yet be advanced, but the survival on the rather isolated North Shore of a forgotten French tradition cannot be ignored as a possibility. Two linen coverlets from the South Shore present the same mastery, but show the strong influence, even copying, of motifs from the imported Bolton luxuries. The similarities will be pointed out when discussing them in detail (fig. 25; nos. 223, 225).

The last type of two-shaft coverlet to be dicussed is simple but handsome, and entirely weft-faced with the warp completely hidden. Two colours are used alternately to produce the characteristic patterns, and these coverlets represent an enormous amount of work in preparing yarns and in weaving. All but two that have been seen come from the neighbourhood of Sherkston in Humberstone Township, Welland County, near the north shore of Lake Erie. This was essentially a Mennonite community and the census returns show that many of the settlers were born in France. Hans Peter, a professional weaver who wove coverlets of this type (nos. 231–2) is known to have been born in Mulhausen. Whether this is the modern Mulhouse in Haut-Rhin, or the village of Mulhausen in Bas-Rhin has not been determined. Of the two examples found outside the Humberstone area, one belonged to a Mennonite family in York County that had connections with the Sherkston community; the other was collected near Milverton in Perth County (ROM 967.220.1), another Mennonite area where some settlers may well have had a similar history. In view of the very localized occurrence of this type of coverlet, it is possible that they represent a practice and tradition brought from Alsace. If this is so, the European antecedents appear not to have survived.

It is an interesting sidelight that very few Mennonites are found listed in the census returns as professional weavers. Hans Peter is one of only four in 1871 and the only one whose work has been identified. Even at the best of times, weaving was not an especially remunerative occupation and the Mennonites undoubtedly found farming a much more satisfying and rewarding method of earning their daily bread. As good farmers, they were quite able to pay to have their weaving done by others.

To produce the characteristic patterns of these weft-faced coverlets, the warp is threaded so that it is alternately single,

FIGURE 25

and in groups of three to five ends that operate as a unit. Arranging the warp in this way produces ribs that are alternately heavy and fine, and which, woven with two colours also used alternately, produces fine ribs in one colour and heavy ribs in the other, on one face, and with the colours reversed on the other. By placing two heavy ribs side by side at regulated intervals, the colouring is reversed producing simple two-block patterns of alternating dominant colour. As each pattern unit is squared, two shots of the same weft are used in succession to change the colouring of the ribs. These points are demonstrated in the diagram (fig. 26), where the weave is shown schematically with the wefts separated to allow the details of the construction of the border, the chessboard block, and the main motif to be seen.

The usual type of warp yarn in these various two-shaft coverlets is a z singles natural white cotton that would have been obtained in imported skeins from pedlars and from local general stores. Like the similar handspun linen that is found in a few examples from French-speaking areas, this would have been sized, probably with starch, before it was put on the loom. Unless otherwise specified in the following descriptions, this is the type and twist of yarn found in these coverlets. The plied cotton warp found in some pieces from Quebec is much finer than the plied cottons found elsewhere in Canada. It more closely resembles the cotton in some possibly Scottish overshot coverlets and may have been imported from Great Britain rather than from the United States.

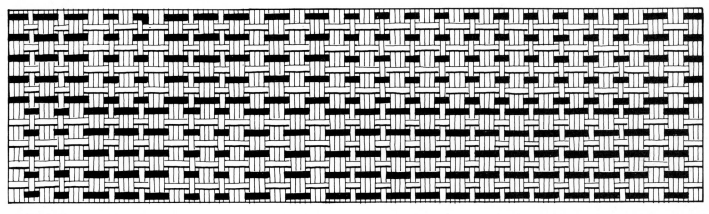

FIGURE 26

196 / Prince Edward Island. Tignish, Prince County. Probably 1825-50
Musée Acadien, Miscouche, PEI. Gift of
Mlle Clothilde Arsenault
Couverture de mariage (bridal coverlet). L. 225cm; w. 159cm, plus fringes

Entirely white linen (warp, z singles; weft, z singles, and z, 3s). Regularly banded with the two weights of yarn, with four shots of fine alternating with two of the heavier to produce a subtle and lovely texture. The added fringes are remarkably handsome. This coverlet was inherited by the donor. There are two other white cotton *couvertures de mariage* in Musée Acadien. One was woven by Mme Irenée Arsenault of St-Chrysostome for her son Larion (Hilarion) who was married about 1870. (Photograph: Heckbert Studio)

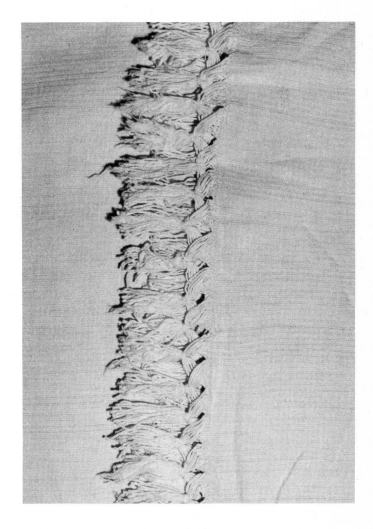

197 / Prince Edward Island. Miscouche, Prince County. About 1840-50
Musée Acadien, Miscouche, PEI. Gift of Mme Arthur (Sophie) Gaudet
Coverlet or overblanket. L. 214cm; w. 175cm

Warp of natural white cotton interspersed irregularly with blue-green, almost completely hidden by black wool weft banded with natural and red-violet wools, and natural white cotton (all z singles). It is not known what was used to obtain the peculiar violet colour, possibly a lichen of the *tripe de roche* family (*Umbillicaria*). It occurs in several pieces from the Maritime Provinces and Quebec that predate the discovery of aniline violet in 1856, the usual source of such shades. It is probable that this material was woven as a skirt length (cf. nos. 75–7) and was made up as a bed covering when traditional styles went out of use. (Photograph: Heckbert Studio)

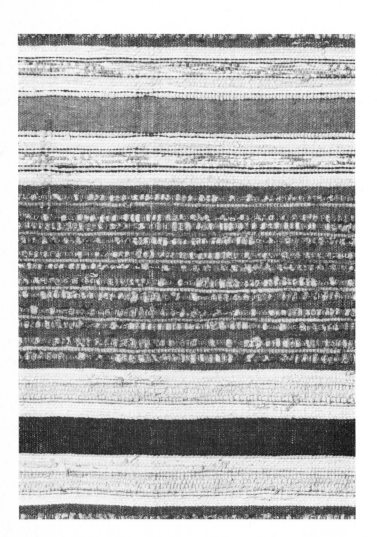

198 / Quebec. Magdalen Islands. About 1900
ROM 970.90.13. Gift of Mrs John David Eaton. Ex coll. CGC
Catalogne coverlet (half). L. 175cm; w. 91cm

Natural white cotton warp (z, 2s) with red, ochre, and purple wools, woollen and cotton cloth strips. Although known from Acadia, no examples of woollen catalogne bedcovers are known that have survived from the Quebec mainland, making this one unique for the province. The length is broken at intervals by bold bands of cotton strips centred alternately by ochre and purple wools. The ground is of red wool combined with strips woven of red wool and white cotton strips. These came from an even older bedcover, the good parts of which have been re-used yet another time showing the value that was placed on all salvageable material.

199 / New Brunswick. Caraquet. 20th century
Musée de Caraquet, Caraquet, NB
Catalogne coverlet. L. 207cm; w. 177cm

Warp of natural white cotton, with regularly repeating
multi-coloured bands: blue, yellow, and red wools, white,
black, pink, and grey cotton strips. At intervals, wider bands
of red or blue wool plied with white cotton give a 'salt and
pepper' effect. This gay coverlet, a late example of traditional
work, shows masterful designing with simple means. (Photograph: Burnham)

200 / Nova Scotia. Belle Côte, Chéticamp, Cape Breton.
19th century, 2nd half
ROM 968.308.4. Gift of Mr and Mrs Harold B. Burnham
Catalogne coverlet (half). L. 208cm; w. 84cm

All white: cotton yarn and cotton strips in regular repeating
bands of eight yarn and five strips on a cotton warp. An all-
white coverlet of this type was an essential part of an Acadian girl's trousseau and was known as a *couverture de
mariage*. In a household, the worn white materials were put
aside and saved for this purpose. It sometimes took a number
of years to save enough for a coverlet.

201 / Nova Scotia. Plateau, Chéticamp, Cape Breton.
19th century, 2nd half.
ROM 968.308.3. Gift of Mr and Mrs Harold B. Burnham
Catalogne coverlet (half). L. 193cm; w. 85cm

All white: cotton yarn and cotton strips on cotton warp.
Another example with an effective use of finely cut cotton
strips in bands of alternating width that are separated by contrasting ones woven with cotton yarn.

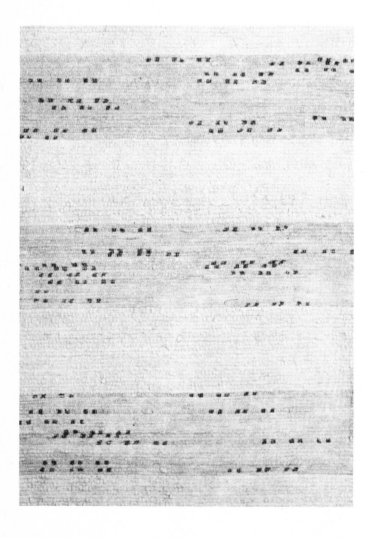

202 / Nova Scotia. Grand Etang, Chéticamp, Cape Breton.
19th century, 2nd half.
ROM 968.308.8. Gift of Mr and Mrs Harold B. Burnham
Catalogne coverlet (half). L. 205cm; w. 85cm

Banded regularly with white cotton strips and natural woollen strips on natural cotton warp. Between each pick of the
cloth strips, two picks of cotton yarns have been used giving
strength and firmness to the fabric. The triple pairs of brown
flecks that show in the woollen bands indicate that these
strips have been cut from blankets of handspun wool that
had three pairs of narrow bands across the ends.

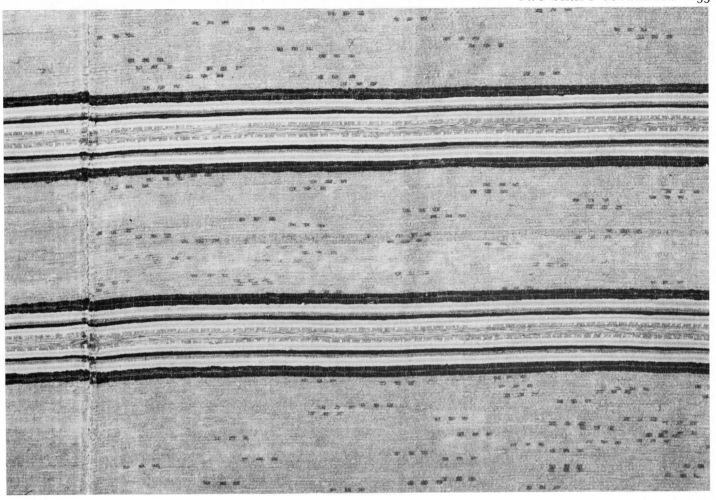

203 / Nova Scotia. Grand Etang, Chéticamp, Cape Breton. Mid-19th century
ROM 968.308.9. Gift of Mr and Mrs Harold B. Burnham
Catalogne coverlet. L. 201cm; w. 172cm

Natural white cotton warp woven with strips of natural wool blanketing banded at regular intervals with stronger colours: black woollen strips, white and red cotton strips, pale pink and dark brown wools. The centre of each pattern band is marked by the use of two cotton strips, one red, the other white, twisted together. This occurs frequently in Acadian work. To either side of this, there is a single shot of a cata- logne strip which, in the photograph, shows a row of white spots across the width. These strips have been cut from an older worn-out coverlet that had been woven with reddish-beige wool banded with single shots of white cotton strips. It is these that show as white dots. The taste and skill of the weaver in using her limited resources to such a full and effective extent are truly masterful.

(in colour PLATE II)

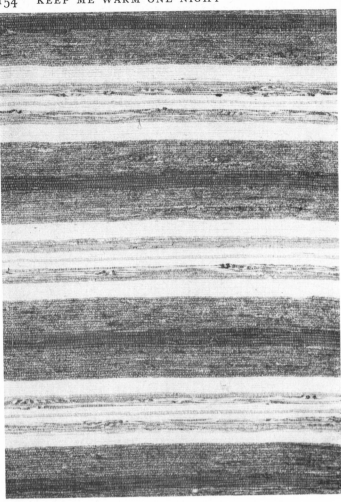

204 / Nova Scotia. Belle Marche, Chéticamp, Cape Breton.
19th century, 2nd half
ROM 968.308.10. Gift of Mr and Mrs Harold B. Burnham
Catalogne coverlet. L. 190cm; w. 175cm

Natural white cotton warp woven with strips of woollen and
cotton cloth, regularly banded with light brown woollen
centred by grey woollen, and grey cotton strips broken by
light brown and grey woollens. The effect appears muted,
but is quite rich: the darks and lights are well balanced in
the banding.

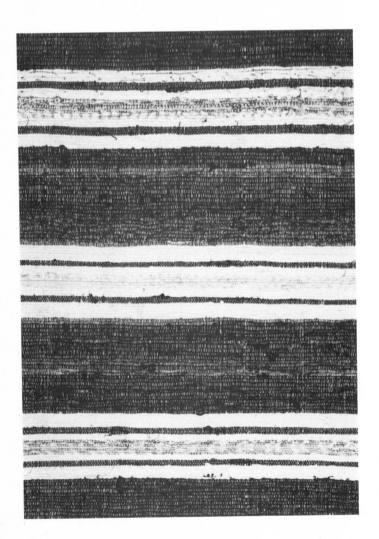

205 / Nova Scotia. Belle Marche, Chéticamp, Cape Breton.
19th century, 2nd half.
ROM 968.308.6. Gift of Mr and Mrs Harold B. Burnham
Catalogne coverlet (half). L. 213cm; w. 89cm

Warp natural white cotton woven with dark woollen strips,
probably from clothing, banded regularly with cotton strips,
the outer bands white, the centre of prints. These are separated by narrow black bands. With the winter conditions on
this coast, warm heavy bedding was essential and coverings
of this type re-using woollen materials were found in every
home. They went out of use only with the introduction of
oil space heaters. When rug hooking was introduced as a
flourishing home industry in the 1920s, it completely supplanted weaving in the area.

206 / Nova Scotia. River Bourgeois, Cape Breton.
About 1880
ROM 970.118.12. Gift of Mr and Mrs Harold B. Burnham
White coverlet. L. 201cm; w. 157cm

Natural white cotton warp and weft, the latter used double, with groups of four bands at intervals formed by using the weft sixfold. This is an example of the white *couvertures de mariage* from this area of Acadian culture, showing the same traditions as at Miscouche and Chéticamp (nos. 196, 200–1). Woven by Mme Tenase Degas.

207 / Nova Scotia. River Bourgeois, Cape Breton.
About 1850–60
ROM 970.118.14. Gift of Mr and Mrs Harold B. Burnham
Coverlet or overblanket. L. 213cm; w. 149cm

Natural white cotton warp woven with natural and faded pink wools. Two narrow bands of dark slate wool repeat regularly. These are edged by a white cotton cloth strip and centred by red and white cotton strips twisted together giving a barber pole effect. Woven by Mme Amable Degas.

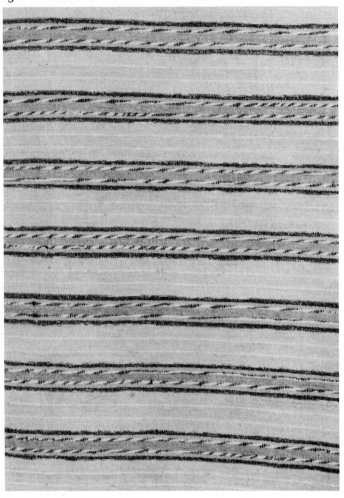

208 / Nova Scotia. River Bourgeois, Cape Breton.
About 1850–60
ROM 970.118.15. Gift of Mr and Mrs Harold B. Burnham
Coverlet or overblanket. L. 200cm; w. 157cm

Natural white cotton warp woven with natural wool broken
by white cotton strips; banded regularly with pink wool
edged with blue and enclosing twisted strips of cotton cloth.
Woven by Mme Amable Degas.

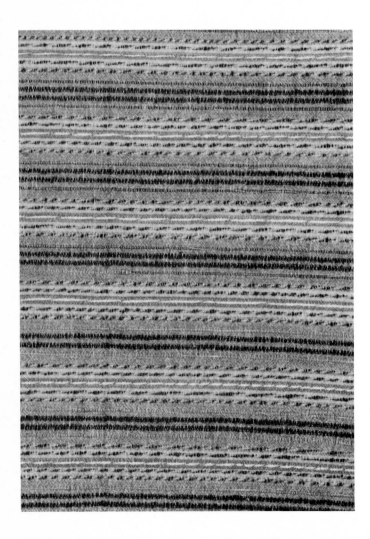

209 / Nova Scotia. River Bourgeois, Cape Breton.
About 1880
ROM 970.118.13. Gift of Mr and Mrs Harold B. Burnham
Coverlet or overblanket. L. 213cm; w. 159cm

Natural white cotton warp regularly banded with warm
colourful yarns in red, pink, and light blue wools, and
black woollen and white cotton cloth strips. The very heavy
bands are of ochre wool and sixfold natural cotton twisted
together and of black wool twisted in the same way with pink.
Similar, but less colourful, blankets are known from Memramcook and Beaubassin in New Brunswick.

210 / Quebec. Ile-aux-Coudres, Cté Charlevoix. 1875-85
NGC 9615
Catalogne coverlet with *à la planche* bands. L. 199cm;
w. 170cm

Natural white cotton warp (z, 2s) woven with cotton cloth
strips of various colours, and with bands of wool in red,
green, magenta, orange, purple, and maroon. Between these
bands, the decoration is in wools in the same colours in a
simple but effective arrangement of a single *à la planche*
block used in combination with narrow bands (fig. 20).
Collected by Dr C.M. Barbeau, whose notes record that it
was woven by Mme Germain-Hilaire Demeules.

211 / Quebec. 1875-90
ROM 970.90.1. Gift of Mrs John David Eaton. Ex coll. CGC
Coverlet patterned *à la planche*. L. 210cm, plus added fringe;
w. 193cm, plus added fringe

White ground of natural white cotton warp (z, 2s) and
bleached linen weft (z singles) and patterned with indigo
blue and red wools (z singles). The pleasant layout of
checked squares and rectangles based on a single *à la planche*
block is basically in blue, with a touch of red across the centre
of each large unit. No firm provenance can be assigned to
this piece.

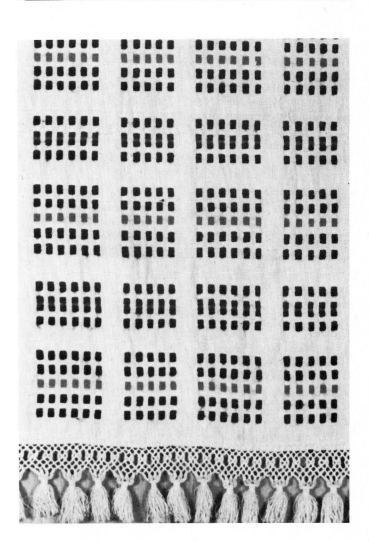

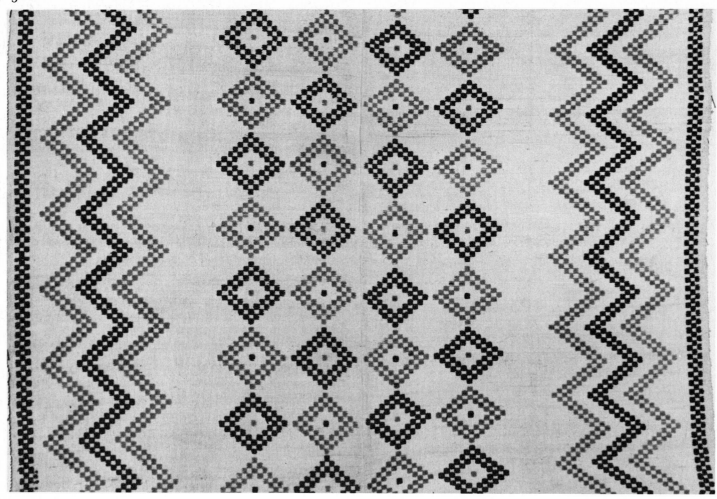

212 / Quebec. Ile-aux-Coudres, Cté Charlevoix.
Late 19th century
NMM A287
Catalogne coverlet patterned *à la planche*. L. 179cm;
w. 169cm

Natural white cotton warp (z, 2s) woven with similar cotton
yarn, and white cotton cloth strips. These are always used
in the same order: two picks of yarn to one of catalogne. The
à la planche motifs are brocaded in brick red and pale green
wools, and always used before and after each shot of catalogne. Collected by Dr C.M. Barbeau from Mme Desgagne,
La Baleine, Ile-aux-Coudres.

213 / Quebec. Ile-aux-Coudres, Cté Charlevoix.
Late 19th century
NGC 9621
Coverlet patterned with *à la planche* and boutonné bands.
L. 214cm; w. 176cm

Natural linen warp with brightly coloured bands in purple,
red, orange, magenta, and blue wools plied with natural linen
tow. These are evenly spaced along the length alternating
with bands decorated on light-coloured cotton strip grounds:
à la planche motifs edged with scarlet woollen strips, and
boutonné bands, both in the same bright wools. Some of the
boutonné wefts travel across the width, others are brocaded
(figs. 22–3). Woven by Mme Germaine Desgagne and collected by Dr C.M. Barbeau.

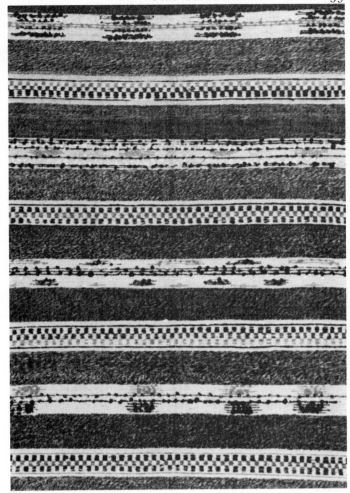

214 / Quebec. Les Eboulements-en-Bas, Cté Charlevoix.
Probably about 1865
ROM 970.90.7. Gift of Mrs John David Eaton. Ex coll. CGC
Boutonné coverlet. L. 204cm; w. 171cm

Natural white cotton warp (z, 2s) woven with various
coloured cotton cloth strips, and olive drab and purple wools.
The ground is formed of light-coloured cotton strips with
two to four picks of stronger colour at regular intervals, one of
which is raised in boutonné loops across the width. Collected
by Dr C.M. Barbeau from Mme François Coulombe in 1937
when she was 86 years of age. She had woven it as a young
girl. The ends are bound with checked cotton.

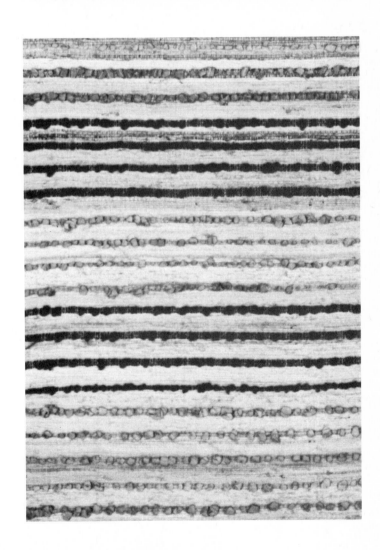

215 / Quebec. Ile-aux-Coudres, Cté Charlevoix.
Traditionally about 1835
ROM 970.90.5. Gift of Mrs John David Eaton. Ex coll. CGC
Catalogne coverlet patterned *à la planche* and with
boutonné. L. 182cm; w. 169cm

Natural white cotton warp (fine z, 2s) woven with light-
coloured cotton strips, some plain, some printed. The *à la
planche* bands are violet, green, red, purple, and yellow
wools used in pairs. The boutonné patterns are in combinations of similar colours and brocaded with the wools turning
on the face (fig. 24). The main chevron lines are laid in after
every fourth pick, but the more solid guards after every second
one. The colours found in this coverlet are definitely of vegetable rather than chemical origin, despite the wide and
unusual palette. The printed cottons in the ground give cre-
dence to the traditional date. They include one in black and
one in purple that are probably copperplate prints that may
well date from the early nineteenth century. The coverlet
was collected by Dr C.M. Barbeau, who reported that it was
made about 1835 and handed down as part of a marriage
dot.
(*in colour* PLATE II)

216 / Quebec. Ile-aux-Coudres, Cté Charlevoix. About 1870
NGC 9612
Catalogne coverlet with *à la planche* and boutonné patterns.
L. 196cm; w. 188cm

Half-bleached linen warp, woven with white cotton strips.
The field is divided into narrow panels by *à la planche* bands
in dyed wools used in pairs of colours: violet and brown, dark
green and violet, and royal blue and gold. Brocaded boutonné
stars and crosses decorate the panels, and there are boutonné
borders down both sides similar to those on no. 215. They are
worked in wools of the same colours as the bands with the
addition of orange, red, and purple. These wefts are laid into
the sheds as required and turn on the face. Collected by Dr
C.M. Barbeau from Phedime Bouchard; woven by Hélène
Desgagne.

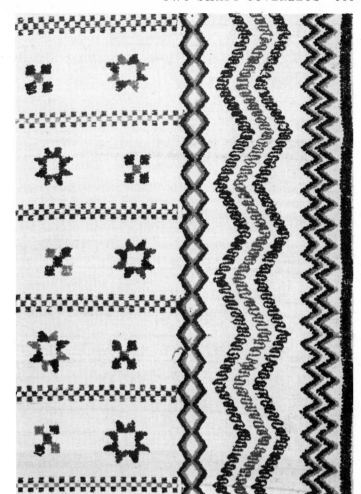

217 / Quebec. Ile-aux-Coudres, Cté Charlevoix. About 1870
NGC 9618
Catalogne coverlet with boutonné patterning. L. 207cm;
w. 154cm

Bleached linen warp, woven with five picks of fine natural
white cotton (z, 2s) alternating with one strip of white cotton cloth. The patterns are in boutonné in coloured wools:
reds, browns, and light blue, and crimson woollen cloth strips.
Occasionally the white cotton strips of the ground are raised
in loops for white pattern details. The boutonné wefts are
brocaded in the shed used for the cotton strips. The stylized
fir and flowering tree are found as traditional motifs in coverlets and hooked rugs from the North Shore of the St Lawrence. Collected by Dr C.M. Barbeau, and woven by Nelsie
Laforest.

218 / Quebec. Baie-St-Paul, Cté Charlevoix. 1870-80
NMM A336
Boutonné coverlet. L. 198cm; w. 180cm

Both warp and main weft are natural linen (z singles) with boutonné pattern forming an allover lozenge lattice regularly banded in natural brown-black and buff (faded aniline violet) wools (z singles, hard twisted, used double). The boutonné weft is carried from selvage to selvage in every seventh shed, and raised in loops as required. Collected by Dr C.M. Barbeau.

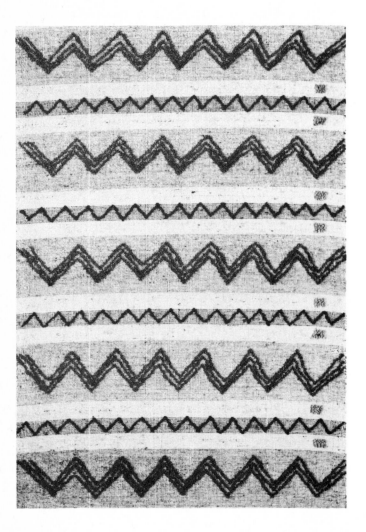

219 / Quebec. Cté Charlevoix. Late 19th century
CGC H153. Gift of Mrs G.W. Birks
Boutonné coverlet. L. 200cm; w. 151cm

Fine natural white cotton warp (z, 2s) woven with similar cotton, and purple wool in the wide bands with triple chevrons, blue wool in the narrow chevron bands, and red wool in the plain bands. The wefts are used with three shots of cotton between each one of wool.

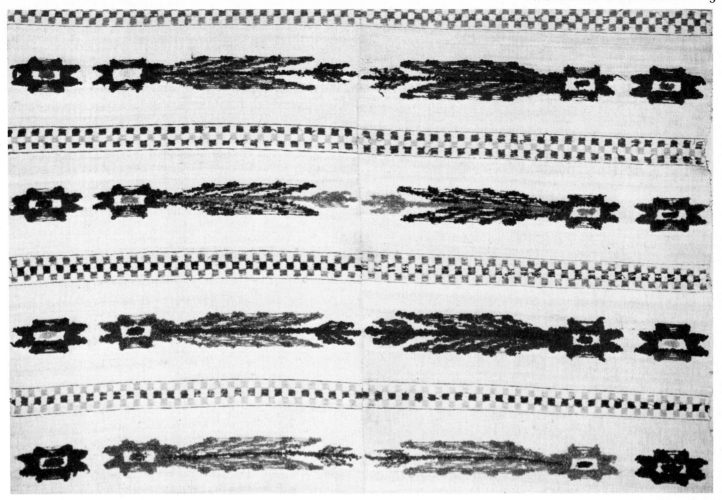

220 / Quebec. St-Urbain, Cté Charlevoix. About 1885
NGC 9626
Catalogne coverlet with boutonné and *à la planche*
patterning. L. 200cm; w. 167cm

Half-bleached linen warp with the ground woven of natural
white cotton cloth strips, and decorated by *à la planche* bands
in pairs of brightly coloured wools: mauve, orange, dark
green, red, yellow, maroon, and dark blue. These alternate
with bands of boutonné motifs, each having a stylized comet

with tail and an eight-pointed star in the same colours, but
supplemented with scarlet and purple cloth strips. This coverlet undoubtedly commemorates the Great Comet of 1882,
which was visible to the unaided eye for some weeks in September of that year and remained in sight for about nine
months (Chambers, 151). A similar coverlet is in the National Museum of Man, Ottawa. Both were collected by Dr
C.M. Barbeau, whose notes state that this one was woven
by Merence Bradette of Baie-St-Paul.

221 / Quebec. Ste-Irénée, Cté Charlevoix. About 1880
ROM 970.90.3. Gift of Mrs John David Eaton. Ex coll. CGC
Boutonné coverlet. L. 199cm; w. 177cm

Fine natural white cotton warp (z, 2s) with ground woven
with natural cotton singles of two weights, and natural wool
used irregularly. The boutonné pattern is brocaded with

rose, blue, and olive wools with every fourth shot of ground
weft. The strange layout of the design is due to the fact that
the coverlet was made for a box bed and so would require
only one border. The photograph of both this and the following one show the coverlets sideways as they would appear in
use when the one border would hang over the side of the bed.

222 / Quebec. Les Eboulements-en-Haut, Cté Charlevoix.
About 1885
NGC 9625
Boutonné coverlet. L. 194cm; w. 186cm

Fine natural white cotton warp (z, 2s) with natural wool
weft. The boutonné patterns are brocaded in yellow, purple,
maroon, red, orange, and blue wools, some of them plied
with cotton. The finer details of the figures are embroidered
in chain stitch. The design with the figures is charming and
quite unusual and the couple may well represent a bride and
groom. A somewhat similar embroidered coverlet from nearby St-Urbain is in the Montreal Museum of Fine Arts and
is known to be connected with a wedding of 1873. In contrast, it has a more balanced layout and a crocheted edging
(*Vie des Arts*, Noël [1961], 30). Collected by Dr C.M.
Barbeau.

223 / Quebec. Ste-Anne-de-la-Pocatière, Cté Kamouraska.
About 1863
ROM 970.90.6. Gift of Mrs John David Eaton. Ex coll. CGC
Boutonné coverlet. L. 252cm; w. 195cm

Bleached linen ground with 6-ply linen weft used, selvage
to selvage, for the boutonné patterning after every two shots
of ground weft. The linen yarns were prepared by the weaver,
Alida Thiboutat, from home-grown and -processed flax. The
coverlet took first prize the first year of the Quebec Provincial
Exhibition about 1870. The standards were obviously high
as it is an excellent piece of weaving of beautiful quality.

Like no. 225, also of linen and from the South Shore, this
coverlet shows the strong influence of the white cotton coverlets woven at Bolton in Lancashire (fig. 25). Many motifs
may be paralleled in the 'Bolton quilts': the patterned eight-
pointed star with its chain edging, the small stylized plants
in the angles formed by the star, the chain frame surrounding
the central field, and also the two borders. The outer border
of connected flowerheads and stars occurs frequently in the
English coverlets, and the wide inner border of opposed
meanders enclosing flowerheads is typical of many examples.
The same is true of the American examples mentioned earlier,
which were unquestionably influenced by the same source.
(*in colour* PLATE II)

224 / Quebec. Ile-aux-Coudres, Cté Charlevoix.
Late 19th century
NMM A337
Boutonné coverlet. L 214cm; w. 160cm

Warp and weft of natural white cotton (z, 2s) patterned
with heavy white candlewick carried from selvage to selvage
with every twelfth shot of ground. The ground is the less
usual 2/2 twill, and the pattern shows the addition of a mal-
tese cross to the familiar motifs of a voided unpatterned eight-
pointed star and stylized flowering trees. The layout of the
motifs in offset rows is unusual. Woven by Mme Nazaire
Tremblay, and collected by Dr C.M. Barbeau.

225 / Quebec. St-Simon, Cté Rimouski. About 1855
ROM 963.88. Gift of Miss D.J. Grant
Boutonné coverlet. L. 235cm; w. 188cm

Bleached linen (warp z singles, main weft the same used
double) with heavier 3-ply linen used for the patterns. This
boutonné weft is carried with the main weft from selvage
to selvage in every third shed. The quality of the handspun
linen gives the coverlet a most beautiful texture. The yarns
were spun and the coverlet woven by Mme Albertine Caron
of St-Simon.

Like no. 223 and another white linen boutonné coverlet
(ROM 970.201.2), both from the South Shore, this coverlet
betrays the strong influence of the imported 'Bolton quilts.'

226 / Quebec. Probably Cté Charlevoix (La Malbaie?).
Late 19th century
ROM 963.186
Boutonné coverlet. L. 182cm; w. 153cm

Natural white ground with fine cotton warp (z, 2s), and
wool weft (z, singles) with boutonné patterns in light blue,
dark blue, and rose-beige wools. The boutonné weft is used
after every sixth shot of ground. In the upper and lower
borders, this pattern weft is carried across from selvage to
selvage; elsewhere it is brocaded in short lengths with the
ends bound into the shed on either side of the motifs. This is
probably an early example of the coverlets woven for sale
at summer resorts on the North Shore of the lower St Lawrence, of which La Malbaie (Murray Bay) was one of the
most popular. As this cottage industry grew, a great number
of boutonné coverlets were produced, and many woven during the 1920s and 1930s are longer than this with a patterned
panel at the top to go over the pillows (ROM 967.162.3).

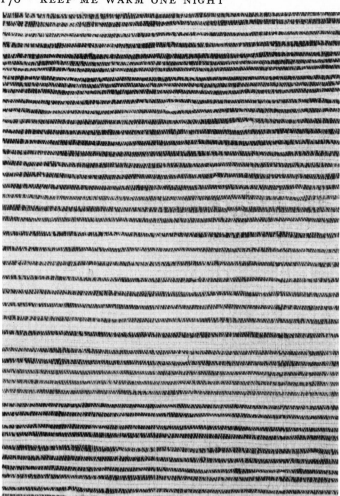

227 / Prince Edward Island. Murray Harbour, King's County. 1840-50
ROM 965.185. Gift of Miss Margaret MacFarlane
Catalogne coverlet. L. 181cm; w. 176cm

Natural white cotton warp, banded with the same white cotton used double, white cotton cloth strips, and green wool. In theory the repeat of the bands appears to be 1 wool, 1 cotton, 1 wool, followed by 1 strip, 1 cotton, 1 strip, but in practice the weaver found this order a little difficult, and the result is a quite delightful irregularity. The re-use of old materials for weaving is found in Scotland, so it is not surprising to find it in the Scottish areas of the Maritime Provinces.

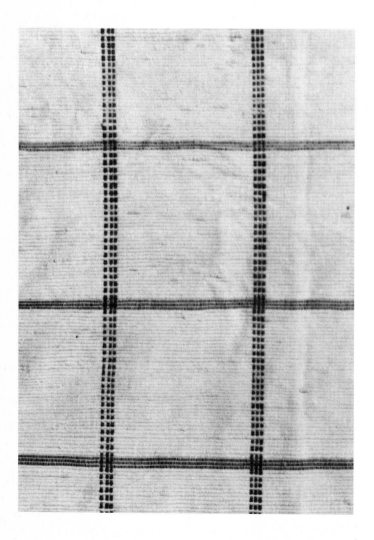

228 / Prince Edward Island. Desable, Queen's County. Mid-19th century
ROM 968.308.12. Gift of Mr and Mrs Harold B. Burnham
Catalogne coverlet. L. 182cm; w. 170cm

Natural white cotton with the same yarn used for weft, and with every third shot of white cotton cloth strips. The large check is formed by three spaced red cotton cloth strips in both warp and weft. Another excellent example of the Scottish tradition of *cloutie*, and the only recorded example in Canada with rags used in the warp as well as in the weft.

229 / Nova Scotia. Troy, Cape Breton. Mid-19th century
Mackley Collection, Sydney, NS
Catalogne coverlet. L. 180cm; w. 171cm

Natural white cotton warp regularly banded with four shots
of white cotton yarn followed by seven shots of white cotton
strips. A simple but unusual and effective decoration is made
by laying short strips of turkey-red cotton rags at regular
intervals in the centre of each band of strips. These are
arranged in half-drop repeat.

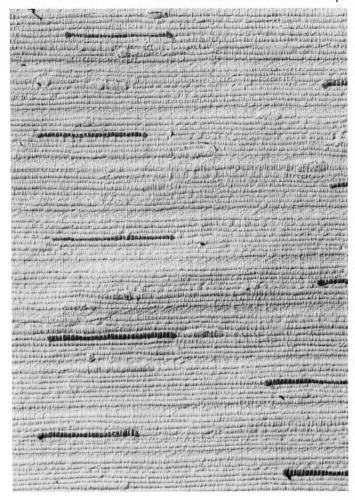

230 / Nova Scotia. Cape North, Cape Breton.
Probably 1885-1900
Mackley Collection, Sydney, NS
Catalogne coverlet with boutonné. L. 172cm; w. 164cm

Natural white cotton warp woven with alternate shots of the
same white cotton and heavy rag strips which are raised in
loops as required to form an allover lozenge lattice pattern.
This coverlet, woven in a Scottish settlement in Cape Breton,
is the only one patterned with weft loops that has been
recorded outside the lower St Lawrence region of Quebec.

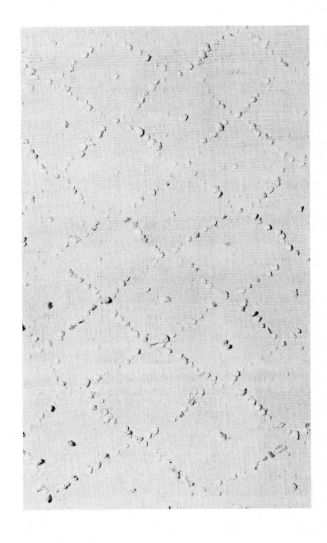

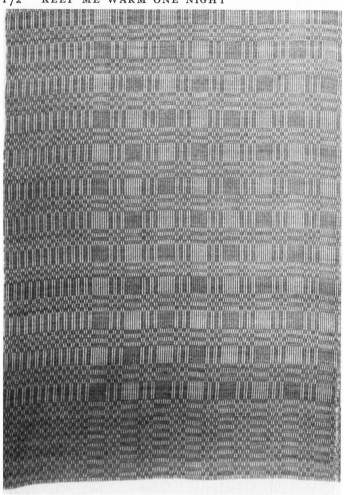

231 / Ontario. Near Sherkston, Humberstone Township, Welland County. 1850-60
ROM 950.93.1. Gift of Mrs Verna Hall
Weft-faced coverlet. L. 211cm; w. 187cm

The warp is natural white cotton entirely covered by fine dark red and dark blue wool wefts. These are used alternately except where a change of colour is needed by the pattern when two shots of red are thrown in succession (fig. 26). This and the following coverlet were woven for the donor's grandmother, Margaret Reeb, by Hans Peter, a professional weaver who lived near Sherkston.

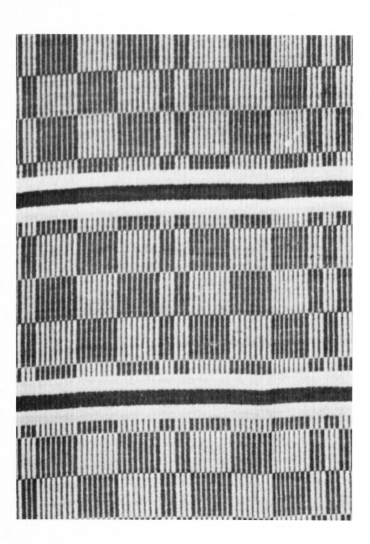

232 / Ontario. Near Sherkston, Humberstone Township, Welland County. 1850-60
ROM 950.93.2. Gift of Mrs Verna Hall
Weft-faced coverlet. L. 165cm; w. 186cm

The warp is natural white cotton entirely hidden by wool wefts in blue, yellow, and green (faded). Technically it is the same as no. 231, and in both the warp is arranged so that a single end alternates with a group of five to produce the vertical ribs of the pattern. The history is identical, this one also having been woven by Hans Peter. The 1871 census lists him as a professional weaver, then 61 years of age, a Mennonite born in France, probably in Alsace.

233 / Ontario. Sherkston, Humberstone Township, Welland County. 1840-50
ROM 968.272.2. Gift of Mr and Mrs Harold B. Burnham
Weft-faced coverlet. L. 216cm; w. 164cm

The warp is natural linen (z, 2s) hidden by a fine wool weft in dull yellow and light brown (probably faded red). Traditionally this and the following example were woven by Mrs Jacob Benner of Sherkston. They are in the same technique as the previous two, but are threaded so that one warp works against a group of three. Although not perhaps quite as expertly woven as the professional work, the spinning of the wool is superb and the linen of beautiful quality.

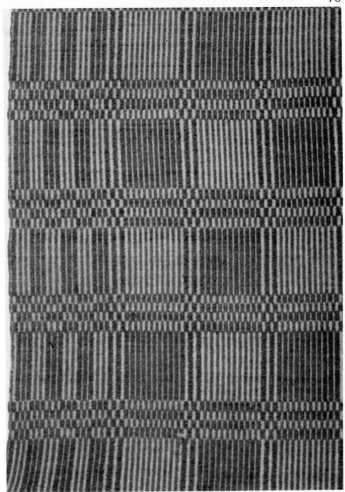

234 / Ontario. Sherkston, Humberstone Township, Welland County. About 1840-50
ROM 968.272.1. Gift of Mr and Mrs Harold B. Burnham
Weft-faced coverlet. L. 213cm; w. 174cm

The warp is natural linen (z, 2s) and the weft is fine brown wool and linen like the warp used alternately in the patterned bands. The bands that separate them are in ochre and black wools and the heading in green and brown wools. This is also believed to be the work of Mrs Jacob Benner. Her family, like Hans Peter, is thought to have come from Alsace. Both were Mennonite. This is a technique that is extravagant of materials and labour, but a good weaver could produce a variety of patterns on a simple two-shaft loom.

Overshot coverlets

Four-shaft overshot coverlets overshadow all other old hand-weaving in North America. More of them were woven than of any other type of coverlet and their chances of survival have been better than that of the thousands of yards of clothing materials, blanketing, and carpeting that were produced and worn out during the nineteenth century. Outside the areas of French tradition, overshot coverlets and pieced quilts were the main decorative bed coverings in the rural areas of the eastern half of Canada. They were known by several other names: draft rugs in Prince Edward Island and draft coverlets in Cape Breton because of the pattern drafts used for threading the loom; in Ontario by the descriptive name 'floatwork' by Samuel Fry of Vineland, and as single coverlets by John Campbell of Komoka, who also wove the more complex doublecloth coverlets on his jacquard loom; and as Chinee coverlids in the Annapolis Valley and Digby County, Nova Scotia, probably because the patterns were blue and white like the coveted ceramics brought from China.

Despite its wide occurrence in North America, the origins of the overshot technique on this continent remain unestablished. In the United States, it has long been called 'Colonial' overshot, but it is more than doubtful whether its use can be dated to the pre-Revolutionary period. It has even been suggested that it is a technique developed independently in the United States, but this theory is totally unfounded.

It is a technique of wide distribution as is shown by investigation and examination of non-American examples. Documented pieces of overshot weave from various parts of Europe exist in museum collections, or have been illustrated in publications: Spain (fig. 27; ROM 970.88.32), Greece (fig. 28; ROM 947.20.16; 959.148.1), Romania (Banateanu, figs. 130 and 334; ROM 970.240.4-.6) where it is still widely used, Ukraine and Byelorussia (MEN), Poland where it is known as 'Upper Baltic' weave (Piwockiego, pls. 90, 91, 106), the Baltic States (Balcikonis, 120, 124, 131), Sweden where it is known as *dälldrall* (NM), Norway where it is called 'Swedish weave' (NFM), and Germany (Galvin, 107).

This list establishes no more than that the knowledge of the technique is widespread, as none of the areas mentioned presents a reasonable source for its occurrence in North America. The regions of Spanish settlement and influence were south of the Rio Grande and there the technique does not appear to be known. Greek, Romanian, and Russian immigration is of late nineteenth- and twentieth-century date, and with few exceptions the same is true of Polish and Balt settlers. Despite the fact that the technique can be reported from Germany, it was not a popular one, more complex weaves that will be discussed later being preferred. The early Swedish settlement in Delaware was of short duration (1638–55), and its main purpose, like those of other nations, was as a base for fishing, for raising tobacco, and as an opportunity for the adventurous in the fur trade. Later immigration from Scandinavia is of late nineteenth- and twentieth-century date.

The two remaining possible sources of origin in North America are France and the British Isles. Nothing in the traditions of French-speaking Canada points to an early use

FIGURE 27

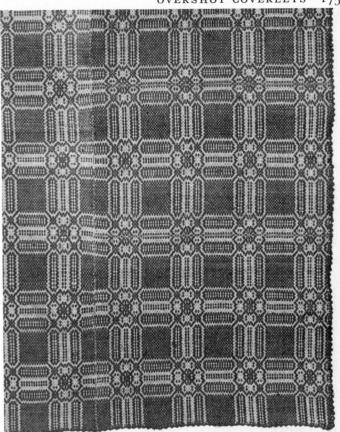

FIGURE 28

of the technique in this country, nor have examples been discovered in the museums of France. A French origin would not account for its widespread occurrence in the United States despite the presence of Huguenot settlers in New England. Nor does an English origin seem likely. Weaving there has been on a commercial basis since the early Middle Ages, and no trace has been unearthed to suggest a use of overshot patterning. It may possibly have existed before the Industrial Revolution, but this would likely have been on a very local basis in isolated rural communities. Of the few English weavers' pattern books that have survived, one from Wiltshire in the Cooper-Hewitt Museum, New York, shows a draft for a coverlet dated 1716 (Titball, 19), but it is a point twill construction.

Before the latter part of the eighteenth century there was little emigration to North America from Ireland, and even less from Wales, but there was considerable settlement of Scottish origin earlier in the century. During the Seven Years' War, Scottish regiments had been involved in North America. With its close in 1763 the whole of the northern part of the continent came under British rule by the Treaty of Paris. Remembering the '45, the English government considered an experienced soldiery too great a danger to be allowed to return to Scotland, particularly the Highlands. The regiments were disbanded on this side of the Atlantic to settle both in the American colonies and in Canada. Once established, these men were often joined by their relatives and clansmen. With the Clearances in Scotland, many Scots found their way across the Atlantic, either by choice or by force. This tide of immigration started in the 1760s and

lasted well into the nineteenth century. Whole uprooted communities re-established themselves, particularly in Canada, 'far from the shieling and the misty island.'

During the recording of coverlets in Canada, a few have been found with a tradition of having been brought from Scotland. A blue and white one found in New Brunswick by Dr Ivan Crowell, but now known only from a photograph, was stated to have been woven at Girvan, south of Ayr, and has a pattern same as no. 342. In addition to others recorded that are still in private hands in Ontario, two with Scottish histories are in the Royal Ontario Museum. Both are red and white, although one has had a hard life and has faded to pink. Both have a cotton fringe across the lower edge, and wool fringes down the sides. The pattern of one is similar to no. 319 (ROM 968.275). It is believed to have belonged to a bride of the 1840s in southwest Scotland. Shortly after her marriage, she lived for a while in Northern Ireland and then came to Canada bringing the coverlet with her. The more worn and faded example shows the same design as no. 350, and was traditionally brought from Skye to Glengarry County in Ontario about 1830 (ROM 962.245). Another in blue and white in the same pattern was brought from the same part of Scotland to Cape Breton, where it is now in the Mackley Collection. The differences between the possibly Scottish ones examined and Canadian examples are found in the yarns. The ground of the former is a fine two-ply cotton both in warp and in weft, in contrast to the plied warp and singles weft that is normal in Canada; they have a pattern weft that usually is decidedly heavier than that found in North American examples. Another point of difference is the red dye used. Although not yet identified, it does not appear to be madder. It is not as fast to water and light as the reds found in North American coverlets and it lacks the rust tone normally associated with madder-dyed wool found on this continent.

The finding of these coverlets gave rise to the thought that the origin of overshot weaving in North America might well lie in Scotland. The history of emigration from that country supported such a view. The timing was right for the appearance of overshot weaving in North America, and the spread of the Scots coincided with the spread of the technique. In Canada, overshot coverlets occur most strongly in areas of Scottish settlement, either Scots- or Gaelic-speaking. Many of those who came were skilled craftsmen and some would have been experienced weavers.

The theory seemed excellent, so the next step was to extend the search to Scotland by a short trip in 1965 and a delightful summer in 1967. Knowledge of the basic technique was established, but proof positive of the type of patterning known from North America could not be located despite a substantial body of circumstantial evidence that was accumulated. In the course of conversations, a number of older informants in southwest Scotland, particularly in Ayr, Kilbarchan, Maybole, and Kirkbean, have described the coverlets that belonged to their grandmothers. There seems little doubt but that these were four-shaft overshot coverlets with patterns similar to the ones known from North America. The majority of informants described the ones they remembered as usually red and white, with a cotton fringe across the lower edge and coloured wool fringes down both sides like the two in the Royal Ontario Museum that have been described above. One told of the curtains and furnishings of her grandmother's box-bed, which were of black and red wool. She drew a sketch and the resemblance to no. 306 from Prince Edward Island was remarkable.

Two pieces seen at The Museum of the Glens at Glen Esk, Angus, showed that the principles of overshot weave were known in Scotland, even if used for simpler patterning. Both employed a pattern weft floating above a tabby ground formed by a linen warp and a natural wool weft. One was patterned with red wool resembling in colour the two possibly Scottish coverlets found in Ontario. The pattern was a simple lozenge diaper of bird's-eye type that was woven from a draft identical to that used for the tablecloth from Pictou County (no. 188). The other was closely related, but had a more extended lozenge diaper of the goose-eye type in natural brown wool (fig. 29). The borders of both were similar, consisting of units of the main pattern between twill guards and divided by twill lines. They bore a resemblance to the borders of some coverlets from Scottish areas in Canada, such as no. 244. The presence of the twill guards was of great interest. This feature is found on a number of Canadian coverlets, where the guards separate the main field from the border, a feature that is particularly noticeable in examples from areas of Scottish settlement in Nova Scotia and Ontario.

There was little history associated with either of the coverlets at Glen Esk, but it seemed likely that they dated from the middle of the nineteenth century. Later, at Knockando in Moray, an informant in her nineties whose family had operated the woollen mill there for some generations said that she remembered coverlets of this type being woven there in her youth, as well as the more elaborate patterns known from North America.

Other coverlets with weft-float patterns are known from Scotland, but none are as close to the North American overshot technique. There are two-block patterns of simple type such as an early nineteenth-century example from Strathspey with cotton warp, natural wool main weft, and indigo blue pattern weft (fig. 30). It is simpler than the only two-block example found in Canada (no. 235), which may have been brought from Skye. A draft of a pattern similar to the Strathspey piece occurs in Alexander Cameron's 'Draft and Cording Book,' possibly from Lochaber, that dates from the eighteenth century. This is now in the National Museum of Antiquities, Edinburgh. Traditional coverlets of the same type are still being woven at Bridgend in Islay.

Three-block patterns were seen at Glen Esk that were certainly not later than the middle of the nineteenth century. These had patterns formed by weft-floats without the half-tones characteristic of overshot weaving, and were woven on a linen warp with a natural wool main weft, and an indigo blue pattern weft. One, of two widths joined by a centre seam, was found in a bothy and showed signs of hard use. It was patterned with repeating bands of small crosses in offset rows. On the outer edges were wide borders composed of two panels of half-motifs separated by a line of full motifs. The other piece was a fragment, still wet from being used as a scrub cloth when seen. The pattern was a lozenge lattice formed of graduated squares with an elongated lozenge in each compartment. Part of the border remained down one side and was based on a straight twill threading. The use of linen warp in both these pieces points to their being woven in the area. Lang Street, between Glen Esk and Edzell, was once a linen-weaving centre, now lost under an air force base, Both pieces required six shafts to produce the three-block patterns.

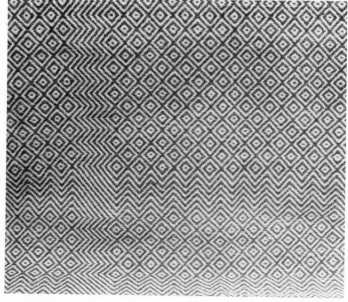

FIGURE 29

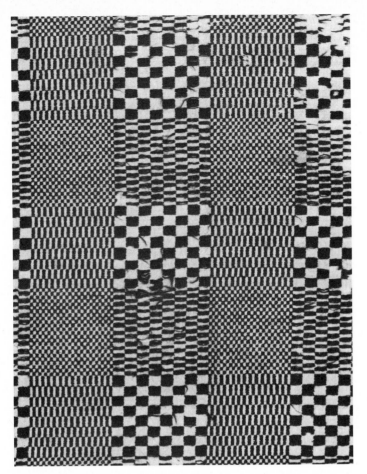

FIGURE 30

Two examples of a different type of coverlet were seen in Edinburgh. These, both with centre seams, had been woven in Lanark and would appear to date from the middle of the nineteenth century, if not earlier. Both were of the same construction, with a contrasting pattern weft above a tabby ground, and may well have been woven at the same time. In one, the tabby ground was of golden brown wool in warp and weft; in the other, the warp was the same, but the weft had been dyed blue. In both, the pattern was in red wool controlled by an eight-point twill treading. The effect was quite different from overshot weaving, but the principle of a contrasting weft above a tabby ground was the same.

Overshot coverlets woven in Scotland would not have been produced on an industrial basis, but rather by the 'customer weavers' mentioned in the parliamentary inquiry of the 1830s on the hand-loom weavers' petitions. These men are described as a 'class ... who are scattered all over the country, but chiefly in the Highlands, who are employed by private families ... to weave yarn supplied to them into coarse fabrics for domestic use. Most are agricultural labourers, and weave only in the intervals of their ordinary avocations ... They supply all the tools and apparatus of the loom themselves' (Report, 5). Unless they limited themselves to simple tweeds and bedding, the use of tartans still being banned at this period, these men would have had pattern books, or at least pattern drafts. Alexander Cameron's 'Draft and Cording Book' is the only example of the former known to have survived, but among the Mackley Collection of overshot drafts collected in Cape Breton, there are some that were

traditionally brought from Scotland when the settlers emigrated. Although this cannot be proved, there is no reason to doubt their origin.

If one accepts the theory that overshot coverlets were woven and used in Scotland, where have they vanished leaving little more than a memory? Several reasons may be considered: industrialization, the Clearances, and the Second World War.

The impact of the Industrial Revolution and the factory system was felt in Scotland much earlier than it affected the pattern of life in North America. It had had profound effects by the middle of the nineteenth century throughout the Lowlands, and by then had probably completely eliminated the 'customer weavers' who had existed a generation earlier. They had been absorbed into the new factory system or into the cottage industries that flourished particularly in the southwest part of the country. This would have meant the end of the traditional pattern of weaving in the Lowlands.

In the Highlands, the Clearances had a disruptive effect on the way of life. The growth of population beyond the limits that the country was able to support was a factor in emigration, but the Clearances were the cause of a mass upheaval of the people. They were an inevitable and tragic aftermath of the destruction of the clan system following the Battle of Culloden, a system on which the entire social and economic organization of life in northern Scotland had been based. The traditional economy vanished, and, together with the displacement of the peoples, meant the end of a way of life that had been sparse but self-sufficient. The areas affected would each have had a local weaver to supply the needs of the community. Those who emigrated would have carried the knowledge of their craft with them to their new homes; those who moved to the Lowlands would have been absorbed into a new way of life. In either case, the traditions would have been lost to much of Scotland: the patterned weaving of the type discussed here would have found a new home across the seas, particularly in North America.

Some of the coverlets described by informants in Scotland would undoubtedly have survived into modern times and have been treasured as family heirlooms of the past. Tucked away in chests and cupboards, they were probably in existence until the outbreak of war in 1939. With the stringent rationing that was essential during the conflict and which survived for some years after the close of hostilities, every scrap of old bedding with any warmth became of essential use during the cold winter nights. Kyst after kyst and cupboard after cupboard was searched for anything that could be used and in the course of the 1940s was worn out. With the passing of clothes rationing, what was left of the old coverlets, quilts, and blankets was discarded as soon as new furnishings could be obtained. It is more than probable that the overshot coverlets that are remembered in Scotland suffered this fate and have left no remnant to prove that they were once made and widely used there in the rural areas.

Turning to North America, the oldest securely dated overshot coverlets found on this continent were woven in the United States. Five are known that appear to be the work of one weaver, probably in the Hudson Valley in New York

State and possibly near Albany. All have dates and some-times initials, woven in one corner. The earliest, dated 1773, was found at Saugerties and is now in Winterthur (HFDM, no. 58.100). One is in Washington dated 1787 (SI 70789). A third in Chicago known to have been woven in Albany County is dated 1800 (AIC 3651; Davison, 734). It resembles no. 301, but has a plain 'table.' The patterns of nos. 310 and 297 are found in the collection of the Coverlet Guild of America (*Swygert*, 24 and 28) and are dated 1784 and 1791 respectively. A number of other coverlets in American collections are traditionally dated to the last quarter of the eighteenth century. No examples appear to be known for which an earlier date than the one at Winterthur may be substantiated. It is on this basis that the statement has been made that the weaving of overshot coverlets does not appear to predate the Revolutionary period, a factor that supports the theory that the origin of the technique was brought from Scotland after the Seven Years' War (1756–63). Coverlets continued to be woven in the United States into the nine-teenth century, but the demand was adversely affected by growing industrialization. Except in isolated rural areas, handweaving was already dying out by the time of the Civil War (1861–5), an event that virtually rang its death knell.

In Canada, no examples comparable to the unique, and fortunately, dated American ones are known that can help in establishing the appearance of overshot weave in this country. The two, and the only two, that have ever been seen here with linen grounds are probably the earliest. No. 236 from Prince Edward Island probably dates from around 1800; no. 296 from the Niagara Peninsula in Ontario may have been woven slightly earlier. The dating of the other Canadian examples illustrated is based on two factors: the existence of a firm family tradition (with the reservation that this may not always be infallible) and a comparison of the cotton yarns in coverlets without a history with those from the same districts for which a traditional date is acceptable.

In this country, overshot weaving occurs most frequently in areas of Scottish settlement and in those originally founded by Loyalists following the American Revolution. These latter were often sparsely settled, but each served as a nucleus to draw new settlers who followed from the United States after 1783, or who arrived from overseas looking for new homes. The areas where these coverlets have been found are the Maritime Provinces, the Eastern Townships of Quebec, and those parts of Ontario where settlement was not predomin-antly German-speaking.

Not until later does overshot weaving make its appearance in the French-speaking parts of the country. It occurs in some Acadian areas: not until the very end of the nineteenth century in western Prince Edward Island and somewhat earlier in southern Nova Scotia. In the Pubnicos, near Yar-mouth, it was a secret possessed by a limited few who would set up the looms for weavers on order. Once a coverlet was woven, the reed and shafts would be removed with the thrums tied in place. When another was needed, the new warp would be tied on to the ends of the old one. In both areas, overshot weaving definitely appears to be a cultural borrowing from neighbouring Scottish communities.

In Quebec the situation is similar. Overshot weaving is known from the Eastern Townships and from Châteauguay County, both areas where English-speaking settlement was dominant. All the older examples from Quebec that have not lost their histories can be traced to English and Scottish families. It is not until the middle of the nineteenth century that overshot weaving makes its appearance in the adjacent dominantly French districts. Compared with the other parts of the country where overshot weaving flourished, the reper-toire of patterns from the French areas of Quebec is very limited, and in the few old examples known does not appear to have been fully understood. Due to an improper balance of ground and pattern threads with a warp setting that was too close, an unusual, but attractive, elongated effect was sometimes produced. With the use of this technique, termed *frappé* or *fleuri*, in the strong revival of weaving as a domestic craft in Quebec in the present century, overshot weaving has come to be considered as having a long tradition in the province. This concept cannot be supported by the evidence, despite the wide knowledge of this method of patterning that has resulted from the work of Oscar Bériau.

In the basically English-speaking parts of Canada, over-shot coverlets were woven and used in quantity. Some pat-terns appear to be of purely local use, but many are known across the eastern part of the country from Cape Breton to the Detroit River. In Ontario, the craft of coverlet weaving passed as the nineteenth century drew to a close in the face of increasing industrialization and the easier accessibility of imported goods. It ceased entirely with the Great War of 1914–18. In Cape Breton, which is only now becoming more generally industrialized, the old traditions lingered on to the present day, but will be gone with the present decade.

One small and unusual group of overshot coverlets, found only in Ontario, requires special mention as they were woven with eight or ten shafts rather than with the usual four. All would appear to be the work of professional weavers who had more complex looms for work such as twill diaper and who adapted patterns to overshot weave to satisfy their customers' demands. With the difference in shedding mechanism of the looms, countermarch rather than counterbalanced, it would have been easier to do this than to strip the looms down to four shafts. These coverlets fall into two groups. One consists of adaptations of known four-shaft overshot patterns (nos. 351–3), and the examples come from York and Wellington Counties. The other eight-shaft coverlets come from Water-loo County (nos. 356–8), and the two ten-shaft examples from Oxford County are related to them (nos. 354–5). These five would appear to be adaptations of twill diaper and doublecloth patterns to the overshot technique. In weaving these coverlets, each pattern unit was entered on a pair of shafts, and additional ties were added to the tie-up preventing long floats of weft and producing the half-tone areas of incidentals that are so characteristic of the normal overshot weave.

A legend that is current today is that the major production of overshot coverlets in Canada was on a domestic level, even that girls of eight or ten years of age wove them in prepara-tion for the day when they would marry. This is pure romanticism. Girls learned to spin at an early age and may well have prepared yarns to be woven into supplies for their future homes, but the weaving of coverlets would have been beyond their physical strength and ability. Admittedly some examples do show that they were domestic productions through mistakes caused by misunderstandings of the drafts and errors in the weaving. An easy criterion to distinguish domestic and professional work is the matching of the centre seam. It can be stated as a general rule that if this seam matches well the coverlet is the work of a fully experienced weaver. The most difficult part of handweaving is to maintain an absolutely even beat throughout an entire length, a facility that only comes through constant practice. In overshot weaving this would mean that there would be no variation in the heights of the repeats of the various motifs. It is only the professional weaver who would have had the opportunity through steady work to develop this skill, and not all weavers achieved this mastery.

In Ontario, the professional weavers were virtually all men, and at least one is listed in almost every rural township in the census returns. In addition, there were other men, basically farmers, who wove professionally during the winter months when outdoor work was slack. There was no need for the young girl or the busy housewife to risk producing an imperfect coverlet by weaving the yarns she had prepared and dyed with so much care. It was much more sensible for her to take them to the local weaver, select the pattern she preferred, and have the work done for her. Once the weaver had his loom set up and threaded, he could easily weave the coverlet in one day. This does not deny the existence of domestic weaving in the home, especially during the winter months when it might be done by either the men or the women of the household. Most sensibly, this work would have been limited to goods where a difference in beat would not be too noticeable: blankets, winter sheets, and simple clothing materials. These call for skill, but not for the mastery that coverlet weaving demanded.

In weaving patterns of the geometric type possible on a shaft loom, the number of pattern units that may be used for decoration is dependent on the construction and the number of shafts available. These units are usually called blocks.

With the limitations of a four-shaft loom, only four blocks are available in the overshot technique. The changes that can be rung by using these in different orders, combinations, and sizes appear to be myriad, but an examination of the patterns to follow will show that all may be reduced to a few easily recognized elements. The simplest arrangement is using the four blocks in order to produce a diagonal line. If repeated, it lengthens the line, and in this form is often found used as a border motif (no. 316) or as a line between other pattern units (no. 310). If the four blocks are used in succession coming to a point, and then reversing, one of the key motifs of overshot patterning, a 'cross,' is formed as may be seen in the lower left of fig. 32. In many of the patterns, this motif may be seen with different sizes of block and different lengths of repeat. It is in simple form in no. 240, slightly longer and larger in no. 241, and with the 'cross' fully extended in no. 245 and similar patterns. It is met again and again as a main

patterning unit, as a link between other motifs, and as a border patterns.

An extension of the 'cross' is the circle or 'wheel.' If at the ends of the 'cross' the order of the blocks is reversed, these close the central motif in on all sides to form a frame. If the blocks are all of the same size, this frame is angular; if the blocks are graduated in size, a rounder form develops that more closely resembles a 'wheel' (no. 323). Here, all four blocks have been employed, but a simple 'wheel' on three blocks may be formed to enclose a motif as shown in no. 319.

The other key motif is known as a 'table.' Two pattern blocks are used repeated a number of times so that a more or less solid square unit results. This occurs in a variety of forms: very simply in no. 241, with uneven sizes of blocks in no. 299, and very often with enlarged corners as in no. 260. The 'table' may be composed of a great number of very small blocks (no. 330) or it is sometimes bisected across and through the centre to form a four-part unit (no. 277). A more precise outline of the parts of the table is seen when the two blocks composing it are drafted 'on opposites' (no. 348; fig. 34). In a few patterns, the 'table' becomes yet more elaborate with a combination of large and small blocks to give a very decorative effect (no. 280). Very occasionally a third block is introduced to give a greater variety (no. 248).

If the two blocks that form a 'table' are only repeated a few times, the resulting motif is referred to as a 'star' (fig. 32, upper right), particularly if the centre block is smaller in size than the outer ones. An excellent example of the basic form is found in no. 239. Occasionally, the central part is doubled making not a true 'table' motif, but rather an extended 'star' (no. 291). Not infrequently, the centre of a 'wheel' is extended to form a 'star' giving emphasis at this point (no. 345).

Another feature of overshot patterns is the submotifs that appear automatically in the ground as the main units are being woven. These may form bars of various types around the main motifs, or ovals sometimes with indented edges, and other incidental forms to fill the ground (figs. 32–3).

Four-shaft overshot weaving is the most flexible loom-controlled method of patterning found in coverlets. It is characterized by a tabby or plain-cloth ground, normally white, over and under which an extra pattern weft, usually heavier and contrasting in colour, is carried or 'shoots.' Warp ends should always alternate on odd- and even-numbered shafts so that, if shafts 1 and 3 are tied to one treadle, and shafts 2 and 4 to another, the use of these two in alternation will produce the tabby weave for the ground. With four shafts there are six possible combinations of pairs. Two of these have been used for the ground, leaving four others (1-2, 2-3, 3-4, 4-1), and these, tied to other treadles, are used to produce the pattern.

Weaving drafts are written in different ways, but most old drafts for overshot give the information in a short but effective form (fig. 31a). This indicates that, starting at the right as is usual in threading the loom, the first six threads are entered on shafts 1 and 2, the next four on 3 and 2; in other words, the first six ends are entered 1, 2, 1, 2, 1, 2, the next four 3, 2, 3, 2, the next two 1, 2, and so on. There are many

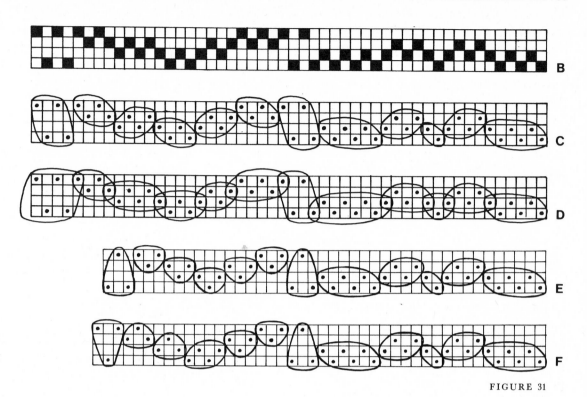

FIGURE 31

ways of writing overshot drafts and the most familiar to hand-weavers of today is that using squared paper with each space that is filled indicating the placing of one warp thread (fig. 31b). This is neat and tidy, but the full information that each block in turn is of a definite number of threads is lost. For this book, a form of notation is being used which, it is hoped, combines the best of the old and the new methods (fig. 31c). Here each pattern block is ringed, making it easier to follow the form of the pattern.

With the blocks following one another as they are in the draft (1-2, 3-2, 1-2, 3-2, 1-2, 1-4, 3-4, 3-2, 1-2, 3-2, 3-4, 1-4), diagonal lines formed by the connecting blocks will run right across the width of the fabric. This is a noticeable charac-teristic of overshot woven in the most traditional manner, nowadays called 'as drawn in.' The draft may be said to show how the warp threads are 'drawn in' on the shafts: if the treadling also takes the thread order and number as a guide, it follows that the weaving is done 'as drawn in.' The older term 'tromp as writ' gives the instructions in vivid and explicit terms. One typical feature of traditional overshot is that successive pattern blocks overlap one another by one thread: by referring to figs. 31–3 it will be evident that each block has threads common to it and to the preceding and following blocks. This feature not only produces overlapping, but also means that instead of the pattern showing up as a clean-cut area on a contrasting ground, every unit is sur-rounded by half-tones caused by incidentals. These occur when the threads that the adjacent blocks have in common with the one being used are depressed by the action of a treadle.

It is possible to arrange the blocks of the pattern so that they do not overlap, but are 'on opposites' to one another. For instance, if a block is on 1-2 and is followed by a block on 3-4, there is no overlapping and there are no incidentals that give the contiguous half-tones characteristic of the usual overshot patterns. This method may be used for a whole design. With only two blocks as in no. 235 or the coverlet from Strathspey (fig. 30), it gives a precise, clean result. If four blocks are used with the pattern drafted 'on opposites,' the motifs are well defined as in fig. 34 and no. 296, but the incidentals cannot be avoided and are apt to confuse the background. At points in these patterns, units must overlap and stronger double-thread incidentals also occur. More often patterning 'on opposites' is used for the centre of a motif to give it clarity, with the rest drafted in a standard way (no. 308), or, in the transition from one motif to another, the adjacent blocks may be put 'on opposites' giving them a stronger separation (no. 290).

'As drawn in' was by far the most common old method of overshot weaving, but there is another way that is equally traditional, although far less usual. This is called 'rose fashion' because the pattern blocks are used so that the pointed 'star' forms become detached rounded forms re-sembling stylized flowerheads or 'roses.' When a pattern is woven 'rose fashion,' the diagonal lines formed by the usual sequence of pattern blocks is lost and each motif stands out separately and independently.

This effect was achieved by reversing the order in which the pattern blocks were treadled. If a 'star' was drafted as in fig. 32, and woven 'as drawn in,' the block entered on shafts

1-2 would be treadled six times, then block 2-3 four, block 1-2 twice, block 2-3 four, and block 1-2 six, completing the motif as shown in the upper right of the figure. In weaving 'rose fashion,' the order in which the blocks were treadled was reversed, but the shuttling order remained unchanged. In other words, the 2-3 block would first be treadled for six picks, then the 1-2 for four, the 2-3 for two, and so on to complete the motif, a 'rose-like' form shown in the upper right of fig. 33. This result could, of course, be accomplished by the weaver making a deliberate change in the treadling order, but it would be simpler to alter the tie-up of the shafts and treadles as shown in fig. 33, so that motifs woven 'rose fashion' would automatically result from a normal treadling order. Rarely, only one of the two pairs of blocks is reversed

with the result that only one motif is woven 'rose fashion' (no. 287); usually both pairs are handled in this way, blocks on shafts 1-2 being exchanged with those of 2-3, and blocks 3-4 with those of 4-1. Some of the old patterns such as 'Whig Rose' (no. 314) are better known in the 'rose fashion' version than 'as drawn in' (no. 313). In no. 315, the main pattern is woven in this special way, whereas the border across the lower edge is woven in the standard way: a most unusual combination.

The 'rose fashion' method in weaving may only be used easily and efficiently when a loom is equipped with lamms. It is only if these are present that the tie-up may be reversed so that this form of patterning results automatically. The great majority of four-shaft looms in eastern Canada are

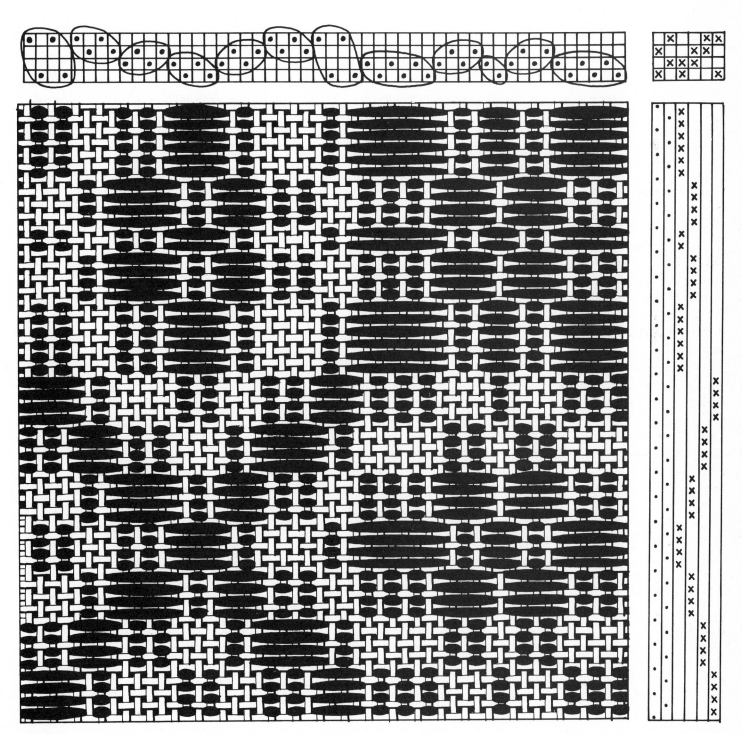

FIGURE 32

without lamms, and depend on a direct tie-up where two feet are needed to depress two shafts. The absence of lamms on most of the looms probably accounts for the comparative rarity of this method of patterning.

One point that is noticeable in many old coverlets is that the patterns are not perfectly balanced: the two halves of a motif are not identical. This is the direct result of the way in which the patterns were drafted and may be understood by comparing figs. 31c and 31d. In the former, it is balanced in appearance, every block consisting of a specific number of ends; if the same draft is taken, and circled to show the floats that will occur in the weaving (fig. 31d), it is obvious that the blocks do not produce floats of the same respective specific lengths. They vary from the basic number to the basic number plus two depending on how the blocks overlap. A

six-end float on one side of the central axis is an eight-end float on the other, while the unit forming the axis is always an uneven number. This point may be clearly seen in the diagram of the weaves shown in figs. 32 and 33.

These controlled irregularities are not errors or mistakes. They are the natural and automatic result of a precise method of drafting. It is from them, and the subtle beauties of the old yarns that the character, quality, and texture of many an old coverlet is due. Modern exponents of overshot weaving are apt to look upon these differences of length of float as sloppy and careless work. When they adapt old patterns for modern use, they rearrange the drafts so that all is in balance. The results often die of perfection. In the pattern used here for demonstration, the problem may be solved very simply by writing the 'cross' motif with three-thread

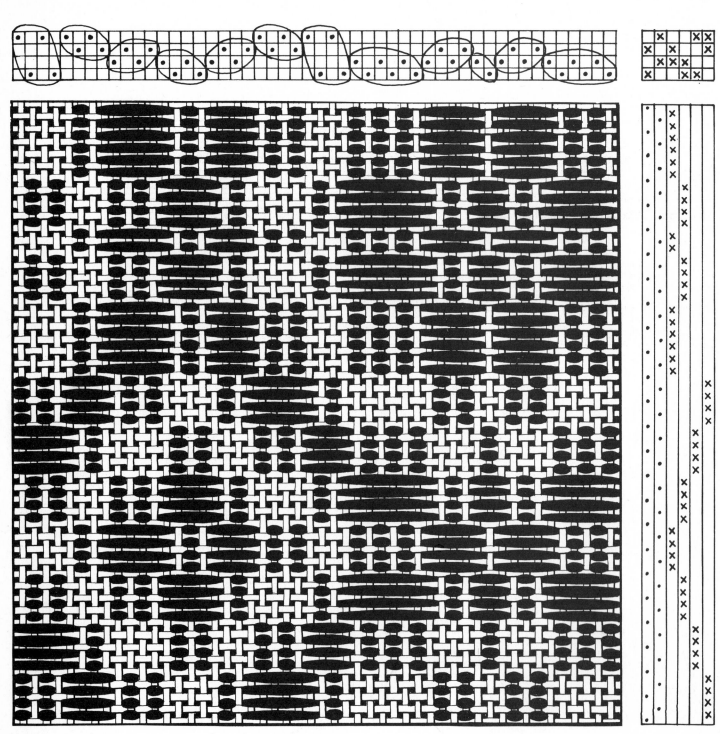

FIGURE 33

blocks instead of four as shown in fig. 31e. This requires an adjustment to form a true tabby ground; it will be seen that the draft begins and ends with a thread on shaft 1. If no adjustment is made, this will result in a doubled thread at this point. This is often found in old coverlets where the tabby has been lost deliberately to control the length of the floats (no. 271). In such a case, the loss of tabby may be adjusted by adding one more thread at the end of the figure (no. 268), or by adding a thread to the block that forms the central axis of the cross as shown in fig. 31f (no. 240). No examples have been found in old coverlets where an attempt has been made to balance the outer units in either 'table' or 'star' motifs.

Many of the old drafts were written with blocks of three, five, seven, or nine threads, or combining odd and even numbers in the blocks of the same draft to produce a balanced result. This practice sometimes took a bit of adjust-ment, but the main point to remember is that the whole principle is flexible. In examining any collection of old coverlets, it is obvious that there were good weavers who were masters of the medium and could obtain the exact effect they wanted, either balanced or unbalanced, while there were many less expert who could take a draft and follow it quite competently without fully understanding what they were doing. There were also, of course, a few domestic weavers who really did not understand what they were doing at all – but did it anyway. It is an interesting sidelight that there are usually more mistakes and misunderstandings in the simple patterns than in the more complex ones.

Two major collections of old Canadian pattern drafts are known (Abercrombie and Fry Collections [ROM], and the Mackley Collection), and these are supplemented by a small group in the Nova Scotia Museum and by photographs of some drafts discovered in New Brunswick by Dr Ivan

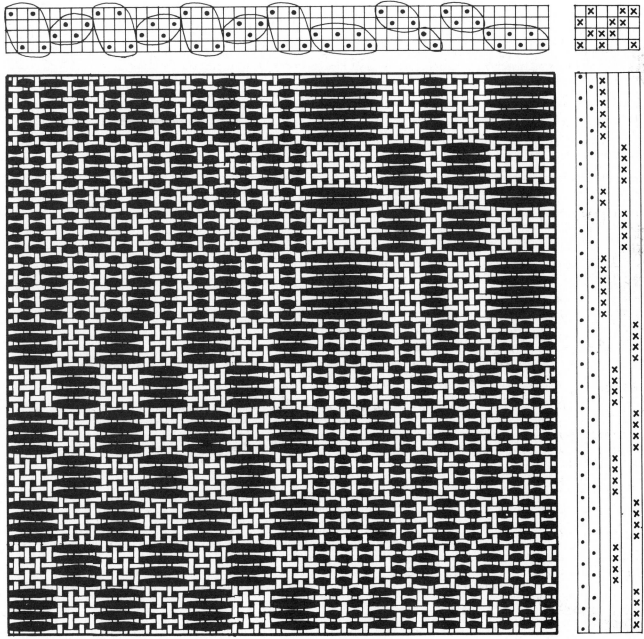

FIGURE 34

Crowell. The majority are written on long strips of paper, often scraps of old letters and accounts pasted and pinned together, or even strips of old wallpaper. They are usually an inch or two wide, and some eight, twelve, or even twenty inches long depending on the pattern, and almost all are riddled with tiny holes. When a pattern was to be woven, the draft was pinned up on the loom and used as a guide for threading; when the first block was threaded a pin was stuck in and as each successive block was completed, the pin was moved along so that the weaver always knew at what point in the draft he was working. Once weaving started, the draft, still on the loom, was also used as a guide for treadling: in theory, each block in turn was woven with the same number of pattern shots as there were warp threads indicated in the draft. Here as well, a pin would be put in and moved along to mark the progress of the work. Even with the most complex drafts a weaver could leave the loom, return later, and know exactly where he had stopped working.

When the old drafts are studied, it is soon realized that they are arranged so that a person with little or no knowledge of arithmetic could end up with a neatly worked out pattern. The old weavers were far too canny to be involved with calculations to make the motifs fit a given width. The majority of patterns start and finish at the centre of a main 'table' motif, and it will be found that the characteristic centre seam of coverlets is most frequently down the centre of this unit of the pattern. The weaver started threading at the side that would eventually be at the centre of the finished piece, and he entered as many repeats of the pattern as would fit the width. Sometimes a pattern stops abruptly when the warp threads ran out; more often, whatever was left after the completion of the pattern repeat, or of a motif, would be used for as many repeats of one of the border patterns as could be fitted in. If a wider border was desired, a motif might be dropped leaving sufficient warp threads for this purpose. One subtle, but effective element that was favoured by weavers particularly in Nova Scotia, but which does appear in strongly Scottish areas of Ontario, is the addition of twill lines separating the field and the border (no. 244). As has already been mentioned, this element was also found in coverlets in Scotland. The same device was standard use at the selvages. Here usually only four threads were involved and served the practical purpose of catching all the pattern threads at the selvage as the shuttle turned.

In old drafts, the 'table' motif might be drafted on any two pair of shafts. In this book, the patterns have been started at the right hand corner of the main 'table' motif and the two blocks forming it have been placed on shafts 1 and 2, and 2 and 3. This has been a quite arbitrary decision, but was done for consistency and so that the various drafts might be compared more easily.

In Ontario, the usual yarns found in overshot coverlets are a z, 2s natural white cotton for warp, a z singles cotton for main weft, and a z, 2s wool for pattern weft. Variations do occur, and, in the descriptions that follow, these are noted. If no mention is made of the twist or ply of the yarns, they are the usual types mentioned. About 1840, the use of a 3-ply warp appears particularly in eastern Ontario, and after about 1850, this type of warp is often combined with a 2-ply main weft. Towards the end of the century, as fewer and fewer coverlets were being woven in Ontario, the use of commercial 4-ply carpet warp is found, normally with a plied weft. The practice of using heavier yarns for the ground of these coverlets was not universal in the province, but regional, and the changes grew slowly; the use of the older types of cotton continued concurrently with the newer ones.

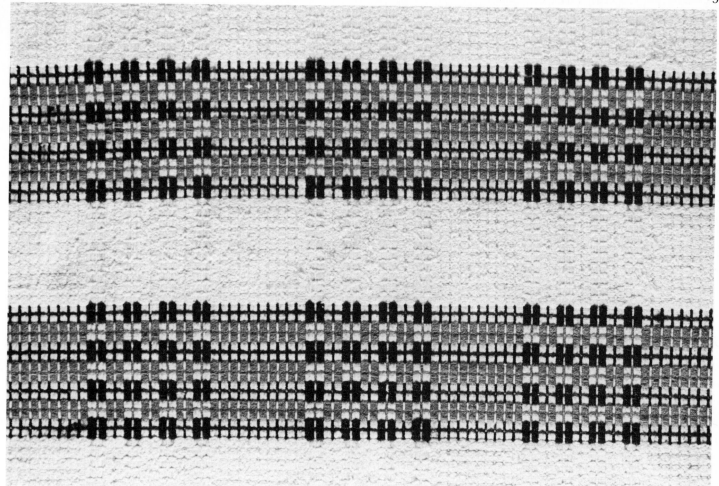

235 / Prince Edward Island (possibly woven in Scotland).
Early 19th century
ROM 968.253. Gift of Mr and Mrs Harold B. Burnham
Overshot coverlet. L. 200cm; w. 178cm

Banded in rust-red and indigo blue wool and white cotton,
on natural white cotton. In 1966, in the course of fieldwork
on the Island, this coverlet was seen and admired. It haunted
us and later we were delighted to acquire it for the Museum.

With only two pattern blocks used, it is a type of patterning
of world wide distribution, often termed 'monk's belt.' It is
the only one of its type found in Canada. The owner's
grandfather, a McLeod, came to Cardigan in 1829 from
Skye as the Presbyterian minister. His father was a professional weaver in the old country, and as this piece is of considerable age, the minister may well have brought it with
him. Bedding was brought for use on the long Atlantic
crossing and then for household needs in the new land.

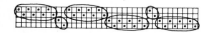

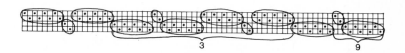

236 / Prince Edward Island. Beginning of the 19th century
ROM 965.198. Gift of Mrs Gerard Brett
Overshot coverlet. L. 192cm; w. 137 cm
(reduced from original size).

Dark brown wool on half-bleached linen (warp and main weft, z singles). The use of linen is a rare and undoubtedly early feature. Designs formed of squares and rectangles are often referred to as 'patch' patterns and occur rather rarely both in the Maritime Provinces and in Ontario. Several pattern drafts similar to this have survived in Cape Breton and are known by the name 'Queen's Delight.'

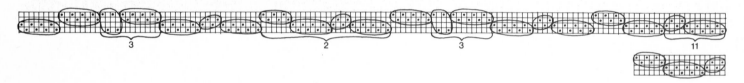

237 / Ontario. Waupoos, Prince Edward County.
Mid-19th century
ROM 968.92.1. Gift of Mrs J.H. Crang
Overshot coverlet. L. 242cm, plus fringe; w. 186cm

Indigo blue wool on natural white cotton. In no. 236, the dark and light areas are broken by pairs of warp threads; here the use of single ends produces a more solid design. Patterns of this type appear to have been popular in Prince Edward County: more have been seen there than in any other part of Ontario. The design of the narrow border is unusual and interesting.

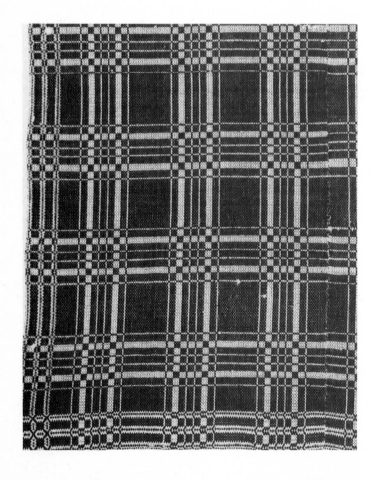

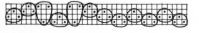

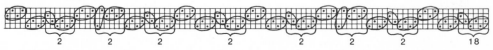

238 / Ontario. Vineland, Lincoln County. About 1875
ROM L965.11.19. The Annie R. Fry Collection
Overshot coverlet. L. 220cm, plus fringe; w. 197cm

Bright red and indigo blue wool on natural white cotton
(warp, z, 3s). This is a somewhat simpler 'patch' pattern

than those just described, but it is expertly woven and uses
the two strong colours to good advantage. There are breaks
'on opposites' between the pattern motifs that help accentuate
the contrast. The coverlet was woven by Samuel Fry, who
farmed near Vineland and wove professionally in the winter
months.

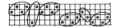

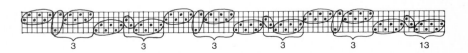

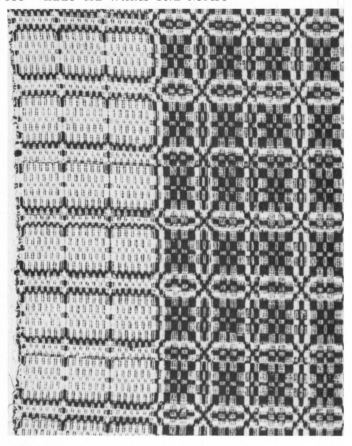

6

239 / Ontario. Saltfleet Township, Wentworth County.
About 1865
ROM 967.168.5. Gift of the Misses Hattie I. and
Charlotte Jones
Overshot coverlet. L. 198cm, plus fringe; w. 155cm

Indigo blue wool on natural white cotton (warp, z, 3s;
pattern weft, s singles). The donors inherited this coverlet
from their father, who was born in 1865. It was used on his
bed when he was a small boy, dating it fairly precisely. The
border is interesting as it uses a threading other than the
usual twill or lozenge arrangements. This and the following
patterns are simple, and consist of a 'star' or a 'table' repeated
vertically and horizontally and joined by a small 'cross.' In
a small 'cross' (as here) the pattern is easy to analyze, but
as the motif lengthens, the design starts to play optical tricks
and ceases to be static. One moment the 'table' and 'star'
are there; the next they are gone and the pattern becomes a
lattice of interlocking circles; this dissolves and the intervening leaf forms emerge. This changeableness is one of the
fascinations of many overshot patterns.

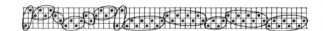

240 / Ontario. Bloomfield, Prince Edward County. 1840-60
ROM 945.33.1. Gift of Mrs Charles H. Mitchell in memory
of her grandmother and mother
Overshot coverlet. L. 239cm; w. 167cm

Indigo blue wool on natural white cotton (warp, z, 3s). This
pattern was of widespread use in Canada. A draft from
Prince Edward County (Abercrombie Collection 954.148.20)
gives a name – 'The Beauty of the Lake.' This county, surrounded by the sparkling waters of Lake Ontario, must have
been breathtakingly lovely when the first settlers came in the
1780s. That beauty is commemorated here. Names for
patterns vary from area to area: an almost identical one
from Cape Breton (Mackley Collection) is 'True Love's
Vine.' Another, dated 1874, from Acadian West Pubnico is
unnamed (NSM).

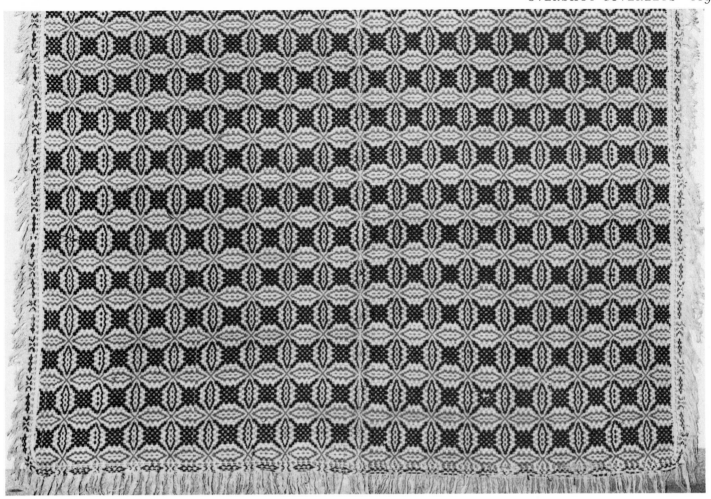

241 / Quebec. Compton County. About 1850
CGC H67
Overshot coverlet. L. 236cm, plus fringe; w. 206cm, plus added fringes

Dark and golden brown wools on natural white cotton. A beautiful example of this simple pattern with a history connecting it to a Loyalist family in the Eastern Townships. The patterned headings give a handsome finish to the fringes. Part of a white coverlet of the same design patterned with heavy linen from Tatamagouche, Nova Scotia, is in the Royal Ontario Museum (ROM 967.88).

3

242 / Ontario. Russell County. About 1880
ROM 962.137. Gift of Miss Sadie M. Fraser
Overshot coverlet. L. 179cm; w. 162cm

Entirely wool, medium indigo blue on strong brick-red (warp and main weft, s singles). From the trousseau of the donor's mother, who was married in 1881. Few all-wool coverlets have survived. A great many must have been made, but being lighter and warmer have been worn out. Some were not bed coverings, but what were called 'storm blankets' in New Brunswick. They were used driving to church in winter and put over the horse while the service was going on.

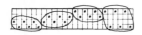
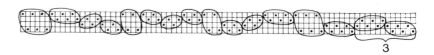

3

243 / Ontario. Williamsburg Township, Dundas County. 1850-60
UCV 67.39.1. From the Heagle family
Overshot coverlet. L. 199cm; w. 168cm

Entirely white cotton (warp and pattern weft, z, 3s). About 1840, commercially produced white cotton 'marseilles' bedspreads became a fashionable import. In response, all-white coverlets were produced by local weavers. These are rare except in eastern Ontario. In this one, the blocks are all of four threads producing a very angular version of 'The Beauty of the Lake.'

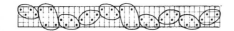

3

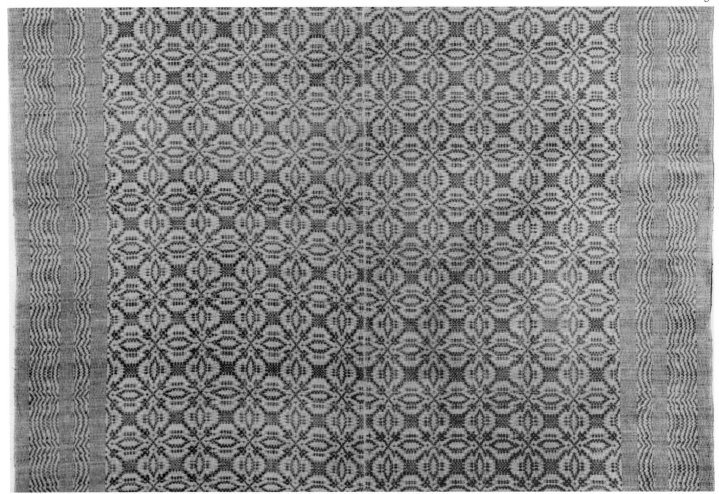

244 / Nova Scotia. Pictou County. 1850-60
ROM 966.158.21. Gift of Mr and Mrs Harold B. Burnham
Overshot coverlet. L. 199cm; w. 173cm

Natural brown linen (z singles) on natural white cotton
(warp, z singles). It was woven by the vendor's grandmother, probably as the best bedspread in her trousseau, and
never used. A draft of the pattern is known from Cape

Breton (Mackley Collection) with the name 'Four Spears.'
It is a variation of 'The Beauty of the Lake' with two extra
blocks forming a bump at each corner, presumably thought
to look like spear heads. Plain twill lines are frequently used
to separate border and field in coverlets from Nova Scotia.
Here the twilling has been increased to form two wide bands
with the border units running in reverse direction on either
side.

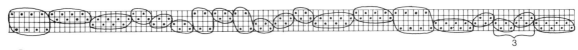

245 / Ontario. Glengarry County. Late 19th century
BCPV 66.83.1
Overshot coverlet, or possibly table cover. L. 206cm;
w. 165cm

Indigo blue, bright red, and rust wools on natural white
cotton. This pattern is similar to 'The Beauty of the Lake,'
but the 'cross' has been lengthened making all the lines
repeat, and the effect is quite dazzling. Almost all overshot
coverlets are woven in two widths joined by a centre seam.
The normal width of a hand loom was governed by the reach
of the weaver who threw the shuttle from one side and
caught it at the other. A comfortable weaving width was
about 40 inches, or 100cm. Most coverlets were woven about

this width giving an allowance for shrinkage. Occasionally
they are found without centre seam, which is often taken as
evidence that they were not handwoven, but this is not
always true. This example, with a full finished width of
165cm, is one of a known group from a Scottish area, Glengarry County, possibly Alexandria. They are the work of a
professional weaver, perhaps trained in Scotland, who had a
wide loom at which two people could work. Others without
centre seam are known from the Niagara Peninsula (no.
350) and from the district around Stratford in Ontario. The
wide borders on four sides point to the possibility that this
may have been a cloth used to cover the dining table between
meals.

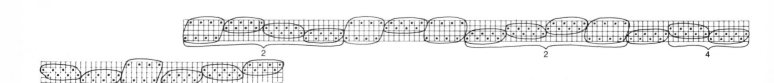

246 / Quebec. Probably Eastern Townships. About 1875
CGC H36
Overshot coverlet. L. 205cm, plus fringe; w. 186cm, plus fringes

Indigo blue wool on natural white cotton (warp, z, 3s). A large group of patterns depend on the repetition of diagonal lines for their effect. The blocks forming these are usually graduated in size, in this example from large to small, but sometimes they swell and then decrease again. The results are vibrating, dancing designs. Coverlets of this type are not uncommon and a number of drafts have also survived. 'Sunrise' or 'Sunburst' is a fairly common general family name. This has an effective fancy 'table' that combines squares and twill lines. Many simpler versions are known from Cape Breton and Ontario. The only history with this coverlet is that it came from a family of English descent in Quebec.

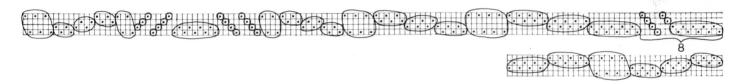

247 / Ontario. Shanly, Edwardsburgh Township, Grenville County. About 1875
NMM D682. Gift of Lois J. Cody
Overshot coverlet. L. 185cm; w. 155cm

Indigo blue wool on natural white cotton (main weft, z, 2s). Another 'Sunrise' pattern, simple in form and expertly woven, but with unusually long floats of twenty-eight ends. Ten or twelve is usually the maximum found. With handspun wool of excellent quality, it is effective, but the durability has been seriously reduced. The border is an interesting variation.

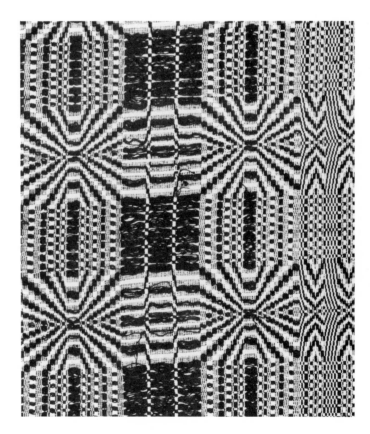

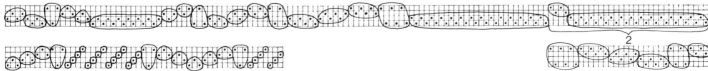

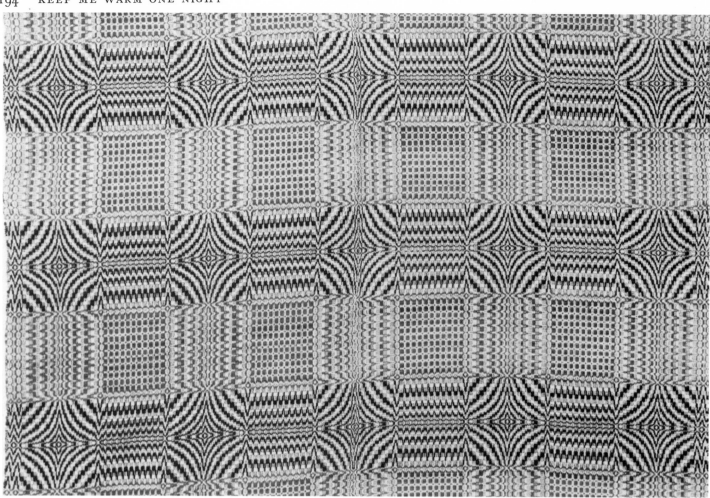

248 / Ontario. Pakenham, Lanark County. 1850-60
ROM 969.152. Gift of Mrs J.H. Crang
Overshot coverlet. L. 180cm; w. 160cm

Rust-red and indigo blue wools on natural white cotton
(warp and main weft, z singles, double). Woven by William
Inglis, born in 1819, in Paisley, Scotland. He came to
Canada as a young man and settled in Pakenham, where he
wove professionally. The use of a singles warp shows his
training in Scotland as a muslin weaver; it required skill to
dress and weave a warp of this type. This is a 'Sunrise' pattern, but has a different 'table,' drafted on three blocks. The
tie-up of the treadles that control the pattern blocks on shafts
1-2 and 3-4 have been exchanged so that the pattern is
partially woven 'rose fashion.'

249 / Nova Scotia. Lunenburg County. Late 19th century
NSM 68.31.1, b
Overshot coverlet (half), or curtain. L. 254cm; w. 107cm

Dark indigo blue wool on natural white cotton. This is one
of two similar pieces, wider and longer than normal, that
may have been woven as curtains, a use for overshot that is
known from the Maritime Provinces in the late nineteenth
century. The tiny border unit is unusual, and effective when
repeated a number of times: doubled threads and loss of
tabby are quite deliberate. Among the Prince Edward
County drafts (Abercrombie Collection 954.148.10), there
is a simpler version called 'Rising Sun,' and similar drafts
come from Cape Breton (Mackley Collection). The name of
one, 'Sunburst or Horse Blanket' suggests that these vibrating
patterns were popular for the wool 'storm blankets' used in
sleighs. Another draft from Cape Breton, 'Wellington's Army
in the Field of Battle,' similar but with the 'table' less widely
split, is a reminder that this part of Canada was being settled
by displaced Highland crofters at the time of the Napoleonic
Wars when the success of Wellington's army was of lively
interest.

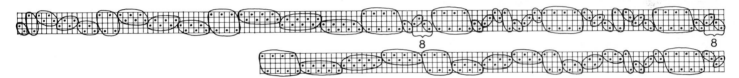

250 / Ontario. Waterford, Norfolk County.
Mid-19th century
ROM 962.11. Gift of the Misses C. and E. Grindley
Overshot coverlet. L. 222cm, plus fringe; w. 184cm,
plus added fringes

Raspberry red wool on natural white cotton. Here the
radiating lines between the 'tables' swell and then contract to
meet at a central point, producing a motif of four leaves. An
additional border has been added down both sides made of
narrow bands woven with extra warp fringe. From the
Perney family.

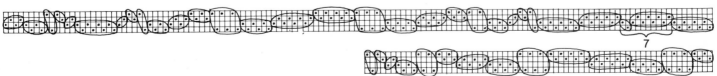

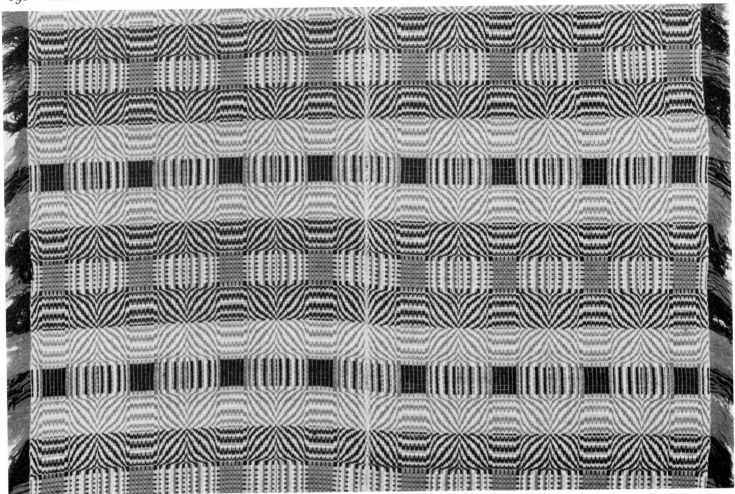

251 / Ontario. North London, Middlesex County. 1840-50
ROM 957.10. Gift of Mr Lewis Smith
Overshot coverlet. L. 211cm; w. 160cm, plus fringes

Banded in indigo blue and dark red wools on natural white cotton. The pattern is similar to the one just described, but the clever use of two colours adds another dimension. The wool wefts are carried out at the sides to form rich fringes.

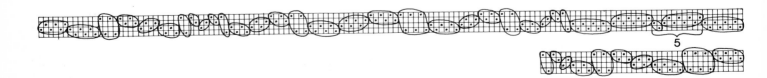

5

252 / Ontario. Wingham, Huron County. 1850-75
ROM 968.65.1. Gift of Mrs J.H. Crang
Overshot coverlet. L. 192cm; w. 165cm

Light indigo blue wool on natural white cotton. The design
is similar to the preceding ones, but is without a 'table.' In
eastern Ontario it is known as 'Turkey Tracks.'

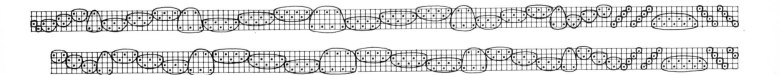

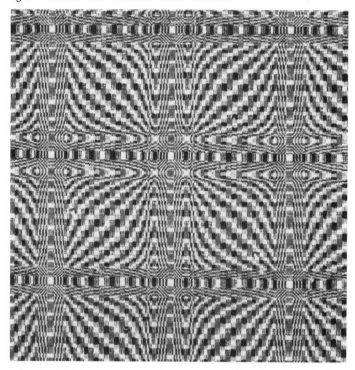

253 / Ontario. Near Altona, Uxbridge Township, Ontario County. 1840-50
ROM 969.229.8. Gift of Mr and Mrs Harold B. Burnham
Overshot coverlet. L. 225cm, plus fringe; w. 167cm

Red and dark indigo blue wool on natural white cotton. This carries the vibrations of 'Turkey Tracks' even further. Extra repeats of twill lines and the two colours in narrow bands add to the dazzling effect. The coverlet is well woven and the pattern well worked out. The treadling follows the draft exactly. The loss of tabby to the side of the large central block occurs regularly, but is completely unnoticeable. It makes the first line of the twilling come 'on opposites' to the large block: this is very effective. Experienced weavers disregarded the loss of tabby if it suited them.

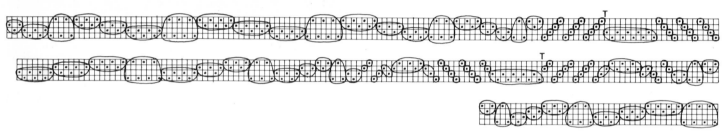

254 / Ontario. Brighton, Northumberland County. 1840-60
ROM 969.111.3. Gift of Mrs J.H. Crang
Overshot coverlet. L. 216cm, plus fringe; w. 167cm

Indigo blue wool on natural white cotton. This variation of 'Turkey Tracks' has an extra radiating line in the centre of each motif. An interesting detail of the drafting is the pairs of blocks on shafts 3 and 4 that bring two threads together and produce doubled threads at these points in the design. The treadling follows the draft exactly. If drafting a pattern from an old coverlet proves difficult, the treadling may be a sure guide to the intentions of the weaver. From the Nesbitt family.

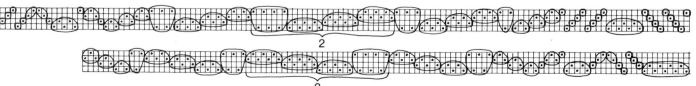

255 / Nova Scotia. Pictou County. Mid-19th century
ROM 968.71. Gift of Mrs J.H. Crang
Overshot coverlet. L. 221cm; w. 171cm

Indigo blue wool on natural white cotton. Although the
effect of the pattern is very different from that of the preceding ones based on radiating lines, an examination of the draft
for no. 252 will show a similarity in concept: there the lines
of the diagonal are larger at the centre than at the ends; here
it is the reverse. The result is that the inner lines form an
effective pattern of concentric circles enclosed in a diagonal
lattice. As was often done in Nova Scotia, twill lines form a
break between the field and the border. This is an excellent
example of how a simple border threading becomes transformed. In the lower corners it is in classic form: a plain
diaper; once the pattern starts, the borders follow the pattern
treadling and the result is something that complements the
main pattern perfectly.

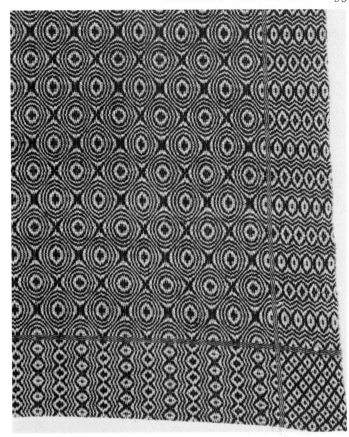

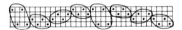 

256 / Ontario (eastern). Probably about 1840-50
UCV 61.8064
Overshot coverlet. L. 210cm, plus fringe; w. 161cm

Entirely of white cotton (pattern weft, z, 3s). Another
eastern Ontario example of the all-white coverlets that were
fashionable in the middle of the nineteenth century (cf. no.
243). This is a larger version of the preceding pattern.

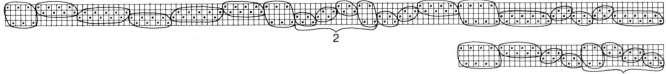

257 / Ontario. Pembroke area, Renfrew County.
Mid-19th century
York Pioneer and Historical Society, Sharon, Ontario. H1026
Overshot coverlet. L. 211cm; w. 182cm

Bright red wool on natural white cotton. The cotton yarns
are interesting: the z, 2s warp is of the weight and type
found in most coverlets, but is so lightly plied that there
would not have been sufficient strength without dressing,
and the same cotton, unplied, is used double for the main
weft. In some ways, this resembles the work of William Inglis
of Pakenham; like him, the weaver may have been trained
as a muslin weaver in Scotland. The pattern is a variation of
the two preceding ones. From the McLean family.

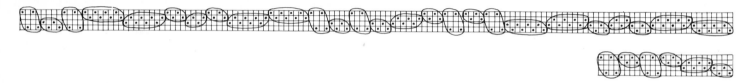

258 / Ontario. Hillsburgh, Wellington County. About 1840
ROM 941.32. Gift of Miss Florence McKinnon
Overshot coverlet. L. 213cm; w. 177cm

Indigo blue wool on natural white cotton. The pattern of this
coverlet has been found widely throughout eastern Canada,
and occurs more commonly than any other coverlet design.
It is known from Cape Breton and Lunenburg County
(ROM 966.158.53) in Nova Scotia, New Brunswick, Château-
guay County in Quebec, and Ontario from east to west. It
comes in various sizes of pattern and range of colours.
Among the drafts in the Mackley Collection from Cape
Breton, there are two with names. Both have been marked
'Monmouth,' although on one this has been changed to
'Monument.' On the other, the inscription reads 'Mrs. Mac-
Leod – April 21, 1868 – Monmouth.'

This name is intriguing. It seems possible that it may refer
to the Duke of Monmouth, son of Charles II, who was be-
headed following his unsuccessful Rebellion against his uncle,
James II, in 1685. He had married the Countess of Buccleuch
and was long remembered in Scotland despite his fate. The

pattern may well commemorate him. It was to his widow as
Duchess of Monmouth and Buccleuch that Sir Walter
Scott's 'The Lay of the Last Minstrel' was supposedly sung.
Coming as it does from a solidly Scottish community, the
name cannot refer to the county in Wales from which the
title derived.

This was the first coverlet to reach the Royal Ontario
Museum and for this reason holds a special place in the collection. Sometimes a simple act like this gift in 1941 sets a
whole chain of events in motion. It started a questioning
about what had been made and used in this country that led
to the launching of the Ontario Textile Research Project over
twenty years ago. It has now led to the publication of this
book. The coverlet may be considered as a typical example
of what was used: it is indigo blue and white like well over
half of all produced, the yarns are of the standard type, and
the pattern is the best known.

The donor said that it was one of nine coverlets woven
from yarns prepared by her grandmother: one for each of
her nine children. That this was a practice has been con-
firmed by other stories of the same type.

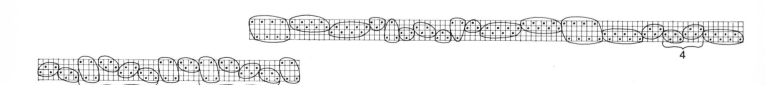

5   4

4

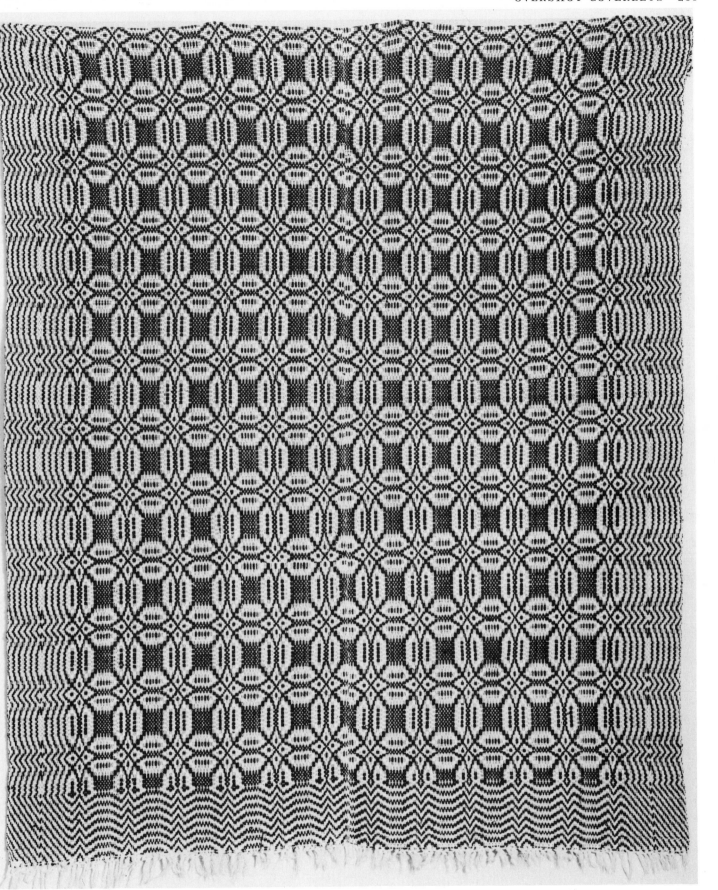

259 / Ontario. Keswick, North Gwillimbury Township, York County. 1839-40
ROM 955.10.1. Gift of Mrs O.D. Vaughan
Overshot coverlet. L. 223cm; w. 180cm

Banded in strong brick-red and light indigo blue wool on natural white cotton (warp, z, 3s). A well-proportioned example of the most usual of all Canadian coverlet patterns. This, and another one in the identical pattern but with the red and blue reversed, both came from the trousseau of Sharlotte Ames. Coverlets were often woven in pairs in this way. The heading, instead of matching the border, has been woven 'on opposites' to make an unusual small-checked pattern.

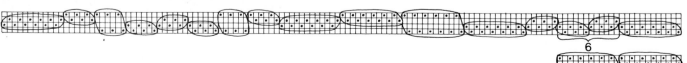

260 / Ontario. Colebrook, Campden Township, Lennox and Addington Counties. 1850-65
ROM 968.267.2. Gift of Mr and Mrs Harold B. Burnham
Overshot coverlet. L. 215cm, plus fringe; w. 180cm, plus added fringes

Black wool on natural white cotton (warp, z, 3s). The bold proportions of this 'Monmouth' pattern, with its twelve-thread blocks and strong contrast, produces a very handsome coverlet. There is an even larger version with sixteen-thread blocks in a group of New Brunswick drafts recorded by Dr Ivan Crowell.

261 / Quebec. Ormstown, Châteauguay County.
Probably about 1850
NMM A1758. Gift of Mrs C.R. Mackenzie
Overshot coverlet. L. 206cm, plus fringe; w. 194cm

All wool, dark green on deep red. The draft is almost
identical to that of no. 259. The illustration shows the reverse
side of this handsome example that is said to have been
woven by the grandmother of the donor, Mrs James Sangster.
One was made for each of the children in her family.

262 / Ontario. Newboyne, Leeds County. Mid-19th century
ROM 968.325. Gift of Mr J.R.M. Peat
Overshot coverlet. L. 212cm; w. 171cm

All wool, deep indigo blue on mixed rust-red and indigo blue
ground. This effective variation of 'Monmouth' has a larger,
more solid 'table' than normal. The donor's family settled in
Newboyne around 1820 and were of Scottish and Irish
origin.

9

263 / Prince Edward Island. Iona, Queen's County.
1820-50
ROM 966.158.16. Gift of Mr and Mrs Harold B. Burnham
Overshot coverlet (half). L. 166cm; w. 74cm

Dark olive-brown wool on natural white cotton (main weft,
z singles, double). This coverlet is full of both threading and
treadling errors, but is fascinating because the weaving
changes abruptly to 'rose fashion' part way down the length.
Suddenly the 'Monmouth' pattern becomes something quite
unfamiliar. Only one other example of the pattern treadled
this way has been seen: in Haliburton House, Windsor,
Nova Scotia.

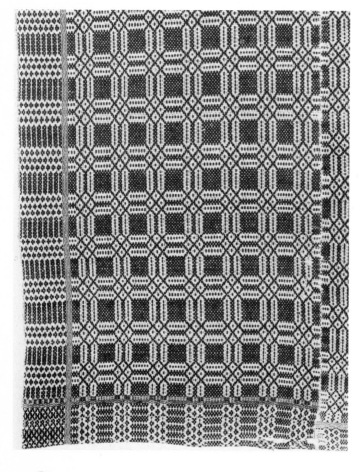

264 / Nova Scotia. Digby County. Mid-19th century
NSM 58.21.2
Overshot coverlet. L. 227cm; w. 160cm

Indigo blue wool on natural white cotton. All pattern blocks
have been reduced to four threads, giving a rather rigid effect
as in no. 243. The twill guards are a noticeable feature of
the design, typical of many Nova Scotian coverlets, making a
distinct break between pattern and border. It is in Digby
County that these blue and white bed coverings were known
as 'Chinee coverlids.'

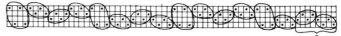

265 / Ontario. Beaverton, Ontario County. 1875-90
ROM 969.213. Gift of Mrs J.H. Crang
Overshot coverlet. L. 207cm; w. 151cm

Medium indigo blue wool on natural white cotton (warp z, 4s). Another stiff variation of 'Monmouth' that has one block less than the normal pattern so that the centres of the lozenges are plain. The z, 4s cotton used is commercially spun and plied carpet warp of late type.

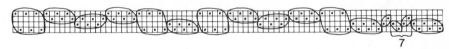

266 / Ontario. Near Aylmer, Elgin County. 1840-60
ROM 968.122. Gift of Mrs J.H. Crang
Overshot coverlet. L. 199cm; w. 176cm

Indigo blue wool on natural white cotton (warp, z, 3s; main weft, z, singles, double). Block by block this pattern is the same as 'Monmouth,' but groups of large blocks have been alternated with small ones and the lozenge pattern has been repeated an extra time between the 'tables,' producing a rather different effect.

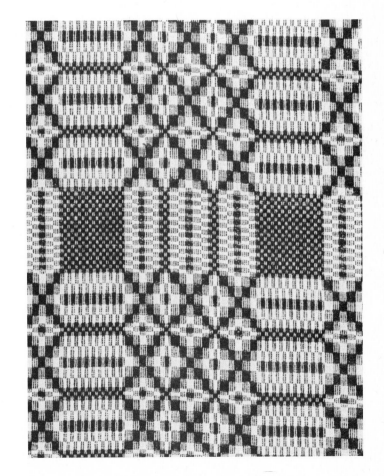

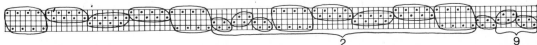

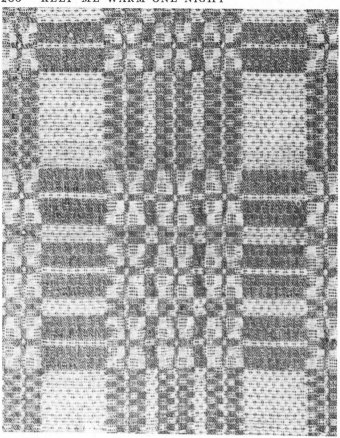

267 / Nova Scotia. Cape Breton. 1840-60
Mackley Collection, Sydney, Nova Scotia
Overshot coverlet (fragment). L. 68cm; w. 75cm

Natural white wool (z singles) on a ground with light blue cotton warp and brown wool weft. There is a close relationship between this draft and the previous one, but with the use of 'opposites' and the pattern light against a darker ground, the effect is completely different. The use of wool for the main weft with a cotton warp has also been found in the work of William Inglis of Pakenham, Ontario, a Scottish-born weaver, and in coverlets in Scotland.

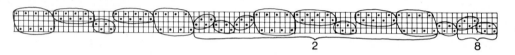

268 / Quebec. About 1860.
From a Scottish-Canadian family
CGC H20
Overshot coverlet. L. 213cm, plus fringe; w. 177cm, plus added fringes

Rust red and indigo blue wool on natural white cotton (main weft, z, 2s). The pattern is an extension of 'Monmouth' with extra blocks forming a longer transition between 'table' and central lozenge. This draft serves to illustrate one of the fine points of traditional drafting. If a 'cross' is drafted on blocks with even numbers of threads, the result is an imbalance in the weave. This can be avoided by drafting with an uneven number of threads. The double cross forming the lozenge is in three-thread units. With the 'table' on even blocks, there must be an adjustment of one thread. Here, a four-thread block was placed to the left of the centre of the 'cross' and a three-thread block to the right, making the rest of the draft run smoothly. Another method is found in no. 240, 'The Beauty of the Lake,' where an extra thread is put in the centre of the cross. In others, a similar problem is dealt with by deliberately departing from the tabby as in no. 271. This is unnoticeable and frequently found in old examples.

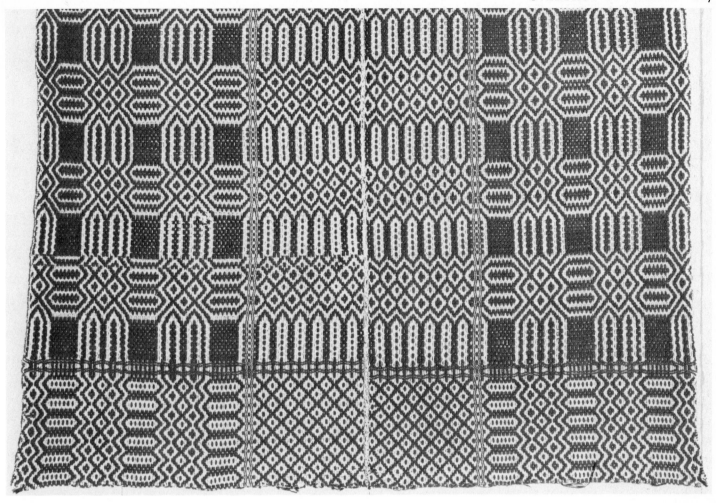

269 / Ontario. Richmond, Carleton County.
Possibly about 1825-50
ROM 966.246. Gift of Mrs J.H. Crang
Overshot coverlet. L. 230cm; w. 143cm

Fine natural white cotton ground with heavy indigo blue
wool (warp and main weft, z, 2s). The history of this
coverlet is that it was woven in Richmond for a member of
the Ferguson family, but the weight and character of the
yarns, both ground and pattern, are unlike those normally
found in Ontario. They are much closer to the possibly Scottish overshot coverlets in the Royal Ontario Museum. The
pattern is a variation of 'Monmouth' with the additional
interest that the wide borders have been sewn together
making a strong central panel.

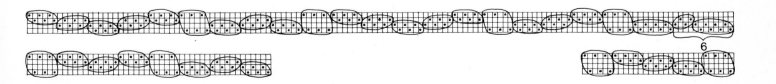

6

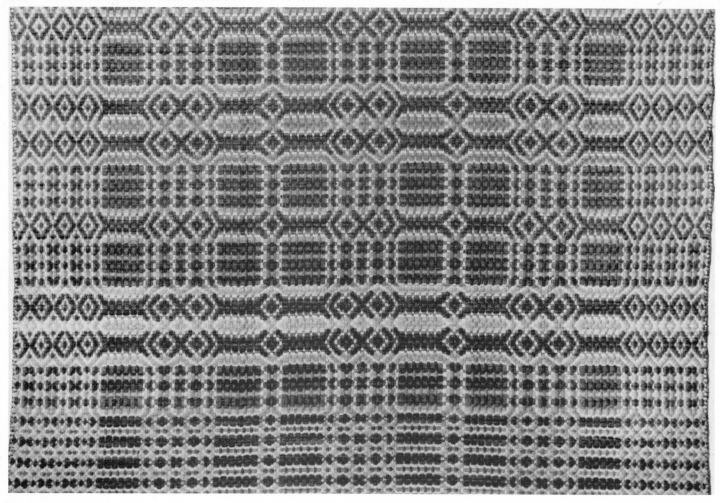

270 / Ontario. Glengarry County. Late 19th century
NMM D588
Overshot coverlet. L. 213cm; w. 163cm

Mauve, orange, and pale yellow-green wool on natural white cotton (warp, and main weft, z, 2s, but the latter is considerably finer), woven double width without centre seam. If the draft of this coverlet is compared with the previous one, it will be found that apart from the 'table' being in four parts, it is almost identical but with slightly larger blocks. The different effect is due to the fact that this coverlet is woven 'rose fashion.' It has no history but is documented by a fragment in the Royal Ontario Museum (954.99.1), which comes from Glengarry County and is identical in every respect except colour. Both are examples of the work of an unknown weaver in this area who had a wide loom. No. 245 is undoubtedly also his work.

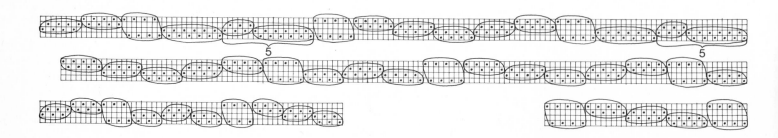

271 / Ontario. Leeds County. 1860-75
ROM 966.158.30. Gift of Mrs J.H. Crang
Overshot coverlet. L. 210cm; w. 129cm

Indigo blue wool on natural white cotton (warp, z, 3s, main weft, z, 2s). This combination of weights of yarn is characteristic of many of the later coverlets from eastern Ontario. The pattern is a further variation of 'Monmouth,' with an extra repeat of the lozenge unit. The tabby loss is deliberate and serves to make an adjustment between the three-thread blocks and the larger ones that are all on an even number of threads.

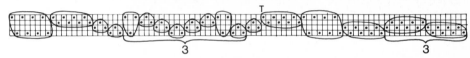

272 / Quebec. Probably 1860-75
ROM 970.90.10. Gift of Mrs John David Eaton. Ex coll. CGC
Overshot tablecloth. L. 163cm; w. 209cm

Warp natural linen (z singles), main weft natural white cotton (z, 2s), pattern weft catalogne (white cotton cloth cut in strips). This was found on a farm, probably south of Montreal, and is definitely of French-Canadian origin. The use of catalogne supports this. The design, another extension of 'Monmouth,' is known from an old draft from Prince Edward County (Abercrombie Collection 954.148.27), and also from Cape Breton (Mackley Collection) where it is called 'Wonder of the World.'

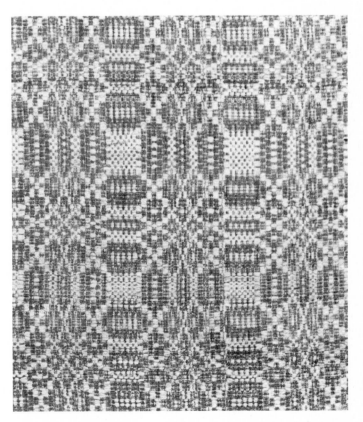

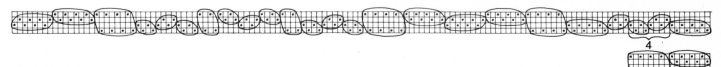

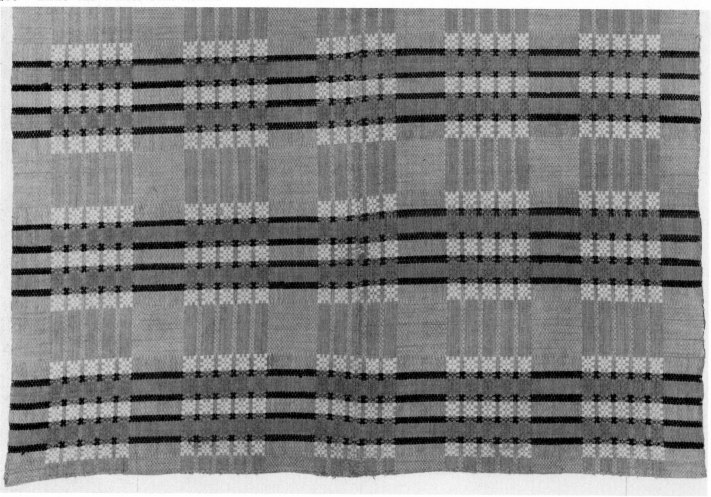

273 / New Brunswick. About 1840
York-Sunbury Museum, Fredericton, NB. 1529. Gift of
Gladys P. Baxter
Overshot coverlet. L. 200cm; w. 178cm

Entirely wool with an unusual colour scheme: pink, natural,
black, and golden-brown banded on light blue. The wool is
of excellent quality and the yarns for the ground have been
combed, rather than carded. A similar draft with sixteen
'stars' comes from Prince Edward County (Abercrombie
Collection 954.148.11). It is called 'M S Morning Star.' The
same pattern, usually with nine 'stars' separated by small
two-block 'crosses' and with 'tables' in different forms, is
known from New Brunswick and Cape Breton as 'Ladies
Delight.' Another version from Cape Breton is called
'Bachelor among the Girls.'

4   17

274 / Ontario. Ameliasburgh Township, Prince Edward
County. About 1840
ROM 950.103. Gift of Mrs H. Williams
Overshot coverlet. L. 252cm; w. 170cm

Indigo blue wool on natural white cotton (warp, z, 3s).
This is a rather odd version of the 'Morning Star' pattern.
On examination, it will be seen that the central star of
the group has been cut in half by a series of twill lines. After
eight three-thread blocks in twill sequence, the normal draft
is resumed. The coverlet was given to the donor's grandfather, Alman Bristol, as payment for teaching school near
Rednersville about 1840.

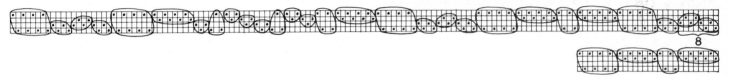

275 / Ontario. Probably Lanark County. 1840-60.
Collected near Perth
NMM D551
Overshot coverlet. L. 211cm; w. 188cm

Banded in dull red and blue-green wool on natural white
cotton. A very neat variation with nine 'stars' and the 'table'
broken into nine parts. In the Royal Ontario Museum's study
collection, there is a fragment of overshot carpeting from
Dundas County with a similar pattern layout. It is much
bolder in scale with 'stars' of extended form.

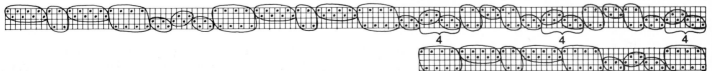

276 / Nova Scotia. River Denys, Cape Breton.
Probably about 1900
Mackley Collection, Sydney, NS
Overshot coverlet. L. 208cm; w. 144cm

Light, dark, and reddish-brown wools on natural cotton
ground (warp, z, 4s; main weft, z, 2s). The coverlet was
woven by a professional weaver in the River Denys district
using yarns coloured with vegetable dyes, showing their late
survival in Cape Breton. The section of the draft marked has
been repeated in the treadling to give a more complex pattern. Another coverlet of similar design was seen there which
the weaver called 'The Flowers of the Field.'

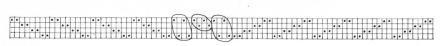

277 / Ontario. Queenston area, Lincoln County. 1825-40
UCV 60.H6226. Gift of Miss Lillian Shaw (ex-estate
Kate Symonds)
Overshot coverlet. L. 220cm; w. 198cm

All wool indigo blue pattern on light brown, possibly faded
red (main weft, s singles). An attractive design with the
'table' divided into four parts that echo the four parts of the
'star' motif. The centre seam does not match exactly, and like
so many all-wool coverlets this one was likely a domestic production. From the Thorburn family.

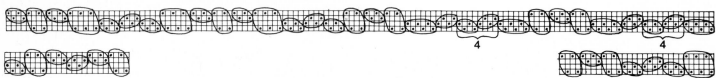

278 / Ontario. Southern Lanark County. 1825-50
ROM 968.202.9. Gift of Mrs J.H. Crang
Overshot coverlet. L. 237cm, plus fringe; w. 163cm

Indigo blue and bright red wool on natural white cotton. A
four-part 'table' and a four-'star' motif broken by a single
block 'on opposites.' Unfortunately, the weaver has not understood the draft and has failed to treadle it correctly at this
point, rather spoiling the effect. The border unit is arranged
so that blocks follow each other 'on opposites,' giving an unusual effect.

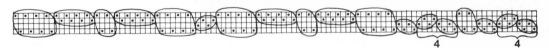

279 / Ontario. Huron County. 1860-80.
Collected at Goderich
ROM 969.32.1. Gift of Mrs J.H. Crang
Overshot coverlet. L. 188cm; w. 191cm

Indigo blue wool on natural white cotton. Again there is a
group of four 'stars,' but the main 'table' is of fancy form and
the motif separating the 'stars' has developed into a small
'table.' The border motif is unusual.

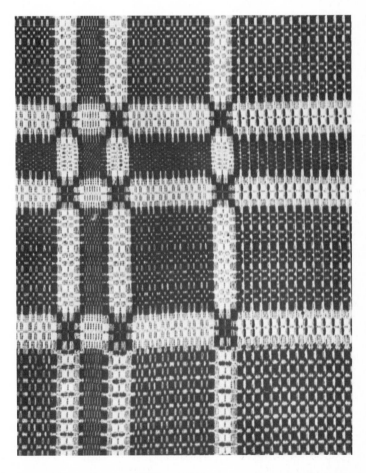

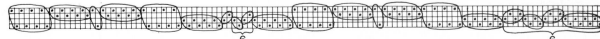

280 / Ontario. Freelton district, Wentworth County.
1835-50
ROM 965.3.1. Gift of Mrs J.H. Crang
Overshot coverlet. L. 212cm, plus fringe; w. 170cm

Dark green wool on natural white cotton. A draft for this
pattern, with one less repeat of the small motif, comes
from Prince Edward County (Abercrombie Collection
954.148.21) and is inscribed 'January 7 1844 The Nine

Roses to Miss Young.' The design differs in appearance from
the previous 'star' patterns because the sizes of the blocks
have been altered. Here the motifs have a large central block
with smaller ones at the corners, giving much more the effect
of the 'rose' of the name. The pattern is of widespread use
from the Maritime Provinces to Lambton County in Ontario
and occurs with nine, sixteen, and even twenty-five 'roses.' In
every case these are combined with the same fancy table.

3   2

281 / Nova Scotia. Cape Breton. Mid-19th century
ROM 969.31.3. Gift of Mrs F.M. Mackley
Overshot coverlet (fragment). L. 87cm, plus added fringe;
w. 79cm, plus added fringe

Indigo blue wool on natural white cotton. A mistake has been
made in threading this piece, one large block having been
omitted from the 'table.' Otherwise, the draft is identical
with 'The Nine Roses' from Prince Edward County. An
added tablet-woven fringe is a rare feature. Two tablets,
threaded in reverse, were used and banded alternately with
blue wool and white cotton.

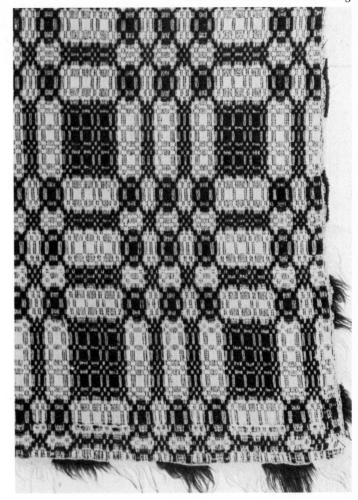

282 / Quebec. Sutton Mountain, Eastern Townships.
About 1900
ROM 970.90.8. Gift of Mrs John David Eaton. Ex coll. CGC
Overshot coverlet. L. 199cm, plus added fringe; w. 186cm,
plus fringes

Bright red, orange, and light turquoise wool dyed with
chemical dyes on natural white cotton (warp and main weft,
z, 2s). Although this coverlet is very late, it is strictly traditional and was woven from an identical draft. The use of
more than one colour gives another dimension to a familiar
pattern. It is the work of an elderly English-Canadian weaver
who lived at Sutton Mountain.

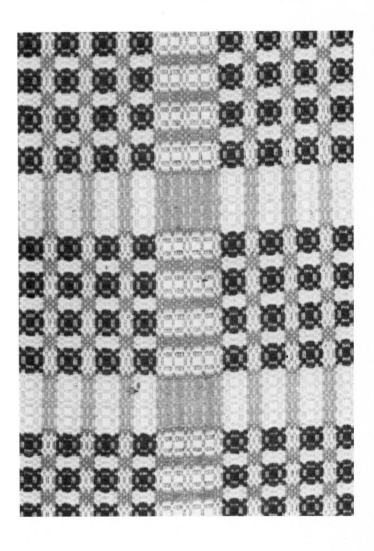

283 / Ontario. Probably Durham County. 1840-60.
Collected at Port Hope
ROM 967.220.10. Gift of Mrs J.H. Crang
Overshot coverlet. L. 223cm, plus fringe; w. 175cm

A curious colour scheme with black-brown, dull yellow, and purple-red wool on natural white cotton. The colours are of vegetable origin, not aniline, despite the unusual purple-red tone. One of Samuel Fry's few overshot drafts, called 'Lady's Delight,' is almost identical. The only difference between this and the pattern of the same name from Cape Breton is that the 'stars' in the Ontario examples are linked by a four-block 'cross,' and in Cape Breton by a two-block (cf. 273).

284 / Ontario. Hastings County. 1850-60
ROM 969.229.6. Gift of Mr and Mrs Harold B. Burnham
Overshot coverlet. L. 204cm, plus fringe; w. 154cm

Indigo blue and rust-red wool on natural white cotton (main weft, z, 2s). Here the 'stars' are separated from the 'table' by a 'half-cross.' A draft from Prince Edward County (Abercrombie Collection 965.148.16) is similar, and has the charming name 'Freemason's Coat of Arms': the strong red motif against the darker blue has a rather heraldic look. Among the drafts from Cape Breton (Mackley Collection), there is a version on a much smaller scale, probably for linen, called 'Snow Drop.'

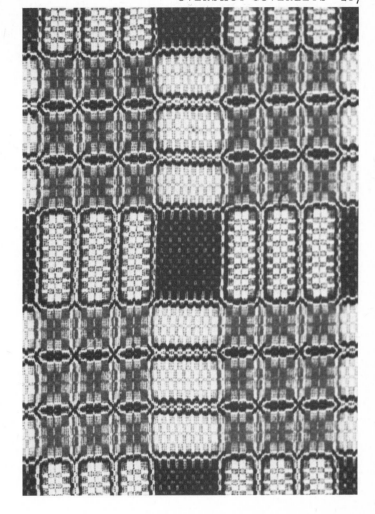

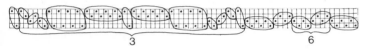

285 / Ontario. Waterloo County, probably New Dundee area, North Dumfries Township. 1860-75
ROM 969.77. Gift of Mrs J.H. Crang
Overshot coverlet. L. 232cm, plus fringe; w. 182cm

Red and indigo blue wool on natural white cotton (warp, z, 3s). This coverlet closely resembles a fragment in the Royal Ontario Museum (961.40.1) with a definite New Dundee provenance. In this pattern, a full 'cross' separates the 'table' from the 'stars' and, as in 'Freemason's Coat of Arms,' also occurs between the stars. Here the first small block of the 'cross' is formed by the corner block of the 'star,' so that the latter takes on a rounded form suggesting the name 'Nine Snowballs' found on a draft for this pattern from Prince Edward County (Abercrombie Collection 954.148.29).

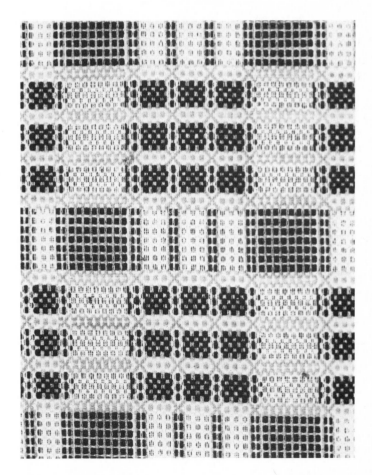

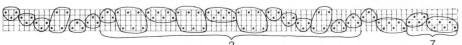

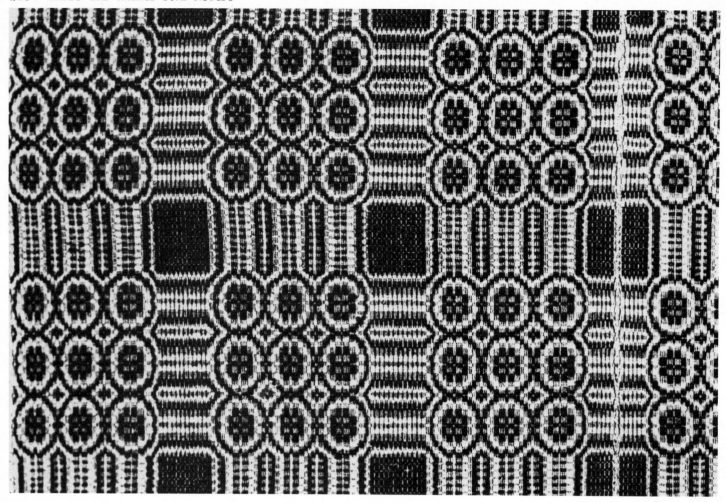

286 / New Brunswick. Hampton, King's County. 1850-60
ROM 966.158.19. Gift of Mrs J.H. Crang
Overshot coverlet. L. 239cm, plus fringe; w. 164cm, plus
added fringes

Indigo blue wool on natural white cotton. This is the same
draft as 'Freemason's Coat of Arms' (no. 284) in slightly
different proportions, but the very different pattern results
from treadling 'rose fashion.' No Canadian name is known.
In the United States it is called 'Nine Snowballs,' the name
for the pattern from Prince Edward County seen in no. 285.
It is impossible to be rigid about names: the same name may
be applied to different patterns in different areas and any one
design may have several names.

287 / Ontario. Glengarry County. About 1863
ROM 945.34. Gift of Mrs J.H. Crang
Overshot coverlet. L. 221cm; w. 142cm

Indigo blue and red wool on natural white cotton. This
particularly effective version of the pattern in two colours has
the 'table' and the two blocks that adjoin it on either side
treadled 'as drawn in'; then where the break comes between
the motifs, the treadling changes to 'rose fashion.' The wool
was spun by Mrs Donald McLennan, and woven by a professional weaver who is said to have come from Scotland.

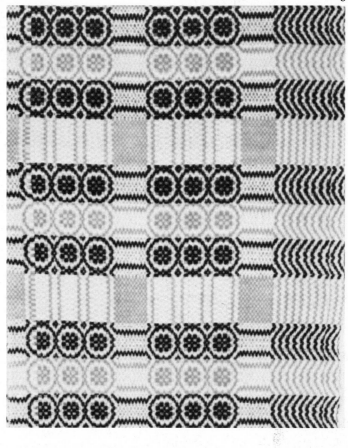

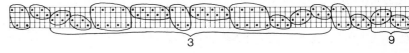

288 / Ontario. Probably Huron County. Late 19th century.
Collected at Goderich
ROM 964.57.15. Gift of Mrs Edgar J. Stone
Overshot coverlet. L. 211cm; w. 160cm

Vivid red (chemical-dyed) wool on natural white cotton
(warp, z, 4s). The use of commercial carpet warp and
chemical dye support the late date, but the use of a singles
main weft shows that the coverlet was still in the old tradition. This is a variation of 'Freemason's Coat of Arms' with
an extra row of 'stars' and a slight extension where they join
the 'table' to form a frame around this motif.

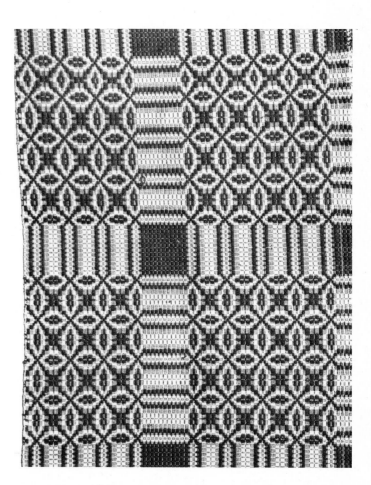

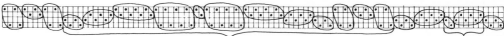

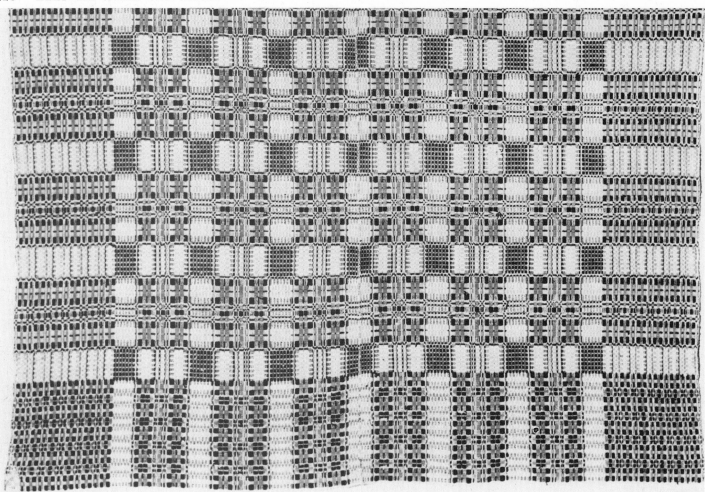

289 / Ontario. Picton, Prince Edward County. 1820-30
ROM 969.229.12. Gift of Mr and Mrs Harold B. Burnham
Overshot coverlet. L. 214cm, plus fringe; w. 164cm

Wool, dark green and terracotta, probably originally black
and red, on natural white cotton (warp, z singles, double;
pattern weft, s singles). The use of singles in the warp suggests that it was woven by a Scot who was probably trained
as a muslin weaver in southwest Scotland, as were William
Inglis of Pakenham (no. 248) and Bollert of Gounston (no.
354). It is a beautiful and expertly woven coverlet, the pattern being a variation of 'Freemason's Coat of Arms' with
only four stars and a large block forming a central point.

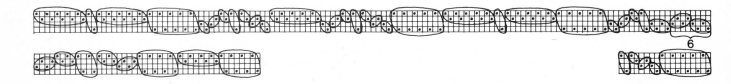

6

290 / Ontario. Wellington, Prince Edward County. Mid-19th century
ROM 969.220.4. Gift of Mrs J.H. Crang
Overshot coverlet. L. 209cm, plus fringe; w. 160cm

Pink (probably faded red) wool on natural white cotton (pattern weft, heavy z singles, tightly spun). A further variation of 'Freemason's Coat of Arms' with a block 'on opposites' making a distinct break between the 'table' and the 'stars.' These latter have a block in common with the 'table' and the 'crosses' between them are longer. These changes give quite a different effect from the previous patterns.

291 / New Brunswick. Probably 1830-50
York-Sunbury Museum, Fredericton, NB 6840
Overshot coverlet. L. 230cm, plus fringe; w. 146cm

Light brown and indigo blue wool on natural white cotton. An attractive pattern with a fancy 'table' and four extended 'stars.' This is drafted on four- and eight-thread blocks, joined by a 'cross' on five-thread blocks. An adjustment is necessary when odd and even numbers are combined in a draft: here the first block to the left of the 'table' is seven instead of eight threads.

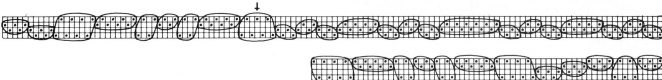

292 / Ontario. Hastings County. 1840-60
ROM 968.202.8. Gift of Mrs J.H. Crang
Overshot coverlet. L. 230cm; w. 164cm

Deep indigo blue and pink-red wool on natural white cotton. The motif here is similar to the nine-'star' unit in 'Freemason's Coat of Arms' (no. 284): in place of the 'table' in that pattern, there is a repeat of the same motif on reverse blocks producing a checkerboard of panels of nine 'stars' in offset rows.

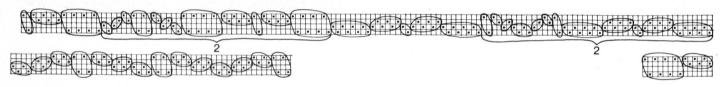

293 / Ontario. Roblin Mills, Sophiasburgh Township, Prince Edward County. About 1825
ROM 968.136. Gift of Mr G.R. Adams
Overshot coverlet (half). L. 251cm, plus fringe; w. 96cm

Deep indigo blue and rust-red wool on natural white cotton. The draft is the same as the preceding one, but with a more imaginative use of colours. The pattern is fully reversible and the illustration shows the reverse patterned with panels of 'roses.' Traditionally woven by Patrick Gibson, great-grandfather of the donor.

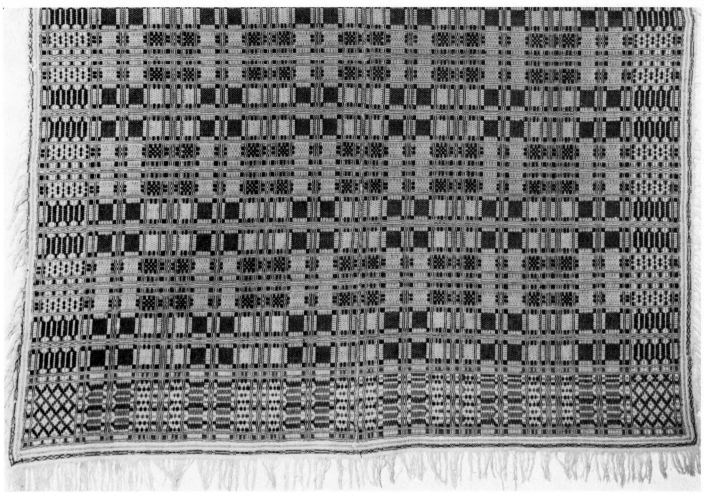

294 / Ontario. Probably Simcoe County. 1840-60
ROM 969.229.3. Gift of Mr and Mrs Harold B. Burnham
Overshot coverlet. L. 215cm, plus added fringe; w. 199cm,
plus added fringes

Raspberry red and green-black wool on natural white cotton
(warp, z, 3s). A handsome coverlet, well finished with pat-

terned fringe across the lower edge and matching fringes
added down both sides. The pattern is a complicated one
with both the group of four 'stars' and the four parts of the
'table' separated by repeated twill lines. The border is used
across the top, as well as down both sides and across the lower
edge.

295 / Ontario. Colebrook, Campden Township, Lennox and Addington Counties, 1825-40
NMM D5326
Overshot coverlet. L. 208cm; w. 156cm

Red and brown-black wool on natural white cotton. A lovely coverlet that is a subtle and imaginative variation of 'Freemason's Coat of Arms.' The extra block on the outside of the 'star' motif is part of the framing of the 'table.' The four-thread block in the centre of the 'cross' joining the parts of the 'table' has three small blocks on either side of it. In order to preserve a balance, the tabby has been deliberately lost at the left. Doubled threads have been used to excellent effect in the centre of the 'crosses' that divide the 'stars.' In the old form of shortened draft this would have been written as two two-thread blocks as shown here, and the treadling follows this. This pattern with all its subtleties is repeated in a coverlet in the Royal Ontario Museum (968.62). The colour scheme differs, but examination proved that both came from the same warp as they had an identical threading mistake. The other coverlet turned up without a history near London. It is a curious chance that brought them together again after more than a hundred years.

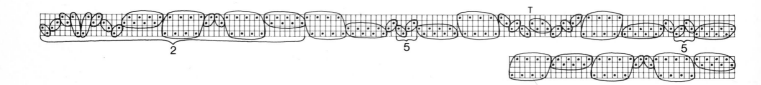

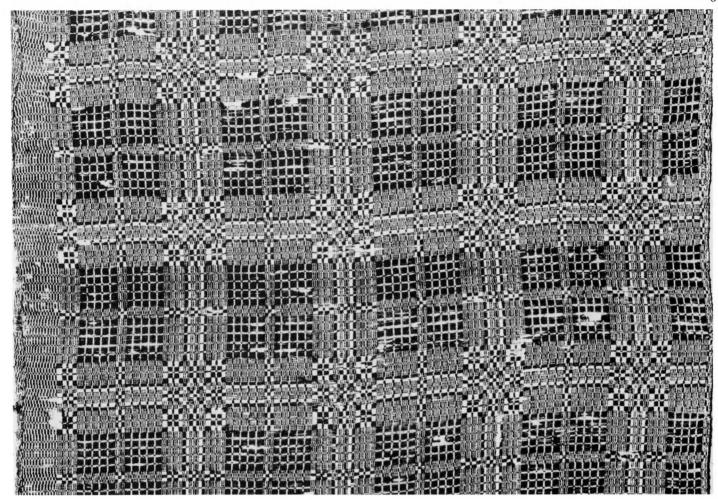

296 / Ontario. Rockway, Louth Township, Lincoln County.
About 1800
ROM 968.286.1. Gift of Miss Marion Houston
Overshot coverlet. L. 223cm; w. 190cm (made from parts
of two matching coverlets)

Indigo blue wool on bleached linen ground (warp and main
weft, linen z singles; pattern weft, wool z singles). A rare
and important coverlet, the only overshot found in Ontario
with an entirely linen ground. It is known to have belonged
to the donor's great-grandmother (née Buckbee) who was
married about 1850. There is no doubt but that it is considerably older than this. The pattern is most interesting and
unusual as it is drafted entirely 'on opposites.' The clean light
and dark of this method is evident, as well as the strange
distribution of incidentals.

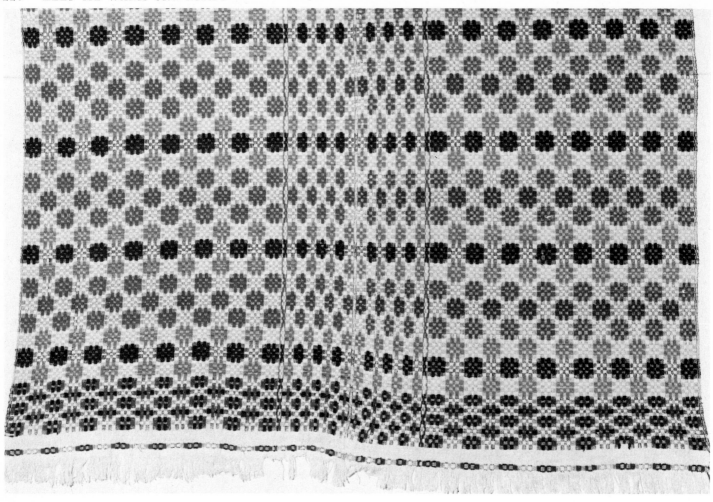

297 / Ontario. Hallowell Township, Prince Edward County. 1840-60
ROM 969.229.5. Gift of Mr and Mrs Harold B. Burnham
Overshot coverlet. L. 216cm, plus fringe; w. 165cm

Banded in four colours of wool, deep and light indigo blue, rust-red, and dark olive-green, on natural white cotton. (Pattern wefts singles, dark blue and red z, olive and light blue s.) This is one of the simplest patterns: a 'star' drafted on two blocks alternating with the same motif on the opposite blocks. This produces an allover lattice of 'stars' in offset rows on the face, and 'roses' arranged in offset rows on the reverse. It is this side that is shown here, the pattern being completely reversible. This aspect of the pattern is sometimes known as 'Dog Tracks,' but no truly Canadian name has been found. The borders formed of a reduced version of the pattern are unusual and have been sewn together giving a wide panel down the centre of the coverlet.

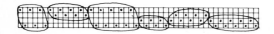

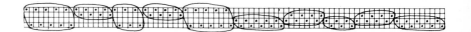

298 / Ontario. Renfrew County. 1840-60
ROM 968.202.11. Gift of Mrs J.H. Crang
Overshot coverlet. L. 207cm; w. 160cm

Green and orange-red wool on natural white cotton. Another
handsome coverlet in the 'Dog Track' pattern, this time
showing the lattice of 'stars.' This version has been seen with
a Canadian name on a 'summer and winter' weave draft
marked 'Thankfulls Fancy,' a name with a Puritan ring.
The wide border is separated from the field by twill guards,
a feature, possibly of a Scottish tradition, found more frequently in Nova Scotia than in Ontario, except in dominantly
Scottish areas such as Renfrew County. It is unusual to find
the border used on all four sides.

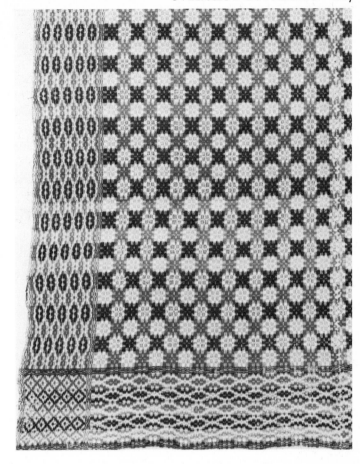

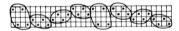

299 / Ontario. Oakville, Halton County. 1850-70
ROM 966.90. Gift of Mr and Mrs W.E. Watt
Overshot coverlet. L. 211cm, plus fringe; w. 141cm

Indigo blue wool on natural white cotton (warp, z, 3s). The
'Dog Track' motif has been used in conjunction with a large
solid 'table.' The small corner blocks of the latter have been
drafted 'on opposites' to the 'star' motif, making the pattern
stand out in clear definition. From the Balmer family.

2   10

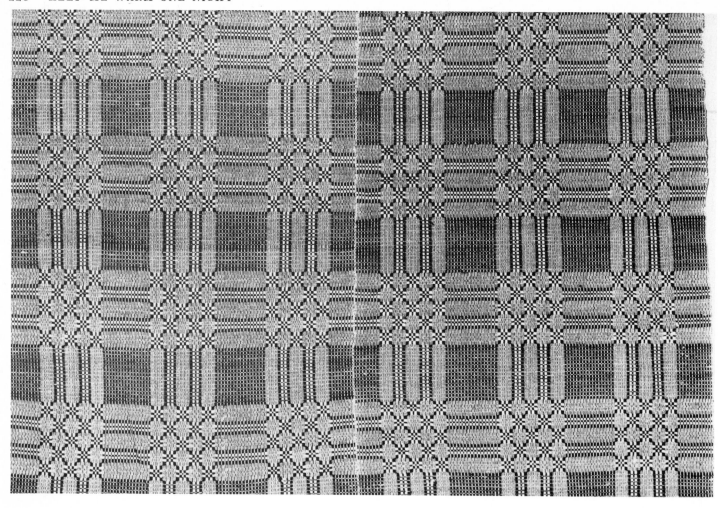

300 / Ontario. Saltfleet Township, Wentworth County.
About 1840
ROM 970.43.2. Gift of Mrs R.L. McFeeters
Overshot coverlet. L. 208cm, plus fringe; w. 178cm

Indigo blue wool on natural white cotton. A similar combination of 'table' and 'Dog Track' motif as in no. 299, but
drafted 'on opposites.' A pair of coverlets in the same pattern
is at Upper Canada Village, one patterned in red and blue,
the other with colours reversed. This was done quite often,
probably because the dye kettle available would only hold
sufficient wool for one coverlet. By using the colours in
reverse proportions, the correct amount would have been
prepared for a pair of coverlets banded in two colours.

2   15

301 / Ontario. Cherry Valley, Prince Edward County.
About 1840
ROM 966.273. Gift of Mrs T.H. Taylor
Overshot coverlet. L. 208cm, plus fringe; w. 163cm

Red, blue, green, and yellow wool on natural white cotton.
This pattern, with its curious and attractive arrangement of
broken 'table' and 'stars,' forms a garland of 'roses' against a
light 'table' on the reverse. It is identical with a draft
from Prince Edward County (Abercrombie Collection
954.148.25) called 'Winter's Rest.' The coverlet was probably woven by Rosanna or Hester Young of Picton, the
original owners of the draft, who were related to the donor's
family. It is certainly expert work of professional standard
with its beautifully matched centre seam.

(in colour PLATE III)

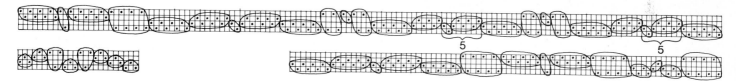

302 / Ontario. Prince Edward County. 1845-50
ROM 968.139. Gift of Miss Naomi McDonald
Overshot coverlet. L. 218cm, plus fringe; w. 195cm, plus
added fringes

All natural white cotton (warp, z singles, double). No draft
is shown for this coverlet as it is identical with no. 301, and is
another example of 'Winter's Rest.' It was made for the
trousseau of Mehitabel (Johnson) McDonald, who was
married about 1850. All-white cotton bedspreads became
fashionable in the 1840s, but overshot ones are rather rare.

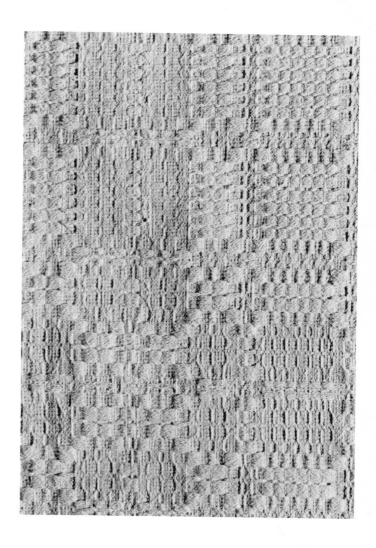

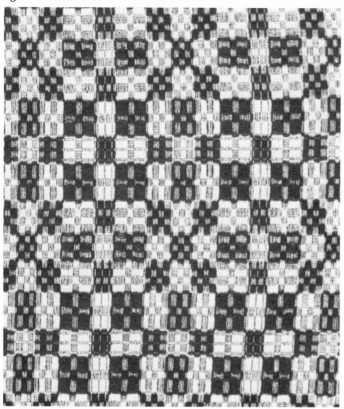

303 / Ontario. Possibly Owen Sound area, Grey County. 1850-70
ROM 968.97. Gift of Mrs J.H. Crang
Overshot coverlet. L. 221cm; w. 156cm

Indigo blue wool on natural white cotton (main weft, z, 2s). This pattern with its tiny 'table,' strangely shaped 'stars,' and checkerboard 'cross' motif is utterly unlike any other overshot coverlet seen, recorded, or found among published examples. The yarns, the dye, and the drafting of the pattern are perfectly correct for Ontario at the date assigned. The coverlet was obtained from a dealer with no history beyond the fact that it was probably collected in Grey County, possibly near Owen Sound. The excellent matching of the centre seam suggests professional work.

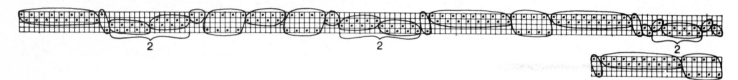

304 / Ontario. Louth Township, Lincoln County. 1860-80
ROM 969.298.1
Overshot coverlet (half). L. 197cm; w. 76cm

Indigo blue wool on natural white cotton (warp, z, 3s). The pattern is interesting as its panels of linked 'stars' repeats in reverse producing rings of 'roses' that alternate with them (cf. no. 310).

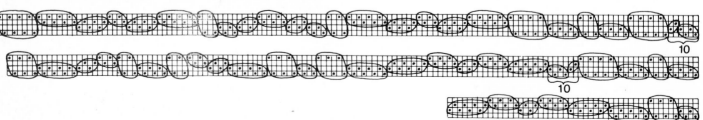

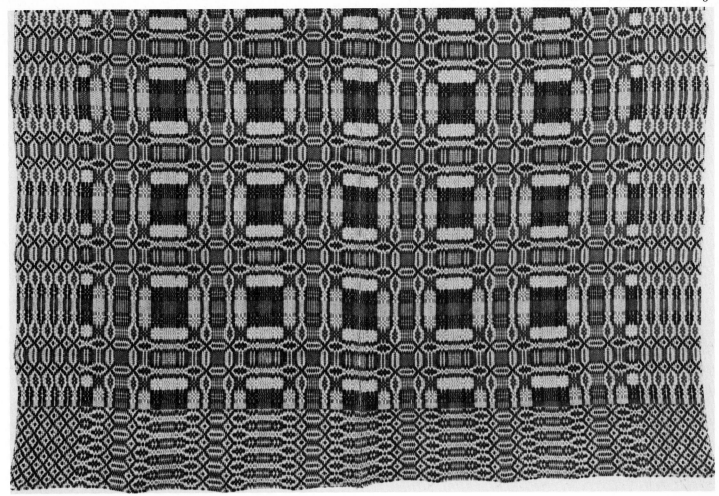

305 / Ontario. Addison, Leeds County. About 1830-50
ROM 968.93.1. Gift of Mrs J.H. Crang
Overshot coverlet. L. 205cm; w. 172cm

Deep red and dark indigo blue wool on natural white cotton.
This is a well-woven coverlet with every appearance of being skilled professional work, but on close examination the small 'table' framed by the 'stars' looks rather odd. The draft shows the reason: every time the 2-3 block was threaded, the shafts were taken in the wrong order resulting in loss of tabby and many doubled threads. The effect is by no means unattractive, but is unlikely to have been intentional.

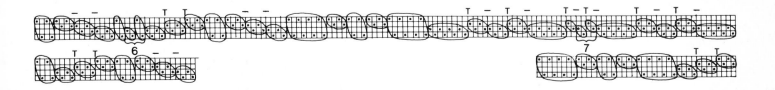

306 / Prince Edward Island. Breadalbane, Queen's County.
1820-40
ROM 966.158.17
Overshot fragment. L. 40cm; w. 47cm

All wool (z singles) in deep red on black. This piece was
found as upholstery on a small pine stool. We were told in the
Island, and in Scotland, of wool overshot of this type being
used as bed curtains and it seems probable that that was the
original purpose of this piece. It is almost too light to serve as
a bed covering. The pattern is a combination of alternating
large and small 'stars,' split into four-lobed motifs by a small
'cross.' No. 191 shows the same pattern used for linen in
Cape Breton. A similar draft, but with the stars used as an
allover pattern (a 'Dog Tracks' variation), is among the
drafts from Cape Breton (Mackley Collection) and has the
name 'My Sweetheart.'

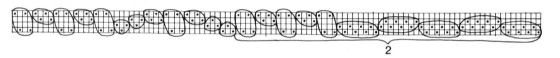

2

307 / Ontario. Hastings County. 1840-60
ROM 968.202.7
Overshot coverlet. L. 224cm, plus fringe; w. 160cm

Indigo blue wool on natural white cotton. This is another
version of a five-'star' motif in 'Dog Tracks' layout. The small
'cross' between the 'table' and the 'stars' provides an effective
frame for the latter. It should be noted that five 'stars' arranged in this way, with smaller ones at the corners, produce
a circular form that will be seen more fully developed in the
following patterns.

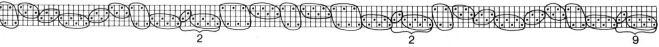

2   2   9

308 / Ontario. Probably Sophiasburgh Township,
Prince Edward County. 1840-60
ROM 969.229.11. Gift of Mr and Mrs Harold B. Burnham
Overshot coverlet. L. 203cm, plus fringe; w. 180cm

Indigo blue wool on natural white cotton. This shows two
interesting technical points. The central 'star' is drafted 'on
opposites' and an examination of the draft will show that
only three of the possible four blocks have been used: a most
unusual feature.

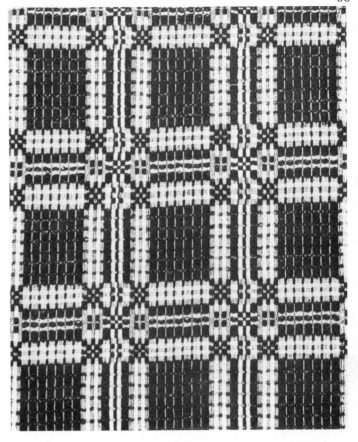

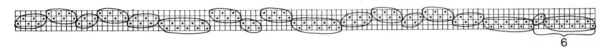

309 / Ontario. Colebrook, Campden Township,
Lennox and Addington Counties. 1840-60
ROM 969.229.9. Gift of Mr and Mrs Harold B. Burnham
Overshot coverlet. L. 211cm, plus fringe; w. 183cm, plus
added fringes

Indigo blue, dull green, and brown wool with details in red
and yellow wool on natural white cotton ground. This
remarkably colourful example has a five-'star' unit as in the
previous patterns, but the central 'star' is considerably larger.
With a small link between the corner 'stars' and the 'table,'
drafted on the same two blocks as the central motif, the
whole unit becomes a large 'wheel.' The drafting of the four-
part 'table' is expert, the pattern well worked out, and the
coverlet superbly woven.

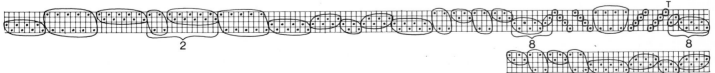

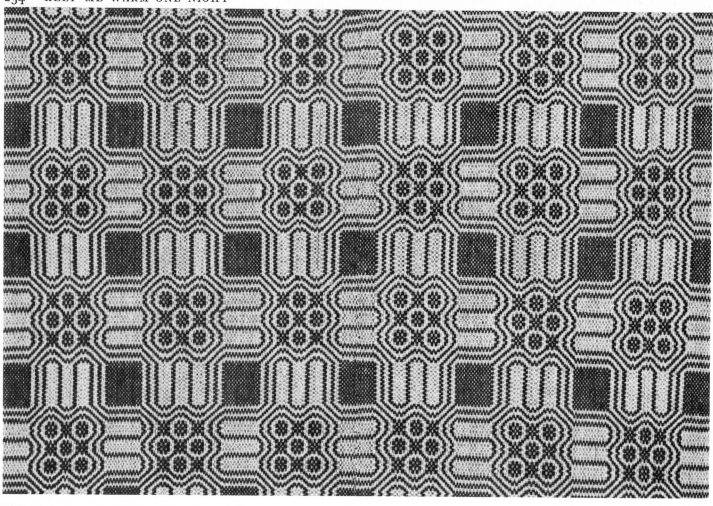

310 / Ontario. Near Adolphustown, Lennox and
Addington Counties. 1800-20
ROM 959.93. Gift of Mrs H.W. Chrysler
Overshot coverlet. L. 232cm, plus fringe; w. 184cm

Dark indigo blue wool on white ground with cotton warp and
bleached linen main weft (z singles). The use of linen is
unusual and rare, indicating an early date. As in no. 304, the
main motif of 'stars' reverses in alternate repeats to produce
a long and tantalizing pattern layout. From the Empy
family.

The pattern is of special interest as it is the same as that
of one of the earliest North American overshot coverlets
known. Dated 1784, and probably from near Albany, New
York, it is in the collection of the Coverlet Guild of America
(*Swygert*, 24).

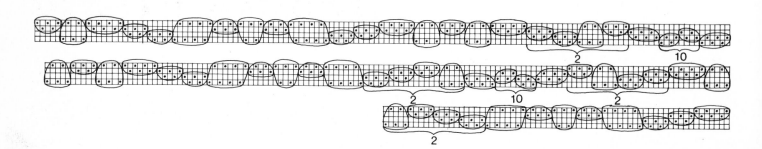

311 / Ontario. York County, probably Markham Township.
1840-60
ROM 966.158.31
Coverlet or carpet fragment. L. 83cm; w. 92cm

Red and green wool on red (now brownish) cotton ground.
The red cotton of the ground is most unusual and may well
indicate that this was made as a floor covering. The cotton
yarn for coverlets was bought from local general stores. Most
of it was natural, but skeins of red or blue were also sometimes available. Such skeins would have been the source of
the colour in the ground of this piece.

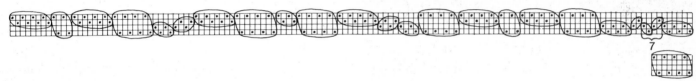

312 / Ontario. Elgin County, possibly Straffordville.
1850-75
ROM 968.123. Gift of Mrs J.H. Crang
Overshot coverlet. L. 217cm, plus fringe; w. 147cm, plus
added fringes

Indigo blue wool on natural white cotton (warp, z, 3s). The
same unit of five 'stars' has again been used, with the linking
and surrounding blocks placed 'on opposites' to give the
'stars' a jumpy, vibrating effect.

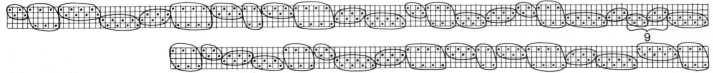

313 / Nova Scotia. Dublin Shore, Lunenburg County.
1850-70
ROM 966.158.26. Gift of Mrs J.H. Crang
Tablecloth. L. 148cm; w. 142cm

Natural brown linen on natural white cotton (all yarns z singles). The five-'star' unit forms a well developed 'wheel,' used here as an overall pattern linked by a 'cross.' This motif is of widespread distribution and is known as 'Single Chariot Wheel' in a draft from Cape Breton (Mackley Collection) when woven 'as drawn in.' The design is more usually treadled 'rose fashion' as in the following example.

314 / Ontario. Chesterville, Winchester Township, Dundas County. 1860-70
UCV 58.H2673. Gift of Mrs H.L. Hough
Overshot coverlet. L. 157cm; w. 161cm

Red wool on natural white cotton. If the previous design is woven 'rose fashion,' this is the result. It is a widely known pattern, surprisingly rare in Canada. It has been usually called 'Whig Rose' in modern weaving books, but the origin of the name is unknown.

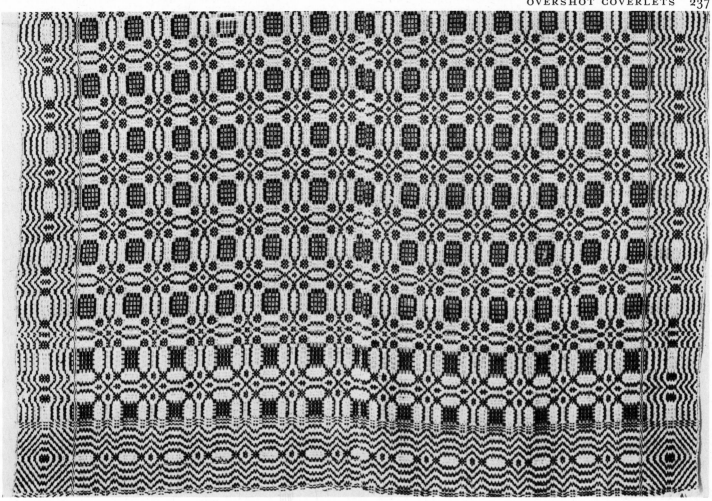

315 / Ontario. Burford, Brant County. 1850-60
ROM 969.229.10. Gift of Mr and Mrs Harold B. Burnham
Overshot coverlet. L. 224cm, plus fringe; w. 176cm

Indigo blue wool on natural white cotton. This again is
'Whig Rose' with an intentional and unusual inner border

across the lower end formed by treadling the draft 'as drawn
in' for two repeats. Here in one coverlet are both versions of
this pattern. The borders are well planned, and show the use
of twill guards, unusual in Ontario. From the Silverthorn
family.

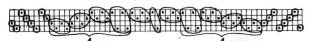

316 / Ontario. Sharon, East Gwillimbury Township,
York County. 1860-75
NMM D308. Gift of Miss A.E. Macphail
Overshot coverlet. L. 234cm, plus added fringe; w. 182cm,
plus added fringes

Indigo blue wool on natural white cotton (warp, z, 3s).
This pattern is quite common in the eastern part of York
County and shows the 'Chariot Wheel' motif used in groups
of four combined with a 'table.' The fringes have been woven
separately, doubled, and sewn on. The draft is similar to one
from Prince Edward County called 'Chariots Wheels' (Abercrombie Collection 954.148.19). The coverlet is said to have
been made by Mrs William Henry Willson, great-grandmother of the donor. It is more probable that she prepared
the yarns and that the coverlet was woven by a professional
who also wove the other examples known. All of these have
fringes of the same type.

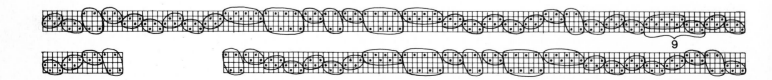

9

317 / Ontario. Kent County. Probably 1820-40.
Chatham-Kent Museum, Chatham
Overshot coverlet. L. 204cm; w. 138cm

Indigo blue wool on natural white cotton (warp and main weft, z singles; pattern weft, s singles). The yarns are all interesting and of early type. This is another version of four 'chariot wheels' with a small 'table' alternating with a lozenge diaper panel. The 'cross' between the 'wheels' has been drafted 'on opposites.' This is one of the very few coverlets from this district that has been recorded.

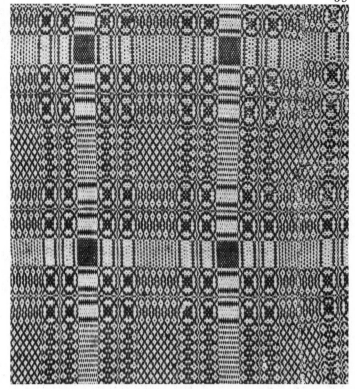

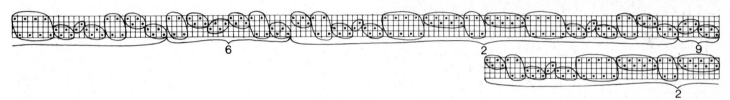

318 / Nova Scotia. Cape Breton. 1850-75
Mackley Collection, Sydney, NS
Overshot coverlet (fragment). L. 84cm; w. 79cm

Dark green wool on natural white cotton. This is another 'wheel' pattern with the motifs joined by a 'cross' extended to produce a lozenge panel. Drafts for a slightly shorter version of the pattern occur in the Mackley Collection of Cape Breton drafts: two with the name 'London Beauty,' and one called 'English Beauty.'

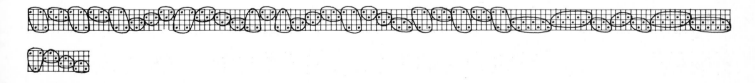

319 / Ontario. Lennox and Addington Counties, Napanee area. 1830-50
ROM 969.229.4. Gift of Mr and Mrs Harold B. Burnham
Overshot coverlet. L. 199cm; w. 164cm

Indigo blue and rose-red wool on natural white cotton. A draft from Prince Edward County is identical (Abercrombie Collection 954.148.24) and has the pleasant name 'Distant Beauty.' Here another form of 'wheel' is seen. Previous circular forms grew from combinations of large and small 'stars' (nos. 313ff.), but here the circle is formed of three blocks used as a 'cross' rounded out at the sides by a return to the two centre ones. This same principle applies to the larger 'wheel' motifs that follow.

9

320 / Ontario. Saltfleet Township, Wentworth County. 1855-65
ROM 967.168.4. Gift of the Misses Hattie I. and Charlotte Jones
Overshot coverlet. L. 208cm, plus fringe; w. 173cm

Indigo blue wool on natural white cotton (main weft, z, 2s). This variant of 'Distant Beauty' with a long 'cross' on two-thread units between the small 'wheels' is a somewhat untidy, but very effective pattern. The border is quite unusual. This coverlet is from the trousseau of Catherine Gage Pettit, who was married in 1865. Another coverlet from the same area and about the same date is patterned in indigo blue, green, and red and is probably the work of the same weaver (ROM 970.43.3). The design is also known from Carleton County (ROM 966.158.57).

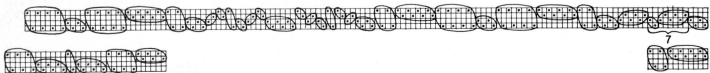

7

321 / Ontario. Richmond Township, Lennox and
Addington Counties. About 1850
ROM 970.257.6. Gift of Mrs Archie Lamont
Overshot coverlet. L. 230cm, plus fringe; w. 175cm, plus
added fringes

Rust-red and medium indigo blue (perhaps originally top-
dyed with yellow) wool on natural white cotton. This is
another, more complex version of the 'wheel' pattern. The
'wheels' are larger here than in the previous examples, and
drafted so that the centres are 'on opposites.' With the 'table'
drafted in the same way, the intervening spaces have a
curious and effective pattern made up of a mixture of single-
and double-thread incidentals that result from this form of
drafting. This was probably woven by Peter Fretz, great-
grandfather of the donor, who lived near Napanee (cf. nos.
27, 40, 55).

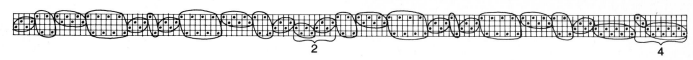

322 / Ontario. Pakenham, Lanark County. About 1865-70
ROM 967.96. Gift of Mr William Inglis Clarke
Overshot coverlet. L. 190cm; w. 205cm

Aniline violet wool on natural white ground (main weft, z
singles wool). This coverlet was woven by William Inglis,
great-great-grandfather of the donor, who came to Pakenham
in the 1840s from Paisley, Scotland. It was made for one of
his daughters and is well woven, short in length but unusually
wide. The pattern is extremely interesting, being a version
of a 'wheel' pattern as in the previous examples, but woven
'rose fashion' to give quite a different effect. Another coverlet
woven by the same weaver in this pattern is in the Royal
Ontario Museum (969.65.1). It is somewhat older and patterned in brown-black wool, but with the same combination
of cotton and wool in the ground.

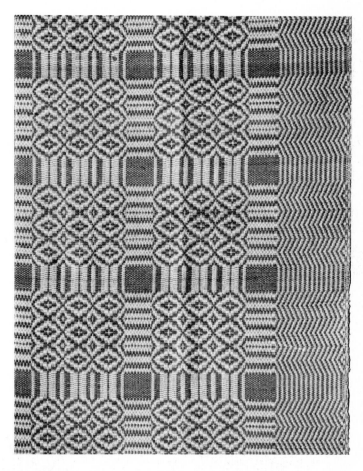

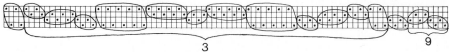

323 / Nova Scotia (?). Possibly Cape Breton.
Late 19th century
ROM 967.34
Pair of overshot curtains. L. 306cm; w. 87cm

All wool with green-black pattern on deep red ground (all yarns z singles). Although found in Victoria, British Columbia, without a history, it is certain that these curtains were taken to the west coast from the Maritime Provinces. In the latter part of the nineteenth century, the weave was used for this purpose in eastern Canada. The pattern is identical with a draft from Cape Breton (Mackley Collection) called 'Cards and Wheels.' The 'wheel' form is fully developed with a long 'cross' reversing at the corners to repeat the centre block and close the circle. It is simple, but effective, with its contrasts of 'tables.'

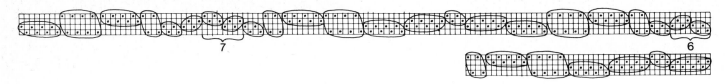

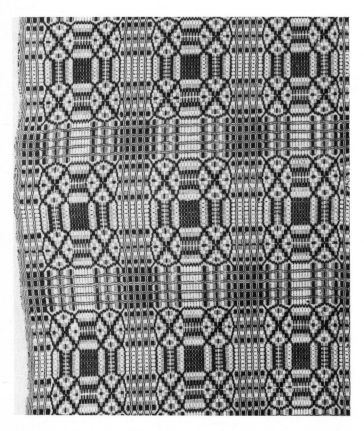

324 / New Brunswick. Mid-19th century
York-Sunbury Museum, Fredericton, NB. 5221B.
Helen Reid Estate
Overshot coverlet. L. 233cm; w. 161cm

Indigo blue wool on natural white cotton. This complex pattern is surprisingly common and with little variation is of wide distribution. A draft from Prince Edward County, Ontario (Abercrombie Collection 954.148.15) has the name 'Freemason's Felicity.' Another, similar and with the same name, comes from Cape Breton (Mackley Collection). An unnamed one from West Pubnico is in the Nova Scotia Museum. The pattern always consists of the same fully developed 'wheel' separated by two types of 'table': one plain, the other fancy.

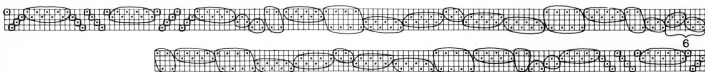

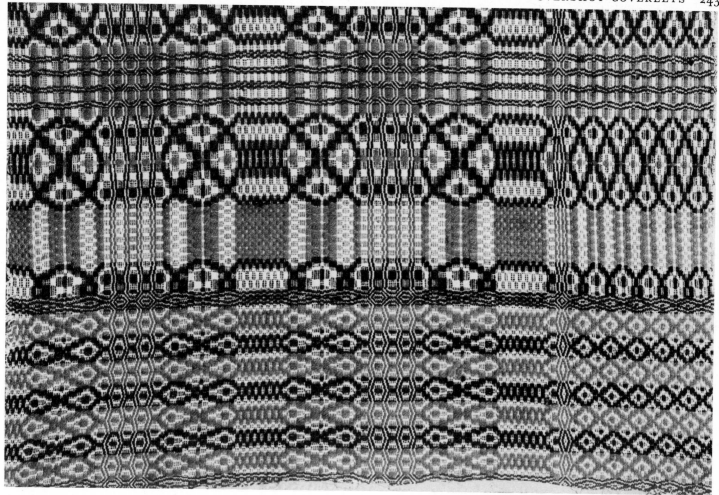

325 / Ontario. Whitechurch, Bruce County. 1850-75
ROM 969.32.2. Gift of Mrs J.H. Crang
Overshot coverlet. L. 220cm; w. 159cm

Deep indigo blue and strong rust-red wool on natural white
cotton (main weft, z, 2s). When found, this was being used
in two halves as curtains in a log cabin, but undoubtedly was
woven as a coverlet. It is another exceedingly handsome
example of 'Freemason's Felicity,' and is work of professional
standard. An all-wool coverlet in this pattern from the same
area is in the Royal Ontario Museum (968.5.2). As the
main draft is identical to no. 324, only the border is shown
here.

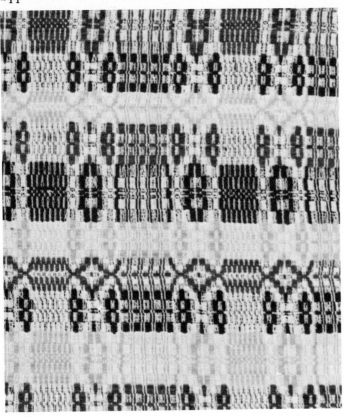

326 / Ontario. Russell County. 1820-40
ROM 946.78. Gift of Mrs H.J. Pennington
Overshot coverlet. L. 176cm; w. 160cm

Medium indigo blue, black, and red (now faded) wool on
natural white cotton. The draft used has been 'Freemason's
Felicity,' but has been treadled in a most unorthodox way.
It was usual for the weaver to pin the threading draft up on
the loom, and follow it exactly for the treadling order. Here
the draft for 'Whig Rose' (no. 314) has been substituted as
a treadling guide, and we shall never know why. Considering
that one draft was used for threading, another for treadling,
and the coverlet woven in three colours, it is no wonder the
effect is unusual and a bit confused.

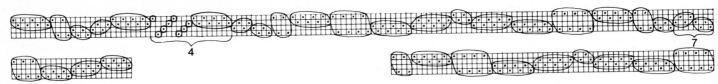

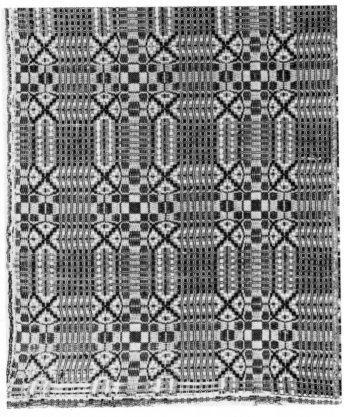

327 / Ontario. Addison, Leeds County. 1830-50
ROM 968.93.2. Gift of Mrs J.H. Crang
Overshot coverlet. L. 219cm, plus added fringe; w. 180cm,
plus added fringes

Indigo blue wool on natural white cotton. This variation of
'Freemason's Felicity' has the plain 'table' split into five parts
and the lead into the other one shortened, making the 'wheel'
incomplete at that side.

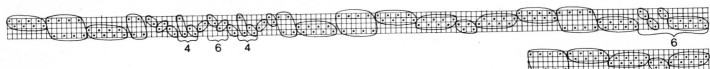

328 / Ontario. Komoka, Lobo Township,
Middlesex County. 1860-75
ROM 949.154.2. Gift of Mr John Campbell
Overshot coverlet. L. 183cm; w. 172cm

Indigo blue wool on natural white cotton. This coverlet was
woven by the grandfather of the donor, John Campbell of
Komoka, who was born and trained in Scotland. He is better
known as a weaver of jacquard coverlets (no. 481). This is
another version of 'Freemason's Felicity' with both sides of
the 'wheels' curtailed so that they resemble 'crosses.' Like
other coverlets from weavers' families, this is quite short and
may well have been fitted on the end of a warp that was not
long enough for a standard marketable coverlet.

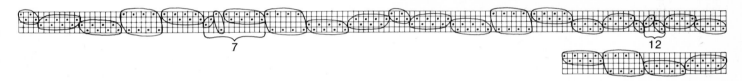

329 / Ontario. Lobo Township, Middlesex County.
Mid-19th century
ROM 969.219. Gift of Mrs Austin Reid
Overshot coverlet. L. 155cm; w. 154cm (considerably cut
down in length)

Indigo blue and brick-red wool on natural white cotton.
Although this appears to be similar to no. 328 woven by John
Campbell, the draft differs, and it is too early in date to be
his work. It may have been woven by one of the other Scottish weavers who settled in this area before Campbell's
arrival in 1859.

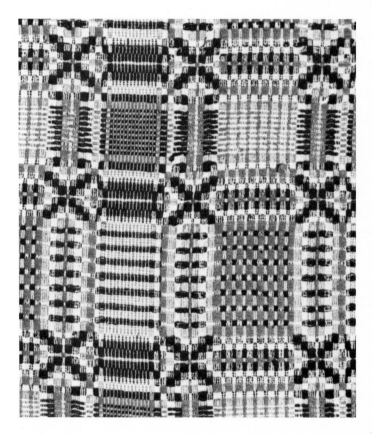

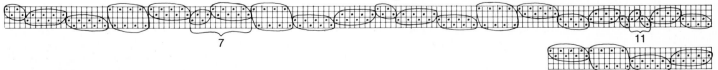

330 / Ontario. Fenelon Township, Victoria County.
About 1875
ROM 966.240. Gift of Mrs A.S. Parrish
Overshot coverlet. L. 204cm, plus fringe; w. 167cm

Red and pale green wool on natural white cotton. This draft starts off in a similar way to 'Freemason's Felicity,' but the larger blocks at the corners give quite a different effect from the 'wheels' of that pattern; instead of a fancy table, the design centres on a series of twill lines. It is a carefully worked out draft, with a necessary loss of tabby at one point. The coverlet was expertly woven by Mrs Caroline Parrish, the mother-in-law of the donor, at Powels Corners, near Fenelon Falls.

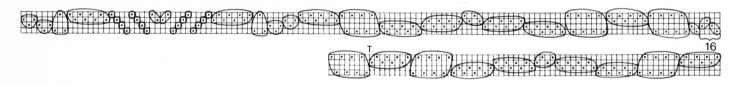

331 / New Brunswick. 1860-80
York-Sunbury Museum, Fredericton, NB. 6804.
Gift of Miss A. Balmain
Overshot coverlet. L. 218cm, plus knotted fringe; w. 192cm

Indigo blue wool on natural white cotton (warp, z, 3s; main weft, z, 2s). The use of these yarns for the ground indicates a fairly late date. The pattern is on a bold scale that seems commoner in New Brunswick than in other parts of Canada. It is well woven and, on close examination, the tabby losses obvious in the draft of the 'table' are unobtrusive in the coverlet. They produce a much better distribution of incidentals.

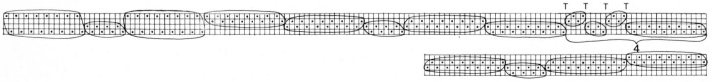

332 / Ontario. Mountain Township, Dundas County.
About 1865
ROM 969.229.2. Gift of Mr and Mrs Harold B. Burnham
Overshot coverlet. L. 207cm; 159cm

Bleached linen (z, 3s) on natural white cotton. The use of
linen for patterns is very rare in Ontario. Like the all-cotton
coverlets, this one probably imitates the fashionable imported
white bedspreads. The flax was raised and processed by the
daughters of Hugh Begg. The pattern is almost identical
with one of the drafts from Prince Edward County (Abercrombie Collection 954.148.32) named 'Indian Plains.' It is
based on four broken 'wheel' motifs that merge into a diamond pattern.

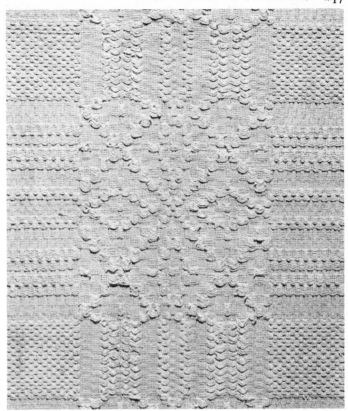

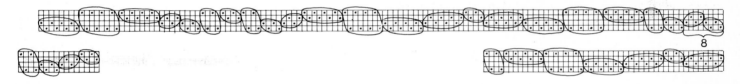

333 / Ontario. Sidney Township, Hastings County.
Early 19th century
ROM 947.69.5. Gift of Mr Macauley Pope
Overshot coverlet. L. 219cm; w. 169cm

Indigo blue wool on natural white cotton (pattern weft, hard
s singles). This is another example of the 'Indian Plains'
pattern with a slightly longer lead from the 'table' to the
main motif. Traditionally, this coverlet is said to have been
woven by Catherine White, after she came from New
England to Canada in 1794.

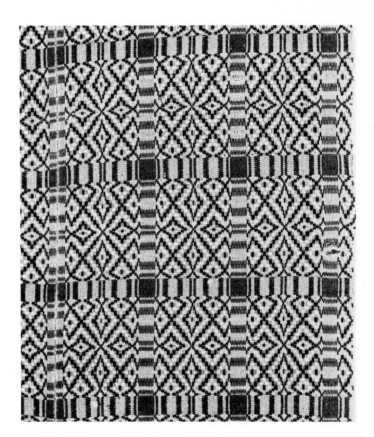

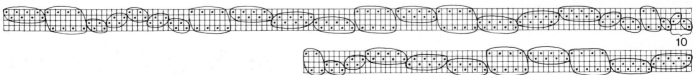

334 / Nova Scotia. Annapolis County. 1850-70
ROM 966.174. Gift of Mrs L.M.W. How
Overshot coverlet (fragment). L. 127cm; w. 84cm

Indigo blue wool on natural white cotton. Four wheels enclose a lozenge panel. Like 'Freemason's Felicity' to which it is related, this is a rather complex pattern known from Nova Scotia, New Brunswick, and Ontario. The name 'Indian Review' is on a draft from Prince Edward County (Abercrombie Collection 954.148.18).

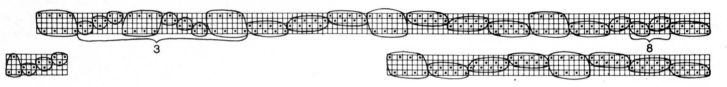

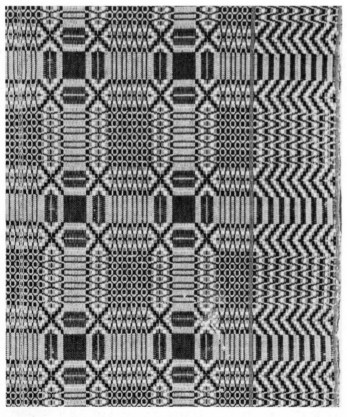

335 / Ontario. Otonabee Township, Peterborough County. 1840-50
Peterborough Centennial Museum, Peterborough. H.62.3. Gift of Mr Dougall Matchett
Overshot coverlet. L. 219cm; w. 169cm

Indigo blue wool on natural white cotton. This variation of 'Indian Review' has a simpler link between the 'table' and the 'semi-wheel' forms; the lozenge pattern is drafted on two-thread blocks rather than three. The simple border becomes most effective as it follows the treadling of the pattern. This coverlet belonged to Jeannette Scott Matchett, who was born in Peterborough in 1820.

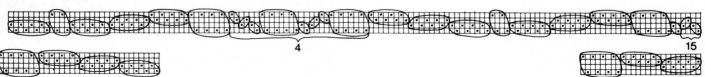

336 / New Brunswick. 1860-80
York-Sunbury Museum, Fredericton, NB
Overshot coverlet. L. 256cm; original width 220cm
(a strip has been cut from one width)

Light brown and chartreuse green wool on natural white
cotton (main weft, z, 2s). This shows the soft shades of the
local vegetable dyes that seem to have been of more common
use in New Brunswick than elsewhere in Canada. Before it
was cut, the coverlet was unusually long and wide. The pattern is similar to no. 335: a variation of 'Indian Review.'

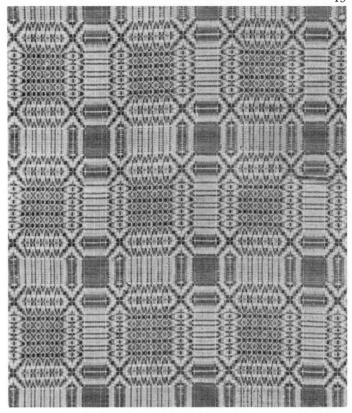

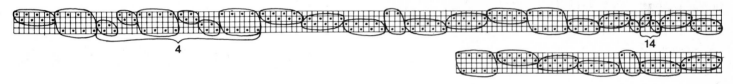

337 / Ontario. Possibly Grey or Bruce Counties. 1860-75
ROM 966.75.2. Gift of Mrs H.C. Smith
Overshot coverlet. L. 180cm; w. 170cm

Indigo blue wool on natural white cotton (main weft, z, 2s).
The pattern has the lozenge lattice without the enclosing
'wheel' forms. This is the most interesting method of drafting
the lattice in this group of coverlets. It is both threaded and
treadled on odd and even numbered blocks, producing a
balanced lattice with doubled threads for emphasis. The
tabby is unnoticeably lost where the two main units meet.

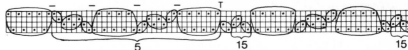

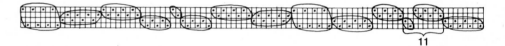

11

338 / Ontario. Dundas, Wentworth County. 1860-80
ROM 949.64. Gift of Mrs George Hils Bowman, in memory of her husband
Overshot coverlet. L. 214cm, plus fringe; w. 166cm

Indigo blue, red, and ochre wool on natural white cotton (warp mixed, z, 2s, and z, 3s). A beautiful and well-woven coverlet with a 'table on opposites' and a 'star,' with the connecting blocks also 'on opposites.' Other coverlets of the same pattern are known that were woven by Mina Misener Morton, a professional weaver at Greensville above Dundas. This is undoubtedly her work.

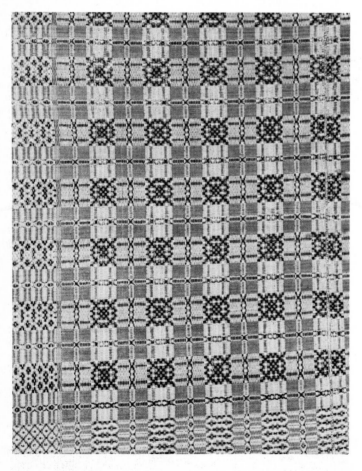

7   7

339 / Ontario. Near Exeter, Huron County. 1835-50
ROM 968.24
Overshot coverlet. L. 197cm; w. 172cm

Brick red and very dark green wool on natural white cotton. A well worked out pattern with four-part 'table' and an intervening 'wheel' centred by a 'star,' in which either side may be equally attractive. Another coverlet in the same pattern from Prince Edward County (ROM 968.195.2) is woven with indigo blue and red wools used in narrow bands throughout the length and deliberately planned so that the reverse of the pattern is the right side.

340 / Ontario. Niagara Peninsula. 1850-65
ROM 969.218. Gift of Mrs Margaret Philip
Overshot coverlet. L. 196cm, plus fringe; w. 168cm

Indigo blue and red wool on natural white cotton (warp, z, 3s). Another attractive version of the same pattern with the four-part 'table' drafted in the same way, but with an extra repeat in the central 'star.' The border is unusual.

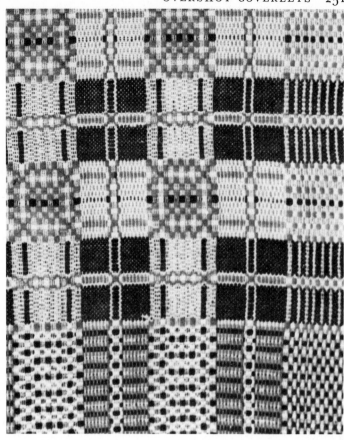

7   7

341 / Ontario. Prince Edward County. 1830-50
NMM D556
Coverlet (part). L. 145cm; w. 87cm

Indigo blue and rust-red wool on natural white cotton. The draft is similar to the previous ones, but differently treadled. The motif between the 'tables' has been shortened by a couple of blocks and partially treadled 'rose fashion.'

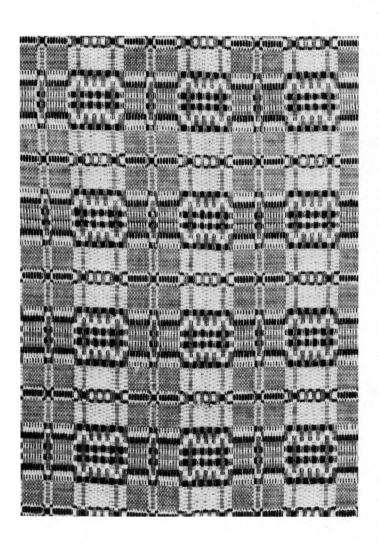

342 / Ontario. Hastings County. 1840-60
NMM D679
Overshot coverlet. L. 222cm; w. 172cm

Indigo blue wool on natural white cotton (warp, z, 3s). An interesting 'table' motif with the central part 'on opposites' and corner sections in contrast to it. The intervening motif leads into a large, rather fancy 'star.' The pattern is the same as that of the coverlet recorded by Dr Ivan Crowell as having been woven at Girvan, Ayrshire, Scotland.

5   5   5

343 / Ontario. Bastard Township, Leeds County.
Late 19th century
ROM 967.85. Gift of Mrs J.H. Crang
Overshot coverlet. L. 199cm; w. 165cm

Medium indigo blue wool on natural white cotton (warp, z,
4s; main weft, z, 2s). The draft runs from the main 'table,'
in this case very small, through a 'cross' to centre on a large
'table' surrounded by a full 'wheel.' The yarn used for the
warp is typical commercial carpet warp, indicating a date at
the end of the nineteenth century.

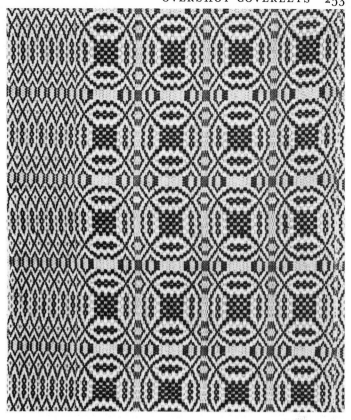

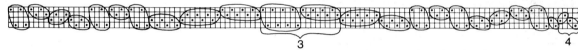

344 / Nova Scotia. Pictou County. 1850-60
ROM 966.158.20. Gift of Mr and Mrs Harold B. Burnham
Overshot coverlet. L. 182cm, plus fringe; w. 175cm

Patterned in bleached linen on natural white cotton. This is
an example of the part-linen coverlets used throughout the
Scottish areas of the Maritime Provinces. The pattern is
similar to no. 343, but the main 'table' is quite large. There
is an unusual point in the way it is drafted and woven:
between the large blocks there are three single shots producing
a stepped line rather than a small block.

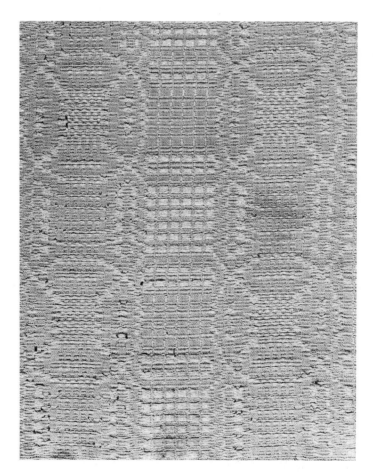

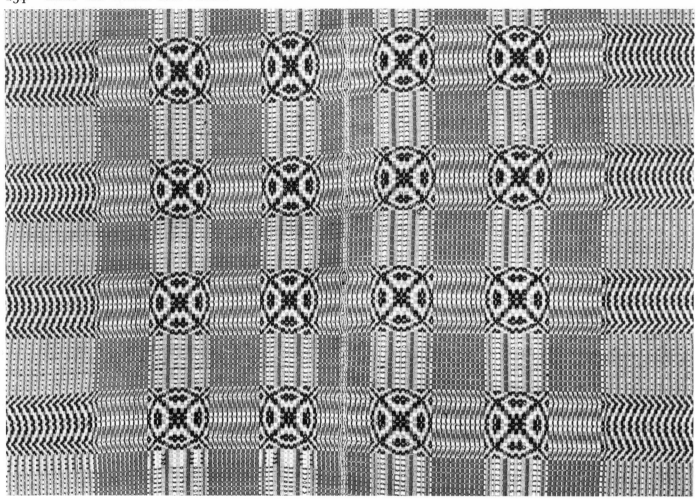

345 / Ontario. Spencerville, Grenville County. 1850-65
ROM 969.229.7. Gift of Mr and Mrs Harold B. Burnham
Overshot coverlet. L. 229cm; w. 177cm

Strong pink-red and dark olive-green wool on natural white

cotton (main weft, z, 2s). The colour of this coverlet is
glorious, matching the strong and effective pattern. It is
another version of 'tables' linked by fully developed 'wheels'
centred, in this case, by a 'star.'

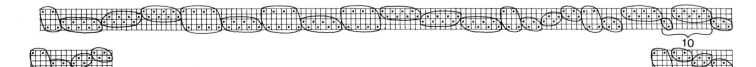

346 / Ontario. Warsaw area, Peterborough County.
1840-60
Peterborough Centennial Museum, Peterborough. H.68.1.
Gift of Miss Mary E. Medd
Overshot coverlet. L. 211cm, plus fringe; w. 182cm

Brick-red and indigo blue wool on natural white cotton
(pattern weft, s singles). Another version of the preceding
pattern with the 'table on opposites' and an interesting subtle
point in the drafting: to the left of the 'table' there is always
a doubled thread producing a better balance between the
two sides.

347 / Ontario. Amherstburg area, Essex County. 1825-50
Hiram Walker Historical Museum, Windsor, Ontario. 58.98
Overshot coverlet. L. 245cm; w. 187cm

Indigo blue wool on natural white cotton. This is a well-
known pattern, widely found with slight variations. It resembles the previous ones, but the 'table' is always split into
several parts, normally nine as here. A draft from Prince
Edward County (Abercrombie Collection 954.148.12) is
labelled 'Chariot Wheels and Church Windows.' Similar patterns occur in Cape Breton (Mackley Collection), one with
the same name, another labelled 'Carpet.' This adds another
piece of evidence that overshot was more widely used for
floor covering than the remaining fragments would indicate.
A coverlet with the same pattern from Saltfleet Township,
Wentworth County, is in the Royal Ontario Museum
(970.43.1).

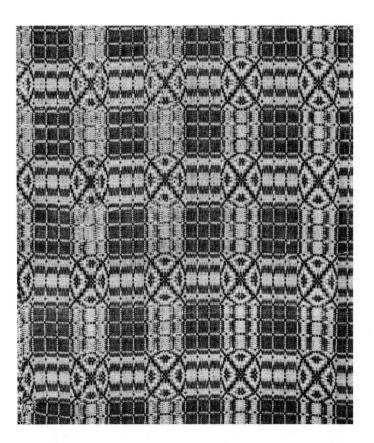

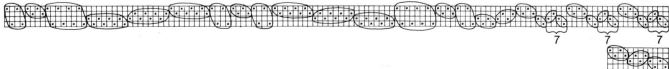

348 / Ontario. Norfolk County. 1820-50
ROM 969.229.1. Gift of Mr and Mrs Harold B. Burnham
Overshot coverlet. L. 206cm, plus fringe; w. 147cm

Rust-red wool on natural white cotton (main weft, fine z, 2s). The wool here is the best handspinning seen in any Canadian coverlet. Although the main weft is plied, the cotton is of an old type. The pattern is a distinctive one that appears to have little relation to other designs, but is in fact a variation of 'Monmouth' with the 'tables' and the centres of the 'crosses' drafted on 'opposites' to produce a very different effect (cf. no. 266). The pattern is of fairly wide distribution, but no Canadian name has been found. It occurs in several parts of Ontario, in Quebec, and is known from the Chignecto Isthmus between New Brunswick and Nova Scotia. One of the coverlets in the Royal Ontario Museum with a Scottish history has the same pattern (962.245). In this, the fine cotton and heavy wool are totally different from those used in Canada, supporting the strong family tradition that it was brought from Skye about 1830 by the donor's grandmother.

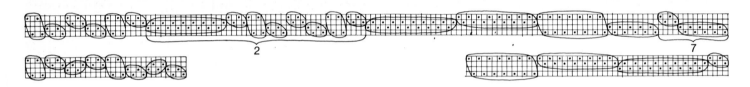

349 / Quebec. Valleyfield, Châteauguay County. 1850-70
ROM 970.228. Gift of Mrs J.H. Crang
Overshot coverlet. L. 213cm; w. 180cm

Burnt orange wool on medium indigo blue cotton (main weft, fine z, 2s). The unusual colour scheme has produced a handsome result. Overshot coverlets with coloured grounds are of rare occurrence. The pattern differs slightly from no. 348, as may be seen by comparing the drafts. The result more closely resembles the two examples seen that had been woven in the Chignecto Isthmus. Both of these are of three, rather than two widths. One is in indigo blue and white, the other, now at Keillor House, Dorchester, NB, is entirely of white cotton. Although the balance of warp and weft has produced a well balanced pattern unlike a number of the earlier overshot coverlets woven by French weavers in Quebec, the centre seam does not divide a pattern unit in the centre as is always found in examples woven in the Scottish tradition. This misunderstanding of the draft supports the fact that it has a French background.

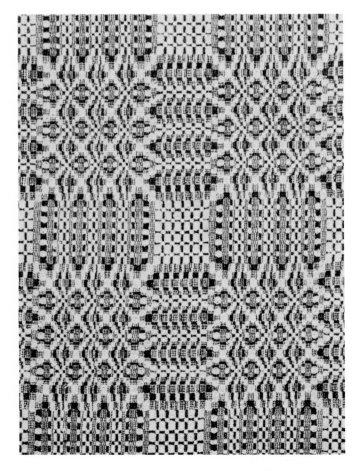

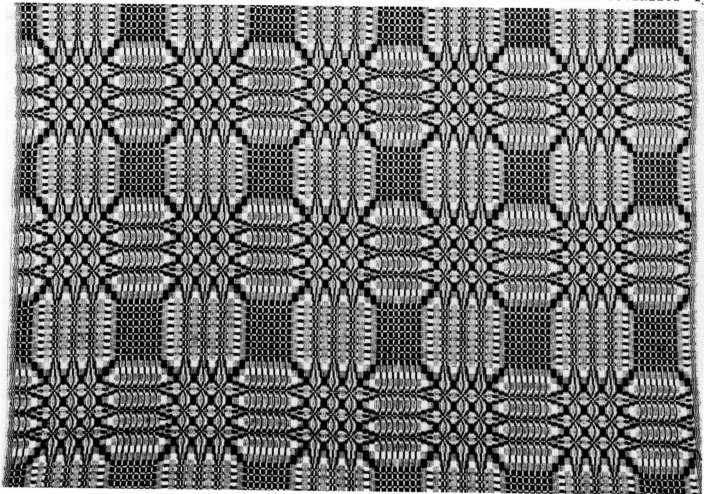

350 / Ontario. Lincoln County, Louth or Clinton
Townships. 1860-75
ROM 964.19. Gift of Mrs J.H. Crang
Overshot coverlet. L. 214cm, plus fringe; w. 181cm

Indigo blue wool on natural white cotton (main weft, z, 2s).
This has a draft almost identical to that of no. 348, but is
woven in one width. The centre seam that occurs in almost
all old coverlets is due to the limited reach of the weaver who
threw the shuttle with one hand and caught it with the other.
Depending on skill and stature, this distance varies with a
maximum of about four feet. This is often taken as the only
infallible proof of handweaving, but nothing is so simple. A
few professional weavers had wide looms in regular use,
equipped with either a flying shuttle with drop box, or
operated by two weavers, one at each side. This coverlet was
handwoven on such a loom.

351 / Ontario. Wellington County. 1860-80
ROM 967.220.9. Gift of Mrs J.H. Crang
Coverlet, eight-shaft overshot. L. 207cm, plus fringe;
w. 178cm, plus fringes

Dark indigo blue, dark green, and red wool on natural white
cotton (warp, fine z, 2s, double). At first glance this seems
a normal overshot coverlet with the same pattern as 'Indian
Plains' (nos. 332–3), but a closer look reveals that eight
shafts were required rather than the usual four. Another
example, technically identical, patterned in dark indigo blue
wool also comes from Wellington County (ROM 959.268).
It would have been easy for a skilled professional weaver to
follow the profile of a normal overshot and thread the loom
on four successive pairs of shafts. The incidentals are created
by tying up the treadles so that single threads from adjacent
or other blocks operated with each patterning combination.
In the drafts the pairs of shafts for each block are marked
with crosses in the tie-up and the additional ties for the incidentals are marked with dots.

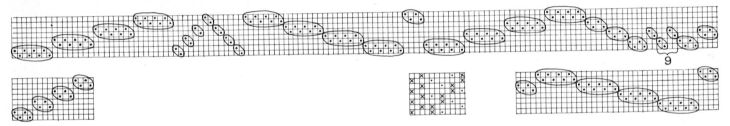

352 / Ontario. York County, possibly North Gwillimbury
Township. 1825-40
ROM 945.36. Gift of Miss Isobel Neilly
Coverlet, eight-shaft overshot. L. 187cm; w. 172cm

Red wool on blue cotton ground (warp and main weft, z,
2s). This is most unusual with its dyed cotton ground. The
pattern appears to be 'Freemason's Felicity' (no. 324), but
as in the previous example eight shafts were required.

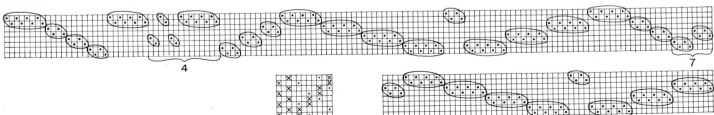

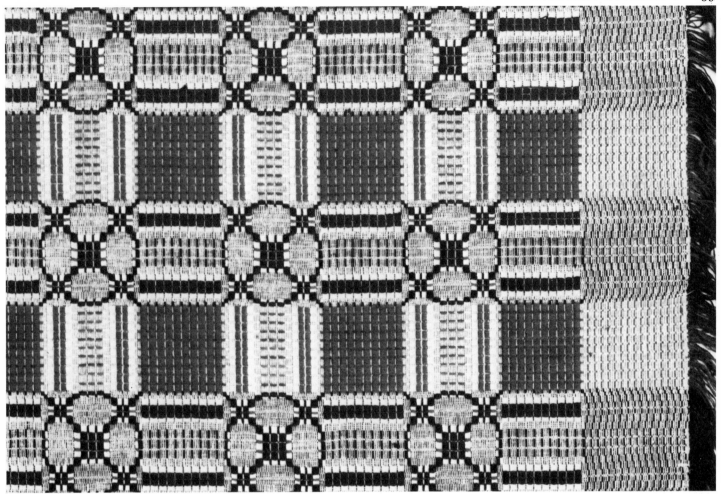

353 / Ontario. Wellington County, collected near Guelph. 1860-80
ROM 962.67.69. Gift of Miss Adelaide Lash Miller
Coverlet, eight-shaft overshot. L. 216cm, plus fringe; w. 186cm, plus fringes

Dark brick-red and dark green wool on natural white cotton

(warp, fine z, 2s, double; main weft, fine z, 2s). This beautiful coverlet uses two basic overshot motifs, the 'table' and the 'wheel,' both 'on opposites.' Another more worn one of the same draft and colour scheme is in the Royal Ontario Museum (955.59). Its history connects it with Freelton, south of Guelph. These and the two described in no. 351 may well be the work of the same weaver.

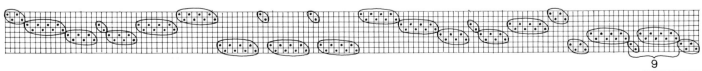

354 / Ontario. Gounston, East Nissouri Township,
Oxford County. 1825-40
ROM 969.113. Gift of Mrs W.A. Murray
Coverlet, ten-shaft overshot. L. 214cm, plus fringe;
w. 176cm, plus fringes

Bright indigo blue wool on natural white cotton ground
(warp and main weft, z singles, double). This and no. 355
are the only overshot coverlets requiring ten shafts that have

been recorded. The design is a version of 'Whig Rose' (no.
392) adapted to a loom of this capacity. The weaver, an
ancestor of the donor, named Bollert, was of Scottish origin
and worked at Gounston. From his use of cotton singles as
warp, it may be assumed that he, like others, was trained as a
muslin weaver before coming to Canada.

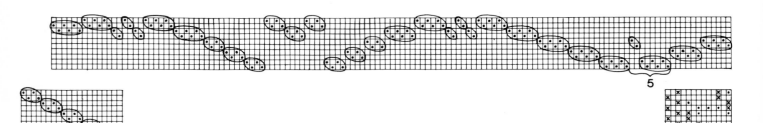

355 / Ontario. Oxford County, collected at Tavistock. 1825-40

ROM 970.118.5. Gift of Mr and Mrs Harold B. Burnham
Coverlet, ten-shaft overshot. L. 223cm, plus fringe; w. 143cm, plus fringes

Pink wool on natural white cotton (warp and main weft, z singles, double). This has been woven from the same draft as no. 354, but the tie-up has been altered, and the weaving follows a different and unorthodox order of treadling. It is undoubtedly the work of the same weaver.

Nos. 351-3 may also be the work of Scots. Trained weavers from the Glasgow district settled in the upper Ottawa Valley of eastern Ontario in the 1820s, but the land was so poor that many moved as soon as they could to Wellington and Simcoe counties, the areas from which these coverlets came.

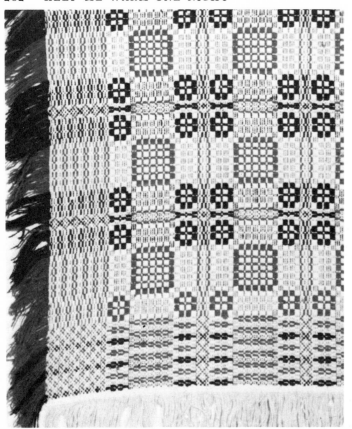

356 / Ontario. Waterloo County, collected at Elmira.
1870-90
ROM 967.220.3. Gift of Mrs J.H. Crang
Coverlet, eight-shaft overshot. L. 222cm, plus fringe;
w. 191cm, plus fringes

Brick-red, indigo blue, and a little turquoise wool on natural
white cotton (warp, z, 3s). A version of the familiar 'Whig
Rose' design woven with eight shafts. The tie-up has been
arranged so that all blocks are 'on opposites' to the adjacent
ones. Waterloo County was an area of extensive German-
speaking settlement with many professional weavers who
used multiple-shaft looms for weaving twill diaper. This
coverlet and the two following appear to be adapted from
designs for this type of work, rather than from normal overshot patterns (cf. 392–3).

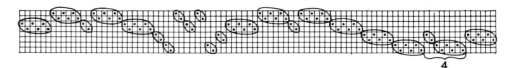

4

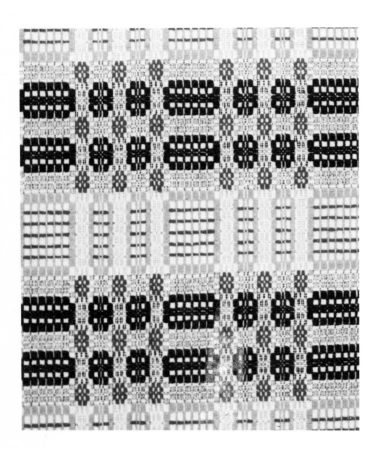

357 / Ontario. Perth County. 1825-40
ROM 964.80. Gift of Mrs J.H. Crang
Coverlet, eight-shaft overshot. L. 211cm, plus fringe;
w. 164cm, plus fringes

Brick-red, indigo blue, and dull yellow wool on natural white
cotton (warp, z, 4s; main weft, z, 2s; both fine). This was
woven for a Scottish bride after she arrived in Canada and
settled near Gad's Hill, not far from Stratford and close to
German-speaking settlements in Perth and Waterloo Counties. It was probably woven by a weaver in this adjacent area.

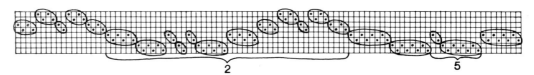

2

5

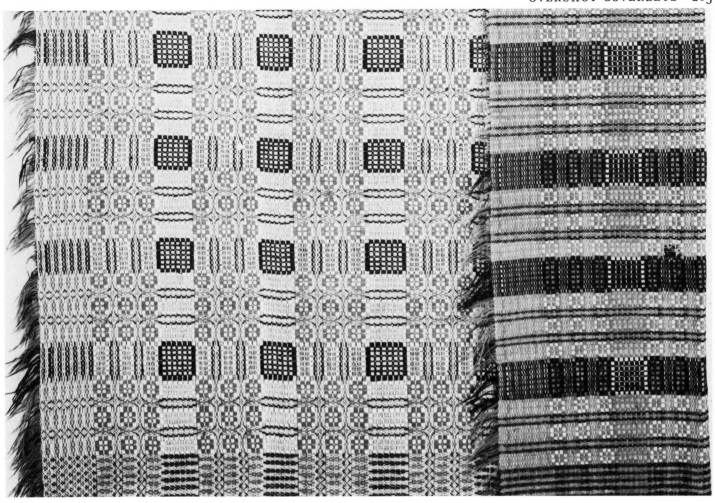

358 / Ontario. Waterloo County. 1850-70
ROM 963.222.2. Gift of Mrs J.H. Crang
Coverlet, eight-shaft overshot. L. 209cm, plus fringe;
w. 164cm, plus fringes

Brick-red and indigo blue wool on natural white cotton
(warp, fine z, 2s, double). The draft is almost identical to
no. 356, but with an extra repeat of the 'rose' unit. The illustration shows both sides of the design. Usually the lighter side
shows the pattern to better advantage, but the reverse can be
very handsome.

  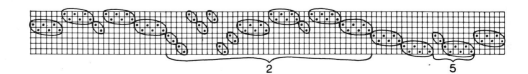

'Summer and winter' coverlets

The occurrence of one type of coverlet weave, usually termed 'summer and winter,' is uncommon and sporadic in Canada. Examples are known from Nova Scotia, New Brunswick, the Eastern Townships of Quebec, and some of the older settled parts of Ontario. It is even difficult to know whether they were at one time more common: it seems probable that, like the doublecloth coverlets, they were only used for best and were always less usual than the simpler constructions. In some twenty years of research, only about fifteen have been seen. All come from a definitely English-speaking and basically United Empire Loyalist background. No trace has been found in areas of French, Scottish, or German settlement. Coverlets in this weave apparently ceased to be made about 1835, and most of those that have survived are even earlier.

The construction is one in which a pattern weft floats over a tabby ground to form a design. As no float is over more than three warp ends, it produces a very serviceable fabric. There is nothing to snag as there is in overshot. 'Summer and winter' coverlets are not as heavy as doublecloth, are firmer than twill diaper, and are as compactly woven as both. The origin of the name by which they are now known appears to be lost, but may stem from the fact that on one face the motifs are in coloured wool on a basically white ground, and on the other they are in white on a coloured field. Traditionally, the lighter side was used for summer, and the darker for winter. It should be pointed out that some other coverlet constructions that are fully reversible, particularly doublecloth, are often mistakenly called 'summer and winter.'

As can be seen in the diagram (fig. 35), the first two shafts must be retained to bind the floats of the pattern weft and every second thread is entered alternately on one or other of these. An additional shaft is needed for each pattern block. The tabby ground is woven by using the two shafts with the binding ends in opposition to all the others. Two treadles are needed for each block of pattern, the first bringing down one set of binding threads and a patterning shaft; the second, the other binding threads and the same patterning shaft. The treadling, as a general rule, follows the threading order exactly, but, as these were made by expert weavers, they varied this order. If they felt that a better effect could be achieved, they used the pattern shots in pairs rather than singly (no. 367), or shortened or lengthened the pattern motifs at will.

All the examples that have been recorded in the course of the Museum's research project are four-block patterns and would have required six-shaft looms. It is possible to produce a two-block pattern with a four-shaft loom. An informant has told us that this was done in New Brunswick. With the addition of extra shafts, more complex patterns may be produced, but none of these with a Canadian history have been seen.

The construction found in these coverlets is related to, and appears to be a descendant of, the weave used for the earliest figured fabrics known to have been woven in the ancient western world. This, now known as weft-faced compound tabby, also occurs with simple geometric patterns. In its simplest form, two weft threads are used, one of which floats on the face while the other floats on the reverse. When they change positions, a pattern is formed. If one of these continues to float on the face or reverse as required, while the second is used to produce a tabby ground, 'summer and winter' weave results. Related to weft-faced compound tabby and virtually contemporary with it is weft-faced compound twill, or samite. Here the weft threads are bound in 1/2 twill. It is interesting to note that this has a descendant today in Finland (Henriksson, 201–2) which resembles 'summer and winter' weave except that the pattern weft is bound in this twill rather than in tabby. It seems possible that these modified versions of the older weaves may once have had a considerable distribution in folk weaving using wool and linen, but the old materials have vanished without a trace.

There are four drafts for 'summer and winter' weave that belonged to Hester and Rosanna Young of Prince Edward County, Ontario, received by them from a weaver in Watertown in northern New York State (Abercrombie Collection,

nos. 954.148.30, .38, .39, .40). One, unfortunately without a name, is the same as that for no. 361. 'Watertown Beauty' was probably woven 'rose fashion' from the form of the draft and would be similar to no. 363. The other two, although not drafted in the same way, are for the same pattern: one is called 'The Chariot Wheel'; the second has a much more intriguing name: 'The Three Wheel Chariot' (no. 71). No 'summer and winter' weave coverlet in this pattern has been seen, but it is based on a lozenge lattice enclosing three circles around a central motif. This principle of patterning is also known from overshot weave and is found in no. 255.

In designing for 'summer and winter' weave, each pattern unit basically consists of four warp threads and the threading principle never varies: two threads are entered in the shafts retained for binding the pattern weft; the other two in the patterning shaft for the unit required. The drafts may be drawn out in extended form as they are in the diagram. Those

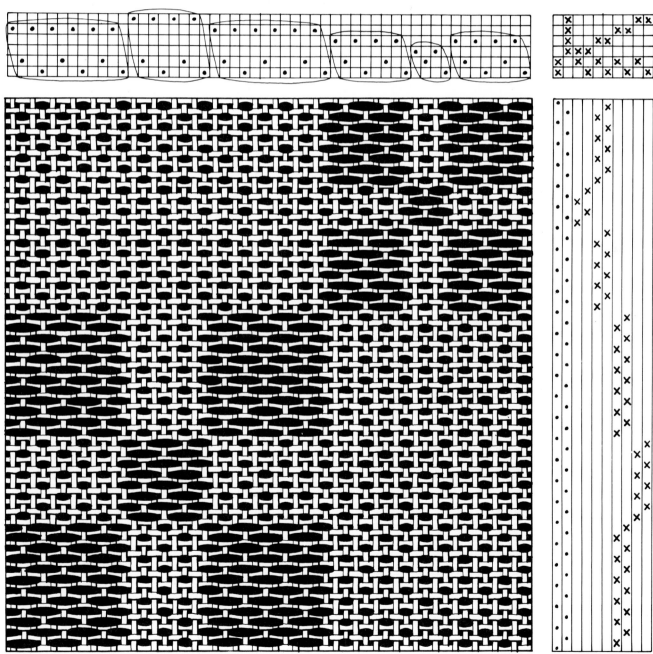

FIGURE 35

in the Abercrombie Collection are done in this way, but using the old-fashioned numerical method. As each pattern unit is constant, a profile draft of the pattern is all that is required once the basic principle is known. Occasionally, only half a basic unit is used intentionally, as in no. 359. For this reason, it has been necessary here to show the drafts with each unit of the profile representing only two threads, or half a basic unit.

As in overshot weave, the tie-up of the treadles must be reversed if a 'rose fashion' pattern is desired. In order to indicate which coverlets have been woven in this way, the drafts are shown here with the characteristic separation of motifs; those that have been woven 'as drawn in' are shown with the motifs linked. This is a convention used by many of the old professional weavers, who produced the more complex patterns. The proper tie-up is shown to the left of each draft in profile form, so that the treadling may follow the draft exactly. Only nos. 363 and 364 are woven 'rose fashion' and are shown with the required reversed tie-up; all the others are woven 'as drawn in' and have their appropriate straight tie-ups.

As in overshot weave, the yarns used in these coverlets are quite consistent. Unless otherwise specified, the warp is a handplied z, 2s cotton, the main weft a z singles cotton, and the pattern weft a handspun z, 2s woollen yarn.

359 / Ontario. South Crosby Township, Leeds County. Probably 1810-15
ucv 60.6439.1. Gift of Mrs R.T. Tamblyn
'Summer and winter' weave coverlet (part). L. 142cm; w. 72cm

Indigo blue wool on bleached linen (warp, z, 2s; main weft, z singles). Uncommon as 'summer and winter' weave coverlets are in Canada, this one, despite its worn and battered condition, is a rare treasure with its bleached linen ground proving its early date. It probably belonged originally to Sarah Bolton, who was married in Canada to Thomas Singleton in 1810.

360 / Ontario. South Crosby Township, Leeds County.
Probably 1815-20
UCV 60.6439.2. Gift of Mrs R.T. Tamblyn
'Summer and winter' weave coverlet. L. 209cm; w. 173cm

Indigo blue wool on natural white cotton. This coverlet, like
the preceding one, comes from the Singleton family. The
ground is of standard early cotton implying that it was woven
slightly later than the one with linen. It is a simpler version
of the same design with the large central unit unbroken. As
the pattern weft in 'summer and winter' weave never floats
more than three threads, there are not the same restrictions to
the size of a pattern block as there are with overshot weave.
Solid blocks like this one may be used without weakening the
construction.

361 / Ontario. Collected in Welland County. 1820-30
ROM 966.33.3. Gift of Mr and Mrs Harold B. Burnham
'Summer and winter' weave coverlet. L. 191cm; w. 214cm

Indigo blue wool on natural white cotton. This is another
version of the same pattern with the large central unit
broken, and a fully developed chessboard motif between the
four 'stars' instead of a 'cross.' The draft of this is identical
to the unnamed one in the Abercrombie Collection from
Prince Edward County (ROM 954.148.38).

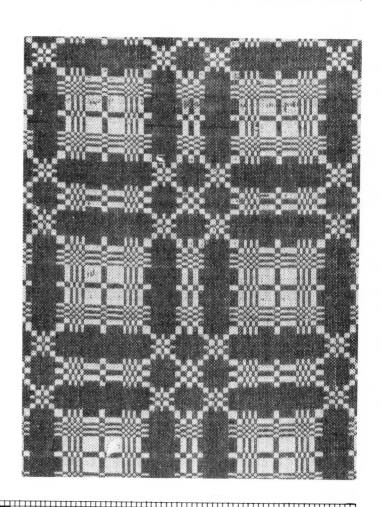

362 / Ontario. Collected near Orangeville, Dufferin County
Probably 1820-35
ROM 966.91. Gift of Mrs J.H. Crang
'Summer and winter' weave coverlet. L. 245cm, plus fringe;
w. 196cm

Indigo blue wool (s singles) on fine natural white cotton.
This is shown with the dark motifs on a light ground, the so-
called 'summer' side. It was collected near Orangeville, but
may well come from an older area of settlement. The fine
plied cotton of the warp more closely resembles that in no.
365 from the Eastern Townships of Quebec, than any of the
others from Ontario or the Maritime Provinces.

363 / Ontario. Collected in Brant County. 1820-30
ROM 952.46.1. Gift of the Ontario Spinners and Weavers
Cooperative
'Summer and winter' weave coverlet. L. 249cm, plus fringe;
w. 209cm, plus added fringes

Indigo blue wool on natural white cotton. The previous patterns are similar in principle to no. 313 in the overshot section, but this one is of the type of no. 314, 'Whig Rose,' that
results when the draft is woven 'rose fashion.' The fringe
border across the lower edge was woven with the piece: first
a narrow patterned band, then a short section of bare warps,
before the main weaving began. After the piece was taken
from the loom, a doubled thread was worked through the
bare warps twisting them in groups to form a run-leno band.
Similar bands were woven separately and sewn to both sides
of the coverlet. This is the only 'summer and winter' weave
coverlet recorded that has a border pattern. It is shown to the
extreme left of the draft.

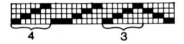

364 / Ontario. Probably Lincoln County. 1810-20
ROM 945.53. Gift of Mr and Mrs Harold B. Burnham
'Summer and winter' weave coverlet (fragment). L. 73cm;
w. 82cm

Indigo blue wool on natural white cotton. This shows a different layout of pattern with 'tables' separated by groups of
nine 'roses,' reminiscent of some of the overshot designs. It
was the first piece of 'summer and winter' weave found for
the Museum's collections: it survived as upholstery on a
chair.

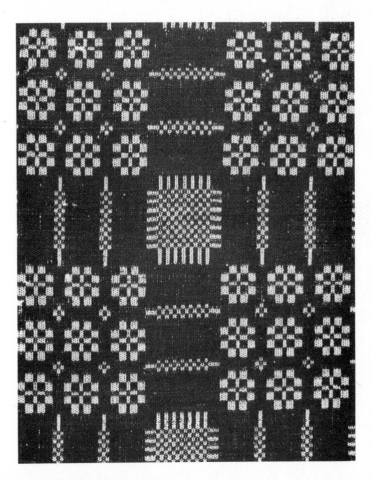

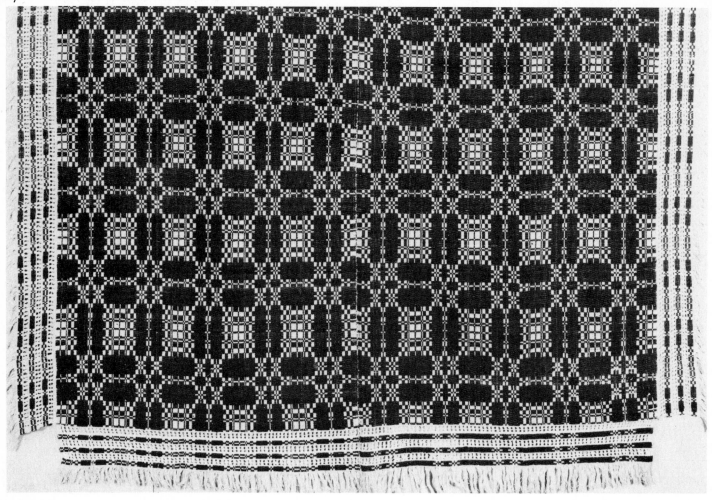

365 / Quebec. Eastern Townships. 1820-30
ROM 950.157.44. Gift of Miss H. Norton
'Summer and winter' weave coverlet. L. 226cm, plus fringe;
w. 198cm, plus added fringes

Indigo blue wool on fine natural white cotton. This is a very
heavy and extremely handsome coverlet. The warp is more
closely spaced than the weft elongating the pattern. The
decorative fringes, spaced at the corners to fit a four-poster
bed, give a beautiful finish. They are worked in the same way
as those on no. 363, but with the patterning repeated three
times. The coverlet has little definite history, but is known to
have been collected in the Eastern Townships, possibly near
Ayer's Cliff. Another 'summer and winter' weave coverlet
from English-speaking Quebec is in the National Museum of
Man, Ottawa (D853).

366 / Nova Scotia. 1800-15
ROM 970.202.8. Gift of Mr and Mrs Harold B. Burnham
'Summer and winter' weave coverlet. L. 231cm; w. 173cm

Indigo blue wool on bleached linen warp (z, 2s) and natural
white cotton. The pattern is based on five 'stars' joined by a
simple 'cross' and should be compared with no. 363. Here,
it has been woven 'as drawn in,' while the other is 'rose
fashion.' As in no. 359, the use of linen in the ground is
clearly indicative of an early date. Another coverlet in the
same weave is in the Nova Scotia Museum, Halifax. It comes
from Elmsdale or Kennetcook in Hants County and is made
up of three, rather than two, widths.

367 / New Brunswick. Collected at Woodstock, Carleton
County. Probably 1820-30
NBM 67.94
'Summer and winter' weave coverlet. L. 242cm; w. 198cm

Indigo blue wool on natural white cotton (main weft, z, 2s).
Although using 'stars' as the main motif in a lozenge lattice,
this pattern varies from the others illustrated in the use of
connecting square blocks, and a 'cross' on small units. The
cotton is of superb quality, possibly sea island, and the use of
a plied main weft strengthens the white areas. The regularity
of the incidentals is the result of the shots of pattern weft
being in pairs rather than alternating.

368 / New Brunswick. Kars, King's County. About 1820
NBM 54.50. Webster Foundation
'Summer and winter' weave coverlet. L. 200cm; w. 178cm

Indigo blue wool on natural white cotton. This was woven by
Mary Anne O'Toole. The pattern is completely different
from any of the others recorded, but is somewhat reminiscent
of the popular overshot ones based on radiating lines. A member of the family remembered three surviving looms that
were used by the weaver. Two were counterbalanced: a
two-shaft one probably for sheeting and clothing materials,
and a four-shaft one suitable for twills such as blanketing.
The third had six shafts, and was a countermarch type with
jacks or coopers, and lamms: each shaft could be raised or
lowered independently of the others. This was the loom on
which this coverlet was woven.

Multiple-shaft coverlets

This section deals with coverlets and horse blankets in various constructions that occur somewhat less frequently than the larger groups described. All have their specific techniques based on the multiple-shaft looms that were used by professional weavers. Most have a pattern weft above a tabby ground, but one type depends solely on the patterning possibilities of a sixteen-shaft point twill.

One distinctive group is known as 'star and diamond' because of the two motifs that are the main pattern elements (nos. 369–73). The first example appeared early in the Ontario Textile Project in the course of fieldwork in the summer of 1948. It was found near Dundas, Ontario, and was unlike anything that had been seen before. It had a centre seam and so was presumably handwoven. The pattern was banded in coloured wools that formed short floats above a cotton ground. The yarns were recognized as typical of those found in older coverlets known to have been woven in the province.

This new and unusual coverlet presented a challenge in determining how it had been made, a problem that would now be less alarming after more than twenty years of research. Bit by bit, a point paper plan of the construction of one complete pattern unit was taken off on graph paper. Then a draft was plotted below, a separate shaft being allowed for each warp thread that moved in identical fashion. After several attempts, the final result was a fully reasonable draft on eighteen shafts, two of which were for the ground and sixteen to control the pattern blocks. Even this was a new type and failed to supply a clue. Having the draft, the tie-up was figured out. The result proved exciting: it was immediately recognized as being of the same type as three tie-ups on a torn piece of paper in Wilhelm Magnus Werlich's pattern book (no. 72). Until then, this document had been an anomaly: there were no drafts, but only a note in German script, some of it fragmentary. The note was deciphered, but was found only to give the basic instructions for setting up this type of pattern: 'At the lower end, a wide star-mat [*Sternenteppich*] is begun with a wreath. 2½ stars in the wreath, then 11 large stars are drawn, then again 2½ stars at the other end for the wreath. It is warped with 1530 threads, and 7 double threads are taken for the selvage at each side.' These instructions were obviously for a piece that was to be woven doublewidth on a wide loom. The use of the term 'wreath' (*Krantz*) undoubtedly implies the border that was drafted on smaller units than the 'large stars' of the field. Borders of this type are characteristic of the 'star and diamond' coverlets that have been seen.

The weave is undoubtedly part of the German tradition in North America. The first example seen, mentioned above, is now known to belong to a small group made before 1850. All appear to be the work of one man, probably in the Hamilton area, perhaps around Stoney Creek. Unfortunately, there are no examples from this group in the public collections in Canada. A drawing of a pattern of this type, without draft or tie-up, is among the loose sheets in Samuel Fry's pattern book, but no example has been seen that might be his work. Far more are known that were woven in the second half of the nineteenth century, and all come from the area of

German-speaking settlement centred on Waterloo County, where many professional weavers worked. 'Star and diamond' weave is also known from the United States, where the typical eight-pointed star sometimes more closely resembles a flowerhead (Reinert, pls. 9, 11, 17; Rogers; ROM 959.65.2).

These coverlets have a firm construction. Reference to the diagram (fig. 36) will show that the basic unit used to build up these patterns is four threads: two on one of the ground shafts, and two on a pattern shaft. This basic unit results in floats that do not exceed five warp threads, but as the ends for the ground are always on the same shaft, units may be diminished to two ends to produce shorter floats and smaller motifs as may be seen in the borders illustrated. Similarly, units may be expanded to six or eight threads producing longer floats for special effects, as in the 'tables' that replace the usual 'diamonds' in no. 373.

Two types of coverlet without specific names are shown in nos. 374–6. Both are based on types of point twill threading and are patterned in coloured wools above a cotton tabby ground. A few examples of each have been seen in Ontario and parallels are known from the United States. In both countries, they are also part of the German-speaking tradition that has made a distinctive contribution to early handweaving on this continent.

The first bears a superficial resemblance to the 'star and diamond' coverlets with its use of eight-pointed stars, but here these motifs are combined with a lozenge-patterned 'table,' and a comparison of the drafts of the two types will show the dissimilarity. This coverlet is based entirely on an eighteen-shaft point twill, using twelve of these to produce the stars, four for the lozenge panel and two for the connecting bars. It is a type reported by Reinert from Pennsylvania (pl. 8), where it is shown from the other side.

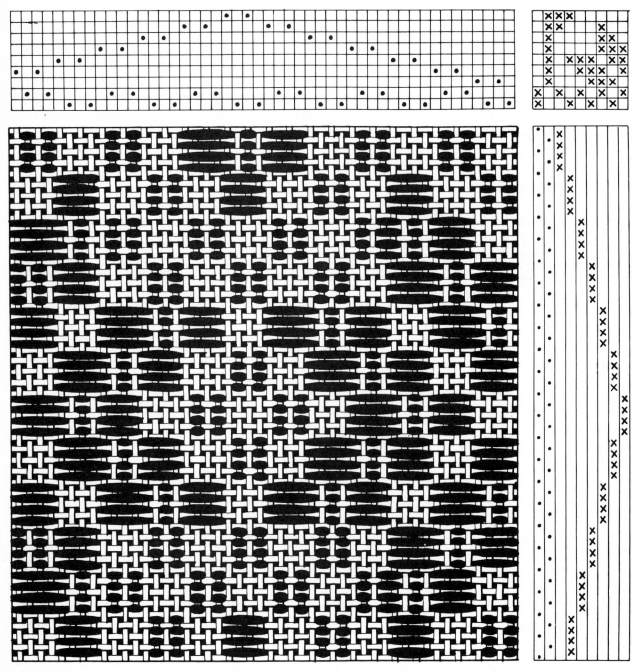

FIGURE 36

The other type occurs in two forms (nos. 375–6) and uses two arrangements of point twills entered in six and ten shafts with two additional ones for the connecting bars for a total of eighteen. The two main elements contribute different units to the design: the former the groups of nine patterned squares, and the latter the lozenge panels. The borders are usually based on a simplified version of the two parts. In no. 375, a full complement of treadles is used. In no. 376, three fewer are needed: the ten-point shaft twill and the connecting bars are 'tromp as writ,' but the part controlled by the other six shafts uses only three treadles that are worked in order as required.

This type of coverlet is of uncommon occurrence. Those like no. 375 turn up sporadically in Waterloo County, but those like no. 376 appear to centre on the Preston area. It is probable that each type is the work of one man, perhaps weavers who had come from the Mennonite areas of Pennsylvania. It is from this part of the United States that American examples are to be found. One like no. 376 is shown by Reinert (pl. 7) and a pair of indigo blue wool and natural white cotton that appear to date from the earlier part of the nineteenth century are in Toronto (ROM 968.18.1, .2).

The three coverlets shown in nos. 377–9 form a unique group that comes from the southern part of Hastings County, perhaps Tyendinaga Township. All were woven before 1850, probably before 1840, and no other examples have been seen. They were woven doublewidth on a wide loom, an unusual feature at such an early date, and must be the work of one man, a trained professional weaver who may only have woven in the off seasons. The design is formed by a pattern weft, indigo blue wool in all three examples, that floats over groups of eight to twelve warp threads. When floating on the face, the pattern weft is bound by a single end between the blocks of the pattern, while on the reverse, it is similarly bound by the adjacent end. Two of the examples are framed on four sides by a chessboard border (nos. 377–8); the third has borders based on diminished units of the main pattern separated by plain stripes.

Each of the pattern blocks in these coverlets would require two shafts and an additional two would be required for the ends that tie the floats. If different blocks are used for the borders, these in turn would require additional pairs of shafts. As the patterns have about ten blocks, this would mean a multiple-shaft loom of considerable capacity. It seems likely that some other method may have been used. Because of the weaving width, pick-up techniques that would be suitable for this weave on a smaller scale are improbable. On the other hand, there is no reason why a double-harness system could not have been employed: one harness for the ground, the other for the pattern. All warp threads would have been entered on four shafts to produce the tabby ground. The pairs of ends needed to bind the pattern-weft floats would have been on two of these and those for the pattern blocks on the other two. The warp threads for these latter would also have been entered in the back harness with one shaft for each pattern block. The front harness would have been controlled by treadles, but the back one by a simple draw system solely

to form the pattern sheds. The third shaft for the ground would always have been used in conjunction with the pattern sheds so that the ends entered on it bound the pattern floats. The use of such a double-harness system would explain the variations found in the motifs on no. 377 and peculiarities in the border of no. 379.

The closest parallel to the construction of these coverlets appears to be a technique used in Lithuania, particularly in the neighbourhood of the city of Vilnius (Balcikonis, 102, 156, 157, etc.). During the Napoleonic Wars, Lithuanians and Poles served in the French forces. A number who were captured were given the choice of enlisting in the British army for service overseas or remaining as prisoners of war. Many chose the more active life and saw duty in India and Ceylon, in the Peninsular War, and finally in North America with the outbreak of the War of 1812–14. With the close of hostilities in 1815, these men were disbanded and received grants of land in Canada (Gaida, 19–24). Some settled in Ontario and it is possible that one of these veterans of Lithuanian origin, originally trained as a weaver, wove these unusual coverlets.

The last group to be considered differs from the others in not having a tabby ground over which the pattern is formed and are horse blankets rather than coverlets. These, in the German-speaking tradition like many of the complex weaves, are based on variations of a sixteen-shaft point twill (nos. 380–2). At first glance, many are quite similar, but variations do occur that possibly indicate the work of different professional weavers. It is known that some were woven by the Noll brothers of Petersburg. Ontario is the only province in Canada where they have been found, and all were made in the Waterloo County area. Judging from the number that have survived, they must have been extremely popular. They are usually multi-coloured, and are known in all wool, in wool on a cotton warp, and checked in wool and cotton. They are related to the multiple-shaft twill table linens known from Pennsylvania, but for which only drafts have been found in Ontario.

The type of sixteen-shaft point twill variation that is found in these coverlets may be seen by referring to the diagram (fig. 37). One would expect a tie-up with all four corners shown as tied, but this was not always done. Two of the corner ties were sometimes omitted intentionally to produce a cleaner break where a colour change occurred (no. 380). Most of these coverlets were woven 'as drawn in,' the treadling following the threading order exactly. Sometimes the treadling order was reversed, either entirely or partially as in no. 382, producing disconnected motifs woven 'rose fashion.'

The woollen yarns in all the examples described in this section are invariably spun z, 2s, and the cottons for the warp are usually of the same twist, but with a z singles for main weft. Variations will be noted, but special mention should be made of the fine plied cotton found quite frequently with the 'star and diamond' construction. As in some of the eight-shaft overshot coverlets, and in many of the jacquard-woven ones from Waterloo County, this yarn is used double and may have been imported from Great Britain rather than from the United States. It was certainly being used in Canada before the outbreak of the Civil War in 1861, but this conflict may easily have resulted in the American loss of the Canadian market for the more usual type of yarn. By the time it was over, British imports, and perhaps yarns produced by the mills that were starting to grow up in Canada, may have captured the market.

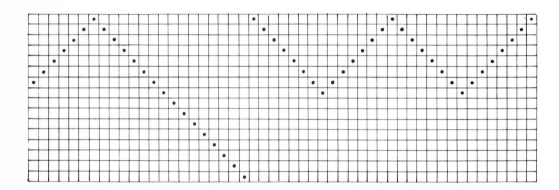

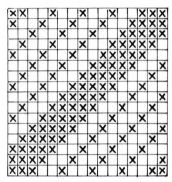

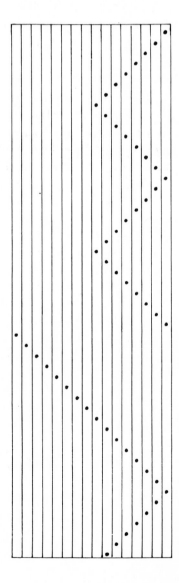

FIGURE 37

369 / Ontario. Perth or Waterloo Counties. 1840-60
ROM 969.63. Gift of Mr and Mrs Frank Baranski
'Star and diamond' coverlet. L. 212cm; w. 179cm

Pink-red wool on natural white cotton (warp and main weft, z, singles, double). This is the simplest version of the 'star and diamond' pattern, and shows the two elements used in their basic form. It was collected in Perth County near the Waterloo County border and may have been woven in either. The use of the singles cotton double in the ground is an unusual and early feature.

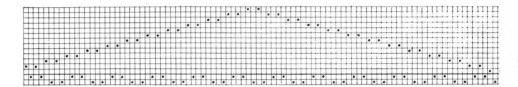

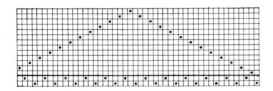

370 / Ontario. Waterloo County, near Kitchener. 1850-70
ROM 957.98. Gift of Mr and Mrs Harold B. Burnham
'Star and diamond' coverlet. L. 180cm; w. 157cm, plus fringes

Indigo blue wool on natural white cotton (warp, fine z, 2s, double). This shows a slight elaboration of the basic diamond element with the more usual form of star not divided into parts. These coverlets are fully reversible: this one shows the motifs reserved on a coloured ground; nos. 371 and 372 show them against the plain ground.

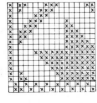

371 / Ontario. Waterloo County. 1850-70
ROM 952.46.2. Gift of the Ontario Spinners and Weavers
Cooperative
'Star and diamond' coverlet. L. 176cm, plus fringe;
w. 177cm, plus fringes

Indigo blue wool on natural white cotton (warp, fine z, 2s,
double). This coverlet shows the most usual pattern found
in Ontario in this weave with voided diamonds at the inter-
sections of a square lattice that form octagonal compartments
for the stars. The characteristic borders based on half-units
show clearly. A number of coverlets from Waterloo County
in this same version of the pattern are in the Royal Ontario
Museum. They have various colour schemes, usually banded,
and date from the second half of the nineteenth century. One
from the last quarter is woven doublewidth without centre
seam. (*in colour* PLATE III)

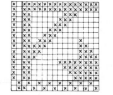

372 / Ontario. Perth County, collected at Stratford. 1870-90
ROM 964.125. Gift of the Hon. Chief Justice D.C. Wells
'Star and diamond' coverlet. L. 205cm, plus fringe;
w. 160cm, plus fringes

Indigo blue and dull maroon wool on natural white cotton
(warp, z, 4s). This again is the most usual pattern found in
these coverlets and like many others is banded in colours. Although the traditional indigo blue has been used, the dull
maroon shade has been obtained from chemical dyes. This
fact combined with the use of commercial carpet warp shows
that it is a later production. The area north of Stratford
where it was woven is contiguous to the Waterloo County
border.

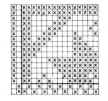

373 / Ontario. Waterloo County. 1860-80
ROM 970.118.7. Gift of Mr and Mrs Harold B. Burnham
'Star and diamond' coverlet. L. 219cm; w. 185cm, plus
fringes

Indigo blue and red wool on natural white cotton (warp, z,
3s). This coverlet shows an unusual variation of the 'star
and diamond' with the stars in groups of four separated
diagonally by 'table' forms rather than the usual diamonds.
This produces a handsome effect on the banded ground.

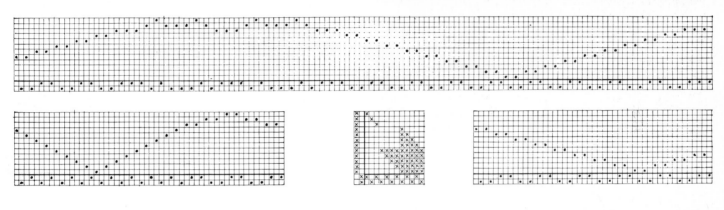

374 / Ontario. Haldimand County, collected in South
Cayuga Township. 1850-75
ROM 970.118.10. Gift of Mr and Mrs Harold B. Burnham
Point-twill coverlet. L. 195cm, plus fringe; w. 184cm, plus
fringes

Indigo blue wool on natural white cotton (warp, z, 3s).
South Cayuga Township, where this coverlet was found, has
one of the smaller Mennonite communities in Ontario and
was settled from Pennsylvania. The star motifs are formed by
floats of weft above the tabby ground, not built up of separate
units as in the 'star and diamond' coverlets.

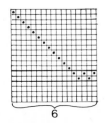

6

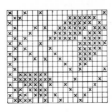

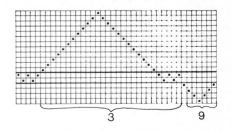

3   9

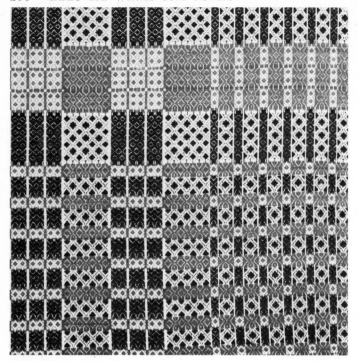

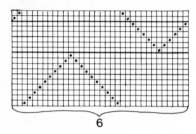
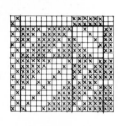

6

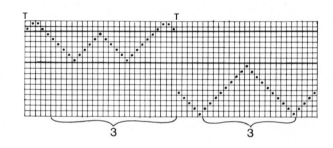

375 / Ontario. Waterloo County. 1850-70
ROM 970.230. Gift of Mrs J.H. Crang
Point-twill coverlet. L. 222cm, plus fringe; w. 190cm,
plus fringes

Dark and light indigo blue, and deep rust-red wool on
natural white cotton (warp, fine z, 2s, double). This and no.
376 shows a different type of point-twill with clear precise
patterning of the highest professional standard. Both use
eighteen shafts for two point-twill threadings to produce an
effect quite different from the preceding example, and also
unlike the sixteen-shaft ones described later (nos. 380–2).
Here, the central thread in the bars is always doubled and an
extra tie has been added to the larger lozenges to modify the
form of the units. The draft has been followed exactly in
treadling. The coverlet has been superbly woven, producing
a most handsome result.

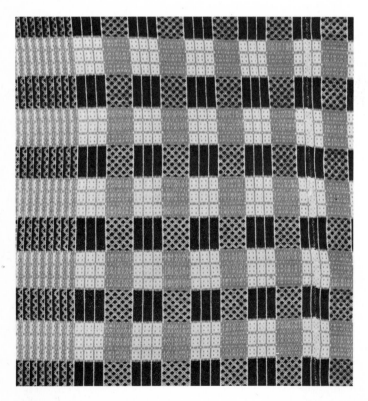

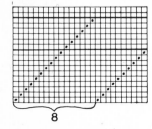

8

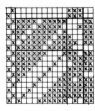

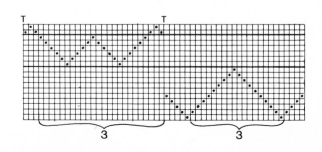

376 / Ontario. Preston area, Waterloo County. 1850-70
ROM 970.118.11. Gift of Mr and Mrs Harold B. Burnham
Point-twill coverlet. L. 217cm, plus fringe; w. 176cm,
plus fringes

Dark indigo blue, terracotta, and soft yellow wool on natural
white cotton (warp, fine z, 2s, double). The draft for this
coverlet is identical to that for no. 375 except for the doubled
thread. An altered tie-up using three treadles less results in a
different effect in the nine-part panels that separate the larger
lozenge-patterned ones. Both this type and no. 375 are rather
rare.

377 / Ontario. Hastings County, possibly Tyendinaga
Township. 1820-40
NMM D574
Weft-patterned coverlet. L. 229cm; w. 193cm

Indigo blue wool on natural white cotton. This and the two
following examples (nos. 378–9) form a unique group that
must be the work of one man. All are woven doublewidth
without centre seam. As previously suggested, the weaver
may have been a Lithuanian mercenary who settled in Hast-

ings County after the War of 1812–14. There are nine pattern
blocks in the main pattern and two separate ones for the
border. The errors that have occurred in forming the pattern
units suggest the use of a simple draw system combined with
a shaft harness to weave the ground. One of these errors appears in the first complete pattern register above the lower
edge, but more noticeable ones occur in other parts. The one
that may be seen would result from failure to raise at the
right time the pattern shaft controlling the centre of the unit.

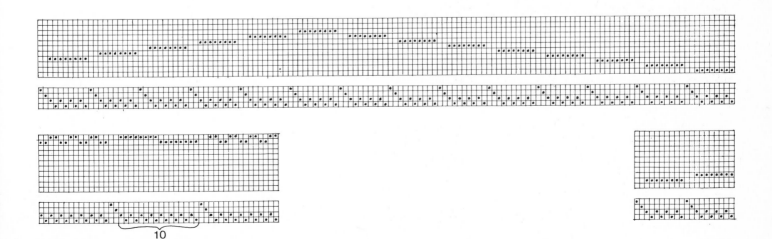

10

378 / Ontario. Hastings County, possibly Tyendinaga Township. 1820-40
York Pioneer and Historical Society, Sharon, Ontario
Weft-patterned coverlet. L. 192cm; ẅ. 154cm

Indigo blue wool on natural white cotton. This simple lozenge pattern would also require nine blocks for the main pattern and two additional ones for the chessboard border. Traditionally it was woven of yarns prepared by a member of the Ostrom family, who were early settlers in the Belleville area.

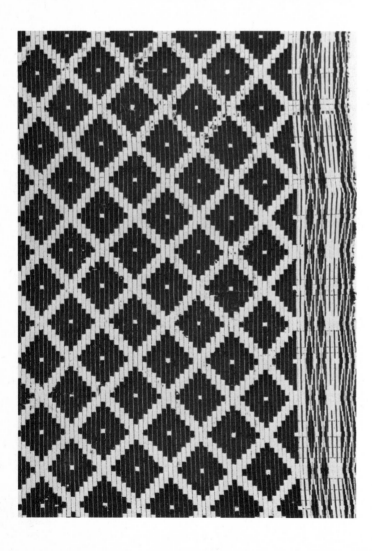

379 / Ontario. Hastings County, possibly Tyendinaga Township. 1820-40
ROM 968.308.1. Gift of Mr and Mrs Harold B. Burnham
Weft-patterned coverlet. L. 226cm; w. 181cm

Indigo blue wool on natural white cotton. This is a simpler lozenge pattern than the preceding example and only requires eight blocks for the motifs in the field. The borders are based on smaller versions of the main units divided down the centre and between the border and the field by plain stripes that would not have been controlled by the pattern harness. In nos. 377 and 378, the pattern blocks were based on eight threads, but here twelve were used.

380 / Ontario. Waterloo County. Dated 1844
ROM 970.118.8. Gift of Mr and Mrs Harold B. Burnham
Point-twill horse blanket. L. 211cm, plus fringe; w. 182cm,
plus fringes

Striped and banded in dark indigo blue and terracotta wool,
and natural white cotton. This is the most handsome example
of the point-twill blankets seen in Ontario and has an added
importance because of the initials and date embroidered in
the same terracotta wool that was used in weaving. These are
worked in cross stitch on either side of the centre seam on a
white band just below the upper edge.

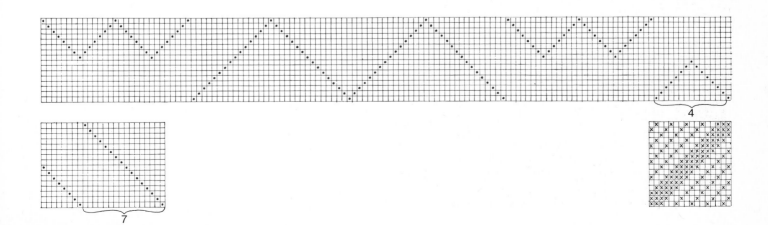

381 / Ontario. Waterloo County. 1840-60
ROM 968.308.2. Gift of Mr and Mrs Harold B. Burnham
Point-twill horse blanket. L. 200cm, plus fringe; w. 185cm,
plus fringes

Striped and banded in dark and medium blue, and bright red
wool. This blanket, using the identical draft and tie-up as no.
380, shows the typical style of patterning found in these
multiple-shaft blankets, professionally woven, and very popular in Waterloo County. They continued to be made until
the end of the nineteenth century. Late examples can be distinguished by the coarser yarns and by the harsher chemical
colours that were then available.

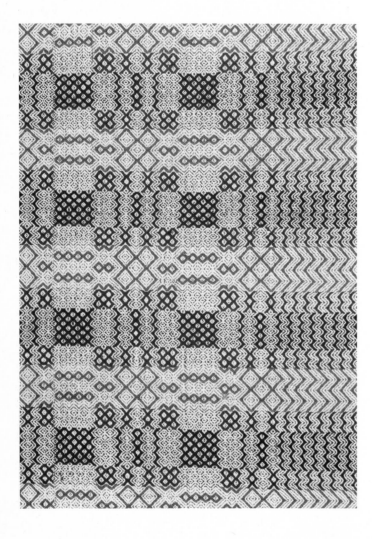

382 / Ontario. Waterloo County. 1850-70
ROM 970.118.6. Gift of Mr and Mrs Harold B. Burnham
Point-twill horse blanket. L. 198cm, plus fringe; w. 169cm,
plus fringes

Dark and medium indigo blue, and terracotta wool banded
on natural white cotton. The strong contrast of the coloured
wools on the white cotton makes the pattern stand out
distinctly. It varies from the previous two examples; the draft
is the same with a slightly different tie-up, but the sixteen-
shaft section of the twill has been treadled in reverse order
producing a different effect.

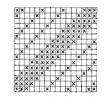

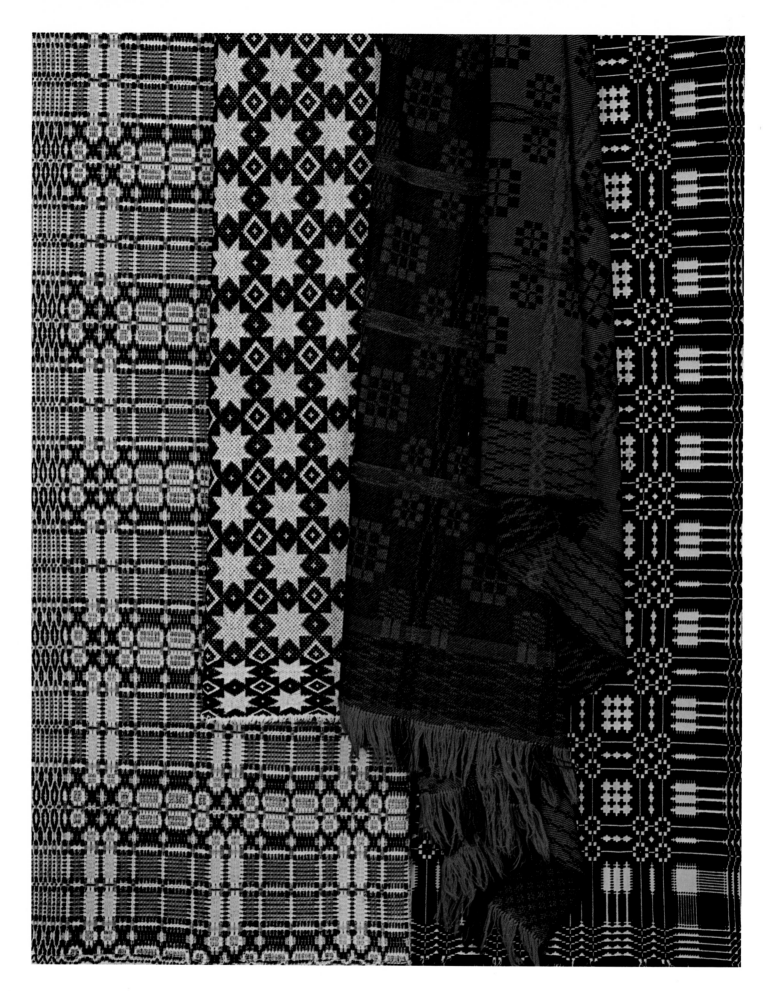

PLATE III

301, 371, 386, 411

Twill diaper coverlets

The use of the term diaper in weaving signifies that the textile is patterned by an allover repeating design. This may be small and simple as in bird's-eye twill, or may indicate larger geometric motifs. It is one of the latter type that is considered here for which the term *twill diaper* is in accepted use. The patterning principle is based on the contrast of the warp and weft faces of an unbalanced weave. In the Canadian coverlets, this is a combination of the 3/1 warp-faced twill, and its opposite, the 1/3 weft-faced one, as may be seen in the diagram (fig. 38). A straight twill is shown as it is the type found in the examples described, but a broken twill is also possible. Although the effect is based on the contrast described, it may be heightened by the use of different colours in warp and weft: the richest results are obtained by the combination of strongly coloured wools. Related to this construction is *damask diaper*, in which the contrast is between the warp and weft faces of a satin weave. This weave is more suitable for finer materials than were woven in Canada, and has only been found in a jacquard-woven coverlet with geometric pattern in the field (no. 488).

Twill diaper has an ancient history. A silk fragment with a two-block pattern found at Palmyra must date from before 278 AD, when the city was destroyed by the Romans (Pfister, pl. 9). Other early examples have been preserved in reliquaries in ancient church treasuries in Europe. Its wide use for table and household linens, both in Europe and North America, has already been mentioned, but the characteristic Canadian examples were woven in Ontario either of wool or of wool and cotton, for decorative bedcovers or horse blankets.

The first piece of a twill diaper coverlet from Ontario that was seen came to light when visiting an elderly cousin who had just completed a braided rug. While admiring it, it became sickeningly obvious that part of an old handwoven bedcover had been used to give the shade of blue that she had desired. On inquiry, this supposition proved true, but all hope was lost of even discovering the pattern. Later in the year, a small piece came to light that had been saved to cover a cushion and was received with delight as a Christmas present. This is now no. 383 in the present series and, like the single example that has turned up outside Ontario (no. 384), must date from around 1800. These two pieces from the Niagara Peninsula and New Brunswick are the earliest of the type that have been found in Canada, both from areas of distinctly English-speaking settlement. They probably belong to a tradition brought by professional weavers from the United States during the latter part of the eighteenth century. The weave was certainly known in New England and a two-block example in red and blue from New Hampshire is also about the same date (ROM 970.158). In Canada, the few professional weavers who made them, as well as the early doublecloth coverlets, came as pioneers. When they died, their skills and this English-speaking tradition died with them. The 'summer and winter' weave coverlets, a part of this tradition requiring a less complex loom, survived a little longer.

Twill diaper coverlets are also known from elsewhere in the United States, particularly from Pennsylvania. It was here that the young Samuel Fry went to serve his apprenticeship as a weaver, probably in Bucks County, one of the strong-

FIGURE 38

holds of Mennonite tradition in that country. He returned to Canada in 1836 with the book of patterns that he had learned there and with his knowledge of the technique. He became a farmer in the Mennonite community near Vineland in Lincoln County, and wove professionally in the off seasons (nos. 385–9).

The area in Ontario where coverlets of this type turn up most frequently is the Waterloo County district where they were popular as horse blankets. It is this part of the province where German influence has been strongest. The main settlement had been Mennonite from Pennsylvania between 1790 and the outbreak of the War of 1812–14. Grafted on this settlement was an influx of German immigrants who came to the new world during the next hundred years, particularly in the middle of the century after the political upheavals of 1848, and with the rise of industrialization. Among these were a number of professional weavers: Wilhelm Magnus Werlich, August Ploethner, Johan Lippert, and many more

whose work cannot now be differentiated. From swatches in Werlich's pattern book, it is known that he had been trained to weave materials in fine cotton in both twill and damask diaper. These were suitable for traditional costume, and for fine household needs in Germany, but there was no demand for them in the new country. There seems no doubt but that the knowledge Werlich possessed would have been adapted to the coarser materials, possibly twill diaper and other complex-weave coverlets for which there was a demand. The same may be equally true of other immigrant weavers, but some may have been trained to weave the coarser materials before emigrating. In Europe, such work might be expected in the folk weaving from areas of German tradition, but no twill diaper coverlets have been seen in that country and only one from Canton Bern, Switzerland.

In the descriptions of the coverlets that follow, the yarns used for both warp and weft are always z, 2s whether wool or cotton, unless otherwise stated.

In the diagram (fig. 38), the twill diaper draft for a four-block pattern is shown expanded in full, but like other complex weaves, from 'summer and winter' on, a profile draft is all that is required once the principle is understood. The basic patterning unit is four warp threads entered in twill on a set of four shafts. Each block of the pattern requires its own set of these and blocks may be combined to produce solid motifs, as will be found in a number of the coverlets from Waterloo County. With the illustrations, each profile draft is shown reading from the right with the border that is found on the respective coverlet to the extreme left; between that and the relative pattern the tie-up is given in profile form. Whether the pattern is to be woven 'as drawn in' or 'rose fashion,' the weaving follows the old tradition of 'tromp as writ.'

383 / Ontario. Lincoln County, perhaps Clinton Township. Probably about 1800
ROM 967.100.1. Gift of Mr and Mrs Harold B. Burnham
Twill diaper coverlet (fragment). L. 47.5cm; w. 49.5cm

Indigo blue wool (s singles) on natural white cotton. This fragment came from the Sumner family of Clinton (now Beamsville) and traditionally was old and worn about 1830 when it was being used on a hired man's bed. This was remembered because he fell asleep while smoking. The bed caught fire and the flames were 'doused with a bucket of swill.' The coverlet was probably woven for Mary Bell, who married Cyrus Sumner, the first doctor in the area, in 1803, but might have been brought by the Bell family when they came from New Jersey in 1790.

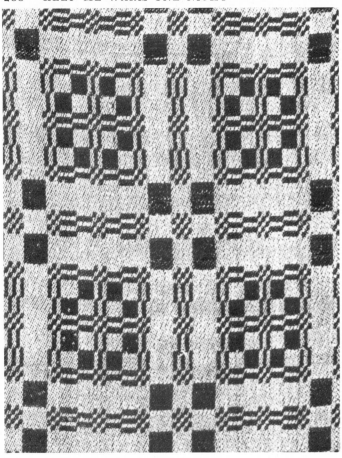

384 / New Brunswick. 1790-1800
NBM
Twill diaper coverlet. L. 158cm; w. 183cm

Indigo blue wool on half-bleached linen. This is the only twill diaper coverlet that has been recorded in Canada with a linen warp, as well as the only one with a three-block pattern. It is probably the work of one of the group of professional weavers who came to New Brunswick as Loyalists, and would have been woven shortly after flax had been raised and processed to spin the linen yarn and sheep were established to supply the wool.

385 / Ontario. Vineland, Lincoln County. 1840-60
ROM L965.11.21. The Annie R. Fry Collection
Twill diaper coverlet. L. 220cm, plus fringe; w. 196cm

Indigo blue wool on yellow wool. The pattern is no. 16 in Samuel Fry's pattern book. The coverlet was woven by him for use in his own family. Another handsome one in pink and blue wools has the identical pattern with a slightly different border (ROM 967.278) and comes from the Burkholder family in Markham Township, York County, another Mennonite community. This community had contacts with the one in Vineland and possibly the coverlet is also the work of Samuel Fry. The pattern occurs in doublecloth (no. 404), a weave that is equally suitable for any of the twill diaper designs.

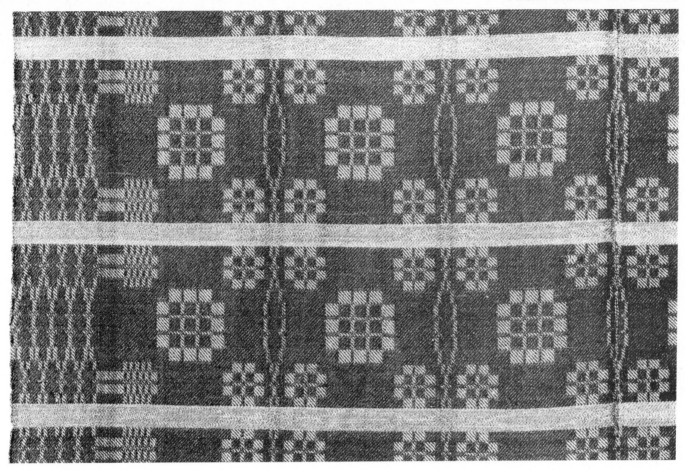

386 / Ontario. Vineland, Lincoln County. About 1860
ROM 955.80.1. Gift of Mr and Mrs Harold B. Burnham
Twill diaper coverlet. L. 207cm, plus fringe; w. 188cm

Indigo blue wool banded with light blue on clear red wool.
On the face, the 'table' and 'roses' show in red against the
dark blue ground with the surrounding interlocking circles

mainly in light blue. It is a beautiful example of Samuel
Fry's expert weaving that is believed to have been made for
his daughter Mary (Fry) Moyer at the time of her marriage
about 1860. This is no. 12 in his pattern book, and is the
same as that he used for the twill diaper tablecloth (no. 194).

(*in colour* PLATE III)

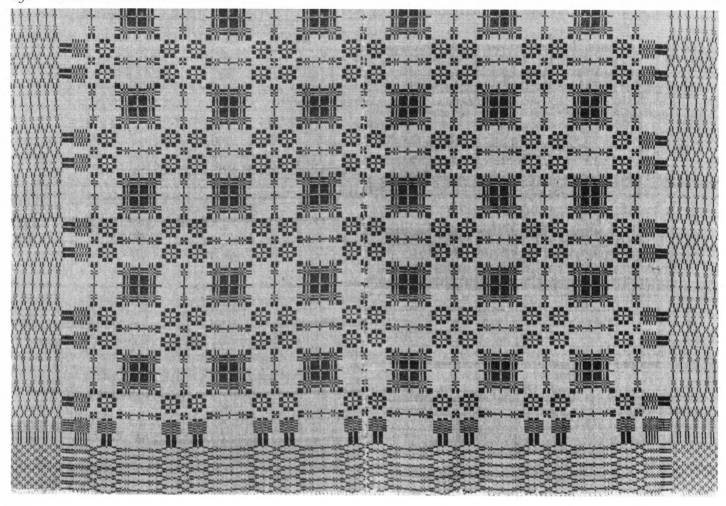

387 / Ontario. Vineland, Lincoln County. 1840-60
ROM L965.11.20. The Annie R. Fry Collection
Twill diaper coverlet. L. 210cm, plus fringe; w. 203cm

Dark green wool on natural white cotton. This is also the work of Samuel Fry and is similar to no. 4 in his pattern book, but with a slightly different 'table.' It was woven for the use of his own family. Like all his work, it is well proportioned and expertly woven. The linear border with an inner row of 'pine trees' is identical to that on no. 386. Borders of this type are a regular feature of both twill diaper and doublecloth coverlets.

388 / Ontario. Vineland, Lincoln County. 1835-50
ROM L965.11.22. The Annie R. Fry Collection
Twill diaper coverlet (fragment). L. 62cm; w. 43cm

Medium indigo blue wool on blue cotton (faded). This is
from a coverlet woven by Samuel Fry and is no. 26 in his
pattern book. It has a reversing pattern: the blocks of the
second 'star' are inverted so that the two connecting stars
produce a panel of two 'stars' and two encircled 'roses.' This
also causes the tables to alternate in form. It is one of a fairly
rare group of patterns of this type, but there are others in
Fry's pattern book. The same principle may be seen in
doublecloth coverlets woven by him (nos. 414–15), and is
also known from overshot coverlets. The fragment was found
under the covering of the ironing board in the Fry home by
Miss Annie R. Fry.

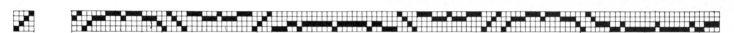

389 / Ontario. Vineland, Lincoln County. Probably 1846
Stone Shop Museum, Grimsby, Ontario.
Gift of Miss Muriel Bonham
Twill diaper coverlet (fragment). L. 35cm; w. 47cm

Dark indigo blue wool on light indigo blue wool striped with
medium blue. The striped effect has no connection with the
pattern. It is probably due to the use in warping of two dye-
lots that have faded differently. As the order of 16 light, 4
medium is regular, it would appear that the weaver, Samuel
Fry, made the warp with twenty threads at a time. The pattern is no. 24 and in the account book there is an entry dated
January 7, 1846: 'to weaving two coverlets, single £2/4/0
for Mr. Moor.' The donor's grandmother was Catherine
Moor, and it is likely that this fragment is from one of them.
Three types of coverlet are mentioned in Samuel Fry's accounts: single (twill diaper), double (doublecloth), and
floatwork (overshot). Most of what he wove was of the first
type.

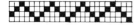

390 / Ontario. Collected in Markham Township,
York County. 1840-60
ROM 964.180.4. Gift of Mr and Mrs Harold B. Burnham
Twill diaper coverlet (half). L. 192cm; w. 84cm

Rust-brown wool on blue cotton (faded). This comes from
the Barkey family, Mennonites in Markham Township. To
date there is no evidence of a weaver who produced twill
diaper coverlets in this area, and this one may have come
from the Vineland area, or from Waterloo County as part of
a bride's trousseau. The use of blue cotton is unusual. It may
indicate the work of Samuel Fry, as it is found in no. 388
woven by him.

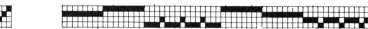

391 / Ontario. Heidelberg, Waterloo County. 1830-50
ROM 964.179. Gift of Mr and Mrs Harold B. Burnham
Twill diaper coverlet (half). L. 225cm; w. 89cm

Red wool (z singles, double) on indigo blue wool (z, 2z).
The ply of the wool in the warp is most unusual and produces an almost bouclé effect with an unusual handle. The
design is simple, but striking, with encircled 'roses' forming
an allover pattern on a bold scale. Apart from Samuel Fry's
work at Vineland, Waterloo County with its German-speaking population was the main centre for twill diaper weaving
in Ontario.

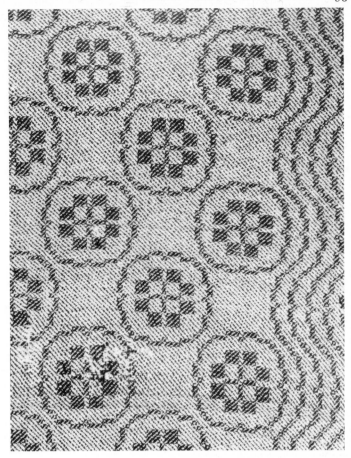

392 / Ontario. Waterloo County. Probably 1850-60
ROM 968.116.1. Gift of Mrs J.H. Crang
Twill diaper horse blanket. L. 160cm, plus fringe;
w. 191cm, plus fringes

Crimson-red wool on dull olive-green wool. This is an excellent example of the 'Whig Rose' pattern, using a slightly
more complex draft than that used by Samuel Fry in no. 386
The use of the two contrasting colours makes the form of the
interlocking circles more obvious. In the Werlich pattern
book, there is an equally good layout of the design with a
note in German script describing it as having 'roses and
wreaths.'

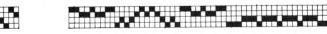

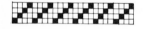

393 / Ontario. Waterloo County. 1830-50
ROM 967.175.4. Gift of Mrs Elton Witmer
Twill diaper coverlet. L. 184cm, plus fringe; w. 183cm

Buff wool banded with medium blue on black wool striped
with red. The wool is all long staple, and combed rather than
carded, a process never found in coverlets after the middle of
the nineteenth century. The pattern is similar to those of nos.
386 and 392, but the overcheck produces an altered effect.

394 / Ontario. Waterloo County, probably Bridgeport.
1830-50
ROM 967.175.5. Gift of Mrs Elton Witmer
Twill diaper coverlet. L. 188cm, plus fringe; w. 202cm

Rose-red wool on dark green wool (now jaspé due to uneven
fading). As in the previous coverlet, the wool is long staple
and has been combed rather than carded. It has been most
expertly spun with a very light twist and an almost imper-
ceptible ply. This is the first pattern shown that has blocks
combined to form a solid motif. In all previous examples they
have been used singly in opposition to one another; here the
central motif, usually called a 'snowball,' has three blocks
combined to produce a solid unit. This is achieved by the
tie-up of the treadles as indicated with the draft.

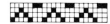 

395 / Ontario. Waterloo County. 1840-60
Doon Pioneer Village, Kitchener, Ontario. 19
Twill diaper coverlet. L. 162cm; w. 170cm

Medium blue and deep rust-red wool on deep indigo blue
wool. As in the previous coverlet, three pattern blocks have
been combined to produce the central 'snowball,' but the
extra repeat of the small intervening motifs makes a richer
pattern. Like several other examples, this one has been cut
down from its original length, probably because of wear
across the upper edge.

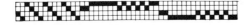

396 / Ontario. Waterloo County. 1860-75
Doon Pioneer Village, Kitchener, Ontario.
Gift of Mr and Mrs Marshall C. Brubaker
Twill diaper horse blanket. L. 196cm, plus fringe;
w. 156cm, plus fringes

Banded in indigo blue and rust-red wool on natural white
cotton. The use of a simple lattice pattern with carefully
arranged bands of colour has produced a blanket of extremely rich appearance that is enhanced by the double
'pine-tree' border. According to tradition, the home-grown
wool was processed, spun, and dyed and the coverlet 'made'
by the women on the farm of the donor's grandfather, Solo-
mon Brubaker. The sixteen-shaft loom required would not
have been domestic equipment, but only owned by a special-
ist. More likely, the prepared yarns were taken to a local
professional weaver, of whom there were over a hundred in
the Waterloo County area at this time. The Noll brothers of
Petersburg are known to have woven horse blankets for the
Brubakers.

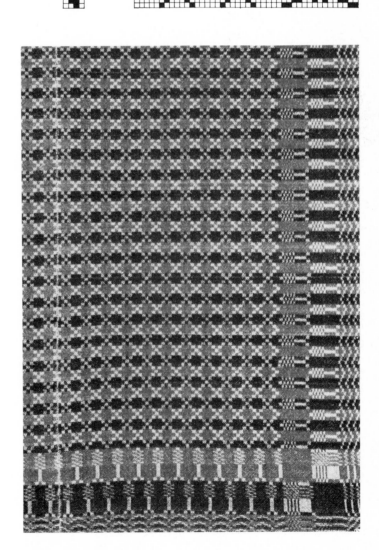

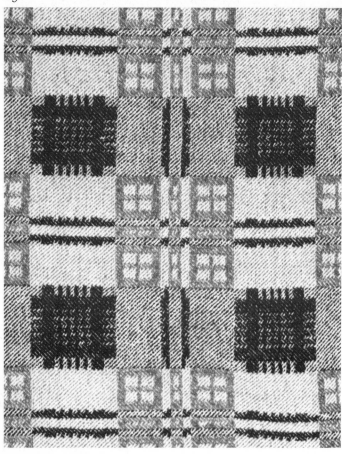

397 / Ontario. Waterloo County. 1850-75
ROM 967.220.11. Gift of Mrs J.H. Crang
Twill diaper coverlet. L. 208cm, plus fringe; w. 182cm,
plus fringes

Banded in reddish-brown and greenish-brown wool on
natural white cotton. The basic layout of the draft resembles
'Whig Rose,' but the tie-up combining blocks produces a very
different result. A draft in Werlich's pattern book combines
blocks to form similar motifs in the same way.

398 / Ontario. Waterloo County, Kitchener district. 1875-90
ROM 950.109. Gift of Mr and Mrs Harold B. Burnham
Twill diaper horse blanket. L. 213cm, plus fringe;
w. 188cm, plus fringes

Banded in red and green wool on greenish-brown wool
striped with red in the outer selvages. This is very heavy in
weight, with neatly knotted fringes down both sides. Pride
has always been taken in outfitting good horses handsomely.
The pattern of simple motifs formed by combined blocks is
most effective, and as it was used by the Noll brothers of
Petersburg specially for this purpose, this blanket was undoubtedly woven by them.

399 / Ontario. Waterloo County. 1850-70
Doon Pioneer Village, Kitchener. K I I
Twill diaper coverlet. L. 154cm; w. 180cm

Banded in indigo blue and medium red wool on light blue
cotton (z, 3s). This unusual pattern with its 'pine tree'
borders is deceptively simple in appearance, with its two plain
little motifs alternating in groups of four against the simulated
check of the ground. When analysed, it is found to be a six-
block pattern requiring a twenty-four shaft loom. All the
other twill diaper coverlets described were woven with sixteen
shafts, the normal loom capacity used by the professional
weavers of this type of work in Waterloo County.

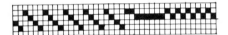

400 / Ontario. Waterloo County, probably Petersburg.
1850-75
ROM 970.118.9. Gift of Mr and Mrs Harold B. Burnham
Twill coverlet. L. 204cm, plus fringe; w. 195cm, plus fringes

Banded in red and medium blue wool on brownish-black
wool. This coverlet shows a combination of two techniques:
twill diaper 'roses,' and panels in six-shaft lozenge twill (cf.
no. 391). It is in a German tradition known from pattern
books printed in that country in the eighteenth century. It is
a type that occurs rarely in Ontario, but was a technique used
by Johan Lippert of Petersburg, who also produced jacquard-woven coverlets. An almost identical example by him
still belongs to his granddaughter.

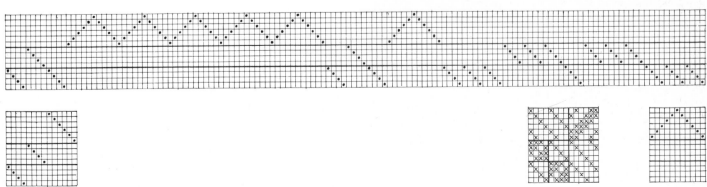

Doublecloth coverlets

The doublecloth coverlets are by far the most handsome of those that were woven on shaft looms. The clean definition of the motifs gives the patterns a clarity that all others lack. Most of those that were woven in Canada are in rich indigo blue and natural white cotton; the few that have been seen that differ from this are all illustrated (nos. 401–3, 419). These coverlets were always made on special order by professional weavers who had multiple-shaft looms. Like the jacquard-woven coverlets that supplanted them, the doublecloth ones were always for best, and sometimes used only on special occasions.

They were more expensive than the other types. Samuel Fry charged £1/2/0 for weaving a twill diaper one or a special bird's-eye blanket, £1/17/0 for an overshot showing the additional labour of handling two shuttles, but £2/6/0 for a doublecloth. Granted that this was York currency that had only half the value of sterling, but the comparison holds good. When Fry started weaving professionally near Vineland in 1836, the doublecloth coverlets were already going out of style; he wove very few of them even though he was working in a conservative Mennonite community. His account book covers the period from 1843 to 1878, and only six of these special orders are listed, the last being in 1851. He had woven others before the first entry was made, and may have made some after 1851 for members of his own family.

In addition to the higher cost of labour, doublecloth coverlets were extravagant of yarn as sufficient was required to weave two separate and independent layers of cloth that changed position to form the pattern motifs. The main period of their production in Canada was the earlier part of the nineteenth century, and almost none have been recorded that have a firm history that dates them after the middle of the century.

The weaving of doublecloth for a variety of purposes has a wide distribution from Scandinavia to pre-Columbian Peru. It has been made using a range of equipment from the simplest looms and a pick-up stick to the highly complex ones of the strictly professional weavers. Special decorative bed coverings with geometric patterns have been the main use in North America, a use which has roots in several parts of Europe. Although the materials used may differ from place to place depending on what was available, the styles and technical knowledge remain the same. In Museum für Deutsche Volkkunde in Berlin, there are examples with four-block patterns in blue and white linen. These come from der Schwalm in Hesse, and include a pillowcase dated 1856 and a complete set of bed furnishings of about the same date consisting of curtains, feather bed tick, and pillowcases. They represent the *Paradebett* from brides' dowers paralleling the use of doublecloth coverlets for best on this side of the Atlantic. Two similar covers are in Germanisches National-Museum in Nürnberg and also from Hesse (Meyer-Heisig, no. 6).

This province appears to be the only part of Germany from which such examples have survived, but they may once have had a wider distribution. German pattern books of the eighteenth century, both printed and manuscript, have patterns mainly for the diaper weaves, but some show doublecloth tie-ups, and make specific mention of the weave. *Neu-hervorkommendes Weber Kunst und Bild Buch* published in Culmbach, Bavaria, in 1727 describes Doppel-Cölnische-Teppiche and gives directions for weaving doublecloth in blue and white. Section no. 19 shows the tie-up for a twelve-shaft, or three-block, pattern, but mentions that doublecloths may be made using as many as twenty shafts. A manuscript pattern book in Nürnberg belonged to George Hauenstein in 1698 and also has the name of Johan Georg Hauenstein with the date 1806, suggesting that it was built up and used over a considerable period. Among the other types of complex weaves, there are two pages with tie-ups and drafts specific-ally for doublecloth (65 and 66). A pattern book published in Nürnberg in 1725 refers to *Doppel-Cölnische-Fussteppiche*, suggesting floor coverings. The same is true of the term *Teppiche* in its modern sense, but the older use survives in the Plattdeutsch of Waterloo County where a coverlet is still known by the dialect form *Depig*. The term 'bed mat' in Scotland is a parallel.

Elias Johan Joachim Mauer, who came to Canada from Waren in Mecklenburg in 1833, kept a small note book in which are tie-ups for complex weaves (ROM 968.32). He settled in Bentinck Township in Grey County, but it is not certain whether he wove there. If he did, no. 423 which was found in that county may be his work, or that of another im-migrant with a similar background. Other examples from areas of definitely German settlement are shown in nos. 418 and 419.

Old Swiss examples from Canton Bern are in Historisches Museum, Bern, and a fragment is in Toronto (ROM 970.-116). Like the German examples, they are woven of blue and white linen, but with three-block patterns that are simple yet effective. One example in Bern is a complete tick for a feather bed together with pillowcase that is dated 1785. It is from this part of the world that the tradition of the use of doublecloth would have been carried by Mennonites to Pennsylvania, and hence to Ontario. It may be seen in the work of Samuel Fry (nos. 414–16) and in no. 417. Even though the materials used in North America differ, the tech-nique and style of patterning remain the same.

Doublecloth is also known from Great Britain, particularly Wales and Scotland. There has been a strong revival in the former country using multi-coloured wools, but three older coverlets in the Welsh Folk Museum at St Fagans near Cardiff are basically indigo blue and white (55.108, 57.-486.1, and .2). The first from Pontypridd, woven of wool and natural white cotton, dates from the early nineteenth century. The other two coverlets from Caerwys, Flintshire, are more probably eighteenth-century. In these the warp is linen, bleached and medium blue, with natural white cotton and dark blue wool wefts, but a red-violet wool is banded with the blue in one of them. These coverlets bear no re-semblance to the modern products. William Jones's pattern book, of which there is a copy at St Fagans, has already been mentioned in dealing with twill diaper linens. The possibility that Wales may have been an origin for doublecloth in North America is remote and must regrettably be set aside. Im-migration from there was always minimal both to the United States and certainly to Canada in the early period when doublecloth coverlets were being made here.

The claims for influence from Scotland are stronger. Im-migration from that part of Great Britain has had a strong impact on life in North America and weavers are known to have come to the new world. A two-block doublecloth pat-tern is found in Alexander Cameron's *Draft and Cording Book* now in Edinburgh, mentioned in connection with over-shot coverlets. A fragment of two-block wool carpeting from the late eighteenth century, traditionally woven by Mrs Cameron of Fassifern but more probably of yarns prepared by her, is in the West Highland Museum at Fort William. Alexander Peddie's *The Linen Manufacturer, Weaver, and Warper's Assistant* was published in Glasgow in 1822. He mentions that the weaving of doublecloth 'is mostly confined to the carpet manufacture, and sometimes on a small scale by customary weavers for bed-covers' (460). John Murphy's *Art of Weaving* was published in Glasgow shortly after Peddie's book, and went through a number of editions. The tenth of 1852 gives patterns and directions for twill diaper and states that all these patterns are equally suitable for doublecloth (96ff.). Murphy also refers to the use of the weave for carpeting and mentions its suitability for bed covers. James Alexander, born in Belfast of Scottish parents, came to the United States in 1798 and settled on a farm in Orange County, New Jersey, where he both farmed and wove (Parslow). His ledger has survived, and is in the col-lections of the New York Historical Association at Coopers-town, New York; scattered through it are drafts and tie-ups for doublecloth and other complex weaves. There are two coverlets in the Everhart Museum in Scranton, Pennsyl-vania: one of these is a drawloom-woven one made by James Alexander for Sally Reeves in 1825. The other is a geometric doublecloth made for the same person and may also be Alexander's work. Two coverlets from definitely Scottish areas in Ontario are illustrated here: no. 407 from Stormont County, and no. 406 from Ayr, North Dumfries Township, in Waterloo County. No. 408 is possibly the work of the weaver of the second of these.

Like 'summer and winter' and early twill diaper, double-cloth coverlets also occur in Ontario in areas of distinctly English-speaking settlement. A knowledge of these techniques would have been brought to the province by professional weavers who came as United Empire Loyalists before 1783 and by others who followed closely on their heels. The same situation existed in New Brunswick, where doublecloth coverlets occur much more rarely (nos. 401–3). The names of a number of professional weavers who came to that prov-ince as Loyalists are known (Wright, 255–345). One was David Pickett from Connecticut, who wove the rare fragment shown in no. 401.

There was at least one man weaving coverlets of this type in the Niagara Peninsula before Samuel Fry set up in business in 1836 in the quite separate Mennonite community near Vineland. He seems to have worked in Lincoln County within range of St Catharines, Grimsby, and Queenston (nos. 409–13). In Woodhouse Township in Norfolk County, James Blayney was the schoolmaster, but also a weaver. He came from Ulster, where Scottish traditions were well known. Overshot coverlets woven by him are still in the possession of his great-grandson, but he also has three sheets from a notebook showing doublecloth and other complex tie-ups. Regrettably, no patterns have survived, but two coverlets shown come from this area and could be his work (nos. 404–5). Doublecloth coverlets have been recorded from the Newmarket area of York County, including nos. 420 and 421, and could be the work of the same weaver who wove the unusual eight-shaft coverlet illustrated as no. 352. Of the others shown, one comes from Prince Edward County, an area of

primary Loyalist settlement (no. 422), and the very handsome no. 424, which unfortunately has no history, may also come from this area.

Unless otherwise stated in the descriptions, the yarns found in the doublecloth coverlets shown here are a handspun woollen (z, 2s), and a natural white cotton that is equal to it in grist, and may be either two- or three-ply. These yarns would have been prepared by the customer who desired a coverlet and handed over to the weaver when she made her choice from his pattern book. In weaving, the two types of yarn were used in the warp alternately, and despite the fact

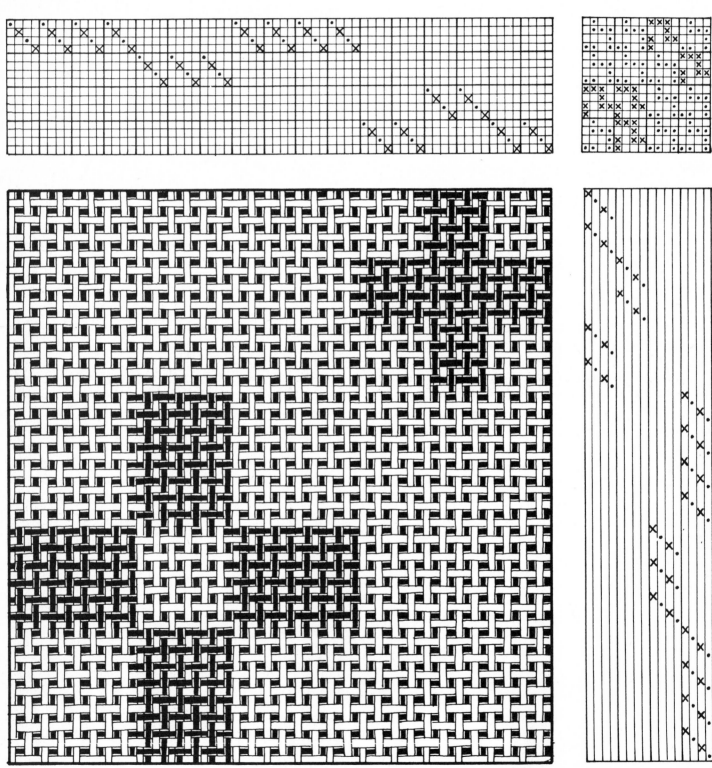

FIGURE 39

that two separate layers of cloth were woven independently, they are considered to be one warp divided into two series as both perform a similar function. Each of these series interweaves with its own weft, which matches it in colour and weight. Due to the difference in elasticity of woollen and cotton yarns, these mixed warps were difficult to handle, and the take-up of the two types of yarn differed. For this reason, doublecloth coverlets were seldom set up and woven more than one or two at a time.

In the accompanying diagram (fig. 39), the drawing of the weave is shown slightly expanded to illustrate that one layer of cloth lies over the other. In any example of doublecloth, this is not obvious: the layer on the face completely hides the one beneath it. The draft in the diagram is of the type used to denote patterns that are to be woven 'rose fashion' with the motifs separated rather than linked as in the draft accompanying the twill diaper diagram (fig. 38). It is

shown treadled in accordance with the draft, using the reverse tie-up required for the 'rose fashion' method. The principle of combining blocks to give a more solid motif is also illustrated at the upper right, a practice found in both doublecloth and twill diaper weaving.

The draft accompanying the diagram is expanded in full, but like other multiple-shaft weaving, a profile is all that is required by an experienced craftsman. Each block of the pattern requires four shafts, and coverlets with three, four, five, and eight blocks are illustrated. Each unit of the profile draft represents four threads, alternately dark and light. It is this colour order and the difference in tie-ups that differentiate the basic plans of twill diaper and doublecloth weaving. The patterns follow the rule of 'tromp as writ,' but there are occasional exceptions. All the coverlets were the work of highly skilled professionals who knew how to utilize slight variations to produce a better result.

401 / New Brunswick. Probably late 18th century
NBM 3549. Gift of Miss Sarah Pickett
Doublecloth coverlet (fragment). L. 70cm; w. 55cm

Indigo blue and yellow wool, and bleached linen (z, 2s). Despite its condition, this is an extremely important piece, and undoubtedly the earliest example of doublecloth weaving to survive in Canada. The use of linen indicates its age, even though much of this has worn away through use. It was woven by an ancestor of the donor, and David Pickett, a Loyalist from Connecticut, is listed as a weaver who settled at Kingston in Queen's County (Wright, 319). This would seem to be an example of his work. Unlike the Loyalists who came overland to Ontario, Pickett would have been able to bring his equipment with him by sea. The fragment is a complete width. Even though it has shrunk considerably, it shows that the multiple-shaft loom the weaver had at this time was a comparatively narrow one.

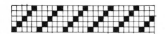 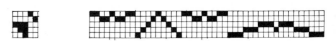

402 / New Brunswick. Collected at St George,
Charlotte County. 1810-25
ROM 966.29.3. Gift of Miss Claire Stenning
Doublecloth coverlet (half). L. 226cm; w. 105cm, plus
added border and fringe

Brown wool and natural white cotton. The pattern is a variation of the 'Whig Rose' design known from overshot and
other techniques, but three of the five pattern blocks have
been combined to produce the dominant central motif known
as a 'snowball.' The brown shade used for the wool was
probably obtained from butternuts, widely used for dyeing
in New Brunswick. The border added down the side is warp-
faced with a simple pattern in the two colours. It would have
been woven on a bandloom, probably of the rigid-heddle
type, and the weft extended on one side to form the fringe.
Part of an indigo blue and white doublecloth coverlet from
this province with the identical design is in the York-Sunbury
Museum, Fredericton.

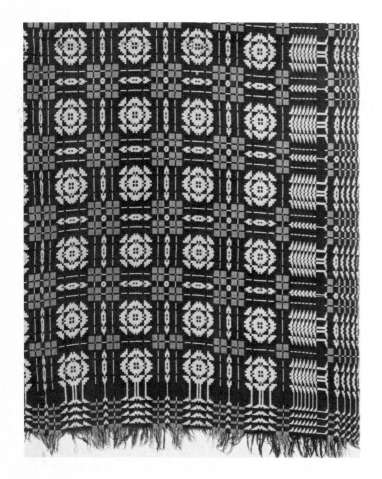

403 / New Brunswick(?). 1810-35
King's Village Historical Settlement, Prince William, NB.
M69.93.1
Doublecloth coverlet. L. 206cm, plus fringe; w. 179cm

Indigo blue wool and pale blue cotton with rust-red wool.
This coverlet was found in Maugerville on the St John River
in New Brunswick, an area where Planters settled about
1760 and were later joined by Loyalists. A combination of
three colours is unusual, but is found in no. 401 and is also
known from the United States. The hope that it was made in
New Brunswick cannot be without reservations until more
detailed research is completed in that province. The pattern
shows a variation of the 'snowball' motif framed on four
sides. The small rust-red squares set off these primary units to
advantage.

3   6

404 / Ontario. From Walpole Township,
Haldimand County. 1815-25
ROM 969.78.1. Gift of Mrs J.H. Crang
Doublecloth coverlet. L. 204cm, plus fringe; w. 191cm

Indigo blue wool and natural white cotton. The pattern is
identical to no. 385, the twill diaper coverlet woven by
Samuel Fry, but is too early to be his work. It is possible that
this and the following example were woven by James Blayney, who was the schoolmaster in Woodhouse Township and
who also wove professionally. Woodhouse is immediately west
of Walpole, although not in the same county.

405 / Ontario. Woodhouse Township, Norfolk County.
About 1820
ROM 960.18. Gift of Mrs F.A. Ballachey
Doublecloth coverlet. L. 207cm, plus fringe; w. 194cm

Indigo blue wool and natural white cotton. This is an example of the reversing patterns that give greater variety to a
design. Ancestors of the donor, named Swayze, settled in
Norfolk County early in the nineteenth century, and this
coverlet is associated with the marriage of the donor's great-
grandmother about 1820. She prepared and dyed the yarns
and took them to the weaver, who was possibly James Blayney
mentioned above.

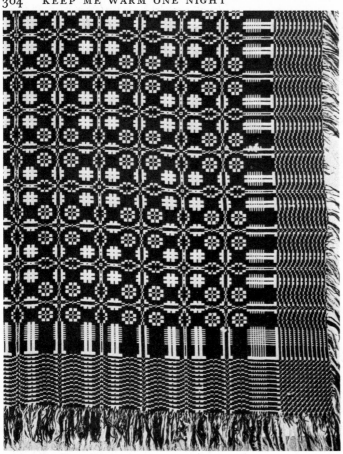

406 / Ontario. Ayr, North Dumfries Township,
Waterloo County. About 1850
ROM 949.250. Gift of Mrs J.H. Crang
Doublecloth coverlet. L. 219cm, plus fringe; w. 171cm, plus
fringes

Indigo blue wool and natural white cotton. The white cotton
is fine, used double, of the type possibly imported from Great
Britain rather than the usual yarn from New England or the
Mohawk Valley bought at the local general store as skeins
of singles. Its use supports the late date for a coverlet of this
type. It is similar to that found in many coverlets from
Waterloo County woven in the German-speaking tradition,
but this example comes from a basically Scottish settlement.
A different effect is given the simple design by combining two
of the pattern blocks.

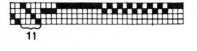 

407 / Ontario. North Valley, Stormont County. About 1825
ROM 947.83. Gift of Mrs J.H. Crang
Doublecloth coverlet. L. 187cm; w. 160cm

Indigo blue wool and natural white cotton. This pattern is
familiar from 'summer and winter' weave coverlets. The
coverlet comes from a distinctly Scottish community and
represents this tradition of doublecloth weaving. All four
sides have been cut and bound, so the present measurements
are no indication of its original size.

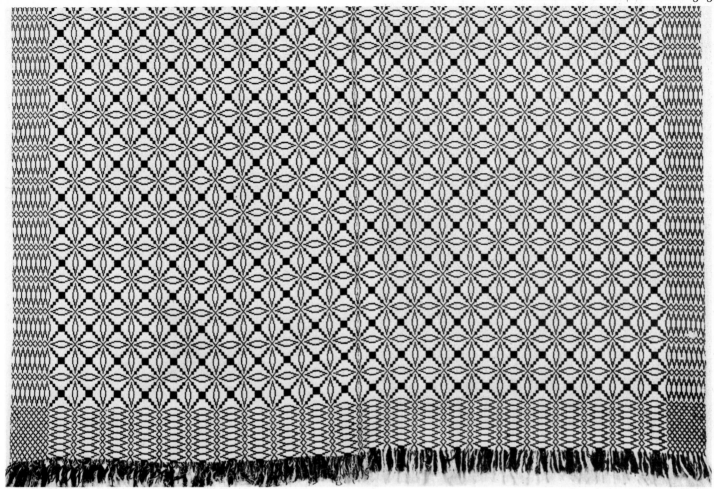

408 / Ontario. Probably Ayr, North Dumfries Township, Waterloo County. About 1850
NMMD 5556
Doublecloth coverlet. L. 228cm, plus fringe; w. 193cm

Dark indigo blue wool and natural white cotton (fine z, 2s, double). The history of this coverlet connects it with the Hamilton area, but the use of the fine cotton, identical to that in no. 406, supports the attribution to the same weaver. The pattern is based on a cross formed by blocks of varying size that produce a simple but effective lozenge lattice.

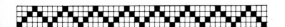

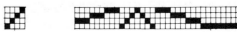

409 / Ontario. Probably Lincoln County. 1815-30.
Collected in St Catharines
ROM 968.235.1. Gift of Mrs J.H. Crang
Doublecloth coverlet. L. 244cm, plus fringe; w. 200cm

Indigo blue wool and natural white cotton. This is the work
of a professional weaver who appears to have lived in the
Queenston-St Catharines area during the early part of the
nineteenth century. He probably came to Ontario shortly
after the American Revolution, and would have woven these
doublecloth coverlets on special order, as well as the plainer
materials for everyday use. The following examples are also
probably his work (nos. 410–12).

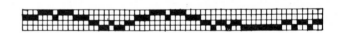

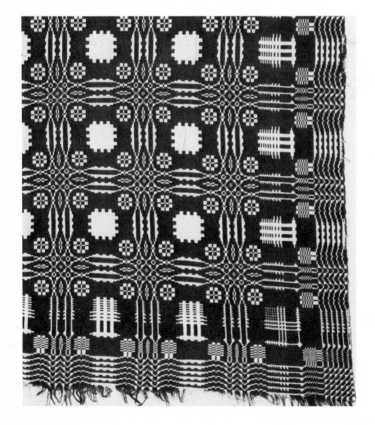

410 / Ontario. Probably Lincoln County. 1815-30
Stone Shop Museum, Grimsby, Ontario.
Gift of Miss Muriel Bonham
Doublecloth coverlet. L. 205cm, plus fringe; w. 177cm

Indigo blue wool and natural white cotton. When a twenty-
shaft loom was available, five pattern blocks could be used
for a design, and some of these could be combined to give
stronger motifs. Here, surrounded by double interlocking
circles, a 'Single Snowball' pattern has a rich effect and is
framed by double 'pine-tree' borders. A twill diaper fragment
(no. 389) comes from the same family. It dates from about
1846, but this coverlet belongs to a previous generation.

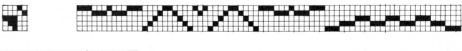

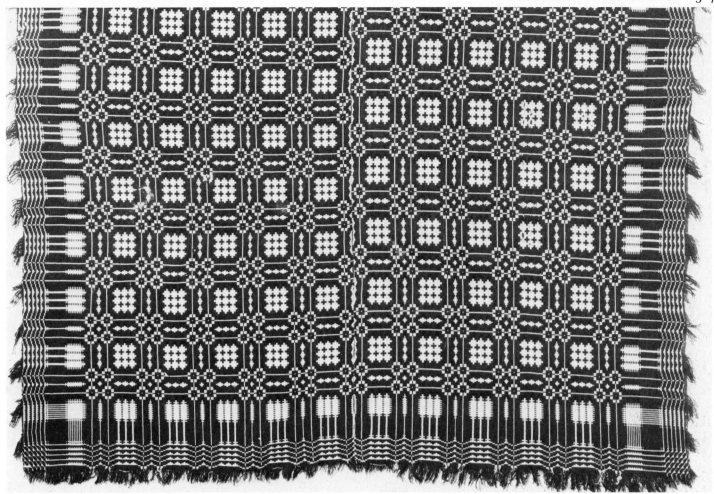

411 / Ontario. Lincoln County. 1815-25
ROM 969.79. Gift of Miss Lillian Shaw
Doublecloth coverlet. L. 236cm, plus fringe; w. 187cm,
plus fringes

Indigo blue wool and natural white cotton. This exceedingly
handsome coverlet was woven for a member of the Thorburn
family in Queenston. It shows another motif formed by combining three blocks that is the simplest form of the pattern
unit sometimes known as 'Lisbon star.' The graceful 'pine-
tree' border supplies a handsome frame.

(*in colour* PLATE III)

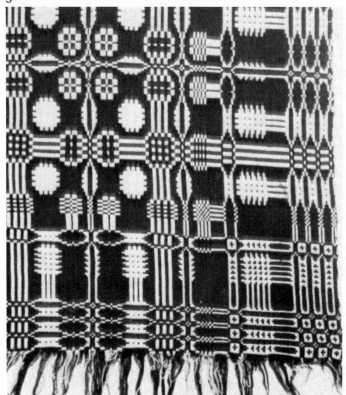

412 / Ontario. Lincoln County. 1820-30.
Collected in St Catharines
ROM 966.33.2. Gift of Mr and Mrs Harold B. Burnham
Doublecloth coverlet. L. 223cm, plus fringe; w. 202cm

Indigo blue wool and natural white cotton. The strong square lattice enclosing 'snowballs' and 'roses' shows the clearly defined patterns available in this technique. The double 'pine-tree' border sets the motifs off to advantage.

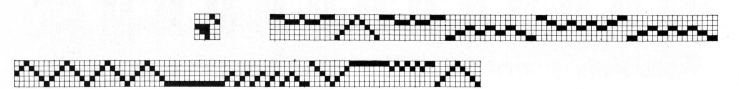

413 / Ontario(?). Perhaps Lincoln County. 1800-15.
Collected in St Catharines
ROM 966.141. Gift of Mrs George Darker
Doublecloth coverlet (fragment). L. 43cm; w. 93cm

Indigo blue wool and natural white cotton. The fragment gives the full weaving width of the coverlet, but barely more than one repeat in height. It is an eight-block pattern requiring a thirty-two shaft loom or a double harness mounting: one to form the pattern and the other for the sheds. Four of the blocks have been combined for the main motif, a fully developed 'Lisbon star.' This fragment has a history of long use in the Niagara Peninsula, but it may originally have been brought from the United States where the pattern is well known and looms of the necessary capacity were used. Two halves of a coverlet with identical pattern are in New Brunswick: one at Fort Beauséjour, Aulac, and the other in the New Brunswick Museum. It is believed to have been brought back to Shediac by a ship's captain trading to New England.

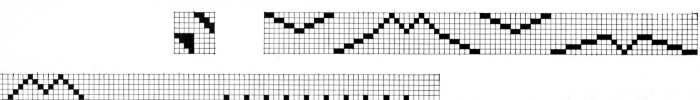

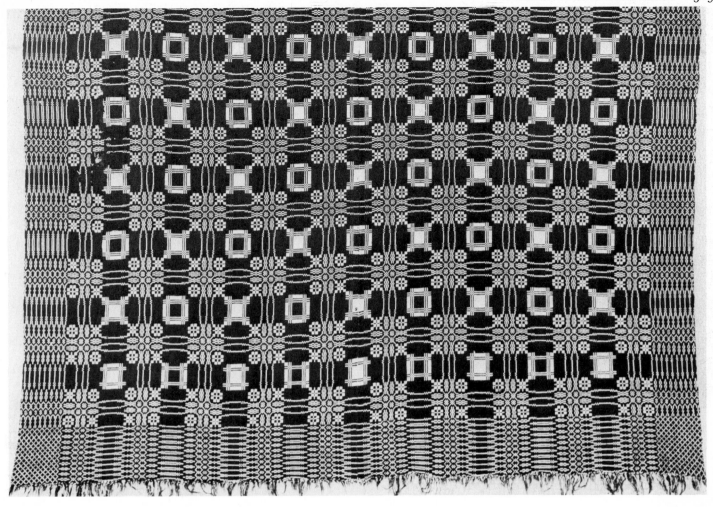

414 / Ontario. Vineland, Lincoln County. About 1840
ROM 967.286. Gift of Mrs Zeta Haist Davis
Doublecloth coverlet. L. 215cm, plus fringe; w. 178cm

Indigo blue wool and natural white cotton (z singles). This
coverlet is associated with a marriage of about 1840 in the
Huntsman family, who lived in the Vineland area of Lincoln

County. The pattern is no. 31 in Samuel Fry's pattern book
and would have been woven by him shortly after he set up in
business. It is not found in his account book as the first entry
there is 1843, but there are records after this date for other
types of work for the same family. The use of cotton singles is
most unusual and has produced a pattern on a finer scale
than in most coverlets of this type.

415 / Ontario. Vineland, Lincoln County. 1836-43
Stone Shop Museum, Grimsby, Ontario. 1031.
Gift of Miss Muriel Bonham
Doublecloth coverlet. L. 173cm, plus fringe; w. 190cm

Indigo blue wool and natural white cotton. This pattern is
Samuel Fry's no. 23 and it seems likely that it is his work, too,
as he wove twill diaper coverlets for the same family. As the
few entries for doublecloth coverlets in Fry's account book
are of no help, this coverlet would have been woven between
1836 when he set up in business, and 1843, the date of the
first entry in the account book.

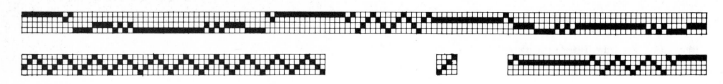

416 / Ontario. Vineland, Lincoln County. 1840-3
Dundurn Castle, Hamilton, Ontario
Doublecloth coverlet. L. 165cm; w. 184cm

Indigo blue wool, and natural white cotton. This handsome
'Nine Snowballs' pattern, with its matching 'pine-tree'
border, is no. 34 in Samuel Fry's pattern book. It was made
for the dower of Cynthia Elizabeth Gage (Mrs James
Nelson Mills), who was born in 1832. It is probably Fry's
work. As there is no corresponding entry in the account book
for the Gage family of Stoney Creek, it would have been
made prior to 1843.

417 / Ontario. Mitchell area, Perth County. About 1854
ROM 968.202.22
Doublecloth coverlet. L. 224cm, plus fringe; w. 170cm,
plus fringes

Medium indigo blue wool and natural white wool. This
coverlet was woven for Margaret Riehl, who lived near
Mitchell in a Mennonite community in Perth County. It is
the only example found in Ontario woven entirely of wool.
The use of a three-block pattern requiring only twelve shafts
is reminiscent of the blue and white linen doublecloth bed
ticks from Canton Bern, the original homeland of the older
Mennonite communities in North America.

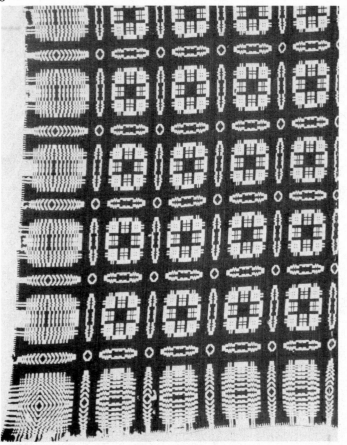

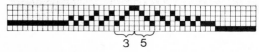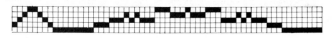

3 5

418 / Ontario. Waterloo County. Probably about 1850
NMMD 5067
Doublecloth coverlet. L. 207cm; w. 154cm

Indigo blue wool and natural white cotton. Both the border
and the main patttern are unusual, but are in a style familiar
both from Wilhelm Magnus Werlich's pattern book and
from some printed in Germany in the eighteenth century. It
differs completely from that of the coverlets with a Scottish
background and from those that appear to have been woven
in a tradition brought from the United States following the
American Revolution. It must be the work of one of the immigrant German weavers who came to Ontario around the
middle of the nineteenth century.

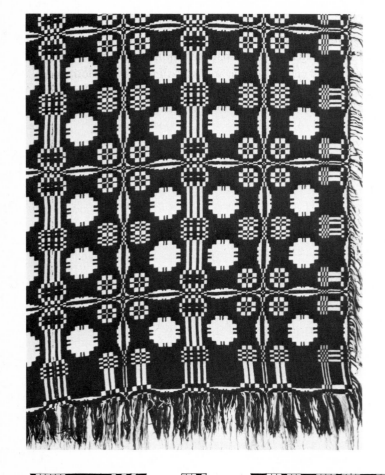

419 / Ontario. Waterloo County. 1825-50
ROM 966.82.1
Doublecloth coverlet. L. 204cm, plus fringe; w. 144cm,
plus fringes

Indigo blue wool and natural white with medium blue cotton. This is the only doublecloth coverlet seen with an Ontario history that is not in the basic dark blue and white. A
medium blue cotton check with the white adds another
dimension. It is one of the very few coverlets found that has
not been 'tromp as writ.' The alteration was made intentionally by the weaver to produce the strong vertical pattern
stripes and a fuller 'pine-tree' border down the sides.

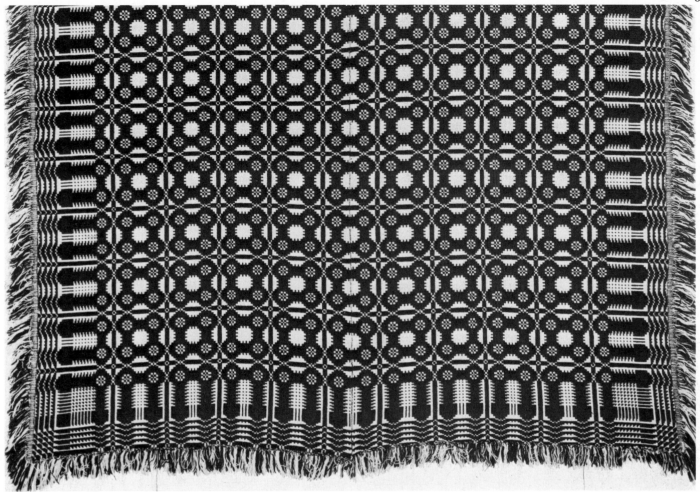

420 / Ontario. Newmarket area, York County. About 1830
ROM 963.129.1. Gift of Miss Helena Daly
Doublecloth coverlet. L. 225cm, plus fringe; w. 198cm,
plus fringes

Indigo blue wool and natural white cotton. This very handsome 'Single Snowball' pattern requires five blocks and a
twenty-shaft loom, as does the following example. Three of
the blocks are combined to produce the main motif and the
slender 'pine trees' in the borders. The coverlet formed part
of the dower of the donor's grandmother, Hannah Doane,
who married Jacob Lundy in 1833.

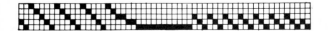

421 / Ontario. York County. About 1840
ROM 951.144
Doublecloth coverlet. L. 226cm, plus fringe; w. 171cm

Indigo blue wool and natural white cotton. This coverlet comes from near Markham, south of Newmarket. The 'Four Snowballs' pattern with 'pine-tree' border requires a loom of the same capacity as no. 420 and is probably the work of the same man. Other coverlets with five-block patterns from York County have been seen, and all would appear to have a com-

mon source that centres on Newmarket. Most doublecloth coverlets with geometric patterns found in Ontario were woven before 1850, a period for which census records are now virtually non-existent. This fact makes it very difficult to discover the name of a weaver working in the earlier part of the nineteenth century even when a body of material obviously the work of the same man turns up in a specific district. Once the jacquard-woven coverlets became available, their more realistic patterns rapidly supplanted the controlled austerity of the geometric ones.

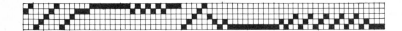

422 / Ontario. Prince Edward County. 1800-20
ROM 968.195.1. Gift of Mrs J.H. Crang
Doublecloth coverlet. L. 210cm; w. 176cm

Indigo blue wool and natural white cotton. The main motif
is the simple 'Lisbon star' formed of three combined pattern
blocks, and these also produce the 'pine-tree' borders. The
primary motifs are separated by four-part tables, a device
known from overshot coverlets. This example was found in
Prince Edward County, an area of early Loyalist settlement,
and was probably woven there.

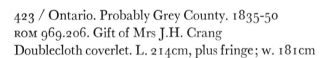

423 / Ontario. Probably Grey County. 1835-50
ROM 969.206. Gift of Mrs J.H. Crang
Doublecloth coverlet. L. 214cm, plus fringe; w. 181cm

Indigo blue wool and natural white cotton. A handsome
combination of the 'Lisbon star' and groups of simple crosses
that gives a lighter effect than many other doublecloth patterns. This coverlet was collected in Grey County and may
possibly be the work of Elias Johan Joachim Mauer, even
though it is in a universal rather than a specifically German
style.

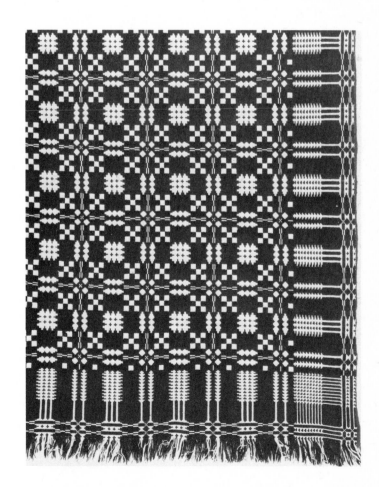

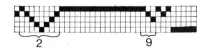

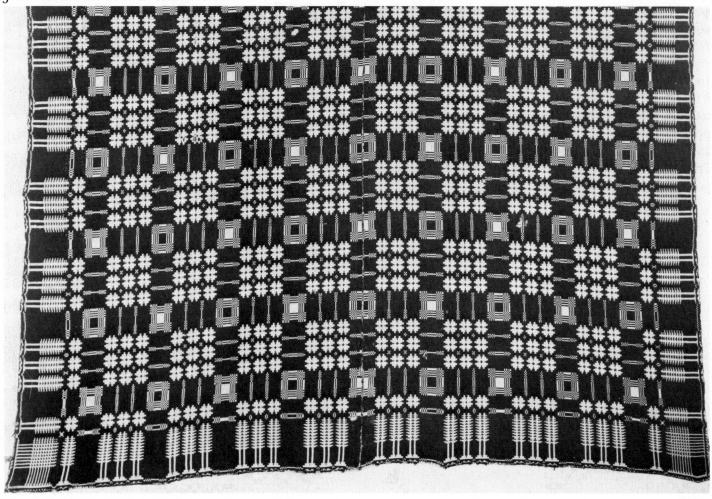

424 / Ontario. 1820-40
ROM 949.253
Doublecloth coverlet. L. 249cm; w. 194cm

Indigo blue wool and natural white cotton. Unfortunately, all that is known about this coverlet is that it was found in Ontario, but there is a strong possibility that it may be from Prince Edward County. The pattern of groups of 'Lisbon stars' and reversing 'tables' has produced a handsome result. A variation from 'tromp as writ' has been made in the treadling that produces x's and o's above the 'pine trees' in the borders and between the elements of the main motifs. It can never now be known whether these enigmatic letters ever had any significance.

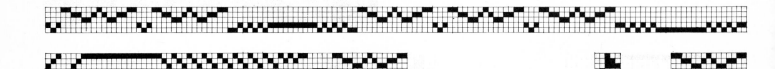

PLATE IV

443, 444, 463

Jacquard coverlets

Until the beginning of the nineteenth century, the drawloom was the means of weaving highly patterned or figured materials. Its origins are still a matter of some dispute, but it probably developed gradually in the Near Eastern area, possibly the Iranian plateau, during the first millennium of the present era, and spread both east and west. Throughout the centuries that it was used, the drawloom was constantly improved, and with it figured silks, the superb damasks and velvets of the late Gothic and Renaissance periods, and the beautiful brocades of eighteenth-century France were woven. It was a highly complicated piece of equipment, requiring the attention of at least two, and sometimes more, workmen for its operation. One of these was the weaver, the other the drawboy who raised the threads necessary to form the pattern. During the eighteenth century, several efforts were made in France to replace the drawboy with a mechanism that could be controlled by the weaver. None were wholly successful until the invention by Joseph-Marie Jacquard of Lyon of the machine that still bears his name. It was first displayed at an industrial exhibition in Paris in 1801, but it was not until he had spent a further five years improving it that the mechanism was ready for use. In 1806, it was declared public property: Jacquard was rewarded with a pension and a royalty on each machine. Despite fierce opposition when it was first introduced in Lyon, it was quickly adopted; in 1812, there are believed to have been eleven thousand jacquard machines in use in France for weaving patterned silks.

Although the term 'jacquard loom' has come into general use, Jacquard's invention could be installed on any loom for weaving figured materials. From France, its use spread and it became known in England and Germany. In 1823, a prosperous Philadelphia merchant, William Horstmann, who had been trained as a weaver in Germany, saw it being used while travelling in Europe (Horstmann, 15). Intrigued by the possibilities it presented, he acquired one and brought it back to the United States in 1824. Little is yet known about its adoption in that country, but it was soon being used to weave coverlets with realistic patterns. Limited use of the drawloom had preceded it there, as is revealed by the work of James Alexander of West Orange, New Jersey, who had come from Scotland in 1797 (Parslow). The new jacquard-woven coverlets proved popular and soon displaced the geometrically patterned doublecloth ones that belonged to the older traditions. From the eastern states, the demand spread west with new settlement as the frontiers expanded, and weavers with jacquard equipment followed the pioneers as far as Iowa. Jacquard coverlets were made in the United States in two widths that were joined by a centre seam, but even as early as the beginning of the 1840s some were woven full width on wide looms. They remained popular until about 1860, when the outbreak of the Civil War put an end to the demand. In 1876, at the time of the Sesquicentennial Exhibition in Philadelphia, a number of commemorative jacquard coverlets were produced commercially, but they failed to prove popular.

Jacquard equipment was first used in Canada in 1834 by Wilhelm Armbrust near Jordan in Louth Township, Lincoln County, Ontario, an area where German-speaking settlers were established. Except that he was a Lutheran born in Germany, and came to Canada from the United States, nothing is known about Armbrust's early history before 1830. In that year, when he was 23, he married Catherine High, a member of a Mennonite family in Louth Township. It may be assumed that he was a fully trained weaver when he arrived in this country and must have acquired experience of the mounting and use of the jacquard mechanism either before leaving Europe, or in the United States. He stopped weaving coverlets in 1848, sold his small farm in 1853, and moved to a larger one at Ridgeville. He lived there until 1904 when he died at the age of 97. Examples of his work are shown in nos. 425–30, including coverlets from both his first and last years of production.

Another weaver, still unidentified, commenced making jacquard coverlets in Welland County in 1835, the year after Armbrust. Examples of his work are shown in nos. 432–8, and he appears to have continued weaving until the early 1850s. Welland County was also an area with communities of German-speaking settlers, so it is probable that this weaver was of the same origin.

More is known of Edward Graf, who was born in Prussia in 1826 of a Bavarian father and a Prussian mother. The family is believed to have come to North America in the early 1840s when the son was in his teens. The parents settled in Buffalo, New York, but most of Edward Graf's life was spent across the Niagara River in Ontario. He married in 1852 and bought half an acre of land at Gasline in Humberstone Township, east of Port Colborne. Here he built a one-storey log cabin. He had a number of children, and as his family grew, a second storey was added to this first home. In 1868, when a new school was built at Gasline, he purchased the old log one, and moved it to his property as a weaving shed. This building has been saved by the Ontario Department of Education and is presently in storage awaiting re-erection in a new location. At the same time he acquired a jacquard loom, probably secondhand from the United States. It was a wide one equipped with a flying shuttle on which Graf could weave coverlets double width without the centre seam characteristic of many handwoven examples.

The older type of coverlet was going out of fashion even in conservative communities and in order to compete with imported products Graf found it necessary to have the wide loom and to produce patterns more to the tastes of the times. Except for his version of the traditional 'Four Roses' pattern, his work shows a new approach to coverlet design. Graf wove until his death in 1904 but, from the time he acquired the wide loom, he was assisted by his son Albert, who continued to make coverlets until 1918. Their production must have been enormous. They still wove on special order using the handspun pattern wefts supplied by their customers in the neighbourhood, but pedlars carried samples across southern Ontario and as far as the Eastern Townships of Quebec. They took orders and delivered finished coverlets on their next round.

Examples of the work done by the Grafs on the wide loom are shown in nos. 447–52, but even when the first of these was woven, the father was a fully competent master of his craft. It seems safe to assume that he was weaving figured coverlets at an earlier date, and nos. 431, 442, and 443 belong to a group that has been assigned to him. The first two represent those marked with a device of two stars, sometimes with a heart between, and the earliest of these recorded is dated 1848. No. 442 represents the stylistic affinity that many of these coverlets have to the work of the unidentified weaver of nos. 432–8. No. 443 belongs to a group dated in the 1860s that is stylistically similar to Edward Graf's later work, and which often employs the same construction. On the basis of these points, the theory is proposed that Graf was apprenticed to the weaver of nos. 432–8. The similarity of the pattern of no. 431 to coverlets known to have been woven by Armbrust suggests that Graf may have acquired this weaver's loom and equipment in 1848. Armbrust ceased weaving in that year; Graf at 22 would have been ready to set up in business for himself.

Moses Grobb was a member of the Mennonite community settled around Vineland, Ontario; he was primarily a farmer and a successful one. In the census returns of the period either this or fruit merchant is shown as his occupation. He had a weaving shed on his farm, is known to have woven himself, and is believed to have employed other weavers on occasion. He produced carpeting, yardage for clothing, and probably blankets. He acquired a jacquard loom in 1853 and for some twenty years thereafter produced coverlets with characteristic patterns and borders (nos. 444–6). A number are known that were woven for his family and relations. These serve as documents of his work, making identification of other examples comparatively easy. It is not known where he learned to handle the complex jacquard equipment, but it might be pointed out that Armbrust had been working only a few miles away. By the time Grobb commenced weaving these coverlets, imported goods were already replacing the handwoven ones in this area, the most prosperous agricultural district in Ontario. His production seems to have been limited in volume, probably due in part to the seasonal nature of his weaving, but also because the demand for such articles was steadily diminishing.

In the parts of Ontario where jacquard coverlets were woven, a number of weavers have yet to be identified. This is as true of the Niagara Peninsula as elsewhere. The examples shown in nos. 439–41 were woven in this area. The first two were made by a man who marked his work with the device of a small lozenge with a flaring tail; the other used a characteristic floral border. As far as has been discovered, both were active for only about five years at the middle of the century. It is possible that both came to Canada for only a short time, or that they had been apprenticed to one of the older weavers at an early age and worked independently for only a few years. In either case, they may have found weaving too unremunerative with the changing fashions and turned their attention to more profitable livelihoods.

Waterloo County has always been an area where conservative traditions have been preserved and new fashions adopted slowly. The weaving of jacquard coverlets commenced here after the middle of the nineteenth century. All that were produced employed a tied doublecloth construction with an all-cotton warp that could be of a considerable length suitable for semi-mass production. The free double cloth with a warp combining wool and cotton, known from the earlier period in the Niagara Peninsula, is never found. To supply a decorative edging, the lower edge was usually hemmed, and a separately woven wool fringe added. This sometimes occurs down the sides as well, but more often the fringes here are formed by the wool pattern weft.

The first jacquard weaver in Waterloo County was Aaron Zelner. He was born in Pennsylvania in 1812, a descendant of a German family (Zöllner) which had settled there in the early eighteenth century. Zelner was trained as a weaver and wove coverlets in Bucks County, Pennsylvania (Lichten, 32), before coming to Canada about 1845. In Canada, he first worked in South Cayuga Township and then moved to Waterloo County about 1855, weaving there until sometime between 1865 and 1871, probably 1868, although he did not die until 1893. Three of his patterns have been recorded, although only one of these is illustrated (nos. 456–7). The other two were both woven in Waterloo County in 1856 and are known from the work of other weavers in Pennsylvania, with different borders (Reinert, pls. 52 and 92). The first has his typical rose spray border, but the second, which was reworked by the Nolls (no. 463), has the bird and bush border that is also found in their work (no. 458). Zelner probably trained John Noll of Petersburg and turned over his equipment and patterns to him. Zelner followed the American practice of including his own name and location in the corner cartouche, as well as the date and the name of the person for whom the coverlet was woven. The type of loom owned by Zelner and the Nolls was the older single-width rather than the newer double-width used by other jacquard weavers in Waterloo County.

John Noll was born in Ontario in 1851 and was weaving professionally by 1871 when he and his brother William, born in 1849, are shown in the census returns of that year as sons of a widow living at Petersburg in Wilmot Township, Waterloo County. From inscriptions on the coverlets, we know that the two brothers were in partnership, but those on the first ones woven in this weaving shop suggest that a younger brother may also have been included at the beginning. The jacquard-woven coverlets were all the work of John, and the earliest known example is dated 1868 (no. 459). Their production ceased in 1905 when John Noll died. Most of his early work is distinguished by a cartouche in one corner giving the brothers' names in one form or other, but unmarked examples that appear to be of later date may be identified as his by the similarity of motifs found both in the corners and in the patterns.

As was usual with the weavers who owned jacquard equipment, these coverlets were a specialty line. The main production of the workshop was for other purposes, and for these they had various other looms equipped with flying shuttles. William Noll, who did not marry and who survived his younger brother, specialized in the handsome horse blankets that were in demand in the area. For these he had a sixteen-shaft loom and wove them in twill diaper (no. 398) and in the point-twill types shown in nos. 380–2. Using the simpler

looms, both brothers produced clothing materials, blankets of cotton and wool and of all wool, as well as cotton sheeting and rag carpeting. Following the death of John Noll, his interest in the partnership was taken over by his son who had been named after him. He ran the general store and was postmaster at Petersburg, and continued to weave professionally until his death about 1930.

Although Petersburg is in Wilmot Township, this is adjacent to Waterloo Township where Zelner worked. Kitchener (then Berlin) would have been the common centre of commerce for both of them. As suggested above, it seems most likely that John Noll learned his craft from Aaron Zelner. He was probably apprenticed to him about the age of twelve, quite normal for the period, and took over the whole of Zelner's equipment, including his patterns, when he was seventeen. Zelner appears to have ceased weaving in the 1860s shortly before the Nolls' earliest known work. Their loom was of the same type and capacity as Zelner's, and some of their work has a strong stylistic affinity to his. The main motifs of no. 463, although an original design, strongly resemble a pattern of Zelner's that has been recorded but is not illustrated. Traditionally, no. 458 was woven at Petersburg for Peter Wilker about 1880. There is no reason to doubt this history, so the coverlet must be the work of the Nolls. The pattern is identical to the one by Zelner seen in nos. 456 and 457, but with a bird and bush border that is the same as that on nos. 459 and 462. The rose-spray border found on Zelner's coverlets is well known from the United States, but is most unusual in Canada. It has been found as a border on one of the Nolls' early coverlets, and as a filler in the corner of several woven by them, such as nos. 458 and 459.

The characteristic cartouche when used by the Nolls appears only in one corner. It gives their name, sometimes the date and the name of the person for whom the coverlet was woven. Various fillers, other than the rose spray mentioned, appear in the other corners and sometimes in both. These serve to identify the Nolls' work when there is no cartouche. The most usual filler is a garland of roses (nos. 461–2), and another is the elaborate diagonal scroll in nos. 463 and 464. Some of their borders are also characteristic, such as in nos. 460 and 461, and nos. 463 and 464. These are not found in the work of other Ontario weavers.

A number of the earlier patterns used by the Nolls appear to have been acquired from Aaron Zelner. Others are original work; it would have been John Noll who was responsible for the designs. In many cases, motifs from older patterns have been incorporated in new ones, but distinctly original work appears to have been inspired by various sources.

Daniel Knechtel was born in the United States, probably Pennsylvania. It is likely that he came to Canada at the time of the Civil War, arriving here as a fully trained weaver. In the 1871 census he is shown as aged 28. His wife, Magdalena, had been born in Germany, but it is probable that they were married in Ontario, where their first child was born in 1870. One pattern that Knechtel wove is firmly identified (no. 473). He undoubtedly had others, four being quite a usual number. Because of identical construction and the similarity of the wild turkeys in the border, no. 474 has also been assigned to him. This pattern occurs frequently in Ontario and is also known from Pennsylvania (Reinert, pl. 33).

Like the Nolls, Johan Lippert and his son George worked at Petersburg, but produced quite different work. The father was born in Germany, but the son in Ontario. The latter's daughter remembered a certain amount about the weaving and stated that they had acquired their wide jacquard loom about 1870 and had had four patterns for the fancy coverlets. They had also produced other types of work, and a lozenge and twill diaper horse blanket that is probably theirs is shown in no. 400. George Lippert continued to weave in Petersburg until 1904, when he disposed of the jacquard equipment and the multiple-shaft loom. It was at this time that he moved to Kitchener, where he continued to weave rag carpeting that was sold in the local stores. Of the four patterns that the Lipperts had woven with the jacquard equipment, George Lippert's daughter could remember the names of two. One was called 'The Garland,' but this is too general a name for the number of designs of this type and cannot be isolated. The other was known as 'The Church,' a much more distinctive name, but which applies equally to two known designs. As one is known to have been woven by Daniel Knechtel (no. 473), the other is undoubtedly that used by the Lipperts (no. 465). For technical and stylistic reasons, nos. 466 and 467 have also been assigned to them.

Two men wove wide jacquard coverlets in Preston: Wilhelm Magnus Werlich and August Ploethner. Both acquired their specialized looms between 1865 and 1870, but they had been professional weavers before and after coming to Canada. Both were born in Germany, Werlich in Wildenspring in Thuringia, and each arrived here about 1850. When he reached Preston, Werlich put up a log cabin which became his weaving shop when he built a house shortly after. He continued weaving until 1912. The weaving shop had an attic with a hole cut in the floor to accommodate the jacquard head, the usual practice so that it could be reached more easily. Werlich's children were strictly forbidden to go up there, and his youngest son never forgot the day that he climbed up to investigate this secret place. August Ploethner had a weaving shed in Preston, but he also operated a shop in Kitchener where he sold his own work, as well as that of other weavers on commission. Two designs used by each of these men have been identified, but they undoubtedly wove others as well.

One pattern definitely known to have been used by Werlich is shown in no. 469. This coverlet was inherited by his grandson, who remembered it being used as a tablecloth. It may easily be the first jacquard coverlet Werlich wove. Because the lower border of palmettes and leafy crosses is the same as the pattern of no. 470, this design is assigned to him. Both are known from an earlier date in Pennsylvania although not always with identical borders (Reinert, pls. 42, 61). Werlich would have acquired the pattern cards for them when he obtained his loom.

The two patterns woven by Ploethner are both known from examples still belonging to his descendants. No. 471 is a palmette design that differs from Werlich's, but it too is known from an earlier date in Pennsylvania (Reinert, pls. 75,

85, 145) and would have been acquired with the loom. An identical coverlet still belongs to his granddaughter, as does the one that identifies no. 472. This piece is banded with a rainbow of colours. Obviously all the odds and ends of wool around the weaving shop were used when it was woven.

Of the remaining doublewidth coverlets produced in Waterloo County and the adjacent areas, none may definitely be assigned to any one weaver. Some tentative suggestions may be made, and any information available will be found with the illustrations of the work of these various men. Most of them purchased their pattern cards in the United States ready for use. The prevalence of distinctly American motifs in a number of patterns definitely supports this view. The individual content of the self-prepared designs found in the work of the Niagara Peninsula weavers, and the sometimes less original work of the Nolls and of Zelner, is gone, and has been replaced by a commercial product.

The Niagara Peninsula and Waterloo County and environs were the main areas where jacquard coverlets were woven in Ontario, but a few men worked in other parts of the province where they depended on individual concepts of design. The unknown weaver of nos. 453–5 was one of these, probably in York or Peel Counties. Elsewhere various men produced distinctive work: William Withers and Christopher Armstrong at Stouffville, William Hunter at Wilfrid, John Campbell at Komoka near London, and a damask weaver north of Whitby.

William Withers was a Scot who came to Canada about 1850 and settled at Stouffville. In the 1861 census he is listed as a weaver, married, aged 36, with four children, the eldest of whom was a daughter. In the 1871 census, the same household is shown with four children, two of them under ten years of age. The eldest was a boy of 17 listed as a weaver, and with them Christopher Armstrong, aged 29, of Irish birth, also a weaver, and a widower. The only additional fact known is that Armstrong obtained his equipment from Withers and continued to weave coverlets until his death in 1910. Taking these data, it seems possible that Armstrong married the eldest Withers daughter in the 1860s, and went into partnership with his father-in-law; that Withers, his wife, his eldest daughter, and one or more younger children died before 1871, possibly in an epidemic, leaving four orphans, and Christopher Armstrong the son-in-law to carry on the business.

William Withers was one of the first weavers in Ontario to have a wide loom, and both his and Armstrong's coverlets that succeeded them are woven full width without centre seam. He definitely appears to have prepared his own designs. The field of the coverlets is divided into rectangular panels, somewhat higher than wide, and the various patterns found in these units were used in a variety of combinations. The most characteristic shows a wreath surrounding four roses, and consisting of thistles, shamrocks, and maple leaves, with birds of paradise. This is seen in the corners of no. 476, which is one of a small group ascribed to Withers: it is also seen as the central motif of no. 477, which is ascribed to Armstrong. The double scrolls of the borders of nos. 477 and 478 are also Withers' design, but are more characteristic of Armstrong's work. Despite the similarity of motifs, the work of the two men may be distinguished by a difference of construction. Both are tied double cloth, but Withers' are woven with a proportion of 2:1 and may have areas of free doublecloth, while Armstrong's are always completely tied and have a proportion of 4:1.

Christopher Armstrong's son remembered his father's weaving shop. He had five other looms in addition to the jacquard. These were used for weaving carpeting, clothing materials, and blanketing, the 'bread and butter' lines of most of the professional weavers. One informant remembered being taken to the Armstrongs as a young girl with the yarns she had prepared. She was shown through the house; every bed in it had a coverlet with a different pattern. It was from these that she chose the design she preferred.

In the census for 1871, William J. Hunter is listed as 32 years of age, born in the United States, married to a wife born in Ontario, and with four children, the eldest of whom was seven. It seems probable that he came to Canada at the time of the Civil War, married about 1863, and settled at Wilfrid in the northern part of Ontario County. He must have been a fully trained weaver at that time, and may well have brought his wide jacquard loom with him. Although it may seem surprising that he settled in what is now only a small hamlet, it was then quite a prosperous town. Two of his patterns are known and examples of each of them are owned by his descendants. One design is shown as nos. 479 and 480; the second is another version of the popular bird of paradise motif.

John Campbell was a Scot, born in Paisley and trained as a weaver there, who emigrated to the United States in 1832 and settled near Syracuse in the northern part of New York State. In 1859, bringing his jacquard equipment with him, he came to Canada. He settled first at Kilworth, and soon moved to Komoka, near London, Ontario. His two looms, one with shafts, the other with jacquard attachment, and his account book have survived and are now at the Ontario Science Centre in Toronto. The account book gives information regarding his production, and the volume he produced is startling. He bought half an acre of land, and wove alone from the time that he settled in Ontario until his death twenty-six years later. During this period filled orders amount to about a thousand jacquard coverlets, mostly one or two at a time. He also lists a number of overshot coverlets, and thousands of yards of carpeting, clothing materials of a wide variety of types, and bordered blanketing. His customers came from an area west to Sarnia and east to Woodstock. He had four jacquard patterns, and the names are known: 'Rose and Stars,' 'Single Rose,' 'Tulip,' and 'Garland.' His customers supplied the necessary yarns and he charged $2.50 for weaving a coverlet. If it was in two colours, it cost $3.00. He charged an extra fifty cents for cutting the special cards for a name, but simplified its inclusion by replacing some of the cards for the inner guard of the border with those specially cut. It is here that the name occurs, somewhat rarely, rather than in the special cartouches known from earlier work. His 'Rose and Stars,' with its heraldic eagle grasping thunderbolt and olive branch, might well be taken for an American pattern (no. 481). It is undoubtedly based on one Campbell used in the United States, the cards for which he brought with him, although he was fully prepared to cut new cards himself when the necessity arose. His loom was a narrow one for weaving single width. The two halves had to be joined by a centre seam.

The work of one weaver in Ontario differs completely from anything else woven in the province. Neither the weaver's identity nor where he worked are definitely known, but the latter was probably in Ontario County between Whitby and Brooklin. Examples of his coverlets turn up both east and west of there, making the location plausible. From the history of some of the coverlets and their style, it appears possible that this weaver started working about 1850 and continued until about 1880, giving a working span of thirty years. The only clue to his identity is a suggestion that he was called 'Weaver Joe.' The only professional weaver listed in the census returns for Whitby Township at this time is John Gibson, an Irish widower living alone, whose age is given as sixty in the 1871 return. It is possible that he is the man being sought.

The construction he used in his coverlets was damask, the weave best known from table linen. The coverlets were woven with coloured wool on a cotton warp. The weaver's mastery of this technique shows that he was fully trained and must have learned his craft before coming to Canada. He used a wide loom and a range of patterns of distinct originality of which six are shown (nos. 484–9). Only two borders have been seen, and their use divides his work into two periods. Both are floral: the earlier one is seen on nos. 484–6, and the later one occurs on nos. 487–9. These always frame all four sides of the coverlets. Stylistically, the patterns of nos. 484 and 485 appear to be earlier than the others. The layout of no. 486 with the earlier border is transitional to the style of no. 487.

In Canada, the only province where jacquard coverlets were woven by hand is Ontario. No evidence of any kind has been unearthed to suggest that they were made locally in any other part of the country. A limited number have turned up in the Maritime Provinces and Quebec, but all of them must be assigned either to Ontario or to the United States. A different group which occurs periodically were woven commercially in England and Scotland and imported into this country. The construction of these coverlets differs completely from all Canadian examples and the yarns have no resemblance to those used here. Virtually all the jacquard coverlets made in Canada were the work of highly trained men who were fulltime professional weavers, although at the very end of the nineteenth century there was a limited mill production in the same styles. These are easily distinguished by the use of only cotton singles in the warp (ROM 967.141.1; 970.229).

The identity of three men who worked in the Niagara Peninsula is now known, and perhaps another five also worked in this area for longer or shorter periods. Most of these men were weaving between 1834 and 1860, although Moses Grobb and particularly the Grafs continued to supply the demand for a longer period. The first jacquard coverlets

FIGURE 40

woven in Waterloo County were produced by Aaron Zelner in the 1850s. He was followed by other weavers, and production continued until the outbreak of the Great War in 1914. In this area the work of six men has been definitely or tentatively established, and there may have been an equal number of others. Outside the main centres of production, some six or eight workshops were scattered in various parts of the province. Adding up these figures, a total of under thirty is reached, and it may safely be stated that between 1834 and 1918, the maximum number of workshops that produced these fancy coverlets did not exceed this figure. The majority of the men who operated them were German born, or of German descent; the remainder were mainly Scots who had come to this country fully trained. If one allows for the fact that jacquard equipment was handed on from one weaver to another, an even smaller number of looms would have existed. Jacquard machines in good condition would have had a capital value; a number were perhaps sold to mills when the handweavers no longer needed them. It is not surprising that only one of the old jacquard hand looms used in Canada has survived: that used by John Campbell of Komoka. It was seen by the Royal Ontario Museum in 1950 still in the weaving shed untouched since Campbell's death in 1885 (fig. 40). The jacquard mechanism may be seen on top of the loom rising through a hole in the attic floor and with the cards still in position. It was presented by the weaver's grandson to the University of Western Ontario, and is now at the Ontario Science Centre. This is the only handloom with jacquard attachment used for weaving coverlets known from the whole of North America.

When perfected in 1806, the device invented by Jacquard was quite simple, with a minimum of moving parts. Its purpose was to simplify the operation of the complex figure harness of the drawloom, used solely for patterning, that was mounted behind a group of shafts needed to produce the ground weave. It retained the lower part of the figure harness, but eliminated the upper part consisting of pulley box, tail cords, simple, and lashes. It dispensed with the services of the drawboy, the weaver's assistant.

The principle of the draw system was that the warp threads could be raised in small units of one or more and that these could be used either singly or in selected groups for the formation of figures. The number of warp threads in each of these units was always small. Each formed a tiny gradation in the pattern known as the warp decoupure which, in the coverlets to be described, may be of one, two, or four threads: the smaller the decoupure, the softer the contours of the motifs.

The figure harness consisted of a number of interrelated parts. Each leash, corresponding to a heddle of the shaft loom, consisted of two loops of cord with a metal, glass, or porcelain eye between them through which the warp threads passed. Each was separately weighted by a small strip of lead, the lingo, attached to the lower end. A cord, the necking cord, was attached to the upper end, and this passed through one of the holes in the comberboard, a set of thin slips of hardwood set in a stationary frame. In these, small holes were accurately drilled to hold each leash in an exact position. A second cord, the pulley cord, was tied to the upper end of each necking cord, but if the pattern was repeated in the width, the necking cords of all leashes performing the same function in the formation of the pattern were tied to the same pulley cord. These were the parts of the drawloom figure harness that Jacquard retained, and basically they remain today the patterning system of any loom with which a jacquard attachment is used.

The invention consisted of five important parts: a square block, the cylinder, with a set of holes drilled in each face; the pattern cards with perforations where required that matched the holes in the cylinder; a set of spring-activated wires, the needles; a series of hooks, one hanging from each needle, and from which the pulley cords of the figure harness were suspended; and a metal plate, the griffe, which served to raise the needles selected by the other parts of the mechanism.

Each pattern card governed a separate pattern shed, so that for any design a large number of cards was required. It was these, laced together in sequence, that controlled the lifting of the warp threads necessary for the figures in the fabric. The cylinder was turned by the action of a treadle, each turn presenting a new pattern card to the needles.

Selected holes were punched in each card, and it was the presence or absence of these perforations that controlled which needles moved and which remained stationary. The needles were in the same plane as the cylinder and pressed against the card on its face. If a hole was present, the needle slipped through the card into the perforation of the cylinder that matched it and automatically moved forward the respective hook with the pulley cord suspended from it. The hooks moved forward were engaged by the griffe, and when this was raised, they with their pulley cords were lifted by it, while those that had not moved remained static. In short, where there were holes in the pattern cards, all the warp threads corresponding to them were lifted, the others remained stationary, and the pattern shed appeared.

In the jacquard attachment, the number of holes on each of the four faces of the cylinder is always identical to the number of needles and of hooks. Although this number varies with different mechanisms, it gives each one a rigidly controlled capacity, and any design prepared to be woven with it is limited to the same number of warp decoupures. For this reason, the jacquard has always remained a less flexible tool than the drawloom.

The loom that John Campbell used at Komoka (fig. 40) shows modifications to the original jacquard mechanism and to the classical form of the figure harness. The device perfected in 1806 had been designed for use with the silk looms of Lyon, but it was soon realized that it could be modified and elaborated to make it suitable for other types of figured weaving. The original became known as the single-lift jacquard as only one griffe was used. The mechanism used by Campbell was called the double-lift jacquard, as two griffes were employed, one beside the other. These were metal plates of special form, sometimes known as lifter-boards. They were drilled with keyhole-shaped perforations, the number in each being the same as that of the number of hooks available for patterning. The two griffes were placed in reversed positions so that the narrow part of the perforations of the front one faced those of the back one. The pulley cords from which the hooks were suspended passed through these holes, and each had a knot situated immediately above the face of the metal plates. This knot would slip easily through the larger part of the perforation, but would be engaged by the narrower tail. When not in operation the cords were positioned so that they passed through the narrower part of the front griffe and the knot was engaged, but through the larger part of the back griffe. Each needle controlled two pulley cords, one in the front griffe and the corresponding and matching one in the back griffe. When by the action of the needles pulley cords were moved into the larger part of the perforations of the front griffe, the corresponding cords in the back one were moved into the narrower part, and the knots in these became engaged. When the front griffe was raised, it lifted all the pulley cords that had remained static; when the back one was raised, it lifted all those that had been shifted. This use of two griffes simplified the weaving of doublecloth and related constructions. As will be explained later, it meant that each pattern card performed two functions, which with the single-lift jacquard would have required two cards.

This elaboration of the jacquard developed in the early nineteenth century, but the modification of the figure harness found in Campbell's loom may date back to at least the eighteenth century and have been used for weaving double-cloth type fabrics on the drawloom. It would have been suitable for weaving the German *Beiderwand* that will be mentioned later, or for the flat-woven carpeting known as kidderminster or scotch ingrain. The production of the latter appears to have commenced at Kilmarnock in southwest Scotland in the 1760s well before the date of Jacquard's invention. In this specialized figure harness, the comber board was no longer rigid, but divided into sections that could be raised and lowered to produce the ground weave. These replaced the shafts that had supplemented the classical figure harness, and combined their function with those of the comber board. Each section consisted of a sturdy length of hardwood drilled like the comber board; these were known as 'journals' in the United States and as 'working comber boards' in Great Britain. A necking cord with leash attached was suspended through each hole and held in position by a knot tied in it that rested on the upper surface of the working comber board.

In the jacquard mechanism, it is the pattern cards working in sequence on the cylinder that control the design being woven. These vary in size with the capacity of the attachment, but all are basically a long rectangle. Two sets of John Campbell's cards have survived. Both use the full capacity of which his jacquard was capable, or 272 hooks governing 272 warp decoupures for each repeat of the design. At each end, and at the centre, there are pairs of large holes used to lace the cards together. The perforations for the pattern are arranged in vertical rows of eight, eighteen of these on each side of the centre. In Campbell's patterns, the repeat in height is identical to the repeat in width, or 272 weft decoupures, each consisting of two picks of ground and two picks of figure for each gradation of the pattern in the weft. As each of the

pattern cards would control one pick of ground and one pick of figure, or technically one pass, 544 of them were required laced together in identical pairs. If Campbell had had a single-lift rather than a double-lift jacquard, 1088 pattern cards would have been needed.

Each set of cards was kept in a wooden box, open at the top, with a division down the centre. As they passed over the cylinder, they were drawn up from one side, and then dropped down into the other. Once the loom was set up with a long cotton warp of the type that Campbell used, it was a simple matter to change the design to be woven. It was merely a matter of changing the set of cards, by removing one box, and replacing it with the new pattern.

The type of double-lift jacquard mechanism that has been described was specifically developed for weaving double-cloth. This construction, as its name implies, is formed by two separate and independent layers of cloth, one above the other, that change position to form a pattern. In describing this weave as used for coverlets, it is easiest to consider the natural white cotton as the ground and the coloured wool layer as the figure. The warp is divided into two series, one for each layer, and each interwoven with its own weft. In the earlier doublecloth coverlets from the Niagara Peninsula, one warp series was cotton for the ground and the other was wool for the figure. In Campbell's coverlets, a variation is found, as both series were cotton – the ground interwoven with a cotton weft and the figure with a coloured wool weft. The warp was entered with the ends of the first series for the ground on the front two comber boards and those of the second series for the figure on the back two. The pulley cords controlling the ground series passed through the front griffe and those for the figure through the back one. When a pick of ground was to be inserted, all the ends of the second series that were to form the figure on the face of the coverlet were lifted by the action of the back griffe, while those that would interweave on the back of the coverlet remained down. One of the front two working comber boards was also raised by the action of the back griffe forming a shed, and a shuttle with cotton weft inserted with the flying shuttle to produce a shot of tabby for the ground. As this griffe returned to its normal position, all the ends of the first series that formed the ground appearing on the face, together with one of the back working comber boards, were lifted by the front griffe and the shuttle with the wool weft thrown by hand to produce a shot of tabby for the figure. It has already been mentioned that the pattern cards were laced together in identical pairs. The second card operated in the same way as the first. The pattern sheds were identical, but the complementary working comber boards were lifted by the griffes producing the opposite sheds necessary for the weft to interweave in tabby.

John Campbell's jacquard mechanism was manufactured by James Lightbody of Jersey City, New Jersey. There is no way of knowing whether it was the type generally employed by the professional coverlet weavers, but it may be safely assumed that it was used by a considerable number in view of its suitability for the purpose. It must be borne in mind that some of the earlier weavers may have had single-lift jacquards, but the necessary evidence is lost.

Two widths of loom with jacquard attachment were used in Ontario. The single-width was the older type and was used by all the weavers in the Niagara Peninsula, with the exception of Edward and Albert Graf after 1868. Outside this area, it was used by Aaron Zelner, the Nolls, and John Campbell. With this loom, both shuttles could be thrown by hand, but a flying shuttle was sometimes used for the ground weft. The coverlets were woven in two widths that had to be joined by a centre seam to make them wide enough for a bed. The double-width on which jacquard-woven coverlets could be made in one piece was first used by William Withers, or the damask weaver who probably lived in Whitby Township. It became the standard type about 1865–70 when the Grafs and the Waterloo County weavers obtained theirs from the United States. With this type, a flying shuttle combined with drop boxes made it possible to weave a shot of ground and a shot of figure alternately without the weaver handling either shuttle. The whole operation remained completely manual as it had been with the single-width looms.

There is a feeling among some that the use of the flying shuttle is not handweaving, but this is absurd and derives from an ignorance of its operation. When first invented by John Kay in 1733, it was activated entirely by handpower and was a manual operation like all the other actions involved in weaving. It was an unmechanized flying shuttle of this type that was steadily adopted by professional hand-weavers and that is still used by them today. The drop box enabling different shuttles to be used at the will of the weaver was also an early invention, by John Kay's son, Robert, in 1760. It was not until the 1790s with Edmund Cartwright's attempts to operate a loom by power that the action of the shuttle was first mechanized, and led to the perfection of power-operated looms suitable for factory use. All the jacquard-woven coverlets described here were woven entirely by hand.

It has already been mentioned that the potential of each jacquard mechanism is rigid. It cannot be increased, but designs not utilizing the full possibilities may be woven by not using some of the hooks. The maximum is generally expressed by the number of hooks available. Mechanisms of varying capacities were used by the professional weavers in Ontario, and a knowledge of these is valuable in differentiating their work. The most important that have been recorded are 240, 256, 272, 300, and 384 hooks. Although two jacquard heads may be mounted on the same loom, for instance one for the border and the other for the pattern, there is no evidence that this was ever done in Ontario in weaving the coverlets discussed here.

A jacquard attachment with a capacity of 240 hooks was used by Wilhelm Armbrust and by the unidentified weaver from Welland County, although Armbrust appears sometimes to have dropped as many as ten hooks, using as few as 230. The main difference in their designing is that Armbrust reserved 60 hooks for the border, while the other man reserved 75. The work of Moses Grobb also reserves this latter number for the border with an attachment of the same capacity.

In Waterloo County, Aaron Zelner and the Nolls both used a jacquard with 240 hooks, and reserved 80 hooks for the border leaving 160 for the pattern. Both used a warp decoupure of 2. This gives additional proof that John Noll apprenticed with Zelner and took over his equipment.

The early work ascribed to Edward Graf appears to have connections with the work of both Armbrust and the Welland County weaver. This group of coverlets is based on a jacquard of the same capacity as their work. No. 431, in the style of Armbrust, uses 60 hooks for the border; no. 442 is closer in style to the work of the Welland County weaver, although probably designed by Graf, and 75 hooks were used for the border. This coverlet supports the suggestion that Graf may have purchased Armbrust's equipment but apprenticed with the Welland County weaver. When Edward Graf and his son acquired their wide loom in 1868 the capacity changed; designs are based on 256 hooks using a warp decoupure of 1.

The jacquard used by John Campbell of Komoka had 272 hooks. Point paper plans have been taken off from the two sets of his pattern cards that are now at the Ontario Science Centre. One of these is shown as no. 483. The outer border required 40 hooks controlling two reversing comber units, the inner 72 for one straight comber unit, and the pattern proper 160, also designed for two reversing comber units. This produced the entire pattern in one width of the coverlet. The effect of the use of the reversing of the parts may be understood by comparing the point paper plan with the coverlet of different pattern shown in no. 481. Here, the same layout and proportions are seen as they appear when woven.

The unknown weaver of nos. 439 and 440 had a jacquard with 300-hook capacity. This would explain his use of a decoupure of 1, unusual in the comparatively narrow width. Others of the same capacity were used for the double-width coverlets with a warp decoupure of 4, and a weft decoupure of 2 passes. These were woven by Werlich and Ploethner of Preston and Knechtel of Roseville. In their work there is only one point repeat of the pattern in the full width. Their looms and equipment were obtained with patterns from the United States. This common denominator of 300 hooks, and the fact that all three used the same construction, presents a major difficulty in differentiating the output of these workshops.

Only one group of coverlets has been recorded that required a 384-hook jacquard. One of these is the pattern suitably called 'The Church' that seems definitely to have been the work of the Lipperts of Petersburg (no. 465). Nos. 466 and 467 have also been assigned to them because of the identical and unusual size of the jacquard attachment and the identical construction found in all three. The manner in which the upper and lower borders have been extended to increase the lengths of the coverlets is also a feature in common.

The capacity of the attachments used by other weavers is of less importance, as the stylistic characteristics of their work make attribution easy. This includes the work of such men as Withers, Armstrong, Hunter, and the damask weaver.

Except for those weavers who obtained their patterns already prepared from the United States, the jacquard weavers prepared their own designs and cut their own cards. In the early days, it must have been difficult to obtain an adequate supply of the right type of heavy paper or sturdy card that would stand up to the constant wear of the needles. Patterns would wear out quite rapidly in use if the material was too light, which accounts for the frequent variations and improvements in similar patterns woven by early weavers such as Armbrust and the man from Welland County. This earlier style of work embraces the coverlets where the date, often the name or initials of the person for whom the coverlet was woven, and sometimes the weaver's distinguishing mark are to be seen in the cartouche in the lower corners. Preparing the special cards for the cartouches for each order also involved cutting the pattern for the lower border of the coverlets. The customer could have selected the border desired to go with the pattern that had been chosen. The side borders were not optional, but incorporated in the cards for the field. To change them, the entire set of pattern cards had to be recut. This was, on occasion, done by the Nolls. In their work, the same pattern is found combined with different borders.

The normal weave for jacquard coverlets in Ontario is doublecloth, either free or tied. The basic construction has been described above in connection with the type of loom used by John Campbell. In the free type, the two layers of cloth lie independently one above the other, and in its basic form the material consists of two equally balanced fabrics, one of wool, the other of cotton. This form occurs in the earlier coverlets from the Niagara Peninsula, but was never used in Waterloo County. It is found in those made by Wilhelm Armbrust, the early unidentified weaver from Welland County, Moses Grobb, and the early work of Edward Graf. In the weaving of all these men, the proportion of the two warp series is always 1 : 1.

A variation of the basic type is found in southwestern Ontario in the coverlets of John Campbell and other weavers. One way in which their work differs is in the use of an all-cotton warp, in keeping with the practice of their times. The other variation is that a balanced doublecloth is not used, but rather one with a warp proportion of 2 : 1 between the series: this is quite satisfactory with the heavy wool weft used for the figures.

The term 'tied doublecloth' used here presents a problem in nomenclature. The result obtained by the weavers may more strictly be considered to be 'lampas,' a weave using two warps, a main one for the ground, and a binding one to tie the pattern weft of the figures. In the jacquard coverlets, the construction would appear to be derived from free doublecloth and is certainly related to it. For this reason, the term 'tied doublecloth' is used. Its origin in North America remains uncertain, but may well be connected with the German *Beiderwand* known from bed furnishings in Schleswig-Holstein and from women's skirts in Mecklenburg. In its classic form, this is a tied doublecloth with free ground and a proportion of 4 : 1.

Different types of tied doublecloth are found used in coverlets made in Ontario. The variations are dependent on the proportion of the warp series (2 : 1 or 4 : 1), and whether the two layers are entirely bound together in the course of weaving, or whether only the figure is treated in this way and

the ground left free. These choices of proportion, and in tying or not tying the ground as well as the figure, result in four different constructions. Once a weaver had decided which of these he would use, it was difficult to change, and it becomes an identifying characteristic of the individual's work. The only man who may have used two is Edward Graf. The coverlets of the 1850s assigned to him, not of free doublecloth, are completely tied with a proportion of 4 : 1. No. 443 dated 1861 is also probably his work, and this, like the coverlets definitely woven by him after he acquired his wide loom in 1868, shows a proportion of 2 : 1 with the figure tied but the ground free.

A proportion of 4 : 1 completely tied is first found in the work of the unidentified weaver in Welland County as early as 1835, of Wilhelm Armbrust from about 1840 on, of the two anonymous weavers around the middle of the nineteenth century who may have trained in Welland County, and in early work of Edward Graf. The appearance of this construction among this group of men, all of whom worked in the Niagara Peninsula, may have a common source, possibly the unidentified weaver from Welland County. It seems probable that he was German, but if more were known of his origins and history, the source of this weave in Ontario might be established. Outside this area, it is only found in the work of one man : Christopher Armstrong of Stouffville, who worked independently at a later date, but who may well have seen examples of older coverlets woven in the Niagara Peninsula and changed to this construction from that used by William Withers, his predecessor.

The other three tied doublecloth constructions are found only in coverlets dating from after the middle of the nineteenth century. A proportion of 2 : 1 with the ground in free doublecloth is characteristic of the work of Edward and Albert Graf after 1868 when they acquired their wide loom, but may have been used as early as 1861 by Edward Graf, as mentioned above. This proportion also occurs in some of the later work of Moses Grobb, in the work of the Lipperts of Petersburg (nos. 465–7), and independently in coverlets woven by William Withers of Stouffville.

Both Aaron Zelner and the Noll brothers used a fully tied doublecloth with a proportion of 2 : 1 ; it is also found in no. 490, which may be the work of a weaver in the Neustadt-Hanover district, an area settled from Waterloo County. This construction produced the firmest and most durable of the tied fabrics.

The use of a proportion of 4 : 1 with free doublecloth ground and a warp decoupure of 4 is characteristic of the bulk of the coverlets woven in Waterloo County after 1870. It is found in the work of Wilhelm Magnus Werlich and August Ploethner of Preston and of Daniel Knechtel of Roseville. Coverlets of this type were woven with looms, equipment, and patterns purchased in the United States. There is no doubt that the use of this construction in Ontario is of American origin, but its introduction into the United States remains to be discovered. Of all the tied doublecloth constructions, it is the closest parallel to the classic *Beiderwand*, which uses a warp decoupure of 1.

Only one other weave is found in the jacquard coverlets

woven in Ontario, and this is the 5-end damask with a warp decoupure of 2 that occurs in nos. 484–9. They are the work of one man who arrived in this country fully trained as a linen-damask weaver, probably from Northern Ireland, but perhaps from Scotland, possibly Dunfermline. If, as has been suggested, John Gibson of Whitby Township proves to have woven them, the former country is the origin of the use of this weave in Ontario.

Many of the experienced weavers who came to Canada had been trained to weave materials for which there was a very limited demand and for which suitable yarns were not available in this country. It was necessary for them to apply their knowledge to satisfy the demands of their immediate market. This is known to have been true of Wilhelm Magnus Werlich from the pattern book that he brought with him with swatches in it of very fine cotton material in twill or damask diaper. Before Werlich acquired a loom with jacquard attachment, he adapted his skills to the weaving of coarser materials. This adaptation appears to be equally true of the weaver of the damask coverlets.

The earlier style of coverlets from the Niagara Peninsula with the date, and often name or initials, were woven on special order one or two at a time. As the customer prepared and supplied both the woollen and cotton yarns, a new warp had to be stretched and mounted on the loom for each order. If the weave was the same as that of the coverlet that had just been taken off the loom, the warp did not have to be entered again, but merely tied on to the ends of the old one. This was a much quicker and easier method than a complete threading of the figure harness. If there was a change in construction to a different weave, there was no choice and the whole loom had to be re-entered. As in the overshot coverlets, the cotton for these jacquards was obtained at the local general store as skeins of singles and plied by hand by the customer to produce the grist specified by the weaver and to match that of the handspun woollen yarn. The weight of the cotton varies and may be either 2- or 3-ply. In the free doublecloth coverlets, the use of a commercially plied cotton occurs only in a very few late ones woven by Moses Grobb. The use of wool in the warp is only found in coverlets woven in the Niagara Peninsula, and is unkown from other parts of the province except in some carpets.

The dating of old material is always a matter of interest and the jacquard-woven coverlets are no exception. They fall into two groups: those with dates woven in that present no problem and those without dates. For the latter, an awareness of the weaving width, and a recognition of the constructions that have been described is of great help, as they have definite periods of use. A knowledge of the easily recognized styles of a number of the weavers serves a similar purpose. Indigo blue, and much less often madder and rarely cochineal red, are the colours found in the earlier coverlets. The former remained a favourite long after the introduction of non-vegetable dyes. Coverlets woven with a range of strong vibrant colours, even if they have faded, may be securely dated to the latter part of the nineteenth century or early in the present one.

Even during the period of semi-mass production and right up to the end of the handweaving of jacquard coverlets in Ontario, the wool pattern weft used on the long all-cotton warps was often handspun and dyed by the customer and brought to the weaver for her coverlet. These were special orders, but the bulk of the work during the late period was for general sale. For this the weavers obtained supplies of prepared and dyed yarn from the local mills that had grown up.

During the last third of the nineteenth and the early part of the twentieth centuries, a new type of cotton yarn appears in the jacquard coverlets, steadily replacing the older type that had been plied by hand. This is a fine 2-ply yarn probably imported from Great Britain, rather than from New England or the Mohawk Valley in New York State. On the other hand, some may perhaps have been produced in Canada. The first cotton mill in the country was established by Wills and Company in Sherbrooke, Quebec, in 1845, followed by one in Thorold, Ontario, in 1847. The latter of these appears to have had financial difficulties for some years. In the census of 1861, another cotton mill is listed at Hillsburgh in Wellington County, but nothing more is known about it. This fine cotton was used double as in some of the eight-shaft overshot, 'star and diamond,' and point-twill coverlets, but is always triple in the jacquard-woven ones assigned to the Lipperts of Petersburg.

The yarn used for the second warp series in the tied doublecloth constructions deserves special mention, and is always specified in the technical notes accompanying the descriptions that follow. It is these threads that interweave with the woollen weft to form the figures and that are used to tie the two layers of cloth together. In the older coverlets from the Niagara Peninsula, this is always of the same type that is used for the first series. In those woven after the middle of the nineteenth century, particularly by the Grafs and the majority of weavers in Waterloo County and its area of influence, it is more usually a fine cotton singles yarn that is quite unnoticeable. It is sometimes natural white, often dyed blue, and occasionally another colour. This use of different yarns for the two series is another connection with the German *Beiderwand*. Here too, the same contrast of colours and a similar balance between the two warp series are usually found.

The practice of the customer supplying the yarns for jacquard coverlets, as well as for those of other types, has given rise to one of the most persistent fables connected with weaving of this kind. The fact that the person whose name or initials occur in the corner cartouches spun and dyed the yarns, becomes altered to the statement that she made them, therefore made the coverlet, and therefore was the weaver. Nothing could be less true, and the fact that a number of these women did have a loom and could weave simple materials for daily use does not alter the facts. From the description of the loom with jacquard attachment, it will be realized that this was never household equipment. The sheer size and expense would have prevented this, let alone the specialized knowledge and physical strength required to set it up and operate it. Every jacquard coverlet woven in Ontario was the work of one of the few competent and trained professionals who gained their livelihood in this way.

425 / Ontario. Near Jordan, Louth Township,
Lincoln County. Dated 1834
ROM L953.8.2. Lent by Miss Florence Lyons
Jacquard coverlet. L. 191cm, plus fringe; w. 181cm

Doublecloth: indigo blue wool and natural white cotton
(decoupure 2). This was woven for Nancy Binkley of Dundas
by Wilhelm Armbrust. He was born in Germany, came to
North America as a young man, and settled near Jordan in
the Niagara Peninsula in 1830, where he married at the age
of 23. He was the first weaver to have a jacquard mechanism
in this country and it is quite possible that he built both it and
the loom himself. In 1834, he advertised in a St Catharines
paper that he was prepared to weave 'Fancy Coverlets on the
New Improved Loom.' This coverlet is probably one of the
first that he wove; none with an earlier date has been found
in Canada. He continued weaving until 1848 and afterwards
moved to Ridgeville, becoming a full-time farmer. He died
there in 1904 at the age of 97. Although his period of activity
as a weaver was only about fourteen years, judging from the
number of his coverlets that have survived his output must
have been large.

'Four Roses' was the most popular of all jacquard patterns
in Ontario and was also known in the United States. Armbrust's coverlets in this design were always for a bride's
trousseau and were usually the standard indigo blue wool and
white cotton. A few that he wove have been recorded that are
all wool, strikingly patterned in red and blue. The lower
border of this coverlet is one that occurs in other examples of
his work, but the side borders with the curious checkerboard
trees are unique and reminiscent of the geometrically patterned coverlets.

The fairly limited range of motifs found in these coverlets –
roses, stars, hearts, flowering trees, and sometimes carnations
– are often considered to be symbolic of a happy marriage.
This interpretation appears to stem from later nineteenth-
century romanticism, and no specific meaning may now be
drawn from them. All are part of the general repertory of
northern European folk art, and are found on ceramics,
painted chests and furniture, small wood artifacts for everyday use, and in printed and manuscript *fraktur* documents.
They are well known from Pennsylvania (Lichten), and
from Switzerland, the original home of the older Mennonite
communities in North America (cf. Rubi, Wyss). Similar
motifs are found in the show towels (nos. 162, 163) and in
German embroideries (cf. Meyer-Heiseg).

426 / Ontario. Near Jordan, Louth Township,
Lincoln County. Dated 1842
ROM 965.190.3. Gift of Miss Adelaide Lash Miller
Jacquard coverlet. L. 212cm, plus fringe; w. 184cm

Doublecloth: indigo blue wool on natural white cotton (decoupure 2). This is one of a pair woven by Wilhelm Armbrust for William and Ann Miller of Niagara-on-the-Lake,
whose initials appear in the corner with the year of their
marriage, 1842. Both show two hearts suspended from a
balance, the device used by Armbrust to mark his bridal
coverlets after about 1838. Modification in the motifs of his
patterns occur frequently, undoubtedly due to the fact that
his jacquard cards wore out and new ones had to be cut.

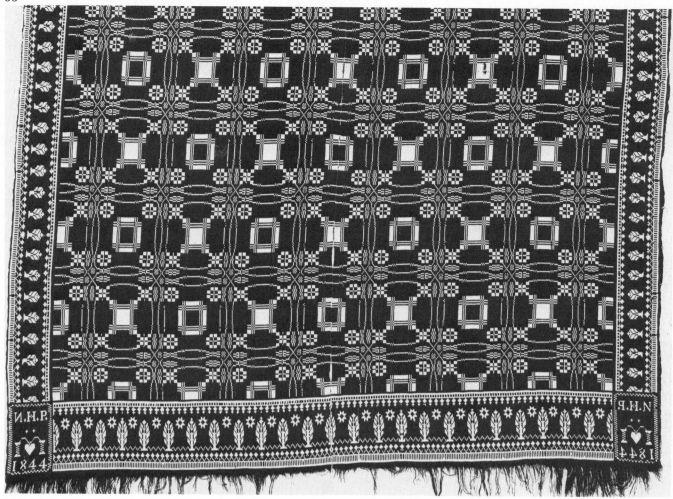

427 / Ontario. Near Jordan, Louth Township,
Lincoln County. Dated 1844
ROM 967.277
Jacquard coverlet. L. 216cm, plus fringe; w. 196cm

Doublecloth: indigo blue wool and natural white cotton (de-coupure 2). This is one of two coverlets woven by Armbrust for boys in the Pawling family, his near neighbours in the Jordan area. Both have main patterns derived from geometric designs suitable for sixteen-shaft looms. This design is almost the same as one woven by Samuel Fry (no. 414). The probable explanation is that the Pawlings had conservative tastes and desired the traditional type rather than the freer floral patterns that could be woven on 'the New Improved Loom.' In the lower corners is another device used by Armbrust to distinguish his work: a heart suspended between two pillars. From the late 1830s on, it is found on all his coverlets except those with four roses, which are always for trousseaus. The simple borders of repeating trees are found on other examples of Armbrust's work.

428 / Ontario. Near Jordan, Louth Township,
Lincoln County. Dated 1847
ROM 968.117.1
Jacquard coverlet. L. 216cm; w. 186cm

Doublecloth: indigo blue wool on natural white cotton (decoupure 2). A late example of Armbrust's work made for
'J.M.F.' The borders and cartouches are similar to the previous coverlet, but the pattern is most unusual. The pairs of
Chinese-style vases with sprays of flowers are quite foreign to
the normal style of jacquard coverlets woven in North
America. Armbrust prepared his own patterns and cut his
own cards, experimenting quite freely with any inspiration
that came his way. Another contemporary coverlet of the
same pattern is in the Lundy's Lane Museum, Niagara Falls.

429 / Ontario. Near Jordan, Louth Township,
Lincoln County. Dated 1840
NGC 9628
Jacquard coverlet. L. 218cm, plus fringe; w. 174cm

Tied doublecloth (proportion 4:1) with free areas: indigo
blue wool with natural white cotton on natural white cotton
(decoupure 2). The cartouche bears Armbrust's device of a
single heart between two pillars, and the initials 'A.J.S.' (possibly Simmerman). The borders are a variant of those on
nos. 425 and 426. The main pattern is unique, employing
the elements found in 'star and diamond' coverlets combined
with suspended hearts and smaller versions of the stylized
trees found in some of Armbrust's borders.

430 / Ontario. Near Jordan, Louth Township,
Lincoln County. Dated 1848
ROM 963.125. Gift of Mrs C. Macdonald Munns
Jarquard coverlet. L. 224cm, plus fringe; w. 159cm

Tied doublecloth (proportion 4:1): indigo blue wool with
natural white cotton on natural white cotton (decoupure 2).
Woven by Wilhelm Armbrust and bearing his device of a
heart suspended between two pillars below the initials 'E.F.'
When this coverlet was first recorded by the museum, the date
'1848' could still be deciphered. This is an excellent example
of a design typical of Armbrust's work. It occurs in a number
of variants woven throughout his career. All have a lattice
reminiscent of 'star and diamond' patterns combined with
small birds and hearts.

431 / Ontario. Probably Welland County. Dated 1850
The Stone Shop Museum, Grimsby, Ontario. L85
Jacquard coverlet. L. 212cm, plus fringe; w. 197cm

Doublecloth: indigo blue wool and natural white cotton
(decoupure 2). This was woven for Mary Grabiel of Wain-
fleet Township. The pattern is similar to some of Armbrust's,
but the coverlet is dated two years after he ceased weaving.
The usual device identifying his work has been replaced by
two stars, known from other coverlets of this date and slightly
later, all of which have been found in Welland County. It
appears to be the work of the weaver who purchased Armbrust's equipment and patterns, probably Edward Graf,
whose work will be illustrated later (nos. 447–52).

432 / Ontario. Probably Welland County. Dated 1837
UCV 60.H.6355
Jacquard coverlet. L. 216cm, plus added fringe; w. 199cm,
plus added fringes

Doublecloth: indigo blue and rust-red wool and natural
white cotton (decoupure 2). The pattern of four lily-like
flowers was second in popularity to the 'Four Roses.' This
example is unusual and very striking with its large check of
coloured wools. The weaver is not yet known, but he appears
to have been active from 1835 until after 1850 in Welland
County. A number of examples of his work have been recorded. His characteristic device is a heart lying on its side,
often showing clearly in the cartouche, but sometimes almost
hidden in the design of the central field as here. Like Armbrust, he was probably a German immigrant who arrived in
this country fully trained.

433 / Ontario. Probably Welland County. Dated 1841
ROM 967.305.1. Gift of Mr and Mrs Hugh Flatt
Jacquard coverlet. L. 222cm, plus fringe; w. 197cm

Doublecloth: indigo blue wool and natural white cotton (decoupure 2). This coverlet was also made by the weaver who
marked his work with a heart lying on its side. Here it is accompanied by a small star, and shows boldly in the cartouche
with the name 'MARY A. HORNING.' Borders with birds and
shrubs or flowering bushes were very popular. The birds are
often referred to as crows, but they are the *Distelfink* (thistle
finch) that is a popular motif in Swiss folk art, and frequently
found in Mennonite work in this country.

434 / Ontario. Probably Welland County. Dated 1838
Jordan Historical Museum of the Twenty, Jordan, Ontario.
L330
Jacquard coverlet. L. 223cm, plus fringe; w. 172cm

Tied doublecloth (proportion 4:1) : indigo blue wool with
natural white cotton on natural white cotton (decoupure 2).
This is the work of the same weaver, incorporating his heart
device in the design. The small star is in the cartouche with
the name 'SARAH MICHNER.' The main motif combines the
stars and branching leaves of many jacquard designs with a
'snowball' motif lifted from a typical geometric pattern.

435 / Ontario. Probably Welland County. Dated 1838
ROM 968.96
Jacquard coverlet. L. 217cm, plus fringe; w. 185cm

Tied doublecloth (proportion 4:1) : indigo blue wool with
natural white cotton on natural white cotton (decoupure 2).
Although this coverlet does not show the heart device, it is
undoubtedly the work of the same man. The small star in the
cartouche is identical to that in previous coverlets and the
digits of the date are in the same script. The quatrefoil centre
of the main motif matches that in no. 434, which has
identical borders.

436 / Ontario. Probably Welland County. Dated 1842
ROM 971.168. Gift of Mrs Joshua Dewitt Smith
Jacquard coverlet. L. 210cm, plus fringe; w. 194cm

Doublecloth: indigo blue wool and natural white cotton (de-coupure 2). This is ascribed to the weaver who used a lateral heart as his mark. Both the border and pattern are similar to those used by him, but the characteristic device has been abandoned and the date is now within a frame open at the bottom. Letters in the names and numerals in the dates of this and other coverlets of identical pattern strongly resemble those in the earlier work (nos. 432–5). The pattern is the most usual version of the 'Four Lilies' design and the borders are the often recurring birds and bushes.

437 / Ontario. Probably Welland County. Dated 1845
ROM 966.193.1. Gift of Mrs Van H. Smith
Jacquard coverlet. L. 220cm, plus fringe; w. 192cm

Doublecloth: indigo blue wool and natural white cotton (decoupure 2). The original owner of this coverlet, 'F.C.,' has not been identified but may have been a member of the Cline family. The lower border is identical to that on no. 436, and the date 1845 with similar numerals is also enclosed in a box open at the bottom. It is certainly the work of the same weaver but the pattern is rather unusual.

438 / Ontario. Probably Welland County. Dated 1856
ROM 965.24
Jacquard coverlet. L. 218cm, plus fringe; w. 189cm

Doublecloth: indigo blue wool and natural white cotton (decoupure 2). This is the work of the same man, the borders being identical to those on no. 437. It was collected near Freelton north of Hamilton, but the family of 'SARAH CARPENTER' for whom it was woven were among the early settlers in Lincoln County. Two contemporary coverlets in the Jordan Historical Museum of the Twenty show the same unusual pattern of a highly stylized flowering tree.

439 / Ontario. Probably Welland County. Dated 1852
ROM 966.25
Jacquard coverlet. L. 208cm, plus fringes; w. 172cm

Tied doublecloth (proportion 4 : 1) : indigo blue wool with natural white cotton on natural white cotton (decoupure 1). This is the work of a jacquard weaver who was active only during the early 1850s. His work can be identified by a device of a diamond with flaring tail found in the cartouche, always small and only in one corner. This coverlet made for 'S.A.N.' is another version of four roses with birds and shrub borders. The softer outlines are due to the warp threads having been controlled singly rather than in pairs by the jacquard mechanism : a warp decoupure of 1, rather than of 2.

440 / Ontario. Probably Welland County. Dated 1852
ROM 969.71
Jacquard coverlet. L. 203cm, plus fringe; w. 172cm

Tied doublecloth (proportion 4 : 1) : indigo blue wool with natural white cotton on natural white cotton (decoupure 1). This was woven for 'S.A.N.' in the same year as no. 439; the pattern is more unusual, but was also used by Edward Graf. The same device is in the cartouche and the warp decoupure of 1 proves that it is the same weaver.

441 / Ontario. Lincoln or Welland County. Dated 1849
BCPV 61.441
Jacquard coverlet. L. 229cm, plus fringe; w. 180cm

Tied doublecloth (proportion 4 : 1) : indigo blue wool with
natural white cotton on natural white cotton (decoupure 2).
Despite the similarity of this pattern to the previous one it has
the more usual decoupure of 2, and is the work of a weaver
other than the one who wove nos. 439–40. It was woven for
'SARAH FARR.' The unusual border is also found on coverlets
patterned with four roses and other designs that date from
the early 1850s. Examples are in the Jordan Historical Museum of the Twenty.

442 / Ontario. Welland County. Dated 1851
ROM 969.318
Jacquard coverlet. L. 239cm, plus fringe; w. 185cm

Tied doublecloth (proportion 4:1): medium indigo blue
wool with natural white cotton on natural white cotton (decoupure 2). This is another version of two popular patterns:
'Four Lilies,' and bird and shrub borders. The name
'CATHERINE F. GEROLD' and the date are framed in both
lower corners above a device of a heart between two stars.
Other contemporary coverlets are known with the two stars
without the small heart as in no. 431, and the latter motif
may denote a bridal coverlet. The earliest of this group with

stars and heart device is dated 1848, the year that Wilhelm
Armbrust ceased weaving. Graf, whose later work is firmly
identified, would have been in his early twenties at this time
and a fully trained weaver. The coverlets with these devices
have been accredited to him. He had come from Germany
with his father some years before. There is no proof, but he
possibly apprenticed with the weaver of nos. 432–8. It is
more than likely that he purchased Armbrust's equipment
and continued to use it until 1868, when he acquired a wide
jacquard loom (cf. nos. 447–52). This theory is supported
by the similarities of the pattern of no. 431 with Armbrust's
work and similarities between this one and nos. 432–8.

443 / Ontario. Welland County. Dated 1861
ROM 959.57.1. Gift of Mrs W.E.P. De Roche
Jacquard coverlet. L. 209cm, plus fringe; w. 167cm,
plus fringes

Tied doublecloth (proportion 2 : 1) with free areas: indigo
blue and red wool with pale blue cotton on natural white
cotton (decoupure 2). This was woven for 'DINAH SAUER' of
Willoughby Township. It may also be attributed to Edward
Graf's early period. The construction is the same as later
documented examples of his work except for a difference in
decoupure. There seems little doubt that Graf, like Armbrust,
drew his own patterns; this would account for the elaborations of familiar themes that are found in his work.

(*in colour* PLATE IV)

444 / Ontario. Near Vineland, Clinton Township,
Lincoln County. Dated 1853
ROM 967.168.1. Gift of the Misses Hattie I. and
Charlotte Jones
Jacquard coverlet. L. 215cm, plus fringe; w. 178cm

Doublecloth: indigo blue wool and natural white cotton (decoupure 2). This was woven for the dower of Catherine Gage
Pettit (Mrs W.I. Jones). At the time she was only fourteen,
but it was customary for girls to be well supplied with bedding and linens long before their marriage. As was usual,
this coverlet would have been her best one, supplemented by
overshot coverlets and pieced quilts for everyday use. It is the
work of Moses Grobb, a connection of Samuel Fry and also
a member of the Mennonite community in the Vineland
area. Both men were basically farmers, weaving in the off
seasons. Grobb himself wove and is thought to have had other
weavers working for him on occasion. His jacquard coverlets
were always dated, the earliest being 1853 and the latest in
the 1870s.   (*in colour* PLATE IV)

445 / Ontario. Near Vineland, Clinton Township,
Lincoln County. Dated 1869
ROM L965.11.23. The Annie R. Fry Collection
Jacquard coverlet. L. 217cm, plus fringe; w. 196cm

Doublecloth: very dark indigo blue wool and natural white
cotton (decoupure 2). This was made by Moses Grobb for
his daughter 'SARAH CATHARINE GROBB,' who married into
the Fry family. Possibly, as in Armbrust's work, the use of
the 'Four Roses' pattern indicates a bridal coverlet. The
scrolling floral borders, the key fret above the date, and the
meander guard across the lower edge are all characteristic of
Grobb's work.

446 / Ontario. Near Vineland, Clinton Township,
Lincoln County. Dated 1873
ROM 969.220.1
Jacquard coverlet. L. 229cm, plus fringe; w. 193cm

Tied doublecloth (proportion 2:1) with free areas: indigo
blue and bright red wool with natural white cotton on natural
white cotton (decoupure 2). This pattern of flower baskets is
known to be by Moses Grobb and shows another version of
his flowing floral borders. Another of the same design
woven for Sarah Catharine Grobb mentioned above still belongs to her descendants. The one shown here was made for
'ALEXANDER COON' in 1873 and is the latest recorded example
of Grobb's work.

447 / Ontario. Gasline, Humberstone Township,
Welland County. 1868-75
ROM 969.13.1
Jacquard coverlet. L. 212cm, plus fringe; w. 190cm,
plus fringes

Tied doublecloth (proportion 2:1) with free areas: indigo
blue wool with pale blue cotton on natural white cotton (decoupure 1). This 'Double Rose Single Flower' is an example
of the work of Edward Graf woven double-width on the wide
loom he acquired in 1868. His earlier work is not documented, but nos. 431, 442, and 443 have been assigned to
him. This is probably one of the first patterns woven on his
new loom, as is an elaborate version of 'Bird of Paradise'.
Both were produced in limited quantity. Almost all his wide
coverlets have the pattern name, rather than the owner's, in
the corner cartouches.

448 / Ontario. Gasline, Humberstone Township, Welland County. About 1870
ROM 968.242
Jacquard coverlet. L. 210cm, plus fringe; w. 190cm, plus fringes

Tied doublecloth (proportion 2:1) with free areas: rose-red, indigo blue, and deep ochre wool with pale blue cotton on natural white cotton (decoupure 1). Although this lacks a pattern name, it has the same construction as documented examples of Edward Graf's work and the rich colour scheme is known from other coverlets woven by him about 1870. The border with the fancy butterflies fitted into scrolls is new and different, without connection with earlier styles.

449 / Ontario. Gasline, Humberstone Township, Welland County. 1875-85
ROM 967.254. Gift of Mrs G.A. Kennedy
Jacquard coverlet. L. 204cm, plus fringe; w. 198cm, plus fringes

Tied doublecloth (proportion 2:1) with free areas: red and green wool with pale blue cotton on natural white cotton (decoupure 1). The bands of colour are placed so that red roses are among green leaves. This 'Double Rose' was one of Edward Graf's most popular designs and replaced that of no. 448. The name of the pattern in the corners facing four different ways is typical of most of his work. It is possible that there was a demand, even at this late date, for the old-fashioned 'Four Roses' as bridal coverlets.

450 / Ontario. Gasline, Humberstone Township, Welland County. About 1875
ROM 950.93.3. Gift of Mrs Verna Hall
Jacquard coverlet. L. 226cm, plus fringe; w. 187cm, plus added fringes

Tied doublecloth (proportion 2 : 1) with free areas: pink-red wool with medium blue cotton on natural white cotton (de-coupure 1). 'Bird's Nest' is another of Edward Graf's popular coverlets. He undoubtedly drew his own patterns, utilizing older motifs with new ones, combining them so that each design was fresh and would appeal to an ever wider clientele. Here he has taken the traditional rose motif, the frame of scrolling leaves in no. 447, and added the bird with her nest of young to fit the taste of the time.

451 / Ontario. Gasline, Humberstone Township,
Welland County. 1875-1900
ROM 968.88
Jacquard coverlet. L. 212cm, plus fringe; w. 187cm,
plus fringes

Tied doublecloth (proportion 2:1) with free areas: deep
pink wool with pale blue cotton on natural white cotton (decoupure 1). This 'Bird of Paradise' design must have been
produced by the Grafs in considerable quantity: many have
survived. Another early version, closer in style to no. 447, is
much rarer, and may well have been more expensive. The
'Bird of Paradise' motif was popular in the United States
around the middle of the nineteenth century. Graf may easily
have drawn his inspiration from an American coverlet, but
has made the design his own. An example with the same pattern as this one is in the Eva Brook Donelly Museum in
Simcoe, Ontario. It has the date '1871' and the initials
'F.A.B.,' for Frances A. Bowlby, embroidered in cross stitch
along the upper edge.

452 / Ontario. Gasline, Humberstone Township,
Welland County. 1885-1900
ROM 964.113. Gift of Mrs D.J. Macdonald
Jacquard coverlet. L. 209cm, plus fringe; w. 202cm,
plus fringes

Tied doublecloth (proportion 2:1) with free areas: deep
raspberry red wool with medium blue cotton on natural white
cotton (decoupure 1). 'Morning Glory,' another of Graf's
designs, belongs to a group that includes 'Flower Pot' and
'Cherubim,' which are not illustrated. They are somewhat
later in date than those just described. Although the Grafs
continued to weave these wide coverlets from 1868 until
1918, the details of their patterns vary much less than do
those of the earlier weavers. Their cards would have been of
more durable material, and the complexity of the designs
allowed for little variation when a new set had to be cut.

453 / Ontario. Possibly Peel or York Counties. 1840-60
ROM 961.96. Gift of Miss Evelyn G. Follett
Jacquard coverlet. L. 215cm, plus fringe; w. 168cm

Doublecloth: indigo blue wool and natural white cotton (decoupure 1). This coverlet and the following one, although
different in style, must be the work of the same weaver, as yet
unidentified. Both have the strange mark of four hands, each

with a heart on the palm, in the lower corners; both have a
warp decoupure of 1, rather than the usual 2. The layout of
the pattern is derived from a simpler geometric design re-
sembling that of no. 414. The borrowing from such a source
is easily recognized in no. 427, but here the elaboration of
detail almost hides the original source. It came from a family
connected with Mono in Peel County.

454 / Ontario. Possibly Peel or York Counties. 1840-60
ROM 966.178. Gift of Mr Thomas E. Fox
Jacquard coverlet. L. 198cm, plus fringe; w. 159cm

Doublecloth: indigo blue wool and natural white cotton (decoupure 1). The history that came with this coverlet was
that it had been brought to Canada from Scotland about
1820. It is certainly later than this and must have been
acquired in this country. Fragments of identical coverlets
with an Ontario history have been seen. The mark in the
lower corners of four hands is the device of the weaver of the
previous coverlet. The layout of the pattern is excellent, and
with a warp decoupure of 1 the drawing of the details is
precise and effective.

455 / Ontario. Possibly Peel or York Counties. 1840-60
ROM 968.146
Jacquard coverlet. L. 221cm; w. 206cm

Doublecloth: indigo blue wool on natural white cotton (decoupure 1). This coverlet has a warp decoupure of 1 like the
previous two and may well be the work of the same weaver.
A pair of coverlets with the same strange design belongs to a
family that used to live in Chinguacousy Township, Peel
County. This pattern again shows the influence of shaft-loom
patterns. The nine 'snowballs' clearly show the source of
inspiration.

456 / Ontario. South Cayuga Township,
Haldimand County. Dated 1850
ROM 966.78. Gift of Mr and Mrs Kurt Sorensen
Jacquard coverlet. L. 185cm, plus added fringe;
w. 178cm, plus fringes

Tied doublecloth (proportion 2:1): red and indigo blue wool with pale blue cotton on natural white cotton (decoupure 2). The cartouche leaves no doubt as to who wove this, where, when, and for whom: 'MADE BY AᴺZELNER Sᴴ CAYUGA TOWNSHIP FOR ROSINA REICHELT 1850.' Aaron Zelner came to Canada about 1845 and first lived in South Cayuga Township. This is the only recorded example of his work in Ontario woven before he moved to Waterloo County about ten years later.

457 / Ontario. Waterloo Township, Waterloo County.
Dated 1858
Doon Pioneer Village, Kitchener, Ontario. 10
Jacquard coverlet. L. 184cm; w. 181cm

Tied doublecloth (proportion 2:1): indigo blue wool with natural white cotton on natural white cotton (decoupure 2). This was woven after Zelner moved to Waterloo County. The cartouche reads: 'MADE BY AᴺZELNER WATERLOO TOWNSHIP FOR MARY GROFF 1858.' Two years earlier Zelner had woven a coverlet here for another member of the same family. The designs of both are identical to no. 456, but in those woven for the Groffs different weights of yarn have produced a better balanced pattern. As with many jacquard coverlets, these are equally good from both sides. In the illustrations, no. 456 is shown with the pattern reserved on the dark ground and this one is shown from the other side. Zelner appears to have ceased weaving by 1868.

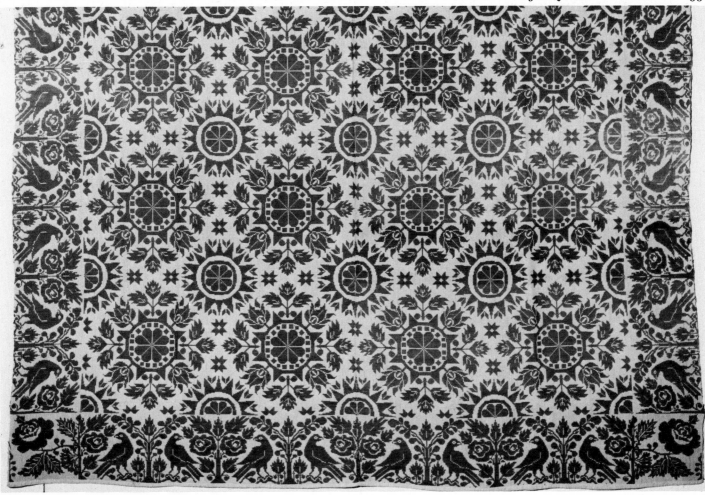

458 / Ontario. Petersburg, Waterloo County. About 1880
Doon Pioneer Village. Kitchener, Ontario. B.69.S.
Gift of the Brandt family
Jacquard coverlet. L. 219cm; w. 189cm

Tied doublecloth (proportion 2 : 1) : bright red wool with
natural white cotton on natural white cotton ground (decoupure 2). This was woven for Peter Wilker of Petersburg
about 1880 by the Noll brothers. The pattern is identical to
that of Zelner just described, but the border is the 'bird and
bush' familiar from the coverlets of the Niagara Peninsula. It
is believed that John Noll apprenticed with Aaron Zelner,
and took over his equipment and patterns about 1868.

459 / Ontario. Petersburg, Waterloo County. Dated 1868
Doon Pioneer Village, Kitchener, Ontario
Jacquard coverlet. L. 218cm, plus added fringe;
w. 193cm, plus added fringes

Tied doublecloth (proportion 2 : 1) : indigo blue, green, and
red wool with natural white cotton on natural white cotton
(decoupure 2). The cartouche of this coverlet reads 'MADE BY
J. NOLL AND BROTHERS FOR MARY DEICHERT 1868.' This
must be one of the first coverlets they wove. John Noll was
seventeen and his older brother William was nineteen. The
pattern is a version of the familiar 'Four Roses' with customary border. It is probably another of Zelner's patterns.

460 / Ontario. Petersburg, Waterloo County. Dated 1872
ROM 965.224.1
Jacquard coverlet. L. 208cm, plus added fringe;
w. 181cm, plus fringes

Tied doublecloth (proportion 2 : 1) : bright red wool with
natural white cotton on natural white cotton (decoupure 2).
This was 'MADE BY WILLIAM AND JOHN NOLL FOR MARIA
BAUER 1872.' Another coverlet of the same pattern has a bird
and bush border (ROM 968.63). In addition to the patterns
acquired from Zelner, the Nolls prepared new designs. This
is a comparatively simple but very effective one and is
probably among their first efforts. The unusual border may
have been adapted from a contemporary china pattern.

461 / Ontario. Petersburg, Waterloo County. 1870-5
ROM 968.86
Jacquard coverlet (half). L. 213cm, plus added fringe;
w. 88cm, plus fringe

Tied doublecloth (proportion 2 : 1) : red and dark indigo
blue wool with natural white cotton on natural white cotton.

The border and the garland of roses in the corner prove that
this was woven by the Nolls. Probably their name and the
date of weaving were on the corner of the other half of the
coverlet. The Nolls wove quite a range of designs of strong
originality and many with elements in common. Their earliest
patterns were taken over from Zelner, but as they matured
their own style emerged.

462 / Ontario. Petersburg, Waterloo County. 1880-90
Lundy's Lane Historical Museum, Niagara Falls, Ontario.
4.3/H250. Gift of Mr S.C. Jackson
Jacquard coverlet. L. 207cm, plus added fringe;
w. 182cm, plus fringes

Tied doublecloth (proportion 2 : 1) : red wool with natural
white cotton on natural white cotton (decoupure 2). This
coverlet may also be ascribed to the Noll brothers. The construction is the one used by them. The garland of roses in the
corners and this version of the 'bird and bush' border are
familiar from a number of examples of their work. The pattern appears to be a composite using disparate elements from
various sources.

463 / Ontario. Petersburg, Waterloo County. 1885-90
ROM 965.66. Gift of Mrs G.T. Cooke
Jacquard coverlet. L. 205cm, plus added fringe;
w. 185cm, plus fringes

Tied doublecloth (proportion 2 : 1) : red wool with natural
white cotton on natural white cotton (decoupure 2). An
identical coverlet has a cartouche 'W. & J. NOLL PETERSBURG
ONT. M. ROSENBERGER 1891' (McCord Museum 965.22).
This coverlet only has the Nolls' name. They filled orders
with names on request, but wove for general sale as well. This
pattern appears to be derived from one that Zelner wove (cf.
Reinert, pl. 92). The small imperial crowns used as fillers
are not found in his work, but they do occur in some of the
Nolls' borders.

464 / Ontario. Petersburg, Waterloo County. 1885-95
ROM 950.191. Gift of Miss G. Robinson
Jacquard coverlet. L. 216cm, plus added fringe;
w. 185cm, plus fringes

Tied doublecloth (proportion 2:1): bright red wool with
natural white cotton on natural white cotton (decoupure 2).
This is another pattern 'FROM W. & J. NOLL PETERSBURG

ONT.' It has the same borders and cartouches as no. 463, and
the pattern is similar in style of drawing and layout. The
Nolls were among the very few weavers in Ontario who were
Roman Catholic. One of their first coverlets was woven for
Father Funken, the parish priest at nearby St Agatha. They
also wove coverlets for the orphanage there: perhaps those
with the inscription 'Herz Maria' inside the garland of roses
in the corner. (*in colour* PLATE IV)

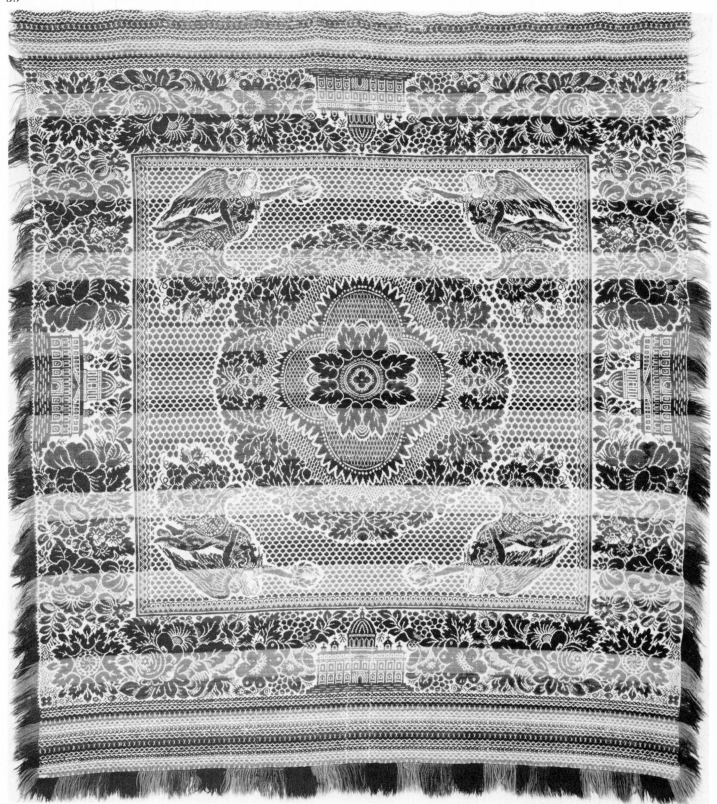

465 / Ontario. Petersburg, Waterloo County. 1875-90
ROM 970.231
Jacquard coverlet. L. 215cm, plus added fringe;
w. 185cm, plus fringes

Tied doublecloth (proportion 2:1) with free areas: indigo
blue, red, and green wool with dark blue cotton on natural
white cotton (decoupure 2). A short distance from the Nolls,
Johan Lippert and his son George had a weaving shop.
Waterloo County was, and still is, an area of prosperous
farms: in the latter half of the nineteenth century there was
plenty of business to keep both families busy. The Lipperts
acquired a wide loom with jacquard attachment about 1870,
together with sets of prepared pattern cards. It was the nineteenth-century equivalent of 'painting by numbers': a considerable amount of know-how was required, but little

originality. A set of cards was mounted on the loom and one
of the overpowering patterns full of fussy detail resulted. It
was one way that a small workshop could compete economic-
ally with mass-produced goods.

The large domed building seen in the borders is also found
in no. 473, woven by Daniel Knechtel, but both the other
details of the design and the construction are different from
his work. The younger Lippert's daughter remembered a
pattern called 'The Church' and her description fits well with
this design. The angels with laurel wreaths standing on
cornucopias in each corner of the field are also known from
another design. In it they are less well drawn and dominate
the field. The lower part of the cornucopias has been omitted,
making them more closely resemble a ship's figurehead of a
Victory. Other somewhat similar angels occur on no. 468.

466 / Ontario. Petersburg, Waterloo County. About 1875
ROM 968.210
Jacquard coverlet. L. 220cm, plus added fringe;
w. 203cm, plus fringes

Tied doublecloth (proportion 2:1) with free areas: bright
red wool with dull blue cotton on natural white cotton (decoupure 2). Because of the identical loom capacity and construction that were needed for nos. 465-7, this and the
following coverlet have been assigned to the Lipperts of
Petersburg. There are also certain stylistic similarities among
the three of them, particularly in supplying longer borders at
both ends. Although in no. 465 such borders are made by
repeating simple geometric motifs, in this one and no. 467,
the heavy scrolled borders are repeated or reversed at the
ends.

467 / Ontario, Petersburg, Waterloo County. 1870-80
ROM 967.220.6
Jacquard coverlet. L. 207cm, plus added fringe;
w. 187cm, plus fringes

Tied doublecloth (proportion 2:1) with free areas: red
wool (faded) with light blue cotton on natural white cotton
(decoupure 2). For technical reasons, as mentioned above,
this coverlet has also been assigned to the Lipperts of Petersburg. Peacocks were sometimes kept as pets on the large

farms of the period and it is not surprising to find them appearing in coverlet designs. The square layout of the main
pattern appears to be more suitable for a tablecloth or carpet,
but adapted for coverlet use by the duplication of the borders. Some of these pieces now called coverlets were used as
tablecloths. In the late Victorian era, it was considered in-
decent for a table to be left naked; it was covered with a
heavy cloth between meals. A large oil lamp was placed in
the centre and around it the family gathered in the evening.

468 / Ontario. Waterloo County. 1875-95
ROM 970.200
Jacquard coverlet. L. 200cm, plus added fringe;
w. 203cm, plus fringes

Tied doublecloth (proportion 4:1) with free areas: indigo blue wool with dark blue cotton on natural cotton ground (decoupure 4). This is the only example that has been recorded of this unusual pattern with its strong religious over-tones. One is tempted to think that it may have been woven as part of a special order for one of the religious institutions scattered through Waterloo County. The crosses surrounded by roses, oak sprays, and grape branches are accompanied by clusters of lilies in the centre of each side. The angel in each corner with a crown of stars and holding out a martyr's wreath is probably derived from the better known pattern seen in no. 465. The *Distelfink* on a rose spray in each corner shows the continued survival and popularity of this old motif.

469 / Ontario. Preston, Waterloo County. About 1865-70
ROM 965.152. Gift of Mr Reginald Werlich
Jacquard coverlet. L. 199cm; w. 199cm, plus fringes

Tied doublecloth (proportion 4:1) with free areas: indigo
blue and soft red wool with light blue cotton on natural white
cotton (decoupure 4). This is the work of Wilhelm Magnus
Werlich, who came to Canada from Germany about 1850 as
a fully trained professional weaver. The pattern book he
brought with him (ROM 955.138) has drafts for a multiple-
shaft loom and swatches of fine cotton materials in twill and
damask diaper of the type he wove in Germany. He adapted
this knowledge to the weaving of complex twill coverlets
after he arrived in Waterloo County. We know that he was

one of the weavers to acquire a wide loom with jacquard
head from the United States after the close of the Civil War.
With this loom he bought cards for a small variety of patterns. Sometimes a person commissioned a coverlet and
provided handspun wool for the weft. Otherwise there was
no personal touch: names and dates were no longer woven
in. There was no reason why coverlets could not be produced
for general sale. This coverlet stayed in the Werlich family
and provides a secure document of one of his patterns. It is
one known from a much earlier date in Pennsylvania
(Reinert, pl. 61). A late nineteenth-century example of the
same pattern is in Toronto (ROM 970.108); it was also woven
by Werlich but is banded in strong colours obtained from
chemical dyes.

470 / Ontario. Preston, Waterloo County. 1870-90
ROM 968.135
Jacquard coverlet. L. 190cm; w. 195cm, plus fringes

Tied doublecloth (proportion 4:1) with free areas: indigo
blue wool with light brown cotton on natural white cotton
(decoupure 4). This is another of Werlich's patterns. If the
lower border of the previous coverlet is examined, it will be
found to be identical with the field of this one. This design is
also known from an earlier period in the United States
(Reinert, pl. 42).

471 / Ontario. Preston, Waterloo County. 1870-90
ROM 968.66.1
Jacquard coverlet. L. 200cm, plus added fringe;
w. 193cm, plus fringes

Tied doublecloth (proportion 4:1) with free areas: indigo
blue wool with light blue cotton on natural white cotton (decoupure 4). This is similar to the previous palmette pattern,
but the secondary motifs and the borders differ. It is the work
of August Ploethner, who was a contemporary of Werlich
and who also worked in Preston. Coverlets of identical designs are owned by the weaver's descendants, one of which
was given by them to Doon Pioneer Village, near Kitchener.
The cards were acquired ready for use; the pattern is known
from an earlier date in Pennsylvania (Reinert, pls. 75, 85,
89).

472 / Ontario. Preston, Waterloo County. 1875-90
ROM 952.137. Gift of Mr John R. MacNicol in
memory of his wife, Maisie MacKinnon
Jacquard coverlet. L. 242cm, plus added fringe;
w. 209cm, plus fringes

Tied doublecloth (proportion 4:1) with free areas: deep red
wool with medium blue cotton on natural white cotton (decoupure 4). August Ploethner purchased a wide loom and
jacquard mechanism about 1865–70. This example is
definitely his work as his granddaughter owns one of identical
pattern. The wide jacquard coverlets from Waterloo County
occur in monochrome, frequently bright red, but the more
characteristic late productions from this area were those
banded regularly in strong bright colours: red, blue, green,
and purple, sometimes combined with brown or black. These
were obtained from chemical dyes that have often faded. As

the nineteenth century drew to a close, the colours became
more strident and the results often garish. Coverlets of this
type were produced in considerable quantity, but have survived in a much more limited area than the Grafs; indicating
that they were made for local sale and not carried farther
afield by pedlars.

Ploethner wove to order using handspun wool supplied by
his customers and also had a small shop on the market square
in Kitchener, where he sold his own work and that of other
men on a commission basis. Fancy coverlets were only a
specialty line with professional weavers; the bulk of their
production was utilitarian, linen for towels (no. 193) and
bedding, clothing materials, blankets and carpeting. As has
already been mentioned, Waterloo County is an area of conservative tastes, and the demand for the Pennsylvania-style
coverlets and the other handwoven goods survived longer
here than elsewhere in Ontario.

473 / Ontario. Roseville, Waterloo County. 1885-1900
ROM 967.298. Gift of Mrs P.G. Hopperton
Jacquard coverlet. L. 206cm; w. 197cm, plus fringes

Tied doublecloth (proportion 4 : 1) with free areas: red wool
with dark blue cotton on natural white cotton (decoupure
4). Daniel Knechtel came to Waterloo County from Pennsylvania about the time of the Civil War as a comparatively
young man and set up in business in the village of Roseville.
The pattern of this coverlet is one he is known to have woven.
The 'church' which appears in the border should be compared with the Lipperts' use of the same motif, although the
construction is different (no. 465).

474 / Ontario. Probably Roseville, Waterloo County.
1875-90
NMM D560
Jacquard coverlet. L. 244cm, plus added fringe;
w. 193cm, plus fringes

Tied doublecloth (proportion 4 : 1) with free areas: indigo

blue, red, and olive-green wools with medium blue cotton on
natural white cotton (decoupure 4). This coverlet is of the
same construction as no. 473 and the wild turkeys found in
the borders of both have a strong stylistic similarity. For these
reasons, it has been assigned to Daniel Knechtel as another of
the patterns he would have woven. The design is also known
from Pennsylvania (Reinert, pl. 33).

475 / Ontario. Probably Preston or Roseville,
Waterloo County. 1870-80
ROM 966.75.1. Gift of Mrs H.C. Smith
Jacquard coverlet. L. 202cm; w. 188cm, plus fringes

Tied doublecloth (proportion 4:1) with free areas: bright red wool with light blue cotton on natural white cotton (decoupure 4). It is not known for certain who wove this pattern, but the possible candidates are Wilhelm Magnus Werlich, August Ploethner, and Daniel Knechtel. All three bought their patterns ready-made from the United States and this one obviously came from there. The birds surmounting the shields with stars and stripes more closely resemble the griffon in *Alice in Wonderland* than the usual American eagle, but there is little doubt but that the latter is the source. Many of these late coverlets from Waterloo County may not be particularly Canadian in content, but they are certainly bright and gay. They must have looked splendid with the heavy dark furniture and large beds of the period.

476 / Ontario. Stouffville, York County. 1855-65
BCPV 59.151
Jacquard coverlet. L. 208cm, plus fringe; w. 185 cm,
plus added fringes

Tied doublecloth (proportion 2 : 1) with free areas: indigo
blue and raspberry red wool with natural white cotton on
natural white cotton (decoupure 2). This is the work of
William Withers, who came from Scotland to Canada about
1850 and settled at Stouffville. He had one of the first wide
looms with jacquard attachment in Ontario and wove coverlets until he died sometime between 1861 and 1871. He
designed his own patterns and cut his own cards. His design
elements seen here are found used in different combinations
in later coverlets from the same workshop. The corner with
roses, thistles, shamrocks, and maple leaves is often found as
the central motif as in no. 477. This union of national em-
blems is an early expression of patriotism.

Many of the motifs found in Withers' designs are reminiscent of the patterns of scotch ingrain carpeting. It is possible
that he had been trained as a carpet weaver before leaving
Scotland. This influence may be seen in the elements of this
pattern but is particularly true of the scrolls and medallions
designed by Withers that occur frequently as borders in the
work of his successor, Christopher Armstrong (nos. 477-8).
Other sources of inspiration may also be recognized. Many
of the families in this part of York County had relations
across Lake Ontario and owned coverlets of earlier date
woven in the Niagara Peninsula. When Withers came from
Scotland he would have seen and been influenced by them.
His earliest known coverlets are of a classic 'Four Roses' type
with borders of tulip bushes and birds (*Distelfink*) woven to
comply with the requests of his Mennonite customers in the
Markham area. In this coverlet, the roses have been taken
over into the new design, but in quite changed surroundings.

477 / Ontario. Stouffville, York County. 1880-90
ROM 963.1.2
Jacquard coverlet. L. 205cm, plus fringe; w. 173cm

Tied doublecloth (proportion 4:1): red, indigo blue, and pale olive-green wool with natural white cotton on natural white cotton (decoupure 2). This is the work of Christopher Armstrong, probably William Withers' son-in-law, who took over his equipment and weaving business when the latter died. He continued in business until 1910. He does not seem to have originated patterns, but took sections of Withers' designs and combined them in different ways. Here the corner motif of no. 476 has been used as the central pattern. Coverlets also occur with three of these motifs across the field, and a narrower border. Both the scrolls and medallions in the border are reminiscent of scotch ingrain carpet patterns.

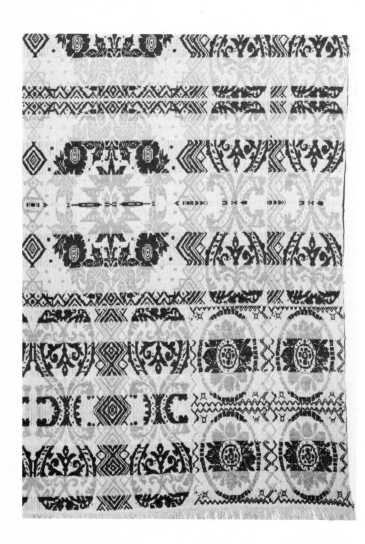

478 / Ontario. Stouffville, York County. 1890-1905
BCPV 60.268
Jacquard coverlet. L. 228cm, plus fringe; w. 177cm

Tied doublecloth (proportion 4:1): dark indigo blue and orange-red wool with natural white cotton on natural white cotton (decoupure 2). This is also the work of Christopher Armstrong, who succeeded William Withers and continued to use his designs, of which this is another. The elaborate star form of the earlier coverlets woven in the Niagara Peninsula has been surrounded by a wreath of stylized roses and lily-like flowers.

479 / Ontario. Wilfrid, Brock Township, Ontario County.
1870-90
York Pioneer and Historical Society, Sharon, Ontario. H1628
Jacquard carpet. L. 207cm; w. 182cm

Doublecloth: all wool in olive-drab and red (decoupure 1).
This carpet was woven by William J. Hunter of Wilfrid.
From the census returns of 1861 and 1871 it is known that
Hunter was born in the United States, must have come to
Canada between these dates, and arrived here fully trained.
It is reasonable to assume that he brought his jacquard
equipment and patterns with him. This piece is typical of his
work. One other design Hunter used is known and is a version
of the bird of paradise motif that caught the public fancy in
the United States about the middle of the nineteenth century.
A coverlet of the design shown here belongs to Hunter's
granddaughter, and one of the second pattern to a great-
granddaughter. Both have natural white cotton grounds.

The demand for handwoven coverlets in the United States
died with the economic disruptions of the Civil War (1861–
65), and William Hunter and John Campbell are two of the
weavers known to have come to Canada about that time. As
the demand for these coverlets in the United States did not
revive when peace came, some enterprising salesman found
a market in Ontario for the idle looms in Pennsylvania. It
was from such a source that the Grafs in the Niagara Peninsula, and Werlich, Ploethner, the Lipperts, and others in the
Waterloo County area obtained their looms and equipment.
For another thirty years or more they were able to compete
in steadily diminishing degree with European and American
commercial imports.

480 / Ontario. Wilfrid, Brock Township, Ontario County.
1890-1910
ROM 968.212
Jacquard coverlet or tablecloth. L. 212cm; w. 197cm

Doublecloth: bright red and aniline purple (faded to greys) wool on cotton warp of the same colours (decoupure 1). This is also William Hunter's work and was probably made for use as a tablecloth. The pattern motifs are identical to those in no. 479, but the yarns are coarser and half a pattern unit has been dropped on either side to make this bolder version fit the loom width. At some point, Hunter's figure harness must have been remounted to fit this coarser scale. This piece was woven towards the end of the period when handwoven coverlets were made in Ontario and when competitive pressure of mass produced commercial goods was becoming intense. The weaving here is very competent; unfortunately the dyes have faded unevenly giving a banded effect where none was intended.

481 / Ontario. Komoka, Middlesex County. 1884
ROM 962.75. Gift of Mrs W.J. Hodder
Jacquard coverlet. L. 217cm, plus fringe; w. 209cm

Doublecloth (proportion 2 : 1) : dull red wool with natural
white cotton on natural white cotton (decoupure 2). This is
the work of John Campbell, who was born in Scotland,
trained there as a weaver, and emigrated to the United States
in 1832. In 1859 he came to Ontario and settled near London, where he wove professionally until his death in 1885.
The order for this coverlet has been found in his account
book, which is at the Ontario Science Centre with his looms.
The donor knew that it was one of a pair woven for Sarah
Kilbourne of Kilworth. The mate is at Upper Canada Village. The entry is dated 1884. According to Campbell's
account book, there were four patterns from which his customers might choose. This is 'Rose and Stars' and is still another variation of the old favourite design. An older version
of this pattern, also woven by Campbell, has a 4 : 1 tied
doublecloth ground and is probably the construction he used
before coming to Canada (ROM 949.154.1).

482 / Ontario. Komoka, Middlesex County. 1869
ROM 970.299. Gift of Mrs Maude Leitch
Jacquard coverlet. L. 230cm, plus fringe; w. 218cm

Doublecloth (proportion 2 : 1) : deep red wool with natural white cotton on natural white cotton (decoupure 2). This is also the work of John Campbell and is the pattern he called 'Single Rose.' It was woven for Mrs Angus Graham, of Lobo, and an entry in the account book in her father's name is dated January 5, 1869. In 1950, the Royal Ontario Museum found John Campbell's jacquard equipment in existence still set up in his weaving shed, untouched since he died (fig. 40).

483 / Ontario. Komoka, Middlesex County.
Probably about 1860
Ontario Science Centre, Toronto
Pattern for jacquard coverlet

Two sets of cards were with John Campbell's loom and are now at the Ontario Science Centre. It was a matter of considerable interest to find what patterns were on them. The holes in each card represent the movement of the warp for one pass of the weaving. It was a tedious process to take the numbered cards in order and to mark the holes in black on a wide sheet of graph paper line by line, but the pattern shown here emerged. No coverlet of this design has been seen. It shows half the pattern for one width. The loom would have been entered so that the narrow part of the border would reverse to the outer edge, making a series of alternating rosettes with double-fan motifs between. The central medallion would also reverse and form a large circle which gave rise to the name 'Garland' known from Campbell's account book. As his coverlets were woven narrow width with a seam down the centre, this would be the design for 1/2 of the coverlet so that in the finished piece there would be 2 garlands in the width, and 2½ or 3 in the length.

The pattern of the other sets of cards, labelled 'Rose and Stars' proved to be that of no. 481. Campbell's fourth pattern is 'Tulip': the design is based on medallions of four stylized flowers with matching smaller versions in the border. On the inner border are eagles as in no. 481 (970.296.2).

484 / Ontario. Probably Whitby Township, Ontario County.
1850-60
Century Village, Lang, Ontario. H.67.31
Jacquard coverlet. L. 196cm; w. 194cm

Damask: indigo blue wool on natural white cotton (decoupure 2). This is one of a unique group of coverlets woven
in 5-end damask that show a considerable variety of designs.
All are the work of one man, who appears to have been active
from about 1850 to 1880. The coverlet shown here was taken
to Peterborough County from near Markham about 1860
when the family who owned it moved to a new farm. The
identity of the weaver is not known, but the latest clues point
to a man who lived just off the Old Stone Road, now Highway 12, between Whitby and Brooklin, and who was known
as 'Weaver Joe.' John Gibson, an Irish widower, is the only
professional weaver shown in the census returns for the township and may have been the man who wove them. A search
in the returns for the neighbouring townships has produced
no better candidate. The detail below shows the damask
weave more clearly.

485 / Ontario. Probably Whitby Township, Ontario County. 1850-60
Manitoulin Historical Society Museum, Gore Bay, Ontario, 64.31. Gift of Mrs W.F. McRae
Jacquard coverlet. L. 208cm; w. 194cm

Damask: indigo blue wool on natural white cotton (decoupure 2). This is another of the damask weaver's patterns. The coverlet was taken from Markham to Manitoulin Island in 1862 when that district was first opened for settlement. It has a similarity of style to no. 484 reminiscent of English design just before the middle of the nineteenth century, and is in contrast to the weaver's later work shown in nos. 486 and 487. The border on this, and on the preceding and following coverlets, is characteristic of his earlier work.

486 / Ontario. Probably Whitby Township, Ontario County. 1860-70
Doon Pioneer Village, Kitchener, Ontario. 21
Jacquard coverlet. L. 231cm; w. 182cm

Damask: indigo blue wool on natural white cotton (decoupure 2). This design by the same weaver has the earlier border, but the chevron panels found in his later work. As in William Withers' corner motifs in no. 476, this pattern combines roses, thistles, and shamrocks but omits the maple leaves. All these damask coverlets were woven with borders on four sides and could equally well have been used on beds or as heavy tablecloths. If the end borders are worn from being pulled up over the shoulders, as they often are, one may be quite certain that they were used as coverlets.

487 / Ontario. Probably Whitby Township, Ontario County. 1865-75
ROM 967.281
Jacquard coverlet or tablecloth. L. 228cm; w. 196cm

Damask: indigo blue wool on natural white cotton (decoupure 2). The damask weaver's later border is seen here. It is heavier, denser, and more confused than the earlier one with its mixed profusion of flowers. The vertical effect of the floral design, broken by chevron bands, is reminiscent of the wallpapers that were becoming very fashionable at this period. It is possible that these designs were produced to complement the decorations of the high-ceilinged bedrooms of the time.

488 / Ontario. Probably Whitby Township, Ontario County. 1865-80
BCPV 67.118.3
Jacquard coverlet. L. 238cm, plus fringe; w. 184cm

Damask: indigo blue and deep red wool on natural white cotton (decoupure 2). This has the same border as the previous coverlet combined with a stunning pattern that appears somewhat alien for the weaver of the other coverlets in this group. It is obviously based on a damask-diaper pattern more suitable for a multiple-shaft loom, and like other jacquard-woven coverlets with geometric patterns was probably produced to satisfy a customer's conservative tastes. Until replaced by figured damask, twill and damask diapers had long been in constant use for table linen. It is probably on his knowledge of these that the weaver based this design.

489 / Ontario. Probably Whitby Township, Ontario County. 1870-80
ROM 968.70
Jacquard coverlet. L. 227cm; w. 190cm

Damask: dark blue-black wool on natural white cotton (decoupure 2). This pattern with well-laden vines has been seen in a number of different colour combinations. Grapes are a difficult motif in textile design, but here have been mastered quite successfully, displaying the weaver's competence as a draftsman. His original patterns show no connection with any other coverlets woven in Ontario; he depended wholly on his own inspiration and ability, undoubtedly adapting his knowledge of linen-damask weaving to this coarser medium to gain a living.

490 / Ontario. Possibly Neustadt-Hanover area.
Grey County. About 1885
ROM 969.70.1. Gift of Mrs R.T. Stinson
Jacquard coverlet. L. 178cm; w. 180cm

Tied doublecloth (proportion 2:1): indigo blue wool with light blue cotton, on natural white cotton (decoupure 2). The name of the weaver of this coverlet is not known, but he may have worked near the southern part of the boundary between Grey and Bruce Counties, a district pioneered by settlers from Waterloo County. In 1910, an informant was taken as a small girl to visit an old jacquard weaver at Neustadt, a short distance south of Hanover. Unfortunately, she did not remember his name. It might be found in the census returns of the late nineteenth and early twentieth centuries, but these are not yet available for research.

This coverlet comes from the same general area and was perhaps woven by this man. Others with different patterns are known that may also be his work. They have the same construction and are also characterized by strong twill lines used as fillers in the ground. Examples are in the Bruce County Museum, Southampton, Ontario.

491 / Ontario. Possibly Rodney, Elgin County.
Dated 1902
ROM 964.150.6. Gift of Mrs Edgar J. Stone
Jacquard coverlet. L. 201cm, plus fringe;
w. 180cm, plus fringes

Doublecloth (proportion 2:1): indigo blue wool with light
blue cotton, and natural white cotton (decoupure 2). This
strange coverlet is one of a small group of which four have
been recorded. All have the same layout with an architectural
motif surrounded by fussy floral detail, and in every case half
of the design has been used for the side borders. A coverlet the
same as this one was dated 1888 and woven for a person who
lived a short distance west of St Thomas in Elgin County.
Two with different patterns, but in the same style, were dated
in the 1890s and came from the general area. The owner of
these did not remember the maker's name, but referred to
him as 'the Dutch weaver.' This is probably the well-known
corruption of *deutsch*, or German.

No weaver of Dutch extraction is listed in any of the
census returns for Ontario, but a search of the last ones that
are open for examination for the area in which these coverlets
have been found has produced the name of one professional
weaver of German birth named George Gaage. In 1871 he
is shown as living at Rodney in Elgin County, aged 31, and
apparently a fairly recent immigrant. He is possibly the
weaver of this unusual group of coverlets.

The example shown here was also collected near St
Thomas and has the latest date, 1902, found on any jacquard
coverlet woven in Ontario. At the opposite end, not shown,
are the initials 'DK,' those of the person for whom it was
woven. Both the date and initials are in reserved frames.
Here they were not controlled by the jacquard mechanism
as in the earlier coverlets, but worked in manually by the
weaver. Nevertheless, they represent the end of a tradition
that began in Ontario in 1834 with Wilhelm Armbrust's first
coverlets.

Select bibliography

MANUSCRIPT SOURCES

Public Archives of Canada Census records. Microfilms of those
  for Ontario are in the Ontario Provincial Archives, Toronto.
Ontario Science Centre Account book of John Campbell of
  Komoka, Middlesex County, Ontario. 1859–85.
Royal Ontario Museum Account book of Samuel Fry of
  Vineland, Lincoln County, Ontario, 1843–78. L965.11.77
  The Annie R. Fry Collection.

PRINTED SOURCES

Aspin, C., and Chapman, S.D. *James Hargreaves and the
  Spinning Jenny* (Helmshore Local History Society, Preston
  1964)
Atwater, Mary Meigs *The Shuttle-Craft Book of American
  Hand-Weaving* (New York 1966)
Balcikonis, J., et al. *Lietuviu Liaudies Menas* (Vilnius 1962)
Ballantyne, Robert Michael *Hudson Bay* (4th ed., London
  1902)
Banateanu, Tancred et al. *Folk Costume, Woven Textiles and
  Embroideries of Rumania* (Bucharest 1958)
Beriau, Oscar *Tissage Domestique* (Québec 1943)
Blanchard, J.-Henri *The Acadians of Prince Edward Island*
  (Charlottetown 1964)
Brett, K.B. *Modesty to Mod, Dress and Underdress in Canada,
  1780–1967*. With patterns and related notes by Dorothy K.
  Burnham (Toronto 1967)
– *Ontario Handwoven Textiles* (Toronto 1956)
Bronson, J. and R. *The Domestic Manufacturer's Assistant in
  the Arts of Weaving and Dyeing* (Utica, NY 1817)
Burnham, Harold B. *Canadian Textiles, 1750–1900. An
  Exhibition* (Toronto 1965)
Carless, William *The Arts and Crafts of Canada* (Montreal
  1925)
Carrothers, William A. *Emigration from the British Isles*
  (London 1929)
Chambers, G.F. *The Story of Comets* (Oxford 1909)
Craig, Gerald M. *Early Travellers in Canada, 1791–1867*
  (Toronto 1955)
Cyrus, Ulla *Handbok i Vävning* (Stockholm 1949)
Davison, Mildred 'Handwoven coverlets in the Art Institute of
  Chicago,' *Antiques* (May 1970), 735–40
Dictionary of Canadian Biography. II, 1701–40 (Toronto 1969)
English, Walter *The Textile Industry: An account of the early
  inventions of spinning, weaving, and knitting machines*
  (London 1969)
Fauteux, Joseph-Noël *Essai sur L'Industrie au Canada sous le
  Régime Français*, 2 vols. (Québec 1927)
Frey, Berta *Designing and Drafting for Handweavers* (New
  York 1958)
Gaida, Pranas, ed. *Lithuanians in Canada* (Toronto 1967)
Galvin, Nellie L., ed. *A German Weaver's Pattern Book*
  (n.p. 1961)
Government of Canada, Board of Registration and Statistics
  Census of the Canadas, 1851–2. 2 vols. (Quebec 1853–4)
– Department of the Secretary of State, Canadian Citizenship
  Branch *The Canadian Family Tree* (Ottawa 1967)
Groves, Naomi Jackson *A.Y.'s Canada* (Toronto 1968)

Hall, Eliza Calvert *A Book of Hand-woven Coverlets* (Boston 1927)

Harvey, D.C., ed. *Journeys to the Island of St-Jean or Prince Edward Island* (Toronto 1955)

Henriksson, Anna *Kankaankudonnan Oppikirja* (Helsinki 1946)

Hoffmann, Marta *The Warp-weighted Loom* (Oslo 1964)

Hooper, Luther *Hand-loom Weaving, Plain and Ornamental* (London 1920)

Horstmann, Wm. H., Company *One Hundred Years: 1816–1916* (Philadelphia 1916)

Hunter, A.F. 'The Ethnographical Elements of Ontario.' *Ontario Historical Society Papers and Records*, III (1910), 180–99

Jamet, Dom Albert, ed. *Marie d'Incarnation, Ursuline de Tours, fondatrice des Ursulines de la Nouvelle France: Ecrits spirituels et historiques*: publiés par Dom Claude Martin. 4 vols. (Paris 1929–39)

Johnson, Stanley C. *A History of Emigration* (London 1913)

Lichten, Frances *Folk Art of Rural Pennsylvania* (New York 1964)

Macdonald, Dorothy K. *Fibres, Spindles and Spinning-wheels* (Toronto 1944)

Mackley, Florence M. *Handweaving in Cape Breton* (Sydney 1967)

Maclaren, George *Antique Furniture by Nova Scotia Craftsmen* (Toronto 1961)

Marshall, Joyce, tr. and ed. *Word from New France: The Selected Letters of Marie de l'Incarnation* (Toronto 1967)

Mauersberger, Herbert R., ed. *Matthews' Textile Fibers* (6th ed., New York 1954)

Meyer-Heisig, Erich *Weberei Nadelwerk Zeugdruck* (Munich 1956)

Miller, Audrey Saunders, ed. *The Journals of Mary O'Brien, 1828–1838* (Toronto 1968)

Murphy, John *Art of Weaving* (10th ed., Glasgow 1852)

Osborn, Bernice B. *Homecraft Course in Pennsylvania German Spinning and Dyeing* (Plymouth Meeting, Pennsylvania 1945)

Ouellet, Fernand *Histoire économique et sociale du Québec, 1760–1850* (Montréal 1966)

Palardy, Jean *The Early Furniture of French Canada* (Toronto 1965)

Parslow, Virginia D. 'James Alexander, Weaver,' *Antiques* (April 1956)

Peddie, Alexander *The Linen Manufacturer, Weaver, and Warper's Assistant, containing a New and Correct Set of Tables, Drafts, Cordings, adapted to the Present State of the Woollen and Linen Manufacturer, and Household Customary Weaving* (Glasgow 1822)

Pfister, R. *Nouveaux Textiles de Palmyre* (Paris 1937)

Piwockiego, Ksawerego *Tkanina Polska* (Warsaw 1959)

Posselt, E.A. *The Jacquard Machine Analyzed and Explained* (Philadelphia, n.d. [about 1868])

Powell, R. Janet *Annals of the Forty*, nos. 3–10 (Grimsby Historical Society, Grimsby 1952–9)

Prebble, John *The Highland Clearances* (London 1963)

Rapport de l'Archiviste de la Province du Québec, 1935–6 (Québec 1936)

Reinert, Guy F. *Coverlets of the Pennsylvania Germans* (The Pennsylvania German Folklore Society, XIII [1948])

Reports from Assistant Hand-Loom Weavers' Commissioners (London 1839)

Riefstahl, Elizabeth *Patterned Textiles in Pharaonic Egypt* (Brooklyn 1944)

Rogers, Grace L. 'Peter Stauffer.' *Handweaver and Craftsman*, VII, 1 (1955–6), 12–14

Roth, H. Ling *Hand Woolcombing*. Bankfield Museum Notes, no. 6 (Halifax, Yorks., n.d. [about 1906])

– *Hand Card Making*. Bankfield Museum Notes, no. 11 (Halifax, Yorks. 1912)

Rubi, Christian *Taufe und Taufzettel im Bernerland* (Wabern 1968)

– *Bauernmalerei* (Bern 1965)

Ryerson, Egerton *The Loyalists of America and Their Times*. 2 vols. (Toronto 1880)

Schwartz, Esther T. 'Early Commercial Weaving in Paterson.' *Antiques* (October 1958), 330–2

Séguin, Robert-Lionel *La Civilisation traditionelle de l'habitant aux XVIIe et XVIIIe siècles* (Montréal 1967)

Spencer, Audrey *Spinning & Weaving at Upper Canada Village* (Toronto 1964)

Start, Laura E. *The McDougall Collection of Indian Textiles from Guatemala and Mexico* (Oxford 1948)

Studio *Peasant Art in Italy: Special Autumn Number* (London 1913)

Swygert, Mrs Luther M., ed. *Heirlooms from Old Looms* (Chicago 1955)

Thompson, George B. *The John Horner Collection of Spindles, Spinning Wheels and Accessories*. City of Belfast Museum and Art Gallery Bulletin, I, 5 (Belfast 1952)

Thomson, William *A Tradesman's Travels in the United States and Canada* (Edinburgh 1842)

Titball, Harriet *Thomas Jackson, Weaver: 17th and 18th century records* (Shuttlecraft Guild, Lansing, Mich. 1964) (The text is in error in ascribing this pattern book to Yorkshire. Its provenance is Wiltshire.)

Traill, Catharine Parr *The Backwoods of Canada* (Toronto 1966)

– / *The Canadian Settlers' Guide* (Toronto 1969)

Watson, William *Advanced Textile Design* (London 1947)

Webster, John Clarence *Acadia at the End of the Seventeenth Century* (Saint John 1934)

White, Margaret E. *Hand-woven Coverlets in The Newark Museum* (Newark 1947)

Wright, Esther Clark *The Loyalists of New Brunswick* (Fredericton 1955)

Wyss, Robert L. *Berner Bauerkeramik* (Bern 1966)

Appendix

ROYAL ONTARIO MUSEUM ACCESSIONS TO WHICH
REFERENCE IS MADE

920.34.1 TOWEL, linen damask diaper.
France. 18th century. L. 71cm; w. 87cm.
Gift of Mrs Frank McMahon

943.24.16 BOUTONNE BEDSPREAD, white cotton with weft-pile
patterns. England. Bolton, Lancs. 1825–50.
L. 279cm; w. 249cm. Gift of Miss Kate Drummond, in
memory of Mr and Mrs Andrew Drummond

945.24.7 NAPKIN, linen damask diaper.
England, dated 1762. L. 74cm; w. 74cm.
Gift of Miss Mary E. Lee

946.14 SPINNING WHEEL with double flyer, stamped 'James
Duff.' Scotland. 19th century.
Diameter of driving wheel 47cm.
Gift of Miss Margaret Robertson

947.20.16 OVERSHOT COVERLET. Mustard yellow wool on
natural white cotton.
Greece. 1920–40. L. 171cm; w. 122cm.
Gift of Mrs H.A. Thompson

948.99 BOUTONNE BEDSPREAD. White cotton with weft-pile
patterns. England. Bolton, Lancs.
Mid-19th century. L. 241cm; w. 220cm.
Gift of Mrs Harold East

949.154.1 JACQUARD COVERLET. Indigo blue wool and natural
white cotton on natural white cotton. 'Rose and Stars'
pattern. Inscribed 'Jessy Campbell' in one corner. Woven by
John Campbell of Komoka, probably near Syracuse, NY,
before coming to Canada. 1840–50.
L. 196cm; w. 166cm.
Gift of Mr John Campbell

951.18 WARP-FACED CARPET (room size; four widths).
Ontario. Ridgetown, Essex County. About 1875.
L. 457cm; w. 259cm. This is identical to the fragment shown
in no. 110 which comes from the same house

954.99.1 OVERSHOT COVERLET (fragment). Rose, green and
buff wool on natural white cotton.
Glengarry County, Ontario. Late 19th century.
L. 37cm; w. 88cm. The pattern is identical to no. 245

955.50 TWILL DIAPER TABLECLOTH. Bleached linen on natural
white cotton. Kitchener area, Waterloo County. 1860–80.
L. 162cm; w. 147cm. Gift of the Hon. Chief Justice D.C.
Wells. The pattern is the same as no. 194

955.59 OVERSHOT COVERLET. Red and black wool on natural
white cotton. Ontario. Probably Wellington County. 1850–75.
L. 214cm; w. 186cm. Gift of Miss Florence Lyons. The
pattern is identical to no. 353

955.138 PATTERN BOOK of Wilhelm Magnus Werlich.
German. Pre-1849. Brought from Wildenspring, Thuringia
about 1850. Gift of Spinners and Weavers of Ontario

956.147.3 SHOW TOWEL. Bleached linen twill diaper.
United States. Pennsylvania. Mid-19th century.
L. 138cm; w. 42cm. Gift of Mrs Edgar J. Stone

959.65.2 STAR AND DIAMOND COVERLET. Dark blue, brick red
and yellow green wool on natural white cotton. United States.
Pennsylvania, Lancaster County. Mid-19th century.
L. 244cm; w. 165cm

959.148.1 OVERSHOT COVERLET. Natural white wool on

natural white cotton. Greece, about 1930.
L. 152cm; w. 172cm. Bequest of Miss Amice Calverley.
The pattern is identical to fig. 28.

959.148.62 TOWEL, cotton, huck-block ground with boutonné borders in pink cotton. Crete. Mere, Gulf of Mirabelle. *c.* 1900. L. 122cm; w. 51cm.
Bequest of Miss Amice Calverley

959.268 OVERSHOT COVERLET. Eight-shaft. Blue wool on natural white cotton. Ontario. Wellington County. 1860–80. Gift of the Arts and Crafts of Georgetown.
L. 216cm; w. 183cm. The pattern is identical to no. 351

959.274.1 SHOW TOWEL. Bleached linen twill diaper. United States. Lancaster County, Pennsylvania. Mid-19th century. L. 131cm; w. 41cm

960.40.1 OVERSHOT COVERLET (fragment). Indigo blue and pale red wool on natural white cotton. Ontario. North Dumfries Township, Waterloo County (New Dundee). L. 63cm; w. 78cm. Gift of Mrs William Hoey. The pattern is identical to no. 285

962.245 OVERSHOT COVERLET. Red (faded) wool on natural white cotton. Scotland, Isle of Skye(?). About 1825. L. 191cm; w. 160cm. Gift of Mr W.K. MacLennan

963.9.57 TABLECLOTH. Linen damask diaper. The Netherlands. About 1895. L. 280cm; w. 176cm. Gift of Miss Adelaide Lash Miller

963.9.58 NAPKIN, linen damask diaper. The Netherlands. About 1895. L. 65cm; w. 68cm. Gift of Miss Adelaide Lash Miller

L965.11.17 BLANKET, 2/2 bird's-eye twill. Checked in brown, dark indigo blue, and bright red wool. Woven by Samuel Fry. Ontario. Vineland, Clinton Township, Lincoln County. 1840–60. L. 214cm; w. 191cm.
The Annie R. Fry Collection

966.33.1 SPINNING WHEEL, with flyer. Stamped 'Peter Nisbet, Coltnes.' Scotland, Lanarkshire. 19th century. Collected in Ontario. Diameter of driving wheel 54cm.
Gift of Mr and Mrs Harold B. Burnham

966.157.14 DISTAFF, oak. Prince Edward Island, Miscouche. 19th century. L. 80cm

966.157.44 SPINNING WHEEL, with flyer. Quebec. Late 19th century. Collected in Chéticamp, Cape Breton, Nova Scotia. Diameter of driving wheel 77cm

966.158.23 TABLECLOTH, four-shaft overshot weave. Bleached linen on natural white cotton. Nova Scotia, Pictou County. 1850–60. L. 217cm; w. 180cm. The pattern is similar to that of no. 189

966.158.53 OVERSHOT COVERLET. Red wool on natural white cotton. Nova Scotia, Lunenburg County. 1850–75. L. 200cm; w. 154cm. The pattern is similar to that of no. 258

966.158.57 OVERSHOT COVERLET. Dark indigo blue and light red wool on natural white cotton. Ontario. Kemptville, Grenville County. 1840–60. L. 184cm; w. 163cm. The pattern is the same as no. 287

966.211.2 BOBBIN WINDER. Quebec. Eastern Townships. 19th century. H. of stand 54cm; diams. of wheels 34, 25, and 8cm. Gift of Miss Emily LeBaron

967.88 OVERSHOT COVERLET (fragment). Bleached linen on

natural white cotton. Nova Scotia, Pictou County. Mid-19th century. L. 108cm; w. 79cm. Gift of Miss Marion Patterson Boa. The pattern is the same as no. 241

967.141.1 JACQUARD COVERLET. Dull green, bright red, blue green, and purple wool on natural white cotton. Doublecloth, proportion 1:1; decoupure 1. Probably mill woven. Ontario(?). Late 19th century. L. 214cm; w. 191cm. Gift of Mrs Edgar J. Stone. The pattern is the same as that of no. 970.229

967.162.3 BOUTONNE BEDSPREAD. Brocaded in light blue wool on natural white cotton and natural white wool ground. Quebec. La Malbaie (Murray Bay). 1920–40. L. 256cm; w. 182cm. Gift of Mrs H.R. Westerfield

967.220.1 WEFT-FACED COVERLET. Light blue and natural white wool on natural white cotton. Ontario. Mid-19th century. L. 192cm; w. 161cm. Collected near Milverton

967.278 TWILL DIAPER COVERLET. Slate grey wool on pink-red wool. Ontario. Collected in Markham Township. Mid-19th century. L. 185cm; w. 182cm. The pattern is the same as no. 385

968.18.1, .2 POINT-TWILL COVERLETS (pair). Indigo blue wool on natural white cotton. Pennsylvania. Early 19th century. L's. 207 and 222cm; w's. 201 and 180cm. Gift of Mrs Paul Hamilton. These are similar in pattern to no. 376

968.32 WEAVER'S NOTE BOOK of Elias Johan Joachim Mauer. Germany, 1830–40. Gift of Mrs Stanley Ashbury. Mauer emigrated to Canada about 1840, and settled in Bentinck Township, Grey County

968.62 OVERSHOT COVERLET. Red, medium indigo blue, and dark olive wool on natural white cotton. Ontario. Colebrooke, Campden Township, Lennox and Addington Counties. 1825–40. The pattern is identical to no. 295

968.63 JACQUARD COVERLET. Deep raspberry red wool on natural white cotton. Ontario. Petersburg, Waterloo County. Woven by John Noll. 1860–80. L. 205cm; w. 179cm

968.93.3 WOOL BLANKET, 2/2 twill. Natural white, bordered down sides and across ends with broken herringbone in indigo blue wool. Ontario. Glengarry County. 1840–60. L. 223cm; w. 187cm

968.195.2 OVERSHOT COVERLET. Indigo blue and strong brick red wool on natural white cotton. Ontario. Prince Edward County. 1830–50. L. 240cm; w. 188cm. The pattern is the same as no. 339

968.259.2 TABLE NAPKINS (3). Linen damask diaper. Scotland. 1825–50. L. 87cm; w. 77cm. Gift of Miss H.M. Armour

968.271 TABLECLOTH, linen twill diaper. Scotland. 1825–50. L. 171cm; w. 170cm

968.275 OVERSHOT COVERLET. Bright red wool on natural white cotton. Southwest Scotland(?). 1830s. Collected in Ontario. L. 210cm; w. 185cm

968.308.5 SKIRT or PETTICOAT LENGTH. Brown, red-brown, natural, red, dark brown, and yellow wools on natural white cotton. 2/2 twill. Nova Scotia. Cape Breton, Chéticamp, Grand Etang. Late 19th century. L. 190cm; w. 87cm. Gift of Mr and Mrs Harold B. Burnham

969.2 BOUTONNE BEDSPREAD. White cotton with patterns in

two heights of weft pile. England. Bolton, Lancs. Dated 1804. L. 240cm; w. 210 cm

970.40.3 SPINNING WHEEL WITH FLYER, painted blue. Stamped 'F.L' on stand. Quebec. About 1850. Diameter of driving wheel 55cm

969.65.1 OVERSHOT COVERLET. Dark brown wool on natural white wool and natural white cotton. Ontario. Lanark County, Pakenham. Woven by William Inglis. 1845–60. Gift of Mr and Mrs Harold B. Burnham

969.144.1 TABLECLOTH. Black woollen tabby ground with boutonné and *à la planche* patterns in magenta, purple, yellow, and red wools. Romania. Transylvania, Village of Prodanesti, Zsibo County, River Szamos Valley. 1880–90. L. 162cm; w. 172cm

969.187.2 NAPKIN, linen twill diaper. Switzerland. Canton Bern. About 1800. L. 96cm; w. 81cm. Gift of Mrs Walter Zuppinger

969.187.3 TABLECLOTH. Linen damask diaper. Two widths with centre seam. Switzerland, Canton Bern. About 1800. L. 238cm; w. 167cm. Gift of Mrs Walter Zuppinger

969.274.2 SPINNING WHEEL with flyer, painted green. Stamped 'Amable Paradis.' Quebec. Kamouraska County. Mid-19th century. Diameter of wheel 56cm

970.43.1 OVERSHOT COVERLET. Indigo blue wool on natural white cotton. Ontario. Wentworth County, Saltfleet Township. 1840s. L. 227cm; w. 167cm. Gift of Mrs R.L. MacFeeters. The pattern is the same as that of no. 347

970.43.3 OVERSHOT COVERLET. Indigo blue, green, and pale red wool on natural white cotton. Ontario. Wentworth County, Saltfleet Township. 1860s. L. 210cm; w. 174cm. Gift of Mrs R.L. MacFeeters. The pattern is the same as no. 320

970.61.1 BOUTONNE RUG (3 widths) with uncut weft pile. Green, red, yellow, and natural white wool on half-bleached linen ground. Spain. La Alpujarra(?). 17–18th centuries. L. 232cm; w. 176cm. Gift of Mrs Edgar J. Stone

970.88.22 BOUTONNE RUG (3 widths) with uncut weft pile. Green wool field patterned in red wool. Spain. La Alpujarra(?). Late 18th–early 19th centuries. L. 230cm; w. 188cm. Gift of Mrs Edgar J. Stone

970.88.23 BOUTONNE RUG (3 widths) with cut weft pile. Red wool ground patterned in red wool. Spain. La Alpujarra(?). Dated 1832. Gift of Mrs Edgar J. Stone

970.88.32 OVERSHOT COVERLET. Red silk on natural white silk. Spain. About 1800. L. 210cm; w. 171cm. Gift of Mrs Edgar J. Stone

970.90.15 WOMAN'S SHAWL (3 widths) checked in indigo blue and natural white wools. Quebec. Mid-19th century. Gift of Mrs John David Eaton

970.108 JACQUARD COVERLET. Green, red, and purple wool with blue cotton on natural white cotton. Tied doublecloth with free areas; proportion 4:1; decoupure 4. Ontario. Preston, Waterloo County. Woven by Wilhelm Magnus Werlich. About 1900. The pattern is identical to that of no. 468

970.115.1 TABLECLOTH, linen broken-twill diaper. England.

Possibly Warwickshire. Dated 1805. L. 184cm; w. 175cm

970.116 FEATHER BED TICK (fragment). Doublecloth, blue and white linen. Switzerland. Canton Bern. About 1800. L. 10cm; w. 36cm. Gift of Dr Michael Stettler

970.158 TWILL DIAPER COVERLET. Indigo blue and red wool on natural white cotton. United States. Concord, New Hampshire. About 1800. L. 232cm; w. 200cm. Gift of Miss Emily LeBaron

970.201.2 BOUTONNE COVERLET. Bleached linen weft pile on bleached linen. Quebec. Probably Rimouski or Kamouraska Counties. 1860–75. L. 247cm; w. 198cm. Gift of Mr and Mrs Harold B. Burnham

970.202.9 SKIRT LENGTH. Grey, natural white, red, pink, and black wool on natural white cotton. Nova Scotia. Chéticamp, Petit Etang. 1870–80. L. 206cm; w. 82cm

970.202.10 SKIRT LENGTH (part). Black, deep red, pink, mauve, light terracotta, and pale grey-green wool on natural white cotton. Nova Scotia. Chéticamp. 1870–80

970.202.27 SPINNING WHEEL with flyer, marked 'R. Stewart.' Nova Scotia. Pictou County. 19th century. Diameter of driving wheel 51cm

970.202.28 SPINNING WHEEL with straight spindle. Nova Scotia (Acadian). Tracadie, Antigonish County. 19th century. Diameter of driving wheel 61cm. Gift of Mrs Edgar J. Stone

970.227.7 BOUTONNE TABLECLOTH. Black wool ground with weft pile patterns in dark red, bright pink, purple, medium pink, red, green, and white wool. Romania, Transylvania. Bistrita-Basaud County, village of Nimigea. About 1900

970.229 JACQUARD TABLECLOTH. Doublecloth, proportion 1:1; decoupure 1. Red cotton and indigo blue cotton. Probably mill-woven. Ontario(?). Late 19th century. L. 225cm; w. 201cm. The pattern is the same as that of 967.141.1

970.240.4 OVERSHOT TABLECLOTH. Red, green, yellow, pink, and blue wool on black wool. Romania. Transylvania, Salaj County, Szamos River Valley. Late 19th century. L. 178cm; w. 181cm. Gift of Mr and Mrs Harold B. Burnham

970.240.5 OVERSHOT CARPET (fragment). Pale brick red, rose-red, and brown-red wool on natural white cotton. Romania. Hurezu, Oltenia. Late 19th century. L. 32cm; w. 59cm. Gift of Mr and Mrs Harold B. Burnham

970.240.6 OVERSHOT FRAGMENT. Brown and natural white wool on grey and black wool. Romania. Transylvania. (Possibly near Cluj.) Late 19th century. L. 39cm; w. 69cm. Gift of Mr and Mrs Harold B. Burnham

970.257.1 WOOL BLANKET, tabby. Initialled 'EAF,' for Edwin A. Fretz, and dated 1834 in cross stitch. Woven by Peter Fretz, near Napanee, Lennox and Addington Counties, Ontario. L. 199cm; w. 180cm. Gift of Mrs Archie Lamont

970.257.2 WOOL BLANKET, tabby. Initialled 'SF,' for Susannah (Vandebogart) Fretz, and numbered '13' in cross stitch. Woven by Peter Fretz, near Napanee, Lennox and Addington Counties, Ontario. 1840–50. L. 180cm; w. 155cm. Gift of Mrs Archie Lamont

970.257.3 WOOL BLANKET, tabby. Initialled 'MAF,' for Mary Almeda Fretz, in cross stitch. Woven by Peter Fretz, near Napanee, Lennox and Addington Counties, Ontario.

1840–50. L. 195cm; w. 159cm. Gift of Mrs Archie Lamont

970.257.7 WOOL BLANKET, 2/2 twill. Natural ground with red and blue check. Woven by Peter Fretz, near Napanee, Lennox and Addington Counties, Ontario. 1825–40. L. 209cm; w. 181cm. Gift of Mrs Archie Lamont

970.257.8 WOOL BLANKET, 2/2 twill. Natural ground checked in red and green. Woven by Peter Fretz, near Napanee, Lennox and Addington Counties, Ontario. 1825–50. L. 222cm; w. 177cm. Gift of Mrs Archie Lamont

970.257.11, .12 PAIR OF TOWELS, bleached linen. M's & O's pattern. Woven by Peter Fretz, near Napanee, Lennox and Addington Counties, Ontario. 1825–35. L's. 85cm; w's. 55cm. Gift of Mrs Archie Lamont

970.257.26 CLOCK REEL of normal type, with clockface for counting on upright of stand. H. stand 77cm; circ. 194cm (app. 79″). Used by Peter Fretz, near Napanee, Lennox and Addington Counties, Ontario. c. 1825. Gift of Mrs Archie Lamont

970.296.2 JACQUARD COVERLET. Doublecloth (Proportion 2:1; decoupure 2). Indigo blue wool and natural white cotton on natural white cotton. 'Tulip' pattern. Woven by John Campbell, Komoka, Middlesex County, Ontario. 1860–80. L. 213cm, plus fringe; w. 214cm

Index

This book

was designed by

ALLAN FLEMING

with the assistance of

ANTJE LINGNER

and was printed by

University of

Toronto

Press